To N. J. T.

*Modern English
and Its Heritage*

Modern English
and Its Heritage

SECOND EDITION

Margaret M. Bryant

Professor of English, Brooklyn College
of The City University of New York

THE MACMILLAN COMPANY, NEW YORK

Macmillan New York, London

A Division of The Crowell-Collier Publishing Company

Second Edition

First Printing

Library of Congress Catalog Card Number: 62–7796

The Macmillan Company, New York
Macmillan New York, London
Brett-Macmillan Ltd., Galt, Ontario

Printed in the United States of America

Contents

III   *Words*

IV   *Grammar and Usage*

Appendix

Preface to the First Edition

Whether or not English becomes eventually the universal auxiliary language for international communication—as predicted confidently in some quarters and striven for in others—there is no gainsaying the fact that World War II has given our tongue greater prestige and wider currency than it ever before enjoyed, thanks to the stationing of British and American troops—especially the latter—all over the globe. The American jeep and bulldozer, chewing gum and candy, are admired and desired throughout the inhabited world today, and in many cases the American names for these commodities have been taken over more or less directly into local languages or dialects.

The war has had another effect. It has brought the Americans into closer contact with the British, Canadians, Australians, New Zealanders, and other users of our common tongue, and it is likely that this association will become more deeply rooted with the passage of years. Proud as we are of our common heritage of individual freedom and political liberty under the law, we can and should be equally proud of the language that we English-speaking peoples share, for it is a noble and eloquent one.

But pride in a thing is not enough for the thinking person; we must understand it and know how to use it to the best advantage. We cannot comprehend fully the status that English enjoys today without knowing something of its position "yesterday"—the yesterday stretching back more than a thousand years. It is with this thought in mind that *Modern English and Its Heritage* has been written.

Part I examines the linguistic heritage historically, from the Indo-European origins down through the Germanic and Anglo-Saxon contributions to the Middle English era and finally to the Modern English period. Part II analyzes the basic elements of the language, the speech sound and the letter, as units of oral and written English. Every effort has been made to handle the technical aspects of phonology with clarity and directness, avoiding the minute distinctions that serve only to bewilder the student being introduced to the science of linguistics.

In Part III, Grammar and Usage, the structure of the language is considered in some detail and the nature of English grammar is set forth. From time to time attention is called to rules or traditions that appear to be based on prejudice or lack of a complete understanding of the amazing flexibility that characterizes our language, as, for instance, the rule against splitting an infinitive. But I have endeavored throughout to make a fair, dispassionate presentation of the subject matter. My own concern is to promote an interest in and understanding of good English on the part of the student and to acquaint him with the rich resources of the language he has inherited, or perhaps learned as a newcomer.

Finally, Part IV, Word Formation, deals with what is perhaps the most fascinating aspect in the whole field of language. Starting with the origin of words, the various chapters show how words have changed their form and meaning over the centuries and how new terms have entered the language. In conclusion, a glimpse is given of that new linguistic science, semantics, which deals with the meanings of words.

I have written this book with two types of user in mind: first, the serious student of the language who will make it a steppingstone to further research in the field, and second, the average college student or general reader who is not interested in linguistics but wishes to gain a deeper knowledge of his mother tongue. By the principles laid down and the examples cited, I have aimed to show that English is dynamic, not static, and that despite its long and varied history it is still growing and still changing.

To add to the book's value for more advanced work, care has been taken to provide for each chapter not only a bibliography but also a list of suggested subjects for further research and class papers. The student is encouraged at every point to consult other sources of information to obtain a broader grasp of the subject than any single textbook can provide.

No writer on any aspect of our language can be insensible of the vast debt owed to predecessors in the field, both among contemporaries and among earlier scholars. The footnotes and bibliographies in this volume can indicate only a small part of this general indebtedness of mine to all the other laborers in the vineyards whose work has come to my attention. We all have three things in common: a love of the language, an enthusiasm for the study of it, and a desire to communicate our own enthusiasm to as many of the coming generations as we can reach.

I am also grateful to Mrs. Georgianna McLarty Voigt for many helpful suggestions in the preparation of the manuscript and to Professor Oscar Cargill who carefully read the manuscript and helped in preparing it for the press.

M. M. B.

New York City

Preface to the Second Edition

Fourteen years have passed since the first edition of *Modern English and Its Heritage* was published, and during that period a great deal of scholarship and investigation has gone on in the field of language. This edition, which represents a revision rather than a rewriting, attempts to take note, so far as limitations of space permit, of the work that has been done during those years. I could not hope to do more than indicate in the body of the text, in the footnotes, or in the bibliographies, those at the end of each chapter and that at the end of the book, the great amount of investigation and its many ramifications. No doubt, I have overlooked or excluded material that will seem important to some, but it is impossible to include everything in a volume of this size.

This book continues the general plan of the first edition and its general aim. A new arrangement, however, has been made. Part III, Grammar and Usage, has been placed at the end, so that those who wish to consider the other parts first and leave the structure of the language for a separate study may do so.

It is my hope that this volume in its revised form may better serve those with an interest in the English language and will continue to encourage its readers to an active observation of the language and a further study of it. I cannot possibly acknowledge in detail here my debt to the many scholars upon whose investigations and explorations I have depended. References within the work must suffice. I wish, however, to thank in particular the following persons who gave valuable advice: Professors James B. McMillan, University of Alabama; Robert C. Pooley, University of Wisconsin; James N. Tidwell, San Diego State College, California; Robert P. Stockwell, University of California at Los Angeles; and others who also made helpful suggestions in preparing this second edition for the press.

MARGARET M. BRYANT

Brooklyn College
The City University of New York

I

The Heritage of
Modern English

1

Indo-European Heritage

1.1 Heir of the Ages "I the heir of all the ages," exultantly proclaims the poet Tennyson in "Locksley Hall." It is for the biological scientist to tell us in what sense, if any, this lyrical sentiment is true with respect to our physical characteristics, and for the psychologist to explain its application to our mental make-up. For the purposes of this book it is enough to say that the phrase was no mere flight of fancy with regard to the language we use. Whether we realize it or not, every word that we speak or write—aside from current catch phrases and slang—is a heritage, and a goodly one, part of it going back beyond the dawn of recorded history.

It is human nature to take for granted the things that come to us without effort, whether they be physical possessions or cultural attainments. It is not surprising, therefore, that most people pay little or no heed to their linguistic heritage. They use their native language as a means of communication with family, friends, neighbors, business or school associates, and acquaintances or strangers, and to them one word is as good as another, just as long as it is not too hard to pronounce or spell.

Most people probably never reflect that even the simplest words they use have a history, often a truly fascinating one. Nor is it words alone that have a history, but our whole pattern of putting words together into phrases and sentences; in short, the language itself.

Every modern language has a history, but in this book we shall deal mainly with our English heritage, the "English" being taken to mean the language spoken and written not only throughout the British Commonwealth, but also in the United States and its possessions.

Nowadays it is the fashion in some circles to "look down" on all forms of heritage. Pride in family ancestry, for instance, is considered snobbish in our democratic society, and even inherited wealth is regarded in some circles as something to be a bit ashamed of. But no user of English needs to be apologetic about his linguistic heritage, because it has given him an excellent vehicle for the communication of his ideas and feelings.

The thesis of this book is that the study of that heritage will prove interesting, and even profitable in a wide sense of the word. This does not mean that ability to trace the verb *love* back to its roots in the earlier languages antedating English is bound to make the student popular with the opposite sex; nor does it mean that this study will inevitably make him a better speaker or writer. After all, it is possible to be expert in the history of music, painting, sculpture, or other arts and crafts without having any artistic or handcraft ability at all. So, too, one can be well versed in the heritage of English without becoming a great orator, novelist, essayist, or even journalist. But, just as a knowledge of the history of the various arts adds to the appreciation and enjoyment of them, so a knowledge of our linguistic heritage adds to our appreciation and enjoyment of the language we use in our everyday life.

1.2 Language Ever Changing   From their struggles with rules of grammar in school, most persons gain the impression that language is something rigid and immutable. It is somewhat of a shock, therefore, to discover that even so recently as the time of Shakespeare, English usage was so different from ours that Shakespearean grammar provides a special field of study. Languages are continually undergoing changes, and their present status is an outgrowth of previous stages of development. There is no such thing as uniformity of language over a long period or a wide area, although the modern emphasis on the printed word and mass oral communication (radio, television, motion pictures) do undoubtedly retard the rate of variation and prevent many localisms from gaining wide currency. Speech differences among various members of a community, and even among individuals in the same family, can be discovered without great difficulty, and still more noticeable are differences in speech ways between communities. This tendency of language to change is abetted by the migratory habits of *homo sapiens*. In earliest times, especially, before written records became general, the inhabitants of a new colony across a river or over a mountain range would almost inevitably develop new words or speech habits if they no longer had communication with the parent group. In the course of time, the language of the original group would also change, but the simultaneous alterations within the two groups would never be in the same direction; nor would a particular difference develop at the same rate of speed in the separate communities, because factors present in the one would be absent in the other.

1.3 Conquest, a Factor in Change   Another condition causing a change in language is conquest. If a defeated tribe or nation has a foreign tongue imposed upon it, some modification is bound to ensue, for at least some of the words of the beaten people will be appropriated by their masters. Change takes place even if the conquerors accept the language of the conquered, as did the Normans in exchanging their Northern speech for the language spoken in what they called Normandy and once again in exchanging the French dialect of Normandy for the Teutonic speech of Britain after the Norman Conquest.

1.4 What Constitutes a Language   In spite of changes due to conquest or other factors, there usually develops a preponderance of likeness in the speech habits of persons inhabiting a particular region at a certain period, and the sum of these individual speech habits goes to make up the language of that locality. On a larger scale, the characteristic speech habits of the dominant group in a nation usually produce a national language, which may be the same as or different from the language spoken in other nations. Thus, English, French, and Spanish, to name only three widely spoken languages, are each the common possession of several nations, sometimes with minor differences, as between British English and American English. Yet even within a nation there may be variations of the language. In the United States, for instance, residents of New England and those of the South each have characteristic dialects, but the two groups have little or no difficulty understanding one another because the common English heritage predominates in both. If the differences in dialect become too great, as with Spanish and Portuguese or German and Dutch, the speakers in one region cannot understand those from another, and two separate languages develop, each with its peculiar traits but each related to the other. Many seemingly dissimilar languages are closely related and are descendants of a parent stock.

1.5 Many Languages We all know, of course, that there are many living languages and several dead ones, and perhaps some of us are fortunate enough to be able to speak or at least understand one or more of these tongues. What few persons except philologists realize, however, is the really large number of languages in existence. Louis H. Gray in his *Foundations of Language* [1] tentatively puts the total number of present-day spoken languages, exclusive of dialects, at 2796. Most of these are localized and of little importance outside their rather narrow geographical limits, except to the student of comparative philology. But the rather staggering total is a hint of the difficulty that will be found in trying to classify all the various tongues. Fortunately, most languages do lend themselves to classification into groups, and only a few "mavericks," such as the Basque of the Pyrenees region of France and Spain, defy exact classification.

Lists of languages are no more exciting than the famous catalogue of ships in Homer's *Iliad* or the list of "begats" in the Bible, yet it is necessary now and then to do a bit of drudgery and assimilate such lists to gain a proper understanding of the subject.

Philologists divide the leading languages of the world into families, all the members of a given family having many, if not most, characteristics in common. Occasionally there is a difference of opinion among scholars as to whether a particular speech belongs to one language group or another, and there is also a lack of uniformity in nomenclature for the various groupings. It is, therefore, difficult to

[1] Louis H. Gray, *Foundations of Language* (New York, The Macmillan Company, 1939), p. 418.

summarize the world linguistic pattern with precision. Broadly speaking, however, the division would include: (1) Altaic, named for the Altai Mountains in central Asia and taking in Mongolian of Mongolia, Manchu of Manchuria (from 1932 to 1945 the Japanese puppet state of Manchukuo), and Turkish of the old Ottoman Empire; (2) Uralic or Finno-Ugric, comprising Finnish, Permian, Ugric, and Samoyede (Nenets), spoken in Finland, Esthonia, northern Sweden, Hungary, on both sides of the Ural Mountains, and as far east as the Tunguska River; (3) Semitic, consisting of Phoenician (the language of the ancient maritime power of that name on the eastern shore of the Mediterranean), Biblical Hebrew, Aramaic (used in Syria and Palestine and the language spoken by Jesus), Arabic, and Amharic, the last-named the official court language of Abyssinia (Ethiopia); (4) Hamitic, taking in ancient Egyptian, Coptic (a neo-Egyptian language which was spoken down to the seventeenth century), and various modern descendants of them in North Africa today; (5) Sudanese, spoken by tribes living generally southwest of the Hamitic area in Africa and by the Bantu groups, south of the Sudanese; (6) Indo-Chinese, spread over Tibet, Burma, Central Vietnam (formerly Annam), Thailand (formerly Siam), and the large areas of China; (7) Korean of Korea and Japanese; (8) Basque of the Pyrenees Mountains of France and Spain; (9) Malay-Polynesian of the Malay Peninsula, Madagascar, Indonesia (formerly Dutch East Indies), Philippines, Hawaii, and small Pacific archipelagos; (10) American Indian of the two American continents, stretching from the Arctic to the Antarctic; (11) Eskimo-Aleut, spoken by the Aleut in the Aleutian Islands and by the Eskimo in Northern Canada, in the western and northern parts of Alaska, in Greenland, and in a small area on the northeastern tip of Asia; (12) a large number of dialects (related in some cases; in others, not) of various peoples in Australia, in Tasmania, New Guinea, and surrounding islands, in India (the Dravidian), in the Andaman Islands in the Bay of Bengal, and in the region surrounding the Caucasus Mountains.[2]

1.6 The Home of the Indo-European Family   Aside from these,

[2] For an outline of the important language groups and languages of the world, see G. W. Gray and C. M. Wise, *The Bases of Speech,* 3rd edit. (New York, Harper & Brothers, 1959), pp. 341–346.

there is one great language "family" that has not yet been mentioned, though it is the one with which this book is primarily
concerned. Formerly known under such names as Aryan or Indo-
Germanic, it is now most generally, and properly, referred to as
Indo-European. It is to this "family" that English belongs.

Naturally enough, the student is likely to wonder whether these
various "families" can be traced to one common ancestor, just as
there has long been speculation about the possibility of all the races
and tribes of mankind stemming from one parentage, as is typified
by the Biblical Adam and Eve. Indeed, anthropologists and archae-
ologists find language study the key to some of their problems, and,
conversely, philologists depend on anthropology, archaeology, and
other sciences to unravel some of the linguistic mysteries. But neither
for races nor languages has a single common ancestor been proved,
scientifically. Whether any will be is another question, quite outside
the scope of this work.

Scholars have been able to demonstrate, however, definite inter-
relationships within a language family, especially in Indo-European.
It has even been possible to construct a theory as to the original
home of the people or peoples who used that primitive tongue.
Formerly it was believed that this primordial home was in Asia, and
the tentative identification of the Tigris-Euphrates valley as the
Biblical Garden of Eden bolstered that theory, but more precise
linguistic study in recent decades has led to the well-nigh universal
conclusion that the language family stems from central or southeastern Europe, somewhere in the region extending from Lithuania to
southern Russia.

The breaking-up of Indo-European into a number of dialects is
thought to have begun sometime between 2000 and 3000 B.C., possibly around 2500 B.C., though this would be frankly a guess. The
types of words common to the various dialects are regarded as a
clue to the geographical location of the original home. The evidence
of language study seems to point to the temperate zone, and more
specifically to an area in the upper part of it and away from the sea,
because of the common word for such ideas as snow, winter, dog,
horse, cow, sheep, wolf, otter, deer, pig, duck, bee, pine, oak, birch,
and willow, whereas there is a lack of such common terminology for

sea, camel, lion, elephant, rhinoceros, tiger, monkey, bamboo, and palm. Professor Bender [3] shows in his excellent study that the honey-bee is indigenous to most parts of Europe and that almost every Indo-European language has a common word for *honey* (Greek *meli*, Latin *mel*, Old English *mildēaw*, "honey-dew," etc.) and for an intoxicating drink made from honey, known as *mead* in English. Professor Bender is careful to point out that the various locations in Asia that have been suggested as the original homeland are not the regions frequented by the honeybee.[4] Another word to which this scholar gives special attention is *beech*, designating what we know as the beech tree in the Latin and the Germanic (Teutonic) languages, but having a different meaning elsewhere: for instance, *oak* in Greek and *elm* and *elder* in other languages. This discrepancy does not invalidate the theory as a whole, but merely emphasizes the difficulty of this kind of detective work. It is almost like a murder mystery in which there are too many contradictory clues. At any rate, after sifting and evaluating all the evidence, Professor Bender regards the modern Lithuania, recently absorbed again into Russia, as the original home of the Indo-European language. He points out that the language of this region has "preserved into modern living speech more of the Indo-European past than any other language on earth" [3] and that "the Lithuanian stock has dwelt in its present location for at least five thousand years, the duration of the Indo-European period, so far as is known." [5]

New arguments, however, have arisen concerning the specific region of origin.[6] But the word for *salmon*, which appears in the Teutonic languages (Swedish *lax*, German *lachs*, etc.), and not in Greek and Latin, has recently been found in one of the Tocharian dialects (*laksi*, meaning "fish," a natural change of meaning for those

---

[3] H. H. Bender, *The Home of the Indo-Europeans* (Princeton, Princeton University Press, 1922), pp. 21–22.

[4] *Ibid.*, pp. 19–21.

[5] *Ibid.*, p. 55.

[6] See, for example, Alexander Jóhannesson, "Um frumtungu Indógermana og frumheimkynni," *Tylgir Árbók, Háskóla Íslands* (1940–1941) (Reykjavik, Gutenburg, 1943). The latest opinion of S. Feist is found in "The origin of the Germanic Languages and the Indo-Europeanizing of North Europe," *Language* (Vol. VIII, 1932), pp. 245–254.

going from an area where salmon was important to one where it did not exist). This evidence also points to a northerly origin.[7]

1.7 The Indo-European Family of Languages Quite apart from its importance to us because it includes English, the Indo-European family is one of the most significant, both in geographical extent and number of users. It takes in several languages in Asia and nearly all those of Europe, and, naturally, those in the New World that have European origins. Also, the Indo-European language system has received greater scientific attention from philologists than any other, but despite this fact, no one can point to the Indo-European language itself, because it has no existence today in written form. Before the dawn of history, this assumed original speech had been broken up into numerous dialects and the original pattern had disappeared. Nevertheless, scholars have been able to reconstruct with a considerable degree of success its inflections and vocabulary by means of a comparative study of the various known languages that form the family. These languages fall into nine main groups exclusive of the Hittite and the Tocharian, two tongues that have recently been identified.[8] The nine groups are:

1 *Indian,* comprising Sanskrit, the ancient literary language (supposedly the nearest representative of the parent Indo-European highly inflected language, with three numbers, three genders, and eight cases of the noun as well as an extremely complicated verbal structure based upon aspect rather than upon tense), in which the Vedas, sacred books of the Brahmins, were written, the oldest going back to about 1500 B.C.; the various literary languages called Prakrits, the chief of which was Pali, which became the recognized language of Buddhism about the middle of the fifth century before Christ; the modern native languages of India, the most important of which are Hindi, Hindustani (a form of Hindi mixed with Persian and Arabic), Bengali, Punjabi, and Mahrati; and Romany, the language of the Gypsies.

2 *Iranian,* including Persian and Avestan or Zend (the language of the Avesta, the sacred book of the Zoroastrians) in their various stages

---

[7] See Paul Thieme, *Die Heimat der indogermanischen Gemeinsprache* (Wiesbaden, 1953, No. 11; *Akademie der Wissenschaften und der Literatur in Mainz, Abhandlungen der Geistes— und Sozialwissenschaftlichen Klasse*).

[8] For a further division into *centum* and *satem* languages, see par. 12.9, pp. 156–157.

from ancient to modern, and related dialects, among them Afghan
and Kurdish.

3   *Armenian,* consisting of Old Armenian, in which the Christian books
of the Armenians were written, dating from about the fifth century
after Christ, and its descendants, the Modern Armenian dialects.

4   *Hellenic,* made up of the ancient Greek dialects, the chief of which
are Attic (from which the common literary language was derived in
the fifth century before Christ), Ionic, Doric, Aeolic, and Modern
Greek, both literary and dialectal.

5   *Albanian,* the language of ancient Illyrian provinces, a limited area
northwest of Greece on the east coast of the Adriatic, now spoken in
modern Albania.

6   *Italic,* consisting of Oscan and Umbrian, known only for place names
and inscriptions which precede Christianity, and Latin with its modern descendants the Romance languages, the most important of
which are French, Spanish, Italian, Portuguese, and Rumanian.

7   *Celtic,* divided into three main branches:
Gallic, the little-known tongue of the ancient Gauls, whom Caesar
conquered; Gaelic, including Irish, Scotch-Gaelic or Erse, known
from about the eleventh century and spoken in the Highlands of
Scotland, and Manx, a dialect of the Isle of Man; and Britannic, the
modern representatives of which are Cornish, generally believed to
be extinct since the eighteenth century,[9] Welsh, and Breton, a dialect of northwest France.

8   *Balto-Slavonic,* falling into two groups:
the Baltic, comprising Lithuanian, the modern tongue most like primitive Indo-European and therefore significant because of its conserva-
tism in preserving some of the ancient traits of the parent language,
Prussian, extinct since the seventeenth century, and Lettic, the speech
of Latvia; the Slavic, breaking up into three parts:
East Slavic or three types of Russian (Great Russian, the tongue of
about 161 [10] million people; White Russian, spoken by approximately 10 [10] million in western Russia and adjoining sections of
Poland; Ukrainian or Little Russian, spoken in the South by about
41 [10] million); West Slavic, including Polish, Czecho-Slovakian, and

---

[9] It is generally believed that Mrs. Dolly Pentraeth, who died in 1777, was
the last Cornish speaker, but Professor John J. Parry has marshalled evidence
to prove that actually Cornish never completely died out. See his illuminating
article entitled "The Revival of Cornish: An Dasserghyans Kernewek" (*Publications of the Modern Language Association,* Vol. LXI, 1946), pp. 258–268.

[10] See *World Almanac,* 1961.

Sorbian or Wend, spoken in a small area in Germany northeast of
Dresden; South Slavic, made up of Bulgarian, Serbo-Croatian, and
Slovenian, the two latter spoken mostly in Yugoslavia.

9   *Germanic* or *Teutonic,* dividing into three groups:
East Germanic, known chiefly through fragments of a fourth-century
translation of the Scriptures (oldest text in a Germanic language) into
Gothic, its main dialect, by Ulfilas, the bishop of the West Goths; North
Germanic, the Scandinavian languages falling into an easterly group,
Old Danish and Old Swedish and their modern representatives, and a
westerly group, Old Icelandic and Old Norwegian and their modern
representatives; West Germanic, with five subdivisions:
(a) High German, spoken originally in the southern highlands of
Germany, in its three periods of Old High German, Middle High
German, and Modern High German, the language of modern Germany; (b) Low German or Old Saxon, spoken in the northern lowlands of Germany, the modern representative of which is Plattdeutsch; (c) Franconian and its descendants, chief of which are
Dutch and Flemish; (d) Old Frisian, the dialect on the continent
most closely related to English, spoken in northwestern Germany
and the coastal areas of the Netherlands, and its descendant, Modern Frisian, surviving in the Dutch province of Friesland, in a small
section of Schleswig, and in adjoining islands; (e) English in its three
periods of Old English, Middle English, and Modern English.

1.8 Common Traits of the Indo-European Languages   These
nine branches of the Indo-European family of languages have certain features in common. They are all inflectional, designating syntactical distinctions such as case, number, gender, tense, and voice
by varying the form of a word. For instance, in English we generally
indicate the plural of a noun by adding -*s* to the singular (*boy, boys*)
and form the present participle by adding -*ing* to the present tense
(*go, going*).[11] Another feature of the Indo-European family is the

[11] It may be interesting to note by way of comparison that languages like
the Chinese (isolating) have no inflection at all but only monosyllabic and invariable roots, the relationship of which depends upon position and variation in
tone. Also agglutinative languages, such as Turkish, Hungarian, and Bantu, have
a type of inflection so different that they must be put into an entirely separate
class. Here the affixing is done by juxtaposition; that is, the primitive words are
run together and combined into compounds, in which the form and meaning of
the component parts undergo little or no change. Then there is the incorporat-
ing language like that of Greenland (Eskimo) in which the concepts of subject,
verb, direct and indirect object may all be expressed in one word.

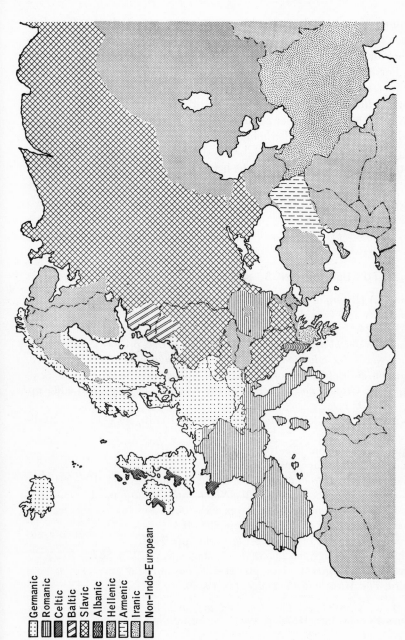

THE INDO-EUROPEAN LANGUAGES IN EUROPE TODAY

After Stuart Robertson and Frederic G. Cassidy. *The Development of Modern English*, 2nd ed., Prentice-Hall.

Germanic
Romanic
Celtic
Baltic
Slavic
Albanic
Hellenic
Armenic
Iranic
Non-Indo-European

common word stock, comprising a number of words not found in other types of languages and formed with similar methods of pronunciation. For example, it is not difficult to observe that Sanskrit *tri*, Persian *thri*, Greek *treis*, Latin *tres*, Celtic *tri*, Slavonic *tri*, Lithuanian *tri*, Gothic *thri*, German *drei*, Icelandic *thriu*, Dutch *drie*, English *three*, all come from a single original root.[12]

There are many other common words that the student may enjoy finding for himself and tracing through the various Indo-European languages with the aid of unabridged English dictionaries and some of the linguistic reference works listed herewith.

For the Student

A. FURTHER READINGS

Baugh, *A History of the English Language,* 2nd edit., pp. 17–46.
Robertson and Cassidy, *Development of Modern English,* 2nd edit., pp. 15–24.
Krapp, *Modern English, Its Growth and Present Use,* pp. 44–48.
Marckwardt, *Introduction to the English Language,* pp. 276–278.
Emerson, *A Brief History of the English Language,* pp. 1–10.
Jespersen, *Growth and Structure of the English Language,* 9th edit., pp. 18–20.
Webster's *New International Dictionary,* 2nd edit., §§ 1–13, pp. lxxxii–lxxxiii.
Sapir, *Language,* pp. 127–156.
Bloomfield, *Language,* pp. 57–73.
Bloomfield, *An Introduction to the Study of Language,* pp. 195–291.
Pedersen, *Linguistic Science in the Nineteenth Century,* pp. 14–98.
Graff, *Language and Languages,* pp. 352–396.
Gray, *Foundations of Language,* pp. 295–418.
Bender, *The Home of the Indo-Europeans,* pp. 9–57.
Whitney, *Language and the Study of Language,* pp. 176–287.
Sheard, *The Words We Use,* pp. 94–128, *passim.*
Laird, *The Miracle of Language,* pp. 19–30.

[12] W. D. Whitney, *Language and the Study of Language* (New York, Scribner's Sons, Inc., 1867), p. 196.

Brugmann and Delbrück, *Grundriss der vergleichenden Grammatik der indogermanischen Sprachen,* 2nd edit.

Hirt, *Indogermanische Grammatik.*

Meillet, A., *Introduction à l'étude comparative des langues indo-européennes,* new edit., corrected and augmented by E. Benveniste.

Meillet and Cohen, *Les Langues du Monde,* 2nd edit.

Schrijnen, *Einführing in das Studium der indogermanischen Sprachwissenschaft,* trans. by W. Fischer.

Meyer, *Die Indogermanenfrage.*

NOTE: More detailed information about each item under "Further Readings" may be found in the bibliography at the end of this volume.

B. FOR CLASS DISCUSSION

1. What is meant by families of languages? Give illustrations.
2. Explain what constitutes a language. Is there any difference between a language and a dialect? Illustrate your answer.
3. What is meant by the Indo-European languages? By the Indo-Chinese? Are these two groups related?
4. What are the theories concerning the home of the Indo-European speech? On what are they based? At what approximate date is Indo-European thought to have become separated into its various related branches?
5. Do scholars have any idea what Primitive Indo-European is like? If so, how did they arrive at their conclusions?
6. What factors enter into the breaking up of a language? Give illustrations.
7. What are the principal branches of the Indo-European family tree? Explain where each branch is spoken.
8. Of the Indo-European languages, which one has preserved most of the parent language?
9. What are the common features of the Indo-European languages?
10. What types of linguistic structure are there? Illustrate. (See Sapir's *Language,* pp. 127–156.)
11. To what type of linguistic structure do the Indo-European languages belong? Explain.
12. What is meant by a common word stock? Can you give examples of cognates in Indo-European languages, in addition to those cited in par. 1.8?
13. What is meant by the *centum* and *satem* groups of languages?

C. SUGGESTIONS FOR RESEARCH PAPERS

1. The Characteristics of French (Latin, Russian, or any other Indo-European language).
2. A Comparison of English with French (Latin, Russian, or any other Indo-European language).
3. Cognates in Indo-European Languages.
4. Cognates in Romance Languages (or any other branch of the Indo-European languages).
5. Cognates in English and Latin (or any other language).
6. A Comparison of an Indo-European Language with Chinese, Turkish, Hebrew, or some other non-Indo-European language.

2

Germanic Heritage

2.1 Judgment of Scholars The point to bear in mind about the classification for the Indo-European language system set forth in Chapter 1 is that while it represents the best judgment of many competent scholars in the field, based on decades of language analysis, there are details about which doubt, if not disagreement, will be found among philologists. Take, for example, the problem of the placing of Albanian in this system. It seems to be a survival of Illyrian, an ancient tongue of the northwestern area of the Balkans. But not only are the outlines of Illyrian hazy, Albanian itself is difficult to define exactly because when it first received the attention of philologists in the seventeenth century its vocabulary was already cluttered up with Latin, Greek, Turkish, and Slavonic elements so that the original Albanian was almost buried from sight. At the outset, it was considered a subordinate tongue in the Hellenic group, and only in the last forty or fifty years has it won recognition as an independent member of the Indo-European family.[1]

[1] The status of Albanian as an independent member of the Indo-European family has been shown convincingly in such scholarly works as the gathering to-

2.2 Another Perplexing Problem   Another difficulty is that of finding a place in the Indo-European system for Hittite and Tocharian, mentioned in Chapter 1. Until recent times, Hittite was known only through incidental references in the Bible, but when the ancient capital of Boghaz-köi (about one hundred fifty kilometers east of Angora) was unearthed in Asia Minor, nearly 10,000 clay tablets, many of them in an unknown language, were found and eventually deciphered. In structure, this language, now referred to generally as Hittite, is almost certainly Indo-European,[2] but the vocabulary seems to be a mixture, as with the case of Albanian. At this time it is impossible to assign a definite niche in the Indo-European group to Hittite.[3] Some scholars hold the Indo-Hittite hypothesis and consider Hittite as co-ordinate with Indo-European. Hittite, no doubt, separated from the Indo-European before any of the other language groups—perhaps some five hundred years before.[4]

Tocharian has been reconstructed from fragmentary texts discovered in Chinese Turkestan in central Asia. It almost certainly is Indo-European and appears to have flourished around the seventh century of the Christian era. Oddly enough, it gives evidence of belonging with the Hellenic, Italic, Teutonic, and Celtic groups rather than with the eastern groups with which it should be connected, on

---

gether of the remains of Illyrian by H. Krahe in his *Die alten balkanillyrischen geographischen Namen* (Heidelberg, 1925) and *Lexikon altillyrischer Personennamen* (Heidelberg, 1929), by the preservation of the ancient Italic dialects with which it was connected (Venetic in the region of Venice, Messapic in the heel of the Italian boot, and Rhaetic in eastern Switzerland and western Austria) in *Prae-Italic Dialects of Italy*, by R. Conway and J. Whatmough (3 vols., Cambridge, Massachusetts, 1933), and especially by the research on the grammar of Albanian itself by G. Pekmezi, A. Leotti, G. Weigand, A. Feizì, S. E. Mann, and G. Meyer, the last-named the author of both a grammar and an etymological dictionary.

[2] Established by the Czech scholar B. Hrozný in 1917 after a thorough study. See E. H. Sturtevant, *An Introduction to Linguistic Science* (New Haven, Yale University Press, 1947), §§ 229–235, for a brief explanation of the Indo-Hittite hypothesis. See also his article "On the Position of Hittite Among the Indo-European Languages," *Language* (Vol. II, March, 1926), pp. 25–34.

[3] See E. H. Sturtevant's excellent *Comparative Grammar of the Hittite Language* (Philadelphia, Linguistic Society of America, 1935). Holger Pedersen has also published a valuable study *Hittitisch und die andern indoeuropäischen Sprachen* (Copenhagen, Levin & Munksgaard, 1938).

[4] See George L. Trager and Henry Lee Smith, Jr., "A Chronology of Indo-Hittite," *Studies in Linguistics* (Vol. VIII, No. 3, September, 1950), pp. 61–70.

the basis of geography alone.[5] The Tocharians apparently migrated with many others from their original home in Europe, perhaps the Balkans, into eastern Asia in the ninth and eighth centuries B.C. From archeological and other available evidence it seems that the Phrygians, Thracians, Illyrians, and Teutons, especially the Scandinavians, joined the migration, which brought about the downfall of the Chou dynasty in China in 771 B.C.[6]

2.3 The Home and Expansion of Germanic Tempting as it would be to pursue further these special problems of classification within the Indo-European system, we must now turn our attention to the Germanic branch of the family, since that is the one to which English belongs. The original home of the *Germani,* so called by the Celts, was probably in northern Germany along the Baltic Sea.[7] From there they spread out in various directions, going north into Scandinavia and settling there as well as extending their territory southward and westward, always pushing the Celts farther and farther back. They branched out so far that they developed the East, North, and West Germanic groups referred to in Chapter 1 (p. 12), each with its own characteristics but all having certain things in common to link them together.

Of the East Germanic dialects, the one of which we have a record is Gothic. A fragmentary translation of the Bible by the Arian bishop Ulfilas and a few other religious texts have been preserved. Ulfilas was a Visigoth (one of the divisions of the Goths establishing themselves in the Balkans in the third century) who lived from about 310 to about 383. Soon after his time the Gothic language of the Balkans became extinct. For a while the Goths played a significant role in European history, including in their vast conquests both Italy and Spain. Italy was conquered by the Ostrogoths and Spain by the Visigoths. In these regions, however, Latin soon took the

[5] See W. Schultz, E. Sieg, and E. Siegling, *Tocharische grammatik* (Göttingen, 1931) and studies by S. Lévi and A. Meillet in *Mémoires de la société de linguistique de Paris,* Vols. XVII–XIX (1912–1916). A. Meillet has also written a brief survey of this language for the *Indogermanisches Jahrbuch,* Vol. I (1914, pp. 1–19).

[6] See Robert Heine-Geldern, "Das Tocharerproblem und die Pontische Wanderung," *Saeculum* (Vol. II, No. 2, 1951), pp. 225–255.

[7] Willem L. Graff, *Language and Languages* (New York, D. Appleton and Company, 1932), p. 384.

place of their language. Gothic survived longest in the Crimea, where vestiges of it were noted as late as in the sixteenth century.

The oldest Germanic records belong to the northern group. They are the runic inscriptions [8] in Scandinavian which go as far back as the third century. The form of the language used then is known as Old Norse. From it emerged in the eleventh century the languages we know today as Icelandic, Norwegian, Swedish, and Danish, each of which has a literature of its own. Icelandic and Norwegian formed the western division and Swedish and Danish the eastern.

The West Germanic group, to which English belongs, has two main subdivisions: High and Low German. In High German, spoken originally in the mountainous region of the southern Germanic area, the sounds *p, t, k, d,* etc. were transformed into other sounds.[9] This change, which did not take place in the lowlands of the north, occurred around A.D. 600. Thus the period from 600 to 1100 is known as Old High German. Then follow the Middle High German (1100 to 1500) and the Modern High German (1500 to the present) periods.

The Low German branch of Germanic divided into Old Saxon, which developed into Modern Low German or Plattdeutsch, spoken in the northern lowlands of Germany; Old Low Franconian, the chief descendants of which are Dutch in Holland and Flemish in northern Belgium; Old Frisian of the northwestern part of the Germanic area, with its descendant Modern Frisian spoken in the Dutch province of Friesland, in a small part of Schleswig, and in the islands near the coast; and Old English, the closest relative of Old Frisian, the two sometimes being classed as the Anglo-Frisian subdivision. The last-mentioned developed through Middle English (1100–1500) to Modern English, the language we speak today.

In summing up the Germanic languages, which sprung from the lost parent language Primitive Germanic, spoken in the period be-

---

[8] The characters of the alphabet in general use by the Germanic peoples from about the third century were known as *runes.*

[9] The portion of the West Germanic affected by the so-called second consonant-shift is the High German; that unaffected by the shift comprises the Low German group.

tween the first century before Christ and the first after Christ, we may present them in this simple outline form:

2.4 Common Features of the Germanic Language This Germanic group has characteristics in common with the eight others in the Indo-European family, but it has its own individual traits, just as the others have theirs. In the Germanic languages, there are four distinguishing features: (1) the development of a weak verb conjugation along with the strong; (2) a twofold declension (strong and weak) of adjectives; (3) a fixed stress accent; and (4) a regular shifting of consonants as described by Grimm's Law, about which more will be said later.

2.5 A Simpler Conjugation of the Verb If we compare the conjugation of a Latin or a Greek verb with that of a Germanic verb, German or English, for example, it is evident that the latter conjugation is much simpler. Latin and Greek are synthetic languages, expressing an idea by changing the form of the root of the verb: as Latin *audiō* (*I hear*), the present tense, and *audīvī* (*I have heard*), the perfect tense. The verbs also have a number of conjugations, distinguished from one another by the vowel of the ending of the present active infinitive. For instance, in Latin, there are, besides the irregular verbs, four regular conjugations typified by *amāre* (*to love*), *monēre* (*to advise*), *regĕre* (*to rule*), *audīre* (*to hear*), the distinguishing vowels being *ā, ē, ĕ, ī*, respectively. The principal parts are four: the present indicative, present infinitive, perfect indicative, and perfect participle, as in *amō, amāre, amāvī, amātus*. From these different stems the full conjugation of the verb may be derived. In turning from Latin to Greek, one finds even more complications, for the verbal system of the latter is nearer to that of the Indo-European verb. There are, to mention a few complexities in Greek, three numbers: singular, plural, and the dual; three voices: active, passive, and the additional middle; and extra tenses, like the aorist.

The Germanic, on the other hand, originally had only two tenses, one expressing past time and one expressing both present and future time, and at an early stage it lost the inflected passive voice. For instance, in Old English, a West Germanic language, one finds surviving the single form *hatte*, "was called," the passive being expressed by combining tense forms, as in the Modern English *I have been heard*. The Germanic verbal system is mainly analytic, expressing the idea of perfect time, for instance, by means of a pronoun, an auxiliary, and a participle, as English *I have sung* and German *ich habe gesungen*.

The outstanding feature of the Germanic verb, however, is its development of a particular type of past in many words. The result has been the grouping of the verbs into two classes: the "weak" and the "strong." If we take the English verb as an example of the Germanic, we find: (1) the weak (constituting the majority of verbs and therefore sometimes called the "regular"), forming its past tense by adding *ed, d,* or *t* to the present or infinitive stem, as *talk, talked, talked;* and (2) the strong, forming its tenses by an internal change of the radical vowel of the verb, as *ring, rang, rung*. The second group is more nearly like verbs of the other languages, but the first is characteristically Germanic. We have come to accept the conjugation of the weak verbs as the normal pattern as well as the simpler form so that a verb being taken into the language or being created is invariably conjugated in this manner. Two examples are the words *camouflage* taken over from the French during World War I and *blitz* borrowed from German in World War II. The principal parts are, respectively, *camouflage, camouflaged, camouflaged* and *blitz, blitzed, blitzed*. An even more striking illustration of this tendency is the making of a weak verb out of the chemical abbreviation *DDT*, to produce such a sentence as "They have DDTed the garbage." [10] So firmly fixed is this type of past that it does not seem strange.

2.6 A Twofold Adjective Declension   Just as the Germanic verb developed a twofold classification, so the Germanic adjective developed a twofold declension. When a demonstrative, a possessive pronoun, or a definite article preceded the adjective, or when it was used substantively, it was declined in one way, called "weak." When, however, the adjective was employed in the predicate relation or alone before the noun, it was declined in another way, called "strong." For instance, in German, where the strong-weak-predicative categories are yet in evidence, one says *das klare Wasser, the clear water,* but *klares Wasser, clear water,* when the article is omitted. *Clear* in German may be *klar, klare, klaren, klarem, klarer,* or *klares,* depending upon the gender, number, case, and whether it is declined in the strong or weak manner.

Modern English, having lost all declension of the adjective, does not distinguish between the weak and strong forms, but Old English, like Modern High German, preserved the full declension. In Modern English there is no change in the adjective form in expressions like *wise men* and *these wise men,* but in Old English the corresponding phrases are *wīse menn* and *þās wīsan menn* and in German *weise Männer* and *diese weisen Männer.* The two forms are distinctively Germanic.

It must be noted that Modern English belongs to the Germanic group because of its history, not because of its present usages. In Old English *good* might be *gōd, gōdes, gōdne, gōdum, gōde, gōdra, gōdre, gōda, gōdan,* or *gōdena,* depending upon whether the grammatical construction called for a masculine, feminine, or neuter, singular or plural, a nominative, genitive, dative, accusative, or instrumental, a strong or weak. All these forms have been lost in Modern English except the first. The English-speaking world can now say *the good man, the good woman, a good book, the good men, the story of a good man, the story for a good man, I like a good book, the book is good* or any similar expression without altering the form of the adjective and without loss of clarity in meaning. Nevertheless, the earlier presence of the twofold adjective declension in English

[10] Allen Walker Read, "The Word Harvest of '45," *Saturday Review of Literature,* June 29, 1946, p. 21.

and its retention in German show both languages to be definitely
Germanic.

2.7 A Fixed Stress Accent   Another trait characterizing the Germanic languages is the fixed accent. Whereas the word stress in
Indo-European was free or variable, in Germanic the stress became
fixed upon the root syllable. The freer accent of Latin, for instance,
may be observed in the conjugation of the present indicative of the
verb *amō* (*I love*): *ámō, ámās, ámat, amāmus, amātis, ámant.* We see
here that the accent shifts from the first syllable to the second in the
first and second persons plural: *amāmus* and *amātis.* The shift of
accent may also be noted in the inflection of a noun like *víctor* (*conqueror*), where the accent is on the first or root syllable in the nominative but on the second in the genitive where the inflectional
ending is added: *victóris* (*of the conqueror*). If, on the other hand,
we turn to a Germanic language, we find the stress fixed upon the
root syllable. Unless the word is a prepositional compound, the first
syllable is almost always stressed. In Modern English, we can generally recognize words which are native as distinguished from those
which have been borrowed from some non-Germanic tongue by noting the stressed syllable when prefixes and suffixes are added to form
new words. For example, observe Modern English *'merry, 'merrily,
'merriness, 'merriment; com'pare, 'comparable, com'parative;* and
*'photograph, pho'tographer, photo'graphic, pho'tography, 'photogra-
'vure.* The native word *merry* keeps the accent on the first syllable,
but *compare* and *photograph,* borrowed from the Latin and Greek
respectively, two non-Germanic languages, shift the accent with the
adding of affixes.

2.8 Grimm's Law   Now we come to the fourth distinctive characteristic of the Germanic languages, the Great (or First) Consonant
Shift, described by "Grimm's Law," as it is called, though the student must always bear in mind that this is no statutory enactment
by any legislative body, but a linguistic principle that was discovered by observation, as subject to error as any generalization is, and
susceptible to modification in the light of further experience. As Professor Leonard Bloomfield has observed, referring to Grimm's discovery as a "law" is in reality a "dangerous metaphor." So the student
must realize that the phenomenon so designated is one that ordinarily takes place, but that exceptions are possible.

The Danish linguist Rasmus Rask and the German scholar Jacob Grimm observed the almost regular shifting of certain Indo-European consonants in the Germanic languages according to a particular pattern. These changes were perhaps first stated by Rask but became generally known through Grimm's formulation of 1822 and thus were given his name. Rask and Grimm observed that Indo-European voiced aspirated stops *bh, dh, gh* became the voiced stops *b, d, g,* respectively; that *b, d, g* became the voiceless stops *p, t, k;* and that *p, t, k* became the voiceless fricatives *f, th, h.*[11]

A simplified presentation of the changes looks like this:

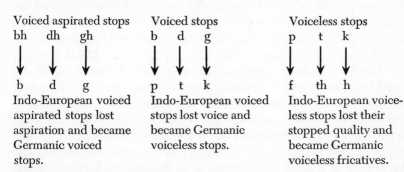

Voiced aspirated stops	Voiced stops	Voiceless stops
bh dh gh	b d g	p t k
↓ ↓ ↓	↓ ↓ ↓	↓ ↓ ↓
b d g	p t k	f th h
Indo-European voiced aspirated stops lost aspiration and became Germanic voiced stops.	Indo-European voiced stops lost voice and became Germanic voiceless stops.	Indo-European voiceless stops lost their stopped quality and became Germanic voiceless fricatives.

Each original group of consonants shifted only once. The entire process is thought to have occurred in three stages. After the change in *p, t,* and *k,* it was then possible for *b, d,* and *g* to shift without producing homophones by the falling together of the sounds which had formerly separated words. Following this second shift, the third change could take place without causing confusion.

Illustrations are Latin *dentem,* English *tooth;* Latin *genu,* English *knee;* Latin *tres,* English *three;* Latin *pater,* English *father;* Latin *cornu,* English *horn;* Latin *cordem,* English *heart.* These illustrations may be added to almost indefinitely from words of Indo-European origin surviving in the Germanic branch; it should be understood, however, that these changes do not always take place since

[11] Sounds are *voiced* when the vocal cords vibrate in their production and *voiceless* when they do not. See par. 7.11. *Aspirated* sounds are those made by blowing the breath out, with a slight drawing together of the throat or oral passage. A *fricative* is a sound produced by forcing the breath, without stopping it entirely, through a restricted opening in the throat or oral passage.

there are many exceptions due to individual developments and influence.

Grimm's Law has been of extraordinary utility in that it has helped linguists in grouping the Germanic languages and finding out the derivation and history of their vocabularies as well as in determining which words are native and which are borrowed. It has also opened the way to later important linguistic laws, one of which is that of the Danish linguist Karl Verner, who observed that many exceptions in applying the principle of Grimm were dependent on accent.[12] It is sufficient to say here that the stress shift which Verner discovered took place later than the consonant shift observed by Grimm, each playing its part in distinguishing the Germanic branch from all other branches of the Indo-European family of languages.[13]

2.9 The Relationship of English and German Many German and English words are practically identical, not because one is derived from the other or borrowed from the other, for the borrowings are few, but because they had their beginnings in a common source known as Primitive Germanic. This, like Indo-European, has been hypothetically reconstructed from a comparative study of the various languages comprising it, for no written records are extant. The differences of English and German arose because each language followed its own course and was exposed to its own particular influences throughout the centuries of growth. The great divergence between the two has been caused by the second consonant shift, which started in southern or upper Germany (hence the name High German) and gradually traveled northward during the sixth, seventh, and eighth centuries. English and German both underwent the first consonant shift explained by Grimm, but the High German consonants have undergone a second change that belongs to that language alone. English *p* generally appears in German (the literary language of today) as *f* or *pf* (*ship, Schiff; pipe, Pfeife*); English *d* as German *t* (*cold, kalt; deep, tief*); English *v* as German *b* in cognates (*over, ober; knave, Knabe*); and *t* often as German *z* or *tz* (*to, zu; ten, zehn;*

[12] See Joseph and Elizabeth M. Wright, *Old English Grammar*, 3rd edit. (Oxford, Oxford University Press, 1925), §§ 229–239, for a full discussion of these two laws, and their *Elementary Old English Grammar* (Oxford, Oxford University Press, 1923), §§ 108–118; also see note in par. 3.17 in this volume for an illustration of Verner's Law.

[13] See pars. 2.4–2.7.

sit, sitzen; cat, Katze). It must be said, however, that, because of the great inflectional leveling that has gone on in English, the inflection of German is much less like that of Modern English than that of Old English, with the twofold full declension of adjectives as well as the full declension of the definite article for gender, number, and case. Also Modern English has many more loan words from other languages than Old English or German, both of which usually expressed new ideas in native terms. As a result of the second consonant shift, Modern English finds itself more like Low German of northern Germany where there was no second shift. Thus Modern English *deep* and *heart* are Low German *deep, Hart,* but their High German equivalents are *tief, Herz.*

American and British occupation troops stationed in northern Germany at the close of World War II were amazed at the ease with which they could understand and make themselves understood by the natives without having studied the language. The soldiers did not realize that those Germans used a dialect that abided by Grimm's Law for a single consonant shift, just as English does. On the other hand, British and American forces stationed elsewhere in Germany could not converse with the inhabitants unless they had studied German in school or unless—like a good many American soldiers—they came from households in which German was spoken as the ancestral tongue. But at least a couple of the "G.I.'s" who had knowledge of German found themselves baffled when two young German girls with whom they had been "fraternizing" with fair success suddenly began talking with each other in the Swabian dialect, a local variation of German spoken in southwest Bavaria, which was completely incomprehensible to the Americans.

2.10 The Relationship of English to Dutch and Frisian Just as Modern English is similar to Low German so it is to Dutch, in which the consonants did not shift a second time and in which there has been a leveling of inflections as in English. For example, English and Dutch have the same word *water* and others that differ very little, as *twenty, twintig; wife, wyf.* The language most nearly akin to English, however, is not Dutch but Frisian, spoken by a few thousand persons in Holland and on the near-by islands of the North Sea. Some scholars have held that Old Frisian and Old English were originally one speech. That English is a Germanic language can

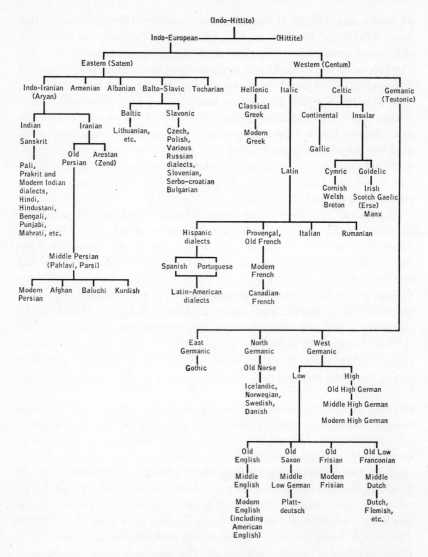

A CHART OF THE INDO-EUROPEAN FAMILY OF LANGUAGES, INCLUDING HITTITE (ACCORDING TO THE INDO-HITTITE THEORY)

easily be seen if only a short time is devoted to comparing it with German, Dutch, and Frisian, West Germanic languages, not to mention the Scandinavian languages and Gothic.

The purpose of discussing the common features of the Germanic languages and the relationship of English to German, Dutch, and Frisian is to stress the Germanic character of the language we speak. Although English has changed its forms and structure radically, has been influenced to a great extent by Latin and French in particular, and has borrowed words from many languages, it is basically a Germanic tongue.

For the Student

A. FURTHER READINGS

Baugh, *A History of the English Language*, 2nd edit., pp. 34–37.
Robertson and Cassidy, *Development of Modern English*, 2nd edit., pp. 25–35.
Krapp, *Modern English, Its Growth and Present Use*, pp. 48–54.
Emerson, *A Brief History of the English Language*, pp. 11–22.
Jespersen, *Language: Its Nature, Development and Origin*, pp. 36–47.
Jespersen, *Growth and Structure of the English Language*, 9th edit., pp. 20–28.
Marckwardt, *Introduction to the English Language*, pp. 278–279.
Webster's *New International Dictionary*, 2nd edit., §§ 14–23, p. lxxxiii.
Graff, *Language and Languages*, pp. 382–396.
Pedersen, *Linguistic Science in the Nineteenth Century*, pp. 30–43.
J. and E. M. Wright, *Old English Grammar*, 3rd edit., §§ 229–239.
J. and E. M. Wright, *An Elementary Old English Grammar*, §§ 108–118.
Gummere and Magoun, *Founders of England*.
Sheard, *The Words We Use*, pp. 94–128, *passim*.
Laird, *The Miracle of Language*, pp. 35–51; 138–140.

B. FOR CLASS DISCUSSION

1. What languages belong to the Germanic, or Teutonic, branch of the Indo-European languages?
2. What are the common characteristics of the Germanic languages?

3. Compare the conjugation of an English verb with that of another Indo-European language and show in what ways they differ.
4. What is meant by the strong and weak verbs? What is the difference between the two? Give examples of each.
5. What is meant by saying that the Germanic verbal system is mainly analytic whereas that of Latin is synthetic? Illustrate.
6. Was there a passive voice in Old English? How does Modern English express the passive?
7. Distinguish between the two declensions of adjectives in the Germanic languages. How does Modern English differ from Old English in this respect?
8. What is the difference between word stress in the Germanic languages and the other Indo-European languages? Give illustrations. Can you think of others in addition to those mentioned in par. 7?
9. Who were Rasmus Rask and Jacob Grimm? See Jespersen's *Language: Its Nature, Development and Origin*, pp. 36–43.
10. State the general principle of Grimm's Law, giving illustrations of the changes.
11. What is the importance of Grimm's Law?
12. What is meant by High and Low German? Illustrate.
13. Compare English with High German. Compare it with Low German. Which is more nearly like English?
14. Compare English with Dutch. Give illustrations.
15. What Germanic language is most like the English language? Where is it spoken?

C. SUGGESTIONS FOR RESEARCH PAPERS

1. Grimm's Law and Its Significance.
2. A Comparison of Old English with Gothic.
3. A Comparison of English with Dutch (or any other Germanic language).
4. Verner's Law and Its Significance.
5. Rasmus Rask and Jacob Grimm as Linguists.
6. A Study of the Adjective (or Verb) in the Germanic Languages.

3

Old English Heritage

3.1 Prehistoric Remains Although English is indubitably a Germanic tongue, as is pointed out in Chapter 2, many other influences have played a part in its development over the centuries. The region known as the British Isles, and particularly the section that forms England, is a very ancient land, from the standpoint of human civilization. Remains of the Old Stone Age as well as of the New Stone Age are abundant in England, and the earliest inhabitants of the area may have arrived via a land bridge from the continent of Europe in prehistoric times, bringing with them some primitive language.

The most famous of the remains from primitive days are those at Stonehenge, ten miles north of Salisbury in Wiltshire. These ruins continue to challenge men's interest and attention, as they have for more than 1000 years. In 1943, while the very future of the British empire was hanging by a thread, the British government purchased 1000 acres to form a National Trust that would preserve this strange collection of huge and small monoliths, dating from somewhere between 1500 and 2000 B.C., when the Neolithic era was being transformed into the Bronze Age.

Stonehenge is one of the most important archaeological remains
in Europe, but its purpose, its time of erection, and the race or races
which built it will probably never be known with certainty.[1]

Space is lacking here for a detailed description of Stonehenge.
In general, it consists of an encircling earthwork and the remains of
four series of stones: viz., an outer circle of sarsens with lintels, an
inner bluestone circle, a horseshoe of five great trilithons, and an
inner ovoid of bluestones.[2] The outer circle consists of thirty large
upright sarsens, of which sixteen remain standing. Their average
height above ground is thirteen and one-half feet, the depth below
ground is four and one-half feet, and the average weight is twenty-
six tons. The height above ground of the largest monolith is twenty-
two feet.

Many and fanciful have been the suppositions as to the object of
this edifice or collection of edifices. The weight of evidence now
leans to the theory that Stonehenge was primarily a place for worship of the sun or was a sepulcher. Not far off are traces of what
Breasted has called "the Late Stone Age racecourse, nearly two miles
long." [3]

If our prehistoric ancestors were men of small stature, as has
been generally believed by scientists, it is inconceivable that they
could have lifted the huge stones into place without machinery or
engineering knowledge. If the Dutch paleontologist, Dr. Ralph von
Koenigswald, is correct in his theory [4] that the races of antiquity
were actual giants, eight or nine feet tall and weighing six or seven
hundred pounds, the mystery of the method of the building of Stonehenge is not so great, but certainly the builders, whether large or
small, must have used language in their cooperation on such an
enterprise. But what language? On this point, the records are silent;
there are no inscriptions on the stones.

[1] *Encyclopedia Americana*, "Stonehenge" (New York, 1957), Vol. XXV,
p. 688.

[2] *Encyclopaedia Britannica*, "Stonehenge" (Chicago and London, 1959),
Vol. XXI, pp. 440–441.

[3] James Henry Breasted, *Ancient Times* (Boston, Ginn and Company,
1916), p. 30.

[4] "Science," *Time Magazine* (October 28, 1946), p. 66.

There is, of course, that "maverick" language, Basque, referred to in Chapter 1. Defying, as it does, identification with any Indo-European language, there would seem to be no reason for its existence in the Spanish and French Pyrenees as an island in the sea of Indo-European tongues unless, as some scholars have suggested, it represents a survival of the speech of some Neolithic (New Stone) Age tribes such as inhabited the British Isles before the dawn of history. Whether the builders of Stonehenge spoke a language that was the ancestor of the modern Basque must remain nothing more than speculation, though a fascinating one.

English itself can boast of no such antiquity. It has been a language for a relatively short time in the history of the world, and did not assume a form of its own until after the invasion of Britain by the Jutes, Angles, and Saxons in the middle of the fifth century after Christ. These three Germanic tribes spoke related Low German dialects when they left Jutland, Schleswig, and Holstein on the continent of Europe for the greener pastures of England. Their speech was similar to Old Frisian and Old Saxon, the ancestor of the present-day Low German.

3.2 Previous Languages in England Before English   The first identified language in England is that of the Celts, which was the first Indo-European tongue known to have been used in the British Isles. When Julius Caesar invaded England in the summer of 55 B.C., he found the Celts there. The Celts have more or less preserved a distinct existence to the present, their speech surviving in the Welsh of Wales, the Irish of Ireland, and the Gaelic spoken in the Highlands of Scotland. In addition there was Cornish, a Celtic speech of Cornwall generally believed to be extinct since the eighteenth century (see p. 11).

The Romans brought with them to Britain their own ways and own speech. Latin, however, did not take the place of Celtic among the common people. It was, no doubt, principally spoken by members of the ruling classes and those dwelling in cities and towns, for after the Roman troops were withdrawn in A.D. 410 its use began to decline, since the language was not general enough to survive as the Celtic has.

The Roman occupation was principally military, and its end left the way open for the Jutes, Angles, and Saxons. The Jutes settled in

Kent and the Isle of Wight, the Angles in the area north from the
Thames to the Firth of Forth (the greatest part of what is now England and Lowland Scotland) with the exception of the district just
north of the mouth of the Thames. This was occupied by the Saxons
along with the area south of the Thames, except the region held by
the Jutes and Cornwall, then held by the Celts. The principal kingdoms of the Angles were Northumbria, East Anglia, and Mercia; of
the Saxons, Wessex (kingdom of the West Saxons), Essex (kingdom
of the East Saxons), and Sussex (kingdom of the South Saxons); and
of the Jutes, Kent. These seven small kingdoms are referred to as the
Anglo-Saxon Heptarchy.

3.3 Divisions in the History of English   The Old English, or
Anglo-Saxon, period begins with the coming of the Jutes, Angles,
and Saxons into England (449) and ends around 1100 after the
Norman Conquest (1066). The earliest recorded forms date back to
the seventh century, and the period from the earliest settlement to
700 is sometimes known as that of Primitive Old English. Few
written records before the late ninth century have been preserved,
however, and of these the oldest might have been composed two
centuries before. The language was constantly changing, and by
1100 many of the inflections had been leveled off. Then began what
is known as the Middle English period, which extends to about 1500.
The time since 1500 is known as the Modern English period, the one
of lost inflections. It must be remembered that there actually were
no definite breaks, such as are suggested by the dates 1100 and 1500,
in the development of English. At times, however, changes are more
rapid than at others because of special circumstances. For convenience in discussing linguistic changes, more or less arbitrary dates are
chosen to set off large general divisions which have special characteristic affecting inflections, sounds, syntax, and words. The development of a language is a continuous process, and English is no
exception.

3.4 Old English Dialects   In Old English there were four main
dialects, two of which were Anglian: the Northumbrian (the language of the first significant literature in English dating from the
late seventh and early eighth centuries), spoken north of the river
Humber; and the Mercian, spoken in the Midlands between the
rivers Humber and Thames. The third was Kentish, spoken by the

Northumbrian

Mercian

Kentish

West Saxon

OLD ENGLISH DIALECTS

Jutes, and the fourth was the chief Saxon dialect, West Saxon, in which are written most of the Old English texts that have come down to us. The reason for this disproportionate survival of West Saxon manuscripts is that most of the prose was originally West Saxon, inspired by the outstanding Anglo-Saxon king, Alfred the Great (871–901), and that the poetry, mainly Anglian, was copied by West Saxon scribes, whose transcriptions have been preserved. Two periods of West Saxon can be differentiated: Early West Saxon, the language of King Alfred, and Late West Saxon, centering around the prose writer Ælfric (*fl.* 955–1025). Traces of these dialects are distinguishable in the provincial speech of England today. In Middle English the West Saxon dialects and Kentish merged as the Southern dialect; the Northumbrian became the Northern; and the Mercian became the Midland, dividing into West Midland and East Midland, the latter of which developed into Modern English. East Midland, the dialect of the metropolis, London, contributed most to the formation of Standard English, since it was not only spoken by more people, but occupied a middle position between the North and the South and shared some of the characteristics of both its neighbors.

3.5 Influence of Celtic on Old English   The influence of Celtic upon Old English was slight. Outside of place names, for example, *Kent, Aberdeen, Dundee, Thames, Avon, Dover, Wye, Bryn Mawr* (*bryn* meaning "hill" and *mawr* meaning "great"), Celtic left fewer than a score of words, such as *broc,* "badger," *binn,* "basket," "crib," *bratt,* "cloak," *cumb,* "valley." A parallel example is that of the American Indian in the United States. There are many Indian place names, such as Arizona, Arkansas, Indiana, Iowa, Minnesota, Mississippi, Missouri, Nevada, Sioux City, Tuscaloosa, Yosemite, but few Indian words in everyday speech.

3.6 Influence of Latin on Old English   The Latin influence in Old English, somewhat stronger than the Celtic, was not great. In Old English, as in Modern German, the tendency was to translate borrowed ideas into Old English instead of borrowing words as later became the tendency in English. It has been estimated that the number of loan words from Latin before 1050 was about four hundred, of which many occur only once, thus making the number actually in use much smaller.[5] This influence was mainly upon the learned language and not on the everyday speech. A few words, however, like *cheese, mile, kitchen, cup, wall, kettle,* and *wine,* were adopted. Another illustration of Latin influence is found in place names, many of which include *castra,* "camp," in its various derivatives, as *Lancaster, Gloucester, Worcester, Chester, Winchester,* the last two palatalizing the *c,* giving *ch.* These borrowings were due to the contact the Anglo-Saxons had with Roman merchants on the Continent, to the words the Romans probably left when they were in possession of England, and to the missionaries following in the wake of Augustine, who introduced the Roman tradition of Christianity into England in 597. The contacts here were not with a conquering race, but with a race which had a higher civilization, the contacts being first commercial and later intellectual and religious.

[5] G. P. Krapp, *Modern English, Its Growth and Present Use* (New York, Charles Scribner's Sons, 1909), p. 216.

3.7 Scandinavian Influence on Old English The third influence upon Old English was Scandinavian. Danish inroads on England began in the late eighth century and continued to the eleventh century when Cnut, King of Denmark, finally obtained the English throne (1017) and from his new seat of power ruled most of the Scandinavian world. During the next twenty-five years Danish kings governed England, and many Scandinavians came into the country and made their homes there. The result of their settling may be seen in the more than 1400 places in England having Scandinavian names, largely in the North and East where most of the invaders settled. Among these are names adding *by*, the Danish word for "town," as *Derby, Rugby, Grimsby;* those adding *thorp*, "village," as *Althorp, Linthorpe;* those adding *thwaite*, "an isolated piece of ground," as *Applethwaite;* and those adding *toft*, "a messuage" (a dwelling house with adjacent buildings and adjoining lands), as *Eastoft* and *Nortoft.*[6] The Anglo-Saxons and the Scandinavians, mostly Danes, soon amalgamated because of the close relationship of the two peoples. The Scandinavians had a great influence upon the language, but in many instances because of the similarity of the tongues it is hard to determine to what extent and in what way Old English was affected. Many of the common, everyday words, such as *man, wife, father, mother, house,*[7] were the same in both languages, but the development of the sound *sk* instead of its palatalized form *sh* (written *sc*) of Old English was Scandinavian. Thus in Modern English we have the native words like *ship, dish, fish* and those borrowed from the Scandinavian like *sky, skull, scrub, scare, bask.* The development of the *g* and *k* in words like *give, get, egg, kid* is also Scandinavian. For instance, we would be saying *yive* as Chaucer did except for the Scandinavian influence, for *g* was palatalized before *e* and *i* in Old English so that the *g* of *giefan*, "to give," was pronounced as a *y*. We have inherited the Scandinavian meaning of some words, for example, *plow*, which in Old English meant a measure of land but in Scandinavian referred to an agricultural implement. The word in

[6] See Allen Mawer, "The Scandinavian Settlements in England as Reflected in English Place-Names," *Acta Philologica Scandinavica* (Vol. VII, 1932), pp. 1–30.

[7] Otto Jespersen, *Growth and Structure of the English Language*, 8th edit. (Leipzig, B. G. Teubner, 1935), p. 60.

Old English for the latter was *sulh*. Most of these words were used in the ordinary daily life, showing that the Anglo-Saxons and the Scandinavians lived side by side as equals, and not in the relationship of ruling class to conquered, as with the Anglo-Saxons and Celts, or of the ignorant to the learned, as with the Anglo-Saxons and Romans.

Thus one can see that the Old English vocabulary was on the whole Germanic, Old English being itself a West Germanic tongue and the chief influence being Scandinavian, the North Germanic branch of languages. The Celtic contribution was slight, including fewer than twenty words aside from place names. And since the Anglo-Saxons were given to applying native words to new concepts instead of borrowing the foreign word, Latin, although it had a much greater influence than Celtic, did not contribute very many words that can rightfully be considered as incorporated into the language. Of the estimated four hundred before the year 1050, many were employed only once in writing and some were purely learned words that would not be counted a part of the everyday speech.

3.8 Old English, a Language of Full Inflections It was previously stated that one of the distinguishing features of the Indo-European languages was inflection (p. 12). These various languages differ in the use they make of inflection, even in the different stages of one particular language, as English. Old English is known as a language of full inflections, Middle English as a language of leveled inflections, and Modern English as a language of lost inflections. It is only in comparison with Middle English and Modern English that Old English can be called a language of full inflections, for Indo-European inflections were disappearing long before the Old English period. Aiken analyzed seven verses of the New Testament, *Mark* 4: 1–7, in Greek, Gothic, Old English, and Modern English (King James Authorized Version, 1611, and Weymouth's translation of the New Testament, 1929) and found that we employ about one-third as many inflected words as did Gothic and Greek. Greek had 62 per cent, Gothic 60, Old English 43, Modern English 23 (Authorized Version) and 21 (Weymouth's translation).[8] Most of the changes in

[8] Janet Rankin Aiken, *English Present and Past* (New York, The Ronald Press Company, 1930), pp. 213–214; 266–271.

inflections in English had taken place by the time of Shakespeare, during the period when the conservative influences of printing and schools were not at work. There have been few losses since 1600, the chief ones being the gradual disappearance of the forms of the sub-junctive mood and the limited use of *ye, thou, thee, thy,* and *thine,* both of which can still be found in literature if rarely ever heard in speech. The tendency toward the loss of inflections continues, as may be observed in the colloquial use of *who* for *whom* in present-day *Who did you hear from?*

3.9 Definition of Inflection Inflection, broadly defined, is a mod-ification (initial, internal, or final) in the form of a word to indicate distinctions of case, number, gender, person, tense, voice, mood, or some like grammatical aspect for the purpose of showing corre-sponding changes in its use and meaning. For example, the plural of Modern English *cap* is *caps,* in which -*s* has been added to *cap* to indicate that there is not one cap but more than one. Every instance, however, is not so simple, for it is often hard to find a line of demar-cation between inflections and other compositional affixes. A com-pound like *horseshoe,* for example, is made up of two independent words, each of which can be used separately, but that is not so with words like *martyrdom* and *freshness* in which -*dom* and -*ness* are not really independent words, but have more meaning as separate elements in the words than generally recognized inflections like the plural -*s* of *caps* or the -*ed* of the past tense *talked.* Other termina-tions of the -*dom* and -*ness* kind are -*ly* and -*like* in *beastly* and *home-like.* For practical purposes, it seems best to distinguish inflectional from compositional elements by finding the varying elements which fulfill the same functions with a fair degree of universality. In Mod-ern English, for example, five living inflections are -*s*, -*ed*, -*ing*, the comparative -*er*, and the superlative -*est*, the first two having several possible pronunciations and spellings. Others which may doubtfully be classed as inflections are the adverbial -*ly* and the *to* of the in-finitive.

3.10 Types of Inflection There are three types of inflection: initial, internal, and final. In Old English the single instance of initial inflection was the prefix *ge-* often added to past participles of verbs as in Modern German. Examples are *gesungen,* "have sung," *geriden,* "have ridden," *gedruncen*, "have drunk." A trace of it remains in the archaic *yclept*, "named," the *y* surviving from the earlier *ge*. The one illustration in Modern English is the sign of the infinitive *to*, which, although it is written separately, might as well be a part of the verb, *toswim* or *totalk*, as the *s* in *swims* or the *ed* in *talked*. If it were, students would not have trouble with that so-called "split infinitive" which still worries the purist. Instances of internal inflection, meaning in practice internal vowel change, are rather common in English, as Old English *mann, menn*, "man, men," *fōt, fēt*, "foot, feet," *swimman, swamm, swummon, swummen*, "swim, swam, swum," the internal inflection in verbs being a survival of the Indo-European ablaut or vowel gradation, and the internal inflection of nouns and a few other types being vowel mutation or umlaut, the fronting and raising of an accented vowel through the influence of vowel sounds in a following syllable, as *tōð, tōðes*, giving *tēð*, "tooth, tooth's, teeth," neither of which is a living process in Modern English. The most common method of inflection is the final, as Old English *camp, campas*, "camp, camps," *disc, discas*, "dish, dishes," *windan*, "to wind," *windep*, "winds." The final inflection is still active in Modern English.

3.11 Old English, a Synthetic Language   There are two types of inflectional languages: synthetic and analytic. In a synthetic language the relationship of words in a sentence depends largely upon inflections whereas in an analytic language the relationship depends upon the use of prepositions and auxiliary verbs and upon the order of words. In Latin, for example, *Agricola amat puellam* means "The farmer loves the girl" and it would have the same meaning no matter in what order the words are arranged, for *agricola* is the form of the nominative case and the ending *-am* of *puellam* designates the accusative no matter at what position in the sentence. In Modern English, however, it makes a great deal of difference whether one says "The farmer loves the girl" or "The girl loves the farmer," for the meaning depends upon the order of words. Modern English is an analytic language, whereas Latin is synthetic. Old English, like Latin, with its numerous inflections, most of which were later to disappear, is synthetic, resembling Modern German in its grammar.

The distinction between synthetic and analytic in language is pointed out by Mario A. Pei in his pamphlet *The Geography of Language*,[9] when he observes that "to the speaker of a language like English the grammatical structure of a language like French is comparatively easy ('I have laid the book on the table' can be translated absolutely word for word into French); German, which says 'I have the book on the table laid' seems a little harder. Latin, requiring 'Book on the table laid-I' is harder still. On the other hand, German *ich habe . . . gelegt* and *das Buch* come considerably closer to English 'I have laid' and 'the book' than French *J'ai posé* and *le livre*, or Latin *librum* and *posui*, with the result that for the example in question the advantage of similarity in French word order is offset by the advantage of similarity in German vocabulary, and the beginner would be tempted to say: 'French and German are about equally difficult.' "

The noun and adjective in Old English are theoretically inflected for four cases in the singular and in the plural, although the forms are not always separate ones. The adjective also has distinctive forms for each of the three genders, as well as a different declension for the weak and strong positions. The definite article, which in Modern English has the one unchanging form *the*, in Old English is elaborately declined for case, number, and gender, just as is the German article *der, die, das*. The conjugation of the verb is not so extensive as that of a Latin or Greek verb, but the various persons, tenses, numbers, and moods have separate endings, and the treatment of the subjunctive is similar to that of German.

3.12 Grammatical Gender   Old English, like Latin, German, and Indo-European languages generally, had what is known as grammatical gender, the placing of nouns into the masculine, feminine, and neuter groups according to the way in which they were inflected without reference to sex. For instance, the words for *hand* and *heart* were feminine, for *foot* and *arm* masculine, but the words for *head, eye,* and *ear* were neuter. Also *mōna,* "moon," *steorra,* "star," were masculine, but *sunne,* "sun," was feminine; *dæg,* "day," was masculine, but *niht,* "night," was feminine. Likewise, *mæden,* "maiden," was neuter as is the cognate from *mädchen* in German. So were

[9] Mario A. Pei, *The Geography of Language* (New York, F. S. Vanni, 1945), p. 15.

wīf, "wife," *bearn,* "child," and *cild,* "child." Modern English has cast aside grammatical gender for natural or logical gender, dependent upon sex. In the Indo-European tongues gender has steadily grown nearer to identification with sex and in Modern English the process has been completed. In Old English many nouns had the same gender they now have in Modern English—for example, *man, boy, ox,* and *lord* were masculine and *woman, lady, cow,* and *queen* were feminine.

3.13 The Noun   The Old English noun falls into two general classes, the vowel and consonant declensions, also called the strong and weak declensions, depending upon whether the stem ended in Germanic in a vowel or a consonant. Each of these classes has several subtypes or classes. For instance, the vowel declension includes stems of nouns ending in *a, ō, i,* and *u* with separate inflections for each. The Old English noun is inflected for number (singular and plural) and case. The case system was somewhat less complicated than that of Latin and some other Indo-European languages, the vocative usually being the same as the nominative and the ablative and instrumental or locative generally identical with the dative. One may get an idea of the somewhat elaborate noun declensions and the synthetic character of Old English from two examples of the vowel declension and one of the consonant: *fisc,* "fish," a masculine *a*-stem; *lufu,* "love," a femine *ō*-stem; and *oxa,* "ox," a masculine consonant stem (so called because the nouns originally ended in these letters): [10]

		STRONG DECLENSION		WEAK DECLENSION
SING.	Nom.	fisc	luf-u	ox-a
	Gen.	fisc-es	luf-e	ox-an
	Dat.	fisc-e	luf-e	ox-an
	Acc.	fisc	luf-e	ox-an
PLUR.	Nom.	fisc-as	luf-a	ox-an
	Gen.	fisc-a	luf-a	ox-ena
	Dat.	fisc-um	luf-um	ox-um
	Acc.	fisc-as	luf-a	ox-an

[10] Since the instrumental is always the same as the dative in the noun, it will not be included in the paradigms.

A summary of the various inflectional endings which the nouns of the different genders and types take follows, in order to show the somewhat complicated system. A dash is used to show words which may appear in certain cases without any inflectional ending.

	SINGULAR		PLURAL
Nom.	___, -u, -a, -e, -o.	Nom.	___, as, -u, -a, -e, -an.
Gen.	-es, -e, -an.	Gen.	-a, -ena.
Dat.	___, -e, -an, -o.	Dat.	-um.
Acc.	___, -e, -an, -o.	Acc.	___, as, -u, -a, -e, -an.

The same ending may appear in more than one case or number. For example, *-e* may be used in any case of the singular or in the nominative or accusative plural, and *-an* appears five times. The endings that are distinctive and occur usually in only one case or number are *-es* of the genitive singular, *-um* of the dative plural, and *-as* which appears only in the nominative and accusative plural, endings that play an important role in the later development of the inflectional system.

3.14 The Adjective The elaborateness of inflection of the Old English adjective contrasts strikingly with the absence of any inflection in Modern English. This loss of inflections in the adjective together with loss of grammatical gender are two major advances scored by Modern English. The Old English adjective inflected for all the forms for which the noun inflected, number, case, gender, and class, and in addition for strong and weak position. As was pointed out previously, the development of the twofold declension of adjectives was an outstanding feature of the Germanic languages, the weak declension being used when a noun was preceded by a definite article, a demonstrative pronoun, or a possessive pronoun, and the strong when it was not. Furthermore, according to the rules of concord, the adjective had to agree in its inflection with the number, case, and gender of the noun it modified. Thus we find in Old English *wīs mann*, "wise man" (nominative singular masculine, strong declension), but *þās wīsan menn*, "these wise men" (nominative plural masculine, weak declension). Some idea of the elaborateness of the inflection may be gathered from the strong and weak declension of *wīs*:

		STRONG DECLENSION			WEAK DECLENSION		
		Masc.	*Fem.*	*Neut.*	*Masc.*	*Fem.*	*Neut.*
SING.	Nom.	wīs	wīs *	wīs	wīs-a	wīs-e	wīs-e
	Gen.	wīs-es	wīs-re	wīs-es	wīs-an	wīs-an	wīs-an
	Dat.	wīs-um	wīs-re	wīs-um	wīs-an	wīs-an	wīs-an
	Acc.	wīs-ne	wīs-e	wīs	wīs-an	wīs-an	wīs-e
	Ins.	wīs-e	wīs-re	wīs-e	wīs-an	wīs-an	wīs-an

* If the stem is short, the adjective ends in *-u* in the feminine nominative singular and the neuter nominative and accusative plural.

		STRONG DECLENSION			WEAK DECLENSION
		Masc.	*Fem.*	*Neut.*	*All Genders*
PLUR.	Nom.	wīs-e	wīs-a, -e	wīs, -e	wīs-an
	Gen.	wīs-ra	wīs-ra	wīs-ra	wīs-ra, -ena
	Dat.	wīs-um	wīs-um	wīs-um	wīs-um
	Acc.	wīs-e	wīs-a, -e	wīs, -e	wīs-an
	Ins.	wīs-um	wīs-um	wīs-um	wīs-um

3.15 The Definite Article   With the adjective should be placed the fully inflected definite article, inflecting like the adjective and the Modern German article for number, case, and gender illustrated below:

		Masc.	*Fem.*	*Neut.*	*All Genders*
SING.	Nom.	sē	sēo, sīo	ðæt *	ðā
	Gen.	ðæs	ðǣre	ðæs	ðāra, ðǣra
	Dat.	ðǣm, ðām	ðǣre	ðǣm, ðām	ðǣm, ðām
	Acc.	ðone, ðæne, ðane	ðā	ðæt	ðā
	Ins.	ðȳ, ðon, ðē [11]		ðȳ, ðon, ðē	ðǣm, ðām

* The symbol *ð*, "eth," also written *þ*, is equivalent to *th*; the symbol *æ*, called the digraph, has the sound of Modern English *a* in *cat*. Old English *a*, as for example *stān*, "stone," has the sound of *a* in Modern English *father*.

Although the usual meaning of *sē, sēo, ðæt* is *the*, it was originally a demonstrative, surviving in the Modern English demonstrative *that*. In Old English it was also used as a relative pronoun (*who, which, that*) and occasionally as a personal pronoun (*he, she, it*).

[11] The adverbial use of the old instrumental case occurs in expressions like "*the* more *the* merrier." It corresponds to the ablative in Latin. For examples of other survivals, see par. 40.1.

3.16 The Personal Pronoun The chief difference between Old English and Modern English personal pronouns is that in Old English we find the dual number, a set of forms for two things or two people, in addition to the singular and the plural. The dual number in the prehistoric stages of the language was probably present in the noun, adjective, and verb. It has been preserved in the verb in Greek and to a certain extent in Gothic. All traces of it have disappeared in Modern English, and the only remnant in Old English is in the personal pronoun of the first and second persons, due, no doubt, to the frequent use of the pronoun and the need for specific reference when employed. The separate accusative forms of early Old English, *mec, ðec, uncit, incit,* also disappeared before the end of the Old English period, being superseded entirely by the datives. Below are listed the inflections of the Old English personal pronoun with the modern English equivalent, if there is one:

	FIRST PERSON		SECOND PERSON	
	SINGULAR		SINGULAR	
Nom.	ic,	"I"	ðū,	"thou"
Gen.	mīn,	"mine"	ðīn,	"thine"
Dat.	mē,	"me"	ðē,	"thee"
Acc.	mē, mec,	"me"	ðē, ðec,	"thee"
	DUAL		DUAL	
Nom.	wit		git	
Gen.	uncer		incer	
Dat.	unc		inc	
Acc.	unc, uncit		inc, incit	
	PLURAL		PLURAL	
Nom.	wē,	"we"	gē,	"ye," "you"
Gen.	ūre, ūser,	"our"	ēower,	"your"
Dat.	ūs,	"us"	ēow,	"you"
Acc.	ūs,	"us"	ēow,	"you"

THIRD PERSON SINGULAR

	Masc.	*Fem.*	*Neut.*
Nom.	hē, "he"	hēo, hīo, hīe, hī, "she"	hit, "it"
Gen.	his, "his"	hiere, hire, hyre, "her"	his, "its"
Dat.	him, "him"	hiere, hire, hyre, "her"	him, "it"
Acc.	hine, hiene, hyne, "him"	hīe, hī, hȳ, hēo, "her"	hit, "it"

PLURAL

All Genders

Nom. hīe, hī, hȳ, hēo, hīo, "they"
Gen. hiera, hira, hyra, heora, hiora, "their"
Dat. him, heom, "them"
Acc. hīe, hī, hȳ, hēo, hīo, "them"

Where more than one form is listed, as in the nominative feminine third person singular, the first form is the most common, but the others appear.

3.17 The Verb The Old English verb differs from Modern English in having more specific forms for the numerous tenses, persons, etc. The verbs were divided into two classes: the strong and the weak. The strong verbs fell into seven classes, the first six having a regular variation of the root vowel to indicate a change of use or meaning (an ablaut series), the seventh being a remnant of an old Indo-European group known as reduplicating verbs. They are illustrated below with a single example of each:

	Infinitive	*Preterite Sing.*	*Preterite Plur.*	*Past Participle*
I.	wrītan, "to write"	wrāt	writon	writen
II.	frēosan, "to freeze"	frēas	fruron *	froren
III.	singan, "to sing"	sang	sungon	sungen
IV.	stelan, "to steal"	stæl	stǣlon	stolen
V.	tredan, "to tread"	træd	trǣdon	treden
VI.	tacan, "to take"	tōc	tōcon	tacen
VII.	blāwan, "to blow"	blēow	blēowon	blāwen

* The change from *s* to *r* in the preterite plural and past participle, known as Grammatical Change, is due to the fact that the accent was originally on the final syllable. This is an illustration of Verner's Law, so named because of the scholar, Karl Verner, who first explained it (see par. 2.8). In Modern English the *r* has been replaced by the *s* through analogy with the other forms.

The verb inflects for three persons; two numbers; two tenses, the present and the past or preterite; three moods, imperative, indicative, and subjunctive, the last having a much wider use than in Modern English; for the infinitive, gerund (the dative case of the infinitive used as a neuter noun after *to*), present and past participle. The personal endings may be illustrated by conjugating the first verb in the above list:

INDICATIVE

PRESENT		PAST	
Singular	*Plural*	*Singular*	*Plural*
ic wrīt-e	wē wrīt-að	ic wrāt	wē writ-on
ðū wrīt-(e)st	gē wrīt-að	ðū writ-e	gē writ-on
hē wrīt-eð, wrītt	hīe wrīt-að	hē wrāt	hīe writ-on

SUBJUNCTIVE

PRESENT		PAST	
Singular	*Plural*	*Singular*	*Plural*
ic wrīt-e	wē wrīt-en	ic writ-e	wē writ-en
ðū wrīt-e	gē wrīt-en	ðū writ-e	gē writ-en
hē wrīt-e	hīe wrīt-en	hē writ-e	hīe writ-en

IMPERATIVE

Sing. *wrīt*
Plur. wrītað

INFINITIVE	GERUND
wrītan	tō wrītenne (-anne)

PRESENT PARTICIPLE	PAST PARTICIPLE
wrītende	(ge) writen

The majority of Old English verbs, the weak verbs, which have come to be the dominant ones in our language, formed their past tense by adding to the present stem *-ede, ode,* or *-de,* and their past participles by adding *-ed, -od,* or *-d.* For instance, the preterite of *styrian,* "to stir," is *styrede* and the past participle *(ge)styred;* of *ðancian,* "to thank," is *ðancode* and *(ge)ðancod;* of *habban,* "to have," is *hæfde* and *(ge)hæfd.* There were three classes. The personal endings need not be given here since they are similar to those of the strong verbs with the exception of the preterite singular. The forms of the present tense were also used to express future time, as is still true in Modern English, as in *I go tomorrow.* In addition to the simple inflectional tenses there were a number of phrasal verbs, as in Modern English, formed by means of joining to the infinitive of the main verb such auxiliaries as *bēon,* "be," *willan,* "will," *sculan,* "shall," and *habban,* "have." Since there was no inflectional passive as in Modern English, the compound or phrasal passive was also formed by joining to the past participle the verb *bēon,* "be," "was," etc. Unlike Modern English, however, the preposition *to* did not merely indicate the infinitive but when employed was followed by the inflected form in the dative case, showing purpose, as in *Ic arās þē tō andettenne,* "I arose to confess [that is, for the purpose of confessing] to thee."

3.18 The Adverb The use of the adverb in Old English is not very different from that in Modern English; in both, it is inflected to show degrees of comparison. There were, however, several inflections employed in Old English for the purpose of forming adverbs. Adding the dative singular ending *-e* to an adjective formed an adverb, as *beorht,* "bright," *beorhte,* "brightly." The addition of this *-e* to adjectives ending in the suffix *-līc,* as *glædlīc,* "glad," *glædlīce,* "gladly," resulted in *līce* becoming an adverbial ending, to be added to adjectives to form them into adverbs, as in *eornost,* "earnest," *eornostlīce,* "earnestly." In time this became the most common of all adverbial endings, living in its shortened form as the adverbial suffix *-ly* in Modern English. Just as the dative singular ending was added, so was the plural *-um,* as in *hwīl,* "time" (Modern English *while*), *hwīlum,* "at times." The genitive singular ending *-es* also had adverbial force, as in *dæg,* "day," *dæges,* "by day." These inflections have gradually disappeared, leaving the archaic form *whilom,* in which the *-um* is present; a survival of the genitive adverb construction in expressions like *He works evenings;* and adverbs without endings, as in *Drive slow* and *Work hard.*

3.19 Passages in Old English Having pointed out many of the inflections in Old English, the syntactical devices which make it a synthetic language, we may look at a few specimens of it. A passage of Old English looks strange to a modern reader because of the two symbols *ð* and *þ,* and the digraph *æ*. Old English also represents the sound of *sh* by *sc,* as *sc(e)ort,* "short," *scip,* "ship," and the sound of *k* by *c,* as *corn,* "corn," *cyssan,* "to kiss," *cynn,* "kin," the letter *k* rarely being found in Old English. Nor do the letters *j, q, v, z* occur, the sounds being represented by *cg,* as in *ecg,* "edge"; the *q* by *cw,* as in *cwic,* "quick," *cwēn,* "queen." The sound of *v* is expressed by *f* placed between voiced sounds, as in *ofer,* "over," *healfe,* "half"; likewise, the sound of *z* is expressed by *s* in the same positions, as *rīsan,* "to rise," *hūsl,* "housel." Thus simple words like *disc,* "dish," *bacan,* "to bake," *bōc,* "book," *cyning,* "king," *bæð,* "bath," and *þæt,* "that," look unfamiliar. A page of French or Italian may look less forbidding at first, but with a little attention one begins to note the similarities to Modern English and can begin to see how the language we use today grew out of the speech of a thousand years ago.

With these points in mind, let us now turn to the first specimen to be presented, the West Saxon version of the Lord's Prayer, the modern form of which is familiar to us from *Matthew* 6:9–13 of the King James version of the Bible.

9   . . . Fæder ūre þū þe eart on heofonum, sī þīn nama gehālgod.

10   Tō becume þīn rīce. Gewurþe ðīn willa on eorðan swā swā on heofonum.

11   Ūrne gedæghwāmlīcan hlāf syle ūs tō dæg.

12   And forgyf ūs ūre gyltas, swā swā wē forgyfað ūrum gyltendum.

13   And ne gelǣd þū ūs on costnunge, ac ālȳs ūs of yfele. Sōþlīce.

The second passage will be the West Saxon version of *Luke* 15: 11–24 with the translation from the King James version of the Bible interpolated.

11   Sōðlīce sum monn hæfde twegen suna.
    . . . A certain man had two sons.

12   Þā cwæð sē gingra tō his fæder, "Fæder, sele mē mīnne dǣl mīnre
    And the younger of them said to his father, "Father, give me the portion of
ǣhte þe mē tō gebyreþ." Þā dǣlde hē him his ǣhta.
goods that falleth to me." And he divided unto them his living.

13   Ðā æfter fēawum dagum eall his þing gegaderode sē gingra sunu ond
    And not many days after the younger son gathered all together, and
fērde wrǣclīce on feorlen rīce ond forspilde þǣr his ǣhta, libbende on his
took his journey into a far country, and there wasted his substance with
gǣlsan.
riotous living.

14 Đā hē hīe hæfde ealle āmierrede, þā wearð micel hungor on þām rīce
    And when he had spent all, there arose a mighty famine in that land;

and he wearð wǣdla.
and he began to be in want.

15 Þā fērde hē and folgode ānum burhsittendum menn þæs rīces; ðā
    And he went and joined himself to a citizen of that country; and

sende hē
he sent

hine tō his tūne þæt hē hēolde his swīn.
him into his fields to feed swine.

16 Đa gewildnode hē his wambe gefyllan of þām bēancoddum þe ðā swīn
    And he would fain have filled his belly with the husks that the swine

ǣton, and him mon ne sealde.
did eat, and no man gave unto him.

17 Þā beþōhte hē hine ond cwæð, "Ēalā, hū fela hȳrlinga on mīnes
    And when he came to himself he said, "How many hired servants of my

fæder hūse hlāf genōhne habbað, ond ic hēr on hungre forweorðe!
father's house have bread enough and to spare, and I perish with hunger.

18 Ic ārīse ond ic fare tō mīnum fæder and ic secge him, 'Ēalā fæder, ic
    I will arise and go to my father, and will say unto him, 'Father, I have

syngode on heofonas and beforan þē;
sinned against heaven and before thee,

19 Nū ic ne eom wierðe þæt ic bēo þīn sunu nemned: dō mē swā ānne of
    and am no more worthy to be called thy son: make me as one of

þīnum hȳrlingum.' "
thy hired servants.' "

20 Ond hē ārās þā ond cōm tō his fæder. And þā gīet þā hē wæs feorr
    And he arose, and came to his father. But when he was yet a great way

off,

his fæder, hē hine geseah and wearð mid mildheortnesse āstyred and ongēan
his father saw him,   and had compassion, and

hine arn ond hine beclypte ond cyste hine.
ran, and fell on his neck, and kissed him.

21 Đā cwæð his sunu, "Fæder, ic syngode on heofon and beforan ðē;
    And the son said unto him, "Father, I have sinned against heaven, and

nū ic ne eom wierþe þæt ic þīn sunu bēo genemned."
in thy sight, and am no more worthy to be called thy son."

22   Ðā cwæþ sē fæder tō his þēowum, "Bringað hræðe þone sēlestan
But the father said to his servants, "Bring forth the best

gegierelan and scrȳdað hine, ond sellað him hring on his hand and gescȳ tō
robe and put it on him; and put a ring on his hand and shoes on

his fōtum;
his feet:

23   Ond bringað ān fætt stierc and ofslēað, ond uton ettan and gewistfullian;
And bring hither the fatted calf and kill it; and let us eat and be merry.

24   For þām þes mīn sunu was dēad, ond he geedcwicode; hē forwearð,
For this my son was dead, and is alive again; he was lost

ond hē is gemētt." Ðā ongunnon hīe gewistlǣcan.
and is found." And they began to be merry.

For the Student

A. FURTHER READINGS

Krapp, *Modern English, Its Growth and Present Use,* pp. 56–74.
Baugh, *A History of the English Language,* 2nd edit., pp. 47–126.
Robertson and Cassidy, *The Development of Modern English,* 2nd edit.,
  pp. 36–51.
Marckwardt, *Introduction to the English Language,* pp. 276–330.
Emerson, *A Brief History of the English Language,* pp. 23–35.
Jespersen, *Growth and Structure of the English Language,* 9th edit., pp.
  31–54.
Bradley, *The Making of English,* pp. 1–13; 47–50.
Moore and Knott, *The Elements of Old English,* 8th edit.
Anderson and Williams, *Old English Handbook.*
Bright, *An Anglo-Saxon Reader,* rev. edit. by Hulbert.
J. and E. M. Wright, *Old English Grammar,* 2nd edit.
J. and E. M. Wright, *An Elementary Old English Grammar.*
Quirk and Wren, *An Old English Grammar.*
Campbell, *Old English Grammar.*
Brunner, *Altenglische Grammatik.*
Webster's *New International Dictionary,* 2nd edit., §§ 1–24, pp. lxxxii–
  lxxxiv.
Stenton, *Anglo-Saxon England,* 2nd edit.

Hodgkin, A *History of the Anglo-Saxons,* 3rd edit.
Jackson, *Language and History in Early Britain.*

B. FOR CLASS DISCUSSION

1. How old is the English language?
2. What is meant by Old English? What is its historical origin? Give the approximate dates of the Old English period.
3. What languages were in England before English? Did they have any influence on English? If so, show in what way.
4. What is the importance of the date A.D. 410 in the history of the English language?
5. What were the various dialects in Old English? Where were they located? How do you account for them?
6. What is Primitive Old English? Do we have records of that period? If not, how do we know what Primitive Old English is like?
7. How did the names *England* and *English* originate? (See Baugh, *History of the English Language,* 2nd edit., p. 57.)
8. Explain how the development of language is a continuous process. Illustrate.
9. In what dialect are most of the Old English manuscripts written? Why?
10. Show the importance of Alfred the Great in the history of the English language.
11. Can you find examples of any other Celtic words that have come down to us in addition to the ones listed in par. 5?
12. What is the importance of the study of place names? Do you know George R. Stewart's *Names in the Land,* rev. edit.? Look into it and find parallel illustrations to those cited in pars. 5, 6, and 7. See also Robert L. Ramsay, *The Place Names of Franklin County, Missouri* (University of Missouri Studies, Vol. 26, No. 3), 1954; "Our Storehouse of Missouri Place Names," *University of Missouri Bulletin* (Vol. 53, No. 34, 1952); Erwin G. Gudde, *California Place Names,* rev. edit. (Berkeley, University of California Press, 1960); F. G. Cassidy, *The Place Names of Dane County, Wisconsin* (American Dialect Society, 1947); articles in *Names,* publication of the American Name Society. How many places can you list that represent different national influences in this country?
13. Of what origin are the place names Winchcombe, Exe, Brockholes, Leicester, Usk, Dorchester, Duncombe, Thoresby, Manchester, Cowperthwaite, Brockhall, Carlisle, Rochester, Holcombe, Brimtoft, Whitby, Bishopsthorpe, Satterthwaite, Langtoft?

14. What is the difference between the type of word borrowed from Scandinavian and that from Latin? How would you account for the difference?
15. What are the three Latin influences on Old English?
16. What is the importance of the date 1017 in the history of the English language?
17. What is the origin of each of the following words: *shall, skill, whisk, shirt, gild, kid, gift, bank, leg, scales, sister, scab, they, them, their?* Give a reason for each answer.
18. What is meant by calling Old English a language of full inflections? Has Old English lost any inflections? If so, how many can you name?
19. What is meant by inflection? Illustrate.
20. Select a piece of prose and eliminate all inflections. Is it comprehensible? Which inflections seem to be necessary? Could any still be lost?
21. Select a page of some foreign language, French, German, or any other that you know, and count the words which are inflected and those that are uninflected. What percentage are inflected? Compare with figures in par. 8.
22. Select a chapter in the King James version of the Bible (1611) and compare it with the same chapter in a modern version. Are there any differences in number and kind of inflections?
23. Can you give any examples of the loss of inflection in colloquial speech?
24. Are *ina* in *czarina* and *ine* in *heroine* inflections? *En* in *children? M* in *whom? Ly* in *joyfully? Like* in *childlike? Ball* in *baesball? Ness* in *neatness? Hood* in *manhood? Ship* in *friendship?* Give reasons for your answers.
25. Can you give examples of initial inflection in other languages besides English? Of internal inflection?
26. What is the difference between a synthetic and an analytic language? Give examples.
27. What is meant by grammatical gender? Illustrate.
28. Why is the loss of grammatical gender a linguistic step forward for Modern English?
29. Look into an Old English grammar and see how many types of declensions of nouns there are. How many kinds are there in the strong declensions? In the weak declensions?
30. Look into an Old English grammar and see the various types of declensions of adjectives. How many advantages can you list for the Modern English adjective over the Old English?
31. How many forms of the definite article were there in Old English? Is the loss of the majority of forms a linguistic advantage? Why?

32. In how many ways was number expressed in Old English? In Modern English? Which has the advantage linguistically? Why?

33. How many of the Old English pronouns have come down to Modern English? Why have so many been preserved?

34. Do you like better the terms *irregular-regular* or *strong-weak* for verbs? Why?

35. At times a strong preterite *snuck* is humorously given to the verb *sneak*. Is the vowel change regular according to the strong classes listed in par. 17? Can you give other examples of strong preterites in slang, funny talk, or colloquial English?

36. Examine the Old English passages in the text and see how many words you can trace into Modern English.

C. SUGGESTIONS FOR RESEARCH PAPERS

1. Scandinavian (Celtic or Latin) Place Names in England.

2. The Inflection of Nouns in Old English and Latin (or any other language).

3. The Conjugation of Strong (Weak) Verbs in Old English.

4. Comparison of the Verb in Old English to the Verb in Latin (or any other language).

5. The Adjective (Adverb, Article, or Pronoun) in Old English and in Latin (or any other language).

6. Gender in Old and Modern English.

7. Self-Explaining Compounds in Old English.

8. Prefixes and Suffixes in Old English.

4

Middle English Heritage

4.1 Continuous Process Although linguistic changes are a continuous process and all dates are a mere approximation, for the sake of convenience the four centuries from 1100 to 1500 are generally regarded as the Middle English period.[1] Certain it is that within that span of years the language developed a pattern that was distinctly different from that of Old English and was the precursor of Modern English. The one factor of overwhelming significance in that period was of course the Norman Conquest at its outset. Without the invasion of William the Conqueror and his cohorts English presumably would have grown along Germanic lines to become even more closely linked to Modern Dutch and Modern German than it is. And if, three centuries after the conquest, the Normans had not lost their land holdings in France, Norman French might have re-

[1] Middle English was, undoubtedly, being spoken much earlier. See Kemp Malone, "When Did Middle English Begin?" *Curme Volume of Linguistic Studies, Language Monograph No. 7* (Baltimore, Waverly Press, 1930), pp. 110–117.

mained in the ascendancy and the dominant language of the British
Isles today would be a variation of French. So much for the "ifs" of
history and linguistics.

4.2 The Conquering Hero   It was in September 1066 that William and some 60,000 Normans landed on English soil, but their
language had actually preceded them. Edward the Confessor, next
to the last of the old Saxon kings, had a Norman mother and had
been reared on the Continent when the Saxon princes were exiled
from Britain during the reign of the Danish usurpers. Proclaimed
king and crowned at the cathedral in Winchester in 1042, Edward
was almost a stranger to the land and the language of his forefathers.
He had brought with him a small group of Normans, and more kept
coming over each year of his reign, so that the Norman tongue even
banished from the palace the Anglo-Saxon, which had become an
object of ridicule to the foreign courtiers, and no flattering discourse
was any longer addressed to the king except in Norman French.

4.3 Infiltration Tactics   This infiltration of Norman French had
gone on, therefore, over a period of nearly twenty-five years before
the arrival of Duke William to wrest the English crown from Edward's successor, King Harold. If the Normans had been defeated at
the battle of Hastings and hurled back to France, the vogue of the
new tongue doubtless would have died out quickly at the English
court, but William's victory naturally made it possible for Norman
French to consolidate its position. Nevertheless, the Norman Conquest was not a national migration, and the modification of English
law, language, and social custom through French influence was a
very gradual process.

4.4 English Not Banned   William did not despise the old language or forbid its use in private affairs and around the family fireside. He even took pains to acquire some knowledge of English, and
the *Anglo-Saxon Chronicle* continued to be written in it for almost
another hundred years—until 1154. Nevertheless, the Venerable
Wulfstan, Bishop of Worcester, was deposed from his See in 1095 as
"an idiot who did not know French." [2] Wulfstan was only a conspicuous example of a process that went on throughout England as

---

[2] "Quasi homo idiota, qui linguam Gallicanum non noverat. . . ." Matthias
Paris, ad ann., quoted by Jean Roemer, *Origins of the English People and of the
English Language* (London, Kegan Paul, Trench & Co., 1888), p. 296.

members of the native clergy were forced to give up their duties and benefices to make way for Norman priests, the result being that French became the language of the churches and monasteries for all secular business. Harsh treatment this undoubtedly was, but from practically contemporary accounts, notably that of Odericus Vitalis, it would seem that a portion at least of the English clergy had become illiterate, even in their own tongue. It is to the credit of William the Conqueror that he brought to England the zest for intellectual affairs that swept over the Continent after its first contacts with the lore of the Arabs and the Far East, a zest that was the precursor of the full-blown Renaissance a few centuries later. "The Conqueror himself patronized and loved letters. . . . Many of the Norman prelates, preferred in England by the Conqueror, were polite scholars," remarks the preface to Warton's *History of English Poety*.[3]

4.5 Effect of Architecture   The invaders also brought with them their delight and skill in erecting imposing buildings in what came to be known as the Norman style of architecture. Doubtless it was English laborers and craftsmen who did most of the manual work on the construction of the imposing cathedrals, monasteries, and manor houses, and in the course of their work they were bound to pick up many words of the new tongue, as did shopkeepers in the towns who had business with the newcomers.

4.6 "Uplandish" Folk   The farmers, herdsmen, and other "uplandish" folk, as the rural dwellers were sometimes called—corresponding to our modern "hillbillies"—clung to the old language, just as the mountaineers of the southeastern United States held on to some of the Shakespearean English of more than three hundred years ago that their ancestors brought over with them. In more thickly settled regions of England the new Norman culture was superimposed on the old, but even there did not drive out the Anglo-Saxon completely, in the way that the Anglo-Saxons had all but obliterated the Britons. In the stratification of society after the Norman Conquest, the Normans were the "high men" and the English, even though called "uplandish" on some accounts, were the "low men," to use the terms employed by Robert of Gloucester in his *Chronicle,* written in 1300. As the chronicler put it,

---

[3] Thomas Warton, *History of English Poetry* (London, Thomas Tegg, 1824), Vol. I.

> . . . The folc of Normandie,
> Among us woneth [dwelleth] yet, and schulleth ever mo. . . .
> Of the Normannes beth thys hey men that beth of thys lond
> And the lowe men of Saxons.

4.7 Ascendancy of French   As was to be expected, it was the language of the "high men" that prevailed, not only because an inferior culture would imitate a superior one, but also because the use of French was enforced by law in public business, in court trials, and, most importantly, in the schools. Robert Holcot, writing in the early part of the fourteenth century, observed that there was no instruction of children in the old English, that the first language they learned was French, through which they were later introduced to Latin, and he added that this practice had been established immediately after the conquest. Or, to quote Robert Gloucester's *Chronicle* again:

> Ɉ þe Normans ne couþe speke þo, bote hor owe speche,
> Ɉ speke French as hii dude at om Ɉ hor children dude also teche.
> So þat heiemen of þis lond, þat of hor blod come,
> Holdeth alle þulke speche that hii of hom nome.
> Vor bote a man conne Frenss, me telþ of him lute.

Students who have not acquired a knowledge of Middle English will need to have this translated in some such fashion as the following: "And the Normans could not then speak any speech but their own; and they spoke French as they did at home, and had their children taught the same. So that the high men of this land, that came of their blood, all retain the same speech that they brought from their home. For unless a man know French, people think little of him."

4.8 Forced on English   This learning of French was compulsory for those children of the English who attended school. This situation brought a complaint from Ranulf Hygden in his *Polychronicon*. A passage, as translated into Middle English by Trevisa, deplores "this apayringe [impairing] of the birthe tonge" resulting in part from the fact that "children in scole, aghenes [against] the usage and maner of alle other naciouns, beth [be] compelled for to leve her [their] owne langage, and for to constrewe her [their] lessouns and her [their] thingis a Frensche. . . ."

4.9 Decline in Quality So, not only was the English language losing quantitatively; it was also felt to be slipping in quality. For one thing, with no formal instructions in the schools and no new literature being created, the language was becoming so diversified in form and utterance—since used only by the "low men"—as to be hardly understood from one district to another. Even at the time of the conquest, the number of Englishmen who could read and write their own language was not large, relatively, and when that generation died out the language, ceasing to be read and written, lost almost all its bookish words, three centuries of misery and national degradation having stripped the native tongue of fully half its vocabulary and left the remainder in utter confusion. Under such circumstances, English must have possessed amazing vitality to survive at all, even if it did become interlarded with French borrowings to replace part of its forgotten vocabulary and to express new concepts that the old vocabulary could not have coped with.

4.10 Impact of History Even linguistic vitality, however, does not go far toward explaining the ascendancy that English finally achieved over Norman French. Recourse must be had to the general history of the times, in its military and political aspects and also in its social and economic trends. A detailed analysis of these factors lies outside the scope of this work, but some general conclusions can bet set forth, bearing on the subject at hand.

4.11 Territory Lost For nearly one hundred forty years after the conquest of England, the Normans expanded territorially as well as linguistically, not only in Britain but also on the Continent. Their influence, if not actual control, extended over two-thirds of France as a result of the weakness of the nominal monarchs of that country and of the valor and ability of William of Normandy and his five immediate successors. But the seventh in this Norman line, King John, was "a trifler and a coward," asserts the brilliant if biased historian, Macaulay, and "just at this conjuncture, France, for the first time since the death of Charlemagne, was governed by a prince of great firmness and ability." [4] King John was driven from Normandy in 1204, and the holdings that the rulers of England retained in the

[4] Thomas B. Macaulay, *History of England*, Vol. I, p. 12, in *The Works of Lord Macaulay*, edited by his sister, Lady Trevelyan (London, Longmans, Green and Co., 1871).

south of France were inconsequential. "The Norman nobles were compelled to make their election between the island and the continent," Macaulay adds. "Shut up by the sea with the people whom they had hitherto oppressed and despised, they gradually came to regard England as their country, and the English as their countrymen."[5]

4.12 The Melting Pot To quote this nineteenth-century historian further, "The stages of the process by which the hostile elements were melted down into one homogeneous mass are not accurately known to us. But it is certain that, when John became king, the distinction between Saxons and Normans was strongly marked, and that before the end of the reign of his grandson it had almost disappeared."[6] Actually, the inhabitants of England, whether of high or low rank in the social scale and whether of Norman or Saxon stock, began to cultivate an interest in all things English that centuries later developed into the insular patriotism that made the modern British the butt of the world's jibes—and envy. The rivalries with France that turned into open and protracted warfare hastened this process. The Hundred Years' War (1337–1453) and the notable victories of English arms at Crécy (1346) and Poitiers (1356) provided new incentives for abandoning the language of the enemy.

4.13 War and Plague Social and economic forces were meanwhile at work toward the same end. As the bitterness of the years immediately after the conquest receded, intermarriage between the Normans and Saxons became frequent, especially in the more isolated sections of the realm, so that more and more Norman courtiers and their descendants acquired a knowledge of the English language. Then, in the middle of the fourteenth century, there came upon the land a great catastrophe, the Black Death, a plague that swept through the length and breadth of the land with awful thoroughness. As usual in such calamities, the fatalities were far larger, both absolutely and relatively, among the lower classes than among the nobles and the wealthy burghers who could get away from pestilential spots. The loss in population was so great that an acute labor shortage developed, wages shot upward, and the working man —and his language, which was English—achieved a new importance

[5] *Ibid.*
[6] *Ibid.*, p. 13.

in the community. This new importance of the old English stock was enhanced further a century later when the Wars of the Roses (1453–1485) between the rival royal houses of York and Lancaster so decimated the ranks of the nobles that they had to turn to the once despised Saxon underlings to recruit their respective forces for continued hostilities.

4.14 Poetry as Clue But even before the Black Death gave the Saxon artisans an enhanced economic and social status, one of the odd poetical customs of the early fourteenth century provides an inkling of the shape of things to come. It became the custom to write verses in bilingual form, with first a couple of lines of French and then a couple of lines of English, the latter not translating the French but continuing the story or sentiment. Thus, a political song of 1311 "On the King's Breaking His Confirmation of the Magna Charta" even maintains a rhyme scheme between French and English sections, as the following lines indicate, the first two in French and the other two in English:

> Nostre prince de Engleterre,
> Par le consail de sa gent
> At Westminster after the feire
> Maad a gret parlement. . . .

4.15 Shift to English But this sort of linguistic and poetic duality could not be maintained indefinitely, in view of the growing trend of the times toward English. In 1356 the Mayor and aldermen of London ordered that proceedings in the Sheriff's Court of that city and Middlesex should be English,[7] and six years later the Chancellor opened Parliament for the first time in English. In 1362 a statute was enacted to require all cases before the King's courts to be pleaded in English instead of in French, and entered and enrolled in Latin. Nevertheless, for another hundred years or more, the laws themselves continued to be drawn up in French, and the first bill of the House of Commons that was written in English bears the date 1485; the House of Lords apparently retained the language of the conquest a few years longer, and some law reports were written in French as late as 1600.

[7] R. R. Sharpe, *Calendar of Letter-Books . . . of the City of London,* Letter-Book G (London, 1905), p. 73.

4.16 Reconversion in Schools   In par. 8 were quoted the remarks of Ranulf Hygden on the compulsory teaching of French in
the schools in the middle of the fourteenth century. Trevisa's translation was made some thirty years after Hygden wrote, so by way of
bringing the situation up to date, as of 1385, the translator added:

"This maner [that is, of instruction solely in French] was myche yused
tofore the first moreyn [that is, before the plague of 1349] and is siththe
som dele [somewhat] yechaungide. For John Cornwaile, a maister of
gramer, chaungide the lore [learning] in gramer scole and construction of
[from] Frensch into Englisch, and Richard Pencriche lerned that maner
teching of him, and other men of Pencriche. So that now, the yere of owre
Lord a thousand thre hundred foure score and fyve, of the secunde King
Richard after the Conquest nyne, in alle the gramer scoles of England children leveth Frensch, and construeth and lerneth an [in] Englisch, and
haveth thereby avauntage in oon [one] side and desavauntage in another.
Her [their] avauntage is, that thei lerneth her [their] gramer in lasse tyme
than children were wont to do; desavauntage is, that now children of gramer
scole kunneth [know] no more Frensch than can her lifte heele [knows their
left heel]; and that is harm for hem [them], and if they schul passe the
see [sea] and travaile in strange londes, and in many places also. Also gen-
tilmen haveth now mych ylefte for to teche her [their] children Frensch."

4.17 A Different French   As a matter of fact, even the English
who did go abroad to strange lands found that Norman French,
which once had set the standard for the language, had undergone so
many changes, due in part to the influence of English on it (especially the tendency to accent the first syllable and slur over the
others), that it was not always easy for the traveler from England
to understand or be understood by speakers of Continental French.
Chaucer's famous pen portrait of the prioress in the *Prologue* to *The
Canterbury Tales* bears witness to this fact:

> And Frensh she spak ful faire and fetisly,
> After the scole of Stratford atte Bowe,
> For Frensh of Paris was to hir unknowe.

That being the case, French had no longer had any inherent claim
to preference as the language of Englishmen, and this was another
factor in accelerating the reestablishment of English as the dominant

tongue. But the English that came again into its own was not the language of four centuries earlier.

4.18 A Different English William Caxton, born in Kent about 1415 and famous as the man who introduced printing to England, saw a tremendous change in the language even in his lifetime. In the preface to his *Eneydos*, translated from the French in 1490, he remarked how some gentlemen had complained that his translations used curious terms which could not be understood by the common people "and desired me to vse olde and homely termes," to which Caxton adds:

"And fayn wolde I satysfye euery man / and so to doo, toke an olde boke and redde therein / and certaynly the englysshe was so rude and brood that I coude not wele vnderstande it. And also my lorde abbot of westmynster ded do shewe to me late certayn euidences wryton in olde englysshe, for to reduce it into our englysshe now vsid / and certaynly it was wreton in such wyse that it was more lyke to dutche than englysshe; I coude not reduce ne brynge it to be vnderstonden / And certaynly our langage now vsed varyeth ferre from that whiche was vsed and spoken whan I was borne / For we englysshe men / ben borne vnder the domynacyon of the mone, whiche is neuer stedfaste / but euer wauerynge / wexynge one season / and waneth & dyscreaseth another season." [8]

4.19 Changes Fundamental If one were to ask in what way the language was altered, the answer must be: "In almost every way." The Normans found English a synthetic, highly inflected language like Greek, Latin, and Modern German, but after a few centuries had passed it had become an analytic language,[9] with rapidly disappearing inflections, like Modern French. Grammatical gender and transposed word order were succeeded by natural gender [10] and the normal word order of present-day English. Grammar was only one aspect of the change. The pronunciation shifted, and the alteration in vocabulary was particularly far-reaching, with thousands of

[8] The crossbar, used in the passage, is found in manuscripts and early printed books as a puctuation mark standing for either a period or a comma.

[9] C. C. Fries, "On the Development of the Structural Use of Word-Order in Modern English," *Language* (Vol. XVI, 1940), pp. 199–208, shows statistically that the change was complete by 1500.

[10] See Samuel Moore, "Grammatical and Natural Gender in Middle English," *Publications of the Modern Language Association* (Vol. 36, March, 1921), pp. 79–103.

French and Latin terms added to the word stock. The whole pattern of the language was modified. The conquest did not account for all these changes, but for many of them.

4.20 Causes of Loss of Inflections   One of the chief reasons for the leveling of inflectional endings in the Middle English period was undoubtedly a change in the method of accenting words. In Old English, although the stress was generally on the root syllable, unstressed vowels were so pronounced as to retain their individual quality, but in Middle English the stress began to be stronger on the first syllables of words, as it is in Modern English, thus making weaker the syllables following. As a result the unstressed *a, e, o,* and *u* in inflectional endings became neutral in sound, the so-called "indeterminate vowel," or *schwa,*[11] usually written as *e.* Also the unstressed distinct endings *-a, -u, -e, -an, -um* were leveled under the vowel *-e,* losing at the same time grammatical distinctions formerly expressed.[12] The first ending to be weakened, beginning in Old English, was *-um* of the dative plural in nouns and adjectives, gradually appearing as *-un, -on, -en,* and *-an,* the last becoming predominant by the end of the Old English period.

4.21 Noun   It has been previously mentioned that there was a leveling of the various Old English vowel endings under the vowel *-e.* The declensions of the few nouns given in par. 3.13 illustrate this change. In the declension of *fisc,* the eight forms of the singular and plural were reduced to three: *fisc, fisces,* and *fisce.* The various declensions of Old English, based on the difference in vowel ending, had largely been abandoned. The endings of Old English shown leveled off in the beginning as follows: [13]

	SINGULAR	PLURAL
Nom.	—, -e.	—, -e, -es, en.
Gen.	-e, -es, -en.	-e, -ene.
Dat.	—, -e, -en.	-en.
Acc.	—, -e, -en.	—, -e, -es, en.

[11] See par. 14.8.

[12] For the chronology of the changes, see Samuel Moore's two articles: "Loss of Final *n* in Inflectional Syllables of Middle English," *Language* (Vol. III, 1927), pp. 232–259; "Earliest Morphological Changes in Middle English," *Language* (Vol. IV, 1928), pp. 238–266.

[13] Compare Old English endings in par. 3.13.

Two classes of nouns remained: the strong and the weak. The strong nouns formed their genitive singular and nominative and accusative plurals in *-es*, whereas the weak nouns had the ending *-en* for these and other forms. With the inflections leveling under *-e*, *-es*, *-en*, the means of distinguishing grammatical gender passed and words began to be used as in Modern English. The inflections below show a typical strong noun in Middle English (*fisc*) and a typical weak noun (*oxe*): [14]

	SINGULAR	PLURAL
Nom.	fisc	fisces
Gen.	fisces	fisce, fisces
Dat.	fisc(e) [15]	fisc(en)e, fisces
Acc.	fisc	fisces

	SINGULAR	PLURAL
Nom.	oxe	oxen
Gen.	oxe(n)	ox(en)e
Dat.	oxe(n)	oxen
Acc.	oxe(n)	oxen

All nouns tended to fall into these two groups, the strong nouns being much more numerous. If a strong noun ended in an unstressed *-e* in the nominative and accusative singular, as in *ende*, *helpe*, and *soule*, the plural and the genitive singular were formed by adding *s* only. Thus in early Middle English there were two main ways of designating the plural: the *-s* or *-es* in the strong declension and the *-en* in the weak. Until the thirteenth century the plural in *-en* was used to a great extent in the South. It was even added to nouns not originally weak.

4.22 Trend in Plurals In the other parts of England, however, the *-s* for the plural and genitive singular, derived from the first declension masculine nouns with the plural in *-as,* was employed much more extensively and became widespread. Even in Old English in the North many nouns originally from other declensions had gone over to this declension. Thus, by the middle of the thirteenth cen-

---

[14] Compare Old English declensions in par. 3.13.
[15] Letters in parentheses were sometimes used, but not always.

tury, *-s* was the usual plural ending for nouns in the North and in the Midlands, and during the fourteenth century this method of forming the plural was accepted as the standard one throughout England. The number of nouns ending in *-en* decreased throughout the Middle English period, so that at the end only a few like *oxen, brethren,* and *children* were left to appear in Modern English.

4.23 The Adjective   As has been stated, the noun lost grammatical gender along with the loss of inflections. With the loss of grammatical gender in the noun went the loss of agreement, so far as gender is concerned, in inflection between the noun and its adjective. At the same time the inflectional endings in the adjective leveled off as they had done in the noun. In both the strong and weak declensions, the nominative singular was extended to all cases in the singular and the nominative plural to all cases in the plural. Thus *wīs,* "wise," would be declined in Middle English as follows: [16]

	STRONG	WEAK
SING.	wīs (all cases and genders)	wīse (all cases and genders)
PLUR.	wīse (all cases and genders)	wīse (all cases and genders)

In the weak declension there was no difference in the singular and plural, both ending in *-e* (*wīsa* became *wīse* and *wīsan* became *wīse*). This was also true of adjectives of the strong declension, ending in *-e*. Thus by about the middle of the thirteenth century there was no distinction between the singular and plural in the strong declension except with a number of monosyllabic adjectives ending in a consonant, as *mad* (sing.), *made* (plur.). In the fourteenth century, the final *e* was no longer pronounced, surviving only in the spelling, and by the end of the Middle English period, the adjective had lost all inflections.

4.24 The Definite Article   Since the majority of the forms of the definite article began with *þ* (*th*), by analogy *þ* was substituted for *s* of *sē* and *sēo* (see par. 3.15), giving in the nominative singular *þē, þēo, þæt.* The vowel of *þēo* became the same as that of *þē* by a regular phonetic development, and with the discarding of grammatical gender in the noun, the neuter form *þæt* was no longer used as an article but the one form *þē* was employed for all three genders, the

[16] Compare with declension in Old English in par. 3.14.

form *þæt* remaining as a demonstrative with a changed value. Analogy extended even further in that *þē* became the one form for all numbers, genders, and cases of the article after the loss of inflections in the noun. Thus one form, giving Modern English *the*, forced out the many forms of the Old English article.

4.25 Personal Pronouns The great loss of inflections found in the noun and adjective did not take place in the personal pronouns. Only they preserved throughout the Middle English period and even in Modern English most of the distinctions existing in Old English (see par. 3.16). The dual number, however, although generally confined to poetic texts, had entirely disappeared by the thirteenth century. Also the dative and accusative cases were merged generally under the form of the dative: *him, her, (t)hem.* It should be pointed out that this merging had already taken place in the first and second persons during the Old English period: *mē, þē*. In the third person neuter, however, since the dative *him* would have been confused with the masculine, the accusative *(h)it* survived, becoming the general objective case, no doubt by analogy with the nominative which had the same form. The forms of the third person plural through normal development should be *hi (he), here, him (hem)* instead of *they, their, them*, but the Scandinavian influence was strong enough in the North to crowd out the Old English forms. The Scandinavian form *þei* first replaced the nominative *hi*, as can be seen from Chaucer who generally used *thei, here, hem.* After *they* was accepted, by analogy the other forms *their* and *them* were adopted so that at the end of the Middle English period the forms *they, their*, and *them* were well established. One other different form is the nominative feminine *she* which had the form *hēo* in Old English. It is thought by some that *hēo* must have been influenced by the nominative feminine *sēo* of the definite article (see par. 3.15), originally a demonstrative, in order to give *she*.

4.26 Verb The division of the verb into strong and weak, or irregular and regular, continued in the Middle English period, but there was a tendency for the strong verbs to become weak, as in the case of *climb, help, flow, weep.* This tendency has continued on into the Modern English period, no doubt, because the weak verbs exemplify the human preference for regularity and simplicity of form. Occasionally by analogy with strong verbs, a strong past tense or past participle was formed, as in Modern English *dive*. This verb has recently developed in the United States a past tense *dove*, by analogy, no doubt, with *drive, drove.* All new verbs in Middle Eng‐ lish formed from adjectives and nouns or brought in from other lan‐ guages were conjugated as weak verbs and still are in Modern English. Thus the number of strong verbs is small in comparison with the ever-increasing stock of weak verbs.

4.27 Strong Verbs Disappear In the early Middle English pe‐ riod nearly a third of the Old English strong verbs died out and to‐ day more than half of them have disappeared. The dropping out of the strong forms was a gradual one. The strong forms continued to be employed while the weak ones were coming into use. For in‐ stance, *climb*, a strong verb of the third class, appeared as a weak verb in the thirteenth century, but the strong past tense *clomb* con‐ tinued in use and can be found in Chaucer, Spenser, and Dryden. The strong forms, surviving from Old English, can even be heard today in illiterate speech. Subtracting the verbs that have been lost and those that have become weak, only sixty-six of the Old English strong verbs are still used.[17] Some of the past participles of strong verbs which developed weak forms have survived, oftentimes used as adjectives, as *molten, shaven, swollen*. While the fluctuation was going on between the strong and weak verbs in the Middle English period, the leveling or changing of the various inflectional vowels to the vowel -*e* was also taking place. The endings -*að* and -*iað* of the present plural merged with the -*eð* of the third singular.[18] In the im‐ perative the endings, -*e*, -*a* and -*að*, -*iað* became -*e* and -*eð* respec‐ tively and in the infinitive the -*an* and -*ian* became -*en*. The gerund ending in -*anne* became -*enne* and the preterite plural endings -*on* and -*don* became -*en* and -*den*. With the present participle ending in -*ende* a different change occurred. The present participle tended to fall in with nouns naming actions that ended in -*ung* or -*ing*, such as *blētsung*, "blessing," so that the participal ending was given up and the noun and present participle both used the ending -*ing*.

4.28 Another Simplification One other simplification of the verb

---

[17] Charles C. Fries, *American English Grammar* (New York, D. Appleton-Century Company, for *The National Council of Teachers of English,* 1940). pp. 60–61.

[18] See conjugation of Old English verb, par. 3.17.

took place in the preterite tenses. In Old English the preterite plural stem of strong verbs often differed from the preterite singular and the past participle frequently was different from both. In giving principal parts of a strong verb in Old English, one therefore gave four forms, as *findan, fand, fundon, funden,* which became in Middle English *finde, found, found.*[19] This simplification did not take place in all strong verbs, for we have a number in Modern English which still have three separate forms, as *write, wrote, written* and *ride, rode, ridden.* It should also be mentioned here that the past tense of surviving strong verbs may be derived from the past tense singular of Old English, as in *rode,*[20] or from the past tense plural, as in *bit.*[21]

4.29 Additions to Vocabulary The conditions following the Norman Conquest were favorable not only to great inflectional and grammatical changes in the language but also to great vocabulary changes.[22] When two languages exist side by side for a long time, as did French and English in England, many words are transferred from one language to the other, especially to the one in the inferior position. So it was with English, which borrowed an incredibly large number of words from the French, enough to change the general character of the language from unilingual to bilingual.

4.30 French as Model English thus began to be influenced by Romance languages as well as by Teutonic, becoming a language made up of two merging strains. Never before or since has English taken in so many words. French, in addition to being the language of the ruling class in England, was also generally regarded as the polite language of Europe. In it was written a great literature which was influencing other nations, especially England. The University of Paris was visited by all the scholars of Europe. Paris itself was considered to be the center of learning and refinement. Parisian French had taken the place of Norman French in the hearts of the English. The admiration for everything French reached its height in the four-

---

[19] See David W. Reed, *The History of Inflectional "n" in English Verbs Before 1500 (University of California Publications in English,* Vol. 7, No. 4), Berkeley and Los Angeles, University of California Press, 1950.

[20] The principal parts in Old English are: *rīdan, rād, ridon, riden.*

[21] The principal parts in Old English are: *bītan, bāt, biton, biten.*

[22] See Hereward T. Price, "Foreign Influences on Middle English," *University of Michigan Contributions in Modern Philology,* No. 10 (Ann Arbor, April, 1947).

teenth century. In attempting to make English as nearly like French as possible, words, phrases, and idioms were borrowed. Many of these took the place of English words, bringing about the obsolescence of the latter. French pronunciations and spellings came in at this time too. For instance, the introduction of *u* after *g* to indicate the hard *g* accounts for Modern English *tongue* from Old English *tunge*, which should give *tung*, like *lung;* it also accounts for spellings like *guest, guilt, guild*, and *language.*

4.31 Types of French Words Borrowed   During the whole Middle English period words of all types, of all parts of speech, and from every sphere of life, came into English, some from Norman and some from Parisian French. In many instances the English word was preserved along with the French, but often on a somewhat less dignified plane, as English *work* but French *labor*, English *town* but French *city*. Many words that were introduced had to do with the table, preparation of food, and eating, such as *dinner, taste, appetite, supper, napkin, pastry, roast, broil*, and *boil*. To these should be added terms dealing with fashions, dress, and social life, including *apparel, gown, veil, cloak, coat, embroidery, kerchief, mitten, taffeta, satin, jewel, ornament, sapphire, diamond, dance, melody, conversation, tournament, palfrey, falcon, checkers, chess.*

As a result of the influence of French life and civilization the English people had a much fuller and more varied life in the fourteenth century than previously, and with it went words of French origin. One would naturally expect many words connected with the court, government, and legal procedures. To mention only a few, among them are *government, reign, court, parliament, tax, revenue, exchequer, traitor, treason, liberty, mayor, treasurer, coroner, duke, duchess, nobility, peer, squire, justice, attorney, plaintiff, jury, verdict, sentence, plead, indict, acquit, assault, libel, fraud.* The church likewise added its share: *prayer, clergy, cardinal, friar, religion, faith, mystery, preach, devotion*, and many others. But many simple, commonplace words were also introduced, such as *fruit, flower, chair*, and *age*. Since war also played a great part in the Middle Ages, many French military terms were introduced, such as *battle, combat, soldier, guard, captain, sergeant, lieutenant, vanquish*, and *besiege.* The arts and formal learning donated their share. There were words connected with architecture, literature, and science, particularly medicine. Among these words are *painting, sculpture, figure, beauty, cathedral, palace, ceiling, chimney, tower, porch, pillar, poet, romance, story, tragedy, prologue, preface, paper, pen, treatise, geometry, grammar, copy, compile, physician, surgeon, malady, anatomy, sulphur, alkali, arsenic, pestilence.* From these lists one can get some idea of the breadth and universality of French influence in the Middle Ages. It contributed words to every walk of life.

4.32 Changes in Words   As has been pointed out, Old English combined native elements into self-explaining compounds and made use of prefixes and suffixes in meeting new needs of vocabulary, but with the influx of thousands of French words—easily acquired new words—the English habits of word formation were weakened. If both the English and French words survived, the meanings were usually differentiated as may be seen from *doom* and *judgment, house* and *mansion, ask* and *demand.* Many of the Old English prefixes gradually fell into disuse. Take, for example, *for-,* employed in Old English to stress the meaning of a verb or to suggest the idea of destructiveness or prejudice. It survived in Middle English, being added even to a few French words, but it died out completely as a formative prefix. In Modern English only a few of the verbs remain, among them *forbear, forbid, forget, forgive,* and *forsake,* all originating in Old English. The prefix *with-,* meaning *against,* made possible *withdraw* and *withhold* in Middle English, which survive in Modern English along with Old English *withstand,* but the prefix *to-* has disappeared entirely. *Over-* and *under-,* greatly weakened in the Middle English period, have, on the other hand, been revived in Modern English. Most of the compounds including these two prefixes belong either to the Old English or to the Modern English period. The prefix *on-* (now *un-*) kept more of its vitality than most prefixes, giving *unfasten, uncover, unwrap* among the Middle English words employed often in Modern English to show the negative. Prefixes of Latin origin, such as *dis-, re-,* and *trans-,* came in to crowd out the Old English ones. With the suffixes, some few remained, among them the noun suffix *-ness* and the adjective endings *-full, -less, -some,* and *-ish,* but most have been lost. A few words were formed in Middle English employing *-dom,* as *dukedom; -hood,* as *manhood, womanhood, likelihood.* The suffix *-hood* has completely died out along with -*ship,* as in *hardship.* The ending -*dom,* on the other hand, has recently been revived. Consider *fandom, filmdom, sportsdom,* and many others, not at all nonce-words. The self-explaining compounds, however, have not suffered the same fate as most of the affixes. The process still goes on even though we borrow many words. We speak of a *gateleg table,* a *tablecloth,* a *gingersnap, sugar beet, sugar cane, sugar maple,* and a host of others.

4.33 Latin Words Borrowed in Middle English   The Latin influence actually increased with the inflow of French words and ideas. During the Middle English period words continued to be borrowed directly from Latin, some from the spoken language of the ecclesiastics and men of learning, but most from the written language. One of the important sources of Latin words which became everyday terms was Wycliffe's translation of the Bible. Many words relating to science, literature, theology, law, and medicine were introduced, the vast majority in the fourteenth and fifteenth centuries. A few may be mentioned: *allegory, legal, mechanical, nervous, prosody, pulpit, rosary, scripture, secular, testify, testimony, ulcer, zephyr.* Among the formative suffixes which became common and still are active are -*able,* -*al,* -*ent,* -*ible,* -*ive,* and -*ous.* In addition poets and writers of prose, chiefly in the fifteenth century, affected a style in which they consciously brought in unusual Latin words, known as "aureate terms." [23] Not a great number but a few of these also dropped into current use. Chaucer in the fourteenth century used some of these words which became common, such as *laureate* and *oriental.* As a result of the French and Latin borrowings, English became a richer language with innumerable synonyms. For instance, one finds *ask* (Old English), *inquire* (French), and *interrogate* (Latin); *bold* (Old English), *valiant* (French), and *audacious* (Latin); *holy* (Old English), *sacred* (French), and *consecrated* (Latin). English has profited greatly by this variety of vocabulary, which enables a person to use a simple, popular style or a more learned, elevated one as the occasion demands.

4.34 Flemish, Dutch, and Low German Borrowings in Middle

[23] G. H. McKnight, *Modern English in the Making* (New York, D. Appleton and Company, 1930), pp. 38–55. See also the standard treatment of the subject by John C. Mendenhall, *Aureate Terms* (Lancaster, Pa., Wickersham Printing Company, 1919).

English Although there was a predominance of Latin and French borrowings in Middle English, one must not disregard the constant intercourse between England and the people of Holland, Flanders, and northern Germany, beginning in the time of William the Conqueror, who married a Flemish wife. During this period many persons from the Low Countries came to settle in England, principally in connection with the trade carried on with the Low Countries. Wool was exported from England to these areas; their expert weavers were urged to come to England and many did. Much travel also went on between these countries and England. As a result of the contacts and intercommunication a number of words were borrowed, among them *deck, dock, freighter, lighter, nap* (of cloth), *furlough, dollar, easel, etching,* and *landscape.* At times it is difficult to tell whether a word has been borrowed or is of native origin because of the similarity of these languages.

MIDDLE ENGLISH DIALECTS

4.35 Dialects in Middle English Roughly, Middle English is divided into four main dialects: the Northern, spoken north of the Humber River; the West Midland and the East Midland, used in the district between the Humber and the Thames; and the Southern, employed in the Kentish and West Saxon areas of Old English, the region south of the Thames along with Gloucestershire and portions of Hereford and Worcestershire Counties.[24] Kentish was a separate dialect of Southern English in the Middle English period.

4.36 Traits of the Dialects A few outstanding traits may be cited here to give an idea of the difference in dialects. In the third person plural the Old English vowel followed by *ð* leveled off to *eð*, retained in the Southern dialect. In the Northern dialect the *-eð* was changed to *-es* and in the Midlands to *-en,* probably taken over by analogy to the corresponding forms of the preterite and the subjunctive or of the preterite-present verbs and the verb *to be*.[25] Thus we find, for example, in the South *serveth,* in the North *serves,* and in the Midlands *serven.* The present participle also had a separate form in each dialect before the ending *-ing* was adopted universally: *servinde* in the South; *servande* in the North; and *servende* in the Midlands. The Midlands and the South accepted the ending *-ing* before the North. As has been pointed out, the Scandinavian forms of the pronouns *they, their,* and *them* were current in the North while the South still used *hi, here* (*hire*), *hem.* There were likewise differences in pronunciation. For instance, *f* and *s* in initial positions were often voiced in the South, giving *v* and *z,* as in Southern *vox, vals, vaste, verst, volk, vorð* for *fox, false, fast, first, folk, forth.* In Modern English one observes the dialectal distinction in *fox* and *vixen.* Another difference is the retaining of the Old English *ā* in the North which

---

[24] See Samuel Moore, Sanford B. Meech, and Harold Whitehall, "Middle English Dialect Characteristics and Dialect Boundaries," *Essays in Studies in English and Comparative Literature* (Ann Arbor, University of Michigan Press, 1935), pp. 1–60; also Mary S. Serjeantson, "The Dialects of the West Midlands in Middle English," I, II, III, *Review of English Studies* (Vol. III, January, April, July, 1927), pp. 54–68; 186–204; 319–332.

[25] W. F. Bryan, "The Midland Present Plural Indicative Ending-*e*(*n*)," *Modern Philology* (Vol. XVIII, January, 1921), pp. 457–473. See also Gösta Forsström, *The Verb "to be" in Middle English* (*Lund Studies in English,* Vol. 15), Lund, C. W. K. Gleerup, 1948 (an exhaustive survey of the forms of the verb *be* in some ninety-four Middle English texts representative of the major chronological and dialect areas in England from *c.* 1150 to *c.* 1450).

developed into ō in the South in such words as *stone* and *home*. Scotland still has *stane* and *hame*. Often too where there was *ch* in the South, the North had *k* as in *kirk* for *church*. With the introduction of printing at the end of the Middle English period these differences were more readily wiped out and certain forms were adopted as standard.[26]

4.37 Standard English Near the close of the fourteenth century a written language developed which was accepted generally in the fifteenth century and became the standard speech. This speech developed in the East Midland district, the most highly populated area, the seat of the capital, London, the metropolitan center of England, important politically, commercially, socially, and intellectually. Into London came the various dialects, finally mingling and merging with the local dialect there to form a standard speech. The Midland dialect, not so conservative as the Southern and not so far advanced as the Northern, held a middle course between the two and developed into the speech which Chaucer used and which was to become the parent of the English we speak today.

4.38 Passages from Middle English The two Middle English passages below have been taken from representative authors who were widely read and had a great deal of influence. Chaucer, sometimes described as "the father of the English language" or "the first finder of our fair language," naturally is included. The selection chosen is his unforgettable description of the Wife of Bath in the Prologue to the *Canterbury Tales*. The other passage is from Wycliffe's translation of the Bible.

THE WYF OF BATHE

> A good Wyf was ther of bisyde Bathe,
> But she was som-del deef, and that was scathe.
> Of clooth-making she hadde swiche an haunt,
> She passed hem of Ypres and of Gaunt.
> In al the parisshe wyf ne was ther noon
> That to th' offring bifore hir sholde goon;
> And if ther dide, certeyn, so wrooth was she,
> That she was out of alle charitee.

[26] McKnight, *op. cit.*, pp. 56–59.

Hir coverchiefs ful fyne were of ground;
I dorste swere they weyeden ten pound
That on a Sonday were upon hir heed.
Hir hosen weren of fyn scarlet reed,
Ful streite y-teyd, and shoos ful moiste and newe.
Bold was hir face, and fair, and reed of hewe.
She was a worthy womman al hir lyve,
Housbondes at chirche-dore she hadde fyve,
Withouten other companye in youthe;
But therof nedeth nat to speke as nouthe.
And thryes hadde she been at Jerusalem;
She hadde passed many a straunge streem;
At Rome she hadde been, and at Boloigne,
In Galice at seint Jame, and at Coloigne.
She coude muche of wandring by the weye:
Gat-tothed was she, soothly for to seye.
Up-on an amblere esily she sat,
Y-wimpled wel, and on hir heed an hat
As brood as is a bokeler or a targe;
A foot-mantel aboute hir hipes large,
And on hir feet a paire of spores sharpe.
In felawschip wel coude she laughe and carpe.
Of remedyes of love she knew perchaunce,
For she coude of that art the olde daunce.

Wycliffe's Translation of *Matthew* 8:1–27

1   Forsothe when Jhesus hadde comen doun fro the hil, many cumpanyes folewiden hum.

2   And loo! a leprouse man cummynge worshipide hym, sayinge, Lord, ʒif thou wolt, thou maist make me clene.

3   And Jhesus, holdynge forthe the hond touchide hym, sayinge, I wole, be thou maad clene. And anoon the lepre of hym was clensid.

4   And Jhesus saith to hym, See, say thou to no man; but go, shewe thee to prestis, and offre that ʒifte that Moyses comaundide, into witnessing to hem.

5   Sothely when he hadde entride in to Capharnaum, centurio neiʒide to hym, preyinge hym.

6   And saide, Lord, my child lyeth in the hous sike on the palsie, and is yuel tourmentid.

7 And Jhesus saith to hym, I shall cume, and shall hele hym.

8 And centurio answerynge saith to hym, Lord, I am not worthi, that thou entre vnder my roof; but oonly say bi word, and my child shal be helid.

9 For whi and I am a man ordeynd vnder power, hauynge vnder me kni3tis; and I say to this, Go, and he goth; and to an other, Come thou, and he cometh; and to my seruaunt, Do thou this thing, and he doth.

10 Sothely Jhesus, heerynge these thingis, wondride, and saide to men suynge hym, Trewly I saye to 3ou, I fonde nat so grete feith in Ysrael.

11 Sothely Y say to 3ou, that manye shulen come from the est and west, and shulen rest with Abraham and Ysaac and Jacob in the kyngdam of heuenes;

12 Forsothe the sonys of the rewme shulen be cast out in to vttermest derknessis; there shall be weepynge, and betynge togidre of teeth.

13 And Jhesus said to centurio, Go, and as thou hast bileeued, be it don to thee. And the child was helid fro that houre.

14 And when Jhesus hadde comen in to the hous of Symond Petre, he say his wyues moder liggynge, and shakyn with feueris.

15 And he touchide hir hond, and the feuer lefte hir; and she roose; and seruyde hem.

16 Sothely whan the euenyng was maad, thei brou3te to hym many hauynge deuelys, and castide out spiritis by word, and helide alle hauynge yuel;

17 That it shulde be fulfilled, that thing that was said by Ysaie the prophete, sayinge, He toke oure infirmytees, and bere oure sykenessis.

18 Sothely Jhesus seeynge many cumpanyes about hym, bad his disciplis go ouer the water.

19 And oo scribe commynge to, saide to hym, Maistre, I shal sue thee, whider euer thou shalt go.

20 And Jhesus said to hym, Foxis han dichis or borowis, and briddis of the eir han nestis, but mannes sone hath nat wher he reste his heued.

21 Sotheli an other of his disciplis saide to hym, Lord, suffre me go first, and birye my fadir.

22 Forsothe Jhesus said to hym, Sue thou me, and late dede men birye her dead men.

23 And Jhesus steyinge vp into a litle ship, his disciplis sueden hym.

24 And loo! a grete steryng was maad in the see, so that the litil ship was hilid with wawis; but he slepte.

25 And his disciplis camen ni3 to hym, and raysiden hym, sayinge, Lord, saue vs; we perishen.

26 And Jhesus seith to hem, What ben ȝee of litil feith agast? Thanne he rysynge comaundide to the wyndis and the see, and a grete pesiblenesse is maad.

27 Forsothe men wondreden, sayinge, what manere man is he this, for the wyndis and the see obeishen to hym?

For the Student

A. FURTHER READINGS

Baugh, *A History of the English Language,* 2nd edit., pp. 127–239; 467–480.

Krapp, *Modern English, Its Growth and Present Use,* pp. 28–35; 74–83; 219–233.

Robertson and Cassidy, *The Development of Modern English,* 2nd edit., pp. 44–51.

Emerson, *A Brief History of the English Language,* pp. 35–51.

Emerson, *A Middle English Reader,* "Grammatical Introduction," pp. xiii–cxxiv.

Mossé, *A Handbook of Middle English,* trans. by James A. Walker, pp. 6–130.

J. and E. M. Wright, *An Elementary Middle English Grammar.*

Kurath and Kuhn (eds.), *Middle English Dictionary* (in progress).

Jordan, *Handbuch der mittelenglischen Grammatik,* 2nd edit.

Brunner, *Abriss der mittelenglischen Grammatik,* 4th edit.

Marckwardt, *Introduction to the English Language,* pp. 239–275.

McKnight, *Modern English in the Making,* pp. 17–69.

Webster's *New International Dictionary,* 2nd edit., § 34, p. lxxxv, § 36, p. lxxxvi, §§ 67–79, pp. lxxxix–xc.

Poole, *From Domesday Book to Magna Carta 1087–1216.*

Coulton, *Medieval Panorama.*

Davis (ed.), *Medieval England.*

B. FOR CLASS DISCUSSION

1. What is the importance of the date 1066 in the history of the English language?

2. What are some of the principal changes that took place in the language from Old English to Middle English?

3. What causes can you give for the leveling of inflections?
4. What are some of the conservative influences working against language? Compare the Middle Ages with the present day in this respect.
5. How are conservative influences overcome? Explain how changes come about.
6. What is meant by the term "good English"? Is "good English" today "good English" tomorrow? Explain. Give illustrations from Middle English.
7. How many languages were spoken in England during the Middle Ages? Where were they used?
8. What was the relationship of the Normans and the English? How did this affect English?
9. Of what significance is the date 1204 in the history of the English language?
10. What factors contributed to the greater use of French? To the greater use of English? Account for the triumph of English. When was it reintroduced?
11. What is the importance of the date 1349 in the history of the English language?
12. How did the Hundred Years' War affect the language?
13. Compare the endings of the nouns in Middle English with those in Old English. List the differences. What simplifications took place?
14. Compare the endings of the adjectives in Middle English with those in Old English. List the differences and tell what simplifications occurred. Do the same for the definite article.
15. Compare the personal pronouns of Middle English with those of Old English. How many have been preserved until the present day?
16. Can you account for the fewer changes in pronouns?
17. Account for the forms *they, them, their,* and *she.*
18. What changes took place in the verb in the Middle English period?
19. What part did analogy play in the development of the verb?
20. When verbs come into the language, are they conjugated as strong or weak verbs? Are there more strong or weak verbs? Give reasons for your answer.
21. What change occurred in gender in Middle English? Illustrate.
22. When did great admiration for everything French reach its height? What types of French words were borrowed? Illustrate.
23. What changes took place in the use of affixes? Illustrate.
24. In addition to the French borrowings in Middle English, what other loan words came in?

25. What are known as "aureate terms"? Illustrate. (See McKnight, *Modern English in the Making*, pp. 38–55, and Mendenhall, *Aureate Terms*, pp. 7–82.
26. What were the main dialects in Middle English? How many differences in them can you list?
27. What dialect did Chaucer use? Why?
28. Out of which dialect did a national language in England develop? Account for this.
29. What effect did the printing press introduced by Caxton have on the English language? (See McKnight, *Modern English in the Making*, pp. 56–69.)
30. Examine the two Middle English selections given in this chapter. To what dialect do the verbs belong? What conclusions would you draw in connection with the pronouns?

C. SUGGESTIONS FOR RESEARCH PAPERS

1. Loss of Grammatical Gender in Middle English.
2. A Study of the Noun (or any other part of speech) in Middle English.
3. A Comparison of the Old and Middle English Verb (or any other part of speech).
4. Self-Explaining Compounds in Middle English.
5. Prefixes (or Suffixes) in Middle English.
6. Latin Borrowings in John Wycliffe.
7. A Comparison of the Northern and Southern Dialects (or any two).

5

Modern English

5.1 The Modern English Period By general agreement among philologists, the year 1500 is regarded as marking the beginning of Modern English, although it cannot be too often insisted that all such dates are mere approximations and that all changes in the use of a mother tongue are gradual and imperceptible to the speakers of it. Furthermore, it is only in a very broad and all-inclusive sense that the English spoken in the sixteenth century can be designated "Modern," for it definitely is not the common, everyday speech of the present, either in Britain or America. The grammar of Shakespeare, whose major works fell within the latter part of the sixteenth century, is sufficiently different from today's to warrant a special treatise on the subject. Furthermore, beautiful and majestic as the cadences of the King James version of the Bible are, the several modern adaptions of recent years [1] are sufficient evidence, if evidence were needed, that the language of that Authorized Version of 1611 is too remote from the speech of the twentieth century to be fully compre-

[1] Notably the Goodspeed and Moffat versions.

hensible at all times. So, when we say that Modern English came into being around 1500, we mean no more than that the fundamental structure of the language as it exists today had developed by that time.

5.2 The Early Modern English Period In the time between 1500 and 1700, known as the Early Modern English period,[2] many of the traits that characterize the language today developed. The chief influence at this time was the great humanistic movement of the Renaissance, which exerted its greatest force from 1500 through the first quarter of the seventeenth century. In this revival of learning the study of the classics was stressed. The influence of Latin and Greek on English was great. Cultivated Englishmen, enthusiastic about the newly rediscovered beauties of Latin and Greek literature, deliberately set out to "enrich" the language by borrowing from these tongues. Style, too, became a matter of great concern, the principal models being such authors as Cicero and Vergil. Native English had to be "made better" by attempts to express ideas as the Latin authors expressed them. Many of the classics were translated in the great endeavor to make the language a better medium.

5.3 The Classicists Among the most famous translations were Sir Thomas North's of Plutach's *Lives of the Noble Grecians and Romans* (1579) and George Chapman's *Homer* which began to appear in 1598. Much earlier Sir Thomas Elyot began to introduce the English people to Plato. He also translated from the Greek *The Doctrinal of Princes, made by the noble oratour Isocrates* in 1534. A Benedictine monk, William Tilley of Selling (d. 1494), was the first Englishman of the period to become well versed in Greek. Others who followed him were Thomas Linacre (1460–1524), William Grocyn (1446–1519), and William Latimer (d. 1545). Another famous student of Greek was Sir Thomas More (1480–1535). Also, the great Dutch humanist Erasmus taught Greek at Cambridge University for several years. All of these men, of course, were facile Latinists and usually did their original composition in that language, as More did with his *Utopia* in 1516. One man who had tremendous influence in spreading the use of Latin was William Lily, first High-Master of St.

2 See Richard F. Jones, *Triumph of the English Language: A Survey of Opinions Concerning the Vernacular from the Introduction of Printing to the Restoration* (Stanford, University Press), 1953.

Paul's School in London, who wrote the famous Latin grammar which Shakespeare and most of his contemporaries used in school, as did generations of schoolboys after him. The direct influence of Latin upon English was much greater than that of Greek during the Renaissance period.

5.4 Reaction Although the humanistic movement was strong, it was not powerful enough to keep down a conservative reaction against "improving" the mother tongue. Some thought their language should depend upon its own resources and preferred to go back to its earlier periods for a renewal of energy instead of reaching out to foreign sources. To them importations from without meant corruption and not improvement. Among those who held this theory was George Pettie, who forcefully stated his position in his translation of Guazzo's *Civile Conversation* (1586). Another was Richard Mulcaster, Head Master of the Merchant Taylors' School, author of *Elementarie* (1582), the chief treatise on English spelling in the sixteenth century, and teacher of Edmund Spenser. Spenser supported his master in upholding the riches of the English language and in augmenting the vocabulary of poetry by consciously employing old words, such as *shend* for "put to shame," *ydrad* for the past participle "dreaded," the intensive prefix *fore-* in *forewasted, fone* for "foes." He also coined new words, many of which were adaptations and derivatives of old ones, as *wrizzled* (probably from "wrinkled" and "frizzled"), *drear* (from "dreary"), *hapless, changeful.* Men like Sir John Cheke, first Regius Professor of Greek at Cambridge University, even though they were classical scholars, were by nature purists and fought the introduction of so-called "inkhorn terms" from Latin and Greek. Cheke was so much opposed that in his translation of the *Gospel of St. Matthew* (c. 1550) he used such words as *hundreder* where the King James version has *centurion, crossed* instead of *crucified, foresayer* instead of *prophet,* etc. A follower of Cheke was Roger Ascham, another Elizabethan schoolmaster, who wrote in English a dialogue on archery, *Toxophilus* (1545), and a more famous work *Scholemaster,* published in 1570, two years after his death. Most scholarly works were written in Latin at this time and those who ventured to write in English were experimenting and were sometimes apologetic, as was Sir Thomas Elyot in his translation of his *Doctrinal of Princes.* In his zealous effort to improve the

English vocabulary by drawing words from Latin, Greek, and French, Elyot used English in what has been called the first book on education printed in English, *The Boke named the Gouernour* (1531), a treatise on the general philosophy of politics and education.

One of the principal objections made to the borrowed terms was their obscurity. The chief person holding this view was Thomas Wilson, author of the popular *Arte of Rhetorique* (1553) and of the excellent satire on the extreme Latinists, entitled *Three Orations of Demosthenes*, published in 1570, in which he gives a letter full of "strange termes," the letter supposedly being from a schoolmate to him: "Pondering, expending, and revoluting with myself your ingent affability and ingenious capacity for mundane affairs, I cannot but celebrate and extol your magnificent dexterity above all other. . . . I doubt not but you will adjuvate such poor adnichilate orphans as whilom condisciples with you and of antique familiarity in Lincolnshire." [3] The poet Gascoigne aligned himself on the side of the conservatives as can be seen from his *Posies*, published in 1575. The author of *The Arte of English poesie* (1589), supposedly the scholar-critic George Puttenham,[4] joined them. Finally, in 1595, Richard Carew wrote his treatise, *The Excellency of the English Tongue*, and we find Sir Philip Sidney praising English as a language equal to any other tongue. The fight of the conservatives was for a lost cause, for the Latinists triumphed, but both movements succeeded in enriching the language, one by borrowing and imitating, the other by developing its own resources.

5.5 Caxton and the Printing Press   One of the greatest influences exerted on the English language has been the printing press, introduced into England in 1476 by William Caxton, an Englishman who lived for a time on the Continent. On his return to England he set up his own printing press and began publishing books, an art he had learned in the Low Countries. Manuscript books began to disappear as movable type came into use. Before 1500, in less than twenty-five years, the number of books issued in Europe had reached the sur-

---

[3] Quoted in Walter Raleigh's "Introduction" to Baldassare Castiglione, *The Courtier*, transl. by Sir Thomas Hoby, 1561 (London, D. Nutt, 1900), p. xliii.

[4] Both George and Richard Puttenham, brothers, have been credited with the authorship of this work.

prising figure of 35,000, most of which were in Latin, but by 1640 in England more than 20,000 titles had appeared in English, including all types of books from mere pamphlets to massive folios. Books were then not for the favored few but began to be available for all. A great force had been released, a force which had a tremendous effect upon English in making it more uniform and in standardizing it. This force was multiplied in strength by the increase in education which began in the later Middle Ages and has continued ever since. Popular education has enabled the printing press to have an influence almost too powerful to describe upon language and thought.

5.6 Caxton, a Latinist Caxton has a greater opportunity than most to influence the language. In seeking material for publication he became a translator, and as author and translator he endeavored to make English as beautiful and as expressive a language as Latin and French seemed to be to him. He therefore introduced many "strange termes" to his readers who were not always pleased. Those unhappy readers he sent to the Latin writers so that they might drink from the fountain of original beauty and thereby gain understanding.

5.7 English as a Scholarly Language English had definitely established itself in England as the spoken language and the language of popular literature in the Middle Ages, but it had a second battle to fight as the language to be used in all fields. The language employed throughout Europe by the educated was Latin, and that fact insured easy communication. It was also felt that the classical languages were near perfection and that such a tongue as English lacked polish, was not mature, and was of limited value in expressing abstract ideas. The élite in education feared the oncoming intrusion of a modern language and voiced their fears, but the popular demand of the people in England to enjoy the benefits of the Renaissance, to share in the ideas of the great civilizations of Greece and Rome, which had much to offer them in their daily lives, won out over the privileged academic group. Gradually books in all fields of knowledge began to be written in English so that the average person could read them. The movement has gone so far that today relatively few avail themselves of the opportunity and privilege of studying Latin, once the accepted language of universal currency in the Western world.

5.8 Changes in Vocabulary in Renaissance Period Despite all
the opposition to the inkhorn terms in the middle of the sixteenth
century, by the end of the Elizabethan period many of the words
had made their way into the vocabulary and were even being used
by the leaders of the opposing group. Some of the words objected to,
like *industry, maturity,* and *temperance,* seem quite commonplace to
us today. In fact, we feel as if we could hardly dispense with many
of them. Such words as *disrespect, excursion, admiration, appropriate, external, education, insane, emancipate, exist,* and *meditate*
came directly from the Latin. Others, among them *emphasis, chaos,
dogma, climax, system,* and *crisis,* are of Greek origin but came in
through the Latin. Many Greek words have come into English
through Latin or French. The added interest in and study of Greek
during the Renaissance, however, brought in directly words such
as *catastrophe, lexicon,* and *anonymous.* Some words like *appendix,
exterior, integer,* and *generator* kept their Latin form, but more often
an ending was dropped, as in *extract* from Latin *extractus,* or
changed to bring the word in line with the accepted English forms.
For instance, the endings of nouns *-antia* and *-entia* were changed
in English to *-ance, -ence,* or *-ancy, -ency,* as in *countenance, confi-
dence, constancy, clemency,* and the ending *-tas* to *-ty* as in *vicinity*
from Latin *vīcīnitās;* the adjective ending *-us* was changed to *-ous* or
was replaced by *-al* as in *frivolous* from Latin *frīvolus* and in *cor-
poreal* from Latin *corporeus* while the ending *-bilis* became *-ble,* as
in *numerable* from Latin *numerābilis, tolerable* from Latin *tolerābilis,*
and *inexorable* from Latin *inexōrābilis.* The Latin past participle
formed the basis for the verbs, many of which ended in *-ate,* as *an-
ticipate* from *anticipātus, dedicate* from *dēdicātus, illustrate* from
illustrātus. At times a word borrowed in the earlier stages of the language was reborrowed with a new meaning as *discus* borrowed in
Old English for *dish* but later reintroduced to give us the words *disc*
and *discus* as well as *dais* and *desk.* During the Renaissance the borrowing of words from Latin was strengthened by the borrowing of
French words that continued from the Middle English period. It
was often hard to tell whether a word came directly from the Latin
or came in through the French, for French was at the same time
taking in many Latin words and passing them on into English.
Sometimes it is easy to tell; for instance, *fact* comes directly from

factum and not from the French *fait*, which gave English at an earlier date the word *feat*. Occasionally two words were borrowed, one from Latin and one from French, as *prejudicate* from Latin and *prejudge* from the French *prejuger*. For many words, however, it is impossible to determine the direct source; we know only that they derive from the Latin originally. In accepting Latin words French may have only set the example which English followed.

5.9 Other Loan Words in the Renaissance Period   In addition to the learned words which came in from Greek and Latin in the Renaissance period, loan words came in from more than fifty languages,[5] the most significant of which were French, Spanish, and Italian. Englishmen who traveled on the Continent brought back Italian words such as *balcony, cameo, piazza,* and *volcano*. Spanish terms such as *alligator, armada, bilbo, hammock, potato,* and *sombrero* were taken in, not to mention the many which had continually come in from the French. In fact, some of the Spanish and Italian terms were received through the French. Many words from various parts of the world came in as a result of the colonization and commerce in which England was engaged. As the British Empire expanded and trade extended, more and more words were borrowed. Word borrowing has continued and has reached vast proportions as inventions have come into being, as science has progressed, and as the world has grown smaller and smaller culturally. All of these forces have affected the English vocabulary.

5.10 Prose of the Renaissance   Along with the liberal policy of borrowing words from Latin in the Renaissance went an imitating of Latin rhetoric. The prose writers made a deliberate effort to adorn English style [6] so as to lift it above ordinary speech. Two outstanding examples of authors who consciously cultivated an artificial language are Sir Philip Sidney in the highly decorated prose of *Arcadia* and John Lyly in his affected style characterized by antithesis, alliteration, far-fetched similes, and other signs of striving after elegance which he used in *Euphues, The Anatomy of Wit* and in *Euphues*

---

[5] *New English Dictionary*, Murray's "Preface" (second page) to Vol. VII, Part II, PH to PY (Oxford, Clarendon Press, 1909).

[6] Even though style is "metalinguistic"—outside the province of linguistics —it involves vocabulary, grammar, and other aspects of language and cannot be disregarded.

and His England. The tendency of literary prose during the Renaissance was toward the ornate with one outstanding exception, the King James version of the Bible brought out in 1611.

5.11 The Bible Literary style in Modern English has been greatly affected by the tradition of Biblical translation, beginning with the first complete translation of the Bible by Wycliffe and Purvey in the fourteenth century. As a result of the Reformation John Tyndale, in 1525, published his translation of the New Testament, to which he later added the Old Testament, a significant work which established a standard of good English, one that was accepted not only by scholars but also by the common people and became the norm for the English-speaking race. Throughout the century, a number of other versions were issued, among them Miles Coverdale's and Cranmer's or the "Great Bible," all based on Tyndale's, which was also the foundation for the King James or the Authorized Version of 1611, produced by a body of English divines. This great monument of English prose owed the quality of its style more to Tyndale than to any other person. It is noted for its Old English diction. The simplicity, dignity, beauty, and strength of the Bible place it in the forefront of English prose writing and make it the greatest single force in the prose style of the last three centuries.

5.12 The Growth of Dictionaries Modern English dictionaries started with glossaries of Latin or some other foreign language and English. The first English dictionaries were those expounding hard words. The earliest was Robert Cawdrey's *The Table Alphabeticall of Hard Words,* a little book published in 1604 explaining some 3000 terms, importations from Hebrew, Greek, Latin, and French as well as archaic native words. Following it in 1616 are John Bullokar's *English Expositor* and in 1623 Henry Cockeram's *English Dictionarie,* both of which went through numerous editions. *The Glossographia* of Blount in 1656, the *New World of Words, or a General English Dictionary* (1658) by Edward Phillips, nephew of John Milton, and subsequent collections dealt only with the more difficult words. In 1721 appeared Nathaniel Bailey's *Universal Etymological English Dictionary,* the dictionary which was first and foremost until Dr. Samuel Johnson's epoch-making lexicon was published in 1755.[7] The

----

[7] See James H. Sledd and Gwin J. Kolb, *Dr. Johnson's Dictionary: Essays in the Biography of a Book* (Chicago, University Press), 1955.

Renaissance period paved the way for the great lexicographical strides made in the eighteenth century and the centuries following.

5.13 Inflections in the Modern English Period Having taken into consideration a number of the important trends of the early Modern English period, let us now observe what was happening to the inflections. The Modern English period is called the period of lost inflections, but only so in comparing it with the earlier periods, for English is still an inflectional language and makes use of a limited number of inflections. The tendencies characteristic of the Middle English period continued to operate: the tendency toward obscuring the vowels in inflectional syllables and the tendency toward simplifying the language by means of analogy, substituting one form for several. But it must be said that changes since 1500 are much fewer than those between the years 1000 and 1250. Changes in Modern English are slow, for it has been a period of regularization and standardization.

5.14 Individualism in English in the Renaissance Period Despite the fact that the early Modern English period had established something in the nature of a uniform standard of language as a result of the printing press and the labors of those who took a conscious interest in the language, there was a great deal of individuality in usage. For example, functional shift,[8] the employment of one part of speech for almost any other, was quite common, as Shakespeare's "repeat and *history* his loss"[9] and "whilst you do *climate* ['dwell'] here."[10] There was no set of conventional rules to which all thought had to conform; rather the language was fitted to the thought. Consequently, variety existed: variations in spelling, pronunciation, and grammatical forms. New words were introduced and experimented with. There were freedom and adventure to a marked degree in matters of language as in other fields during the Renaissance.

5.15 Authority in English As progress was made toward a uniform standard in the English language, freedom decreased. Rules began to be formulated, efforts began to be made to fix the language, to determine what was right and what was wrong, to prescribe the

[8] See par. 24.7.
[9] *Henry IV*, IV, i.
[10] *Winter's Tale*, V, i.

goal to be attained. This attitude reached its height in the eighteenth century, the age in which reason and logic were uppermost. Formerly, the paramount issues were the use of English instead of the traditional Latin for certain words, the adoption of a large number of loan words into the language, and the making of a better system of spelling, but in the eighteenth century attention was turned to grammar so as to codify and regularize the language, making it orderly to eliminate uncertainty. Attempts were made to settle questions logically, and authoritative examples were desired. Many demanded an English Academy, similar to those of France and Italy, to legislate on matters of language, to eliminate all impurities, and to determine what was correct.[11] Chief among the advocates were men like Dryden, Defoe, and Swift. The desire was to give English a permanent form and not allow it to be corrupted. Swift went so far as to address *A Proposal for Correcting, Improving, and Ascertaining the English Tongue* in 1712 to the Earl of Oxford, Lord Treasurer of England, complaining of the corruptions in the language and appealing to him to take some action in setting up a group of the best qualified persons to consider the language problems in imitation of the French. In other words he was suggesting an English Academy based on the French Academy, which had been founded in 1635 to give definite rules to the language and "to render it pure, eloquent, and capable of treating the arts and the sciences" (see par. 31.3). Fortunately, Swift's proposal failed. The English, for the most part, desired independence in their use of the language. Nevertheless, they felt a great need for a dictionary and a grammar to use as a standard.

5.16 Dr. Johnson's Dictionary One of the great language needs was filled in 1755 when Dr. Samuel Johnson published his *Dictionary* in two folio volumes. He confessed in the Preface that he once had some idea of fixing the language, but by the time he had finished his great work he realized that it could not keep the language from changing and that he objected to establishing an Academy. He wrote, "With this hope, however, academies have been instituted, to guard the avenues of their languages, to retain fugitives, and repulse

---

[11] See Allen Walker Read, "Suggestions for an Academy in England in the Latter Half of the Eighteenth Century," *Modern Philology* (Vol. XXXVI, November, 1938), pp. 145–156.

intruders; but their vigilance and activity have hitherto been vain; sounds are too volatile and subtile for legal restraints; to enchain syllables, and to lash the wind, are equally the undertaking of pride, unwilling to measure its desires by its strength. The French language has visibly changed under the inspection of the academy . . . and no Italian will maintain, that the diction of any modern writer is not perceptibly different from that of Boccace, Machiavel, or Caro." Even though Dr. Johnson opposed an Academy, his dictionary served practically the same purpose, setting for the eighteenth century a standard, an authority to which the public could turn.[12] Johnson himself considered that his dictionary did for the English language what the dictionary of the French Academy did for French. In matters of spelling, accent, and meaning he assumed the responsibility of legislating. Boswell spoke of Johnson as "the man who had conferred stability on the language of his country." He undoubtedly was voicing the opinion of his day. Despite the defects of ridiculous etymologies, prejudiced definitions,[13] and the inclusion of words which should scarcely be considered as belonging to the language,[14] his work of seven years was a great step forward in lexicography in setting a standard for spelling, in supplying quotations illustrating the use of words, and in giving a better idea of the English vocabulary than had been done previously. It was a great achievement. Johnson said in his *Dictionary*, "When I took the first survey of my undertaking, I found our speech copious without order, and energetick without rules: wherever I turned my view, there was perplexity to be disentangled, and confusion to be regulated." Out of the disorder he established order.[15]

[12] See Harold B. Allen, *Samuel Johnson and the Authoritarian Principle in Linguistic Criticism*, 1940 (University Microfilm, No. 381, Ann Arbor, Michigan).

[13] For example, he defined *oats* as "a grain given in England to horses and in Scotland to the people" and *pension* as "an allowance made to anyone without equivalent. In England it is generally understood to mean pay given to a state hireling for treason to his country." It may be well to mention here also his fondness for long words as in his definition of *network* as "anything reticulated or decussated at equal distances with interstices between the intersections" and of *cough* as "a convulsion of the lungs, vellicated by some sharp serosity."

[14] He included such words as *opiniatry, ariolation, assation, conclusible, cubiculary, incompossible, incompossibility, indigitate.*

[15] For a fuller treatment of the subject, see G. H. McKnight, *op. cit.,* pp. 351–376.

5.17 The Grammarians of the Eighteenth Century   Great interest in English grammar developed in the eighteenth century. Earlier grammatical treatises had been written, but generally for the purpose of giving foreigners some idea of the language or for serving as an introduction to the study of Latin grammar. The eighteenth-century grammarians attempted to formulate rules for deciding matters of syntax and usage. They also tried to improve the language by pointing out errors that were to be avoided. The grammarian was a lawgiver who passed judgment on the correctness and incorrectness of words and expressions.[16] One of the most popular grammars was Robert Lowth's *Short Introduction to Grammar* published in 1762 which went through many editions and was widely imitated. Three years later William Ward set forth the many prescriptions to which Lindley Murray gave currency in his grammar in 1795. These were prescriptive grammars. Rules were set forth without considering actual usage, thus separating written English more and more widely from spoken. There were some grammarians in the latter half of the century, however, who realized that usage was the most significant linguistic criterion. These men were the forerunners of the modern doctrine of usage, fundamental in all sound investigations of matters linguistic. The philosopher Joseph Priestley set forth this doctrine in 1761 in his *Rudiments of English Grammar* as well as in his lectures on the *Theory of Language* written the next year. This point of view was also propounded by George Campbell in his *Philosophy of Rhetoric* (1776). These two men knew that all linguistic problems could not be solved by logic, but that the forces surrounding them were often too complex to analyze. The prescriptive grammarian had no knowledge of the processes of linguistic change, for the historical study of English was just beginning.

5.18 Borrowings of the Eighteenth Century   Since the eighteenth century was concerned with the purity of the language, it was natural that there was objection to the introduction of foreign words. French, however, was used at almost all the courts in Europe and was spoken by the upper classes in England, who also traveled in France. Consequently, the relations between England and France

---

[16] See Sterling A. Leonard, *The Doctrine of Correctness in English Usage, 1700–1800* (Madison, University of Wisconsin Studies in Language and Literature, No. 25), 1929.

were so close that French words continued to be borrowed, not so many as formerly, but words that fill a real need, such as *dentist, routine, brunette, ballet, publicity.* Many other words besides French came in with the expansion of the British Empire. The Indians in America contributed words like *hominy, papoose, raccoon, skunk, totem, tomahawk, wigwam;* the Mexicans, through Spanish chiefly, *chili, coyote;* South Americans, *alpaca, llama, pampas, quinine, tapioca, cayenne, petunia;* the Indians in the East, *bandanna, bungalow, calico, cashmere, chintz, curry, jungle, tom-tom, verandah, gingham, indigo;* the Africans, *chimpanzee, voodoo, zebra;* the Australians, *boomerang* and *kangaroo.* The colonization served to make the English vocabulary more and more cosmopolitan in its character.

5.19 A More Liberal Attitude After the Eighteenth Century The conservative eighteenth century was followed by a period of greater liberalism in literature and in language. The Romantic era was an age of individualism, and various writers revived obsolete words, coined new words, and introduced dialect into their writing. Great changes were also taking place in society, putting it on a more democratic basis. The industrial reforms of the nineteenth century brought the upper and lower classes closer together, allowing greater economic and cultural opportunities to the populace. The first cheap newspaper in 1816 and cheap postage in 1837 aided greatly in this process as did the rapid strides made in science. The means of communication and travel were improved by the telephone, the telegraph, the radio, the railroad, the steamship, the automobile, and the airplane, thus bringing the world closer and closer together and increasing the English vocabulary by words borrowed from other countries.

5.20 Progress Reflected in Language With the progress in science went the development of the vocabulary, for words are but symbols by which ideas are expressed. Each new invention brought with it a new stock of words. For instance, a few terms that came in with the automobile, either as new words or as new meanings, are *steering wheel, radiator, hood, windshield, chassis, spark plug, self-starter, shock absorber, clutch, gas.*[17] Thus the vocabulary has grown

---

[17] These are the terms used in American English. One may find other terms in British English; for instance, *windscreen* instead of *windshield, bonnet* instead of *hood,* or *petrol* instead of *gas.*

by leaps and bounds as one invention after another has taken place
in the nineteenth and twentieth centuries.

5.21 Dictionaries Since Dr. Johnson's The aim of Dr. Johnson
was to give the correct spelling, accent, and meaning of all words in
good usage at that time. The matter of giving the exact pronunciation was left for later lexicographers, the first of whom was William
Kenrick, who indicated the vowel sounds for the first time in a general dictionary in his *New Dictionary* of 1773. Previously two Scotsmen, James Buchanan and William Johnston, had published pronouncing dictionaries in 1757 and 1764 respectively. The precedent
of indicating pronunciation has been followed ever since by lexicographers, both British and American. The most important American
lexicographers of the early nineteenth century were Noah Webster
and J. E. Worcester. Webster's *Compendious Dictionary of the English Language* first appeared in 1806. It was revised from time to
time and was the chief authority for the greater part of the nineteenth century. Professor George Philip Krapp described the 1828
edition, *An American Dictionary of the English Language,* as "the
most significant contribution to English lexicography between Dr.
Johnson and the appearance of the first volume of the New English
Dictionary." [18] The first edition of this dictionary to be termed
Unabridged appeared in 1864. The second edition, *Webster's New
International Dictionary,* appeared in 1934 and the third in 1961.
Two competitors of Webster's in the latter part of the nineteenth
century were the *Century* and the *Standard.* The most eminent work
in the field of lexicography, however, was the *New English Dictionary (NED)* or *Oxford (OED),* [19] a dictionary built on historical principles, begun under Sir James Murray and finished under Sir William
A. Craigie, both Scotsmen. The first volumes appeared in 1884 and
the last in 1928. A supplementary volume appeared in 1933 containing the accumulated additions and corrections of the forty-four
years during which the original work was being published. The original work treated within its volumes 450,000 words, 240,165 main
words with their derivatives. The publication has had a far-reaching

---

[18] G. P. Krapp, *English Language in America* (New York, The Century
Company, for the Modern Language Association of America, 1925; republished,
New York, Frederick Ungar Publishing Co., 1960), Vol. I, p. 362.

[19] Both titles are used. The *NED* was the original and the *OED* the reissue in 1933.

effect upon the study of language by showing the history of words and idioms, giving their various forms and spellings, and indicating changes in meaning through the centuries. This dictionary enables one to realize the rise and fall of words and the importance of usage.

5.22 Attitude toward Dictionaries With the rise of the middle class there was great concern about "correctness" in speech. Dictionaries and grammars, therefore, gained a great deal of respect in the eighteenth century as the final arbiters in matters of speech.[20] More recent dictionaries do not profess to settle questions of language but merely to record usage. Actually, the practice of lexicographers is not so different from that of the eighteenth-century dictionary makers, for the recordings in dictionaries lag behind usage. New words or changes in spelling or pronunciation find it difficult to enter the authoritative quarters. Nevertheless, dictionaries are still held as the final authority by most persons, especially by Americans, who seem to have inherited the conservative attitude of the eighteenth century. Perhaps the *New English Dictionary* has done more than anything else to help weaken the great love for authority in language and to establish the proper respect for usage, for what is actually happening in the language.

5.23 Modern English Dialects In addition to Standard English, spoken by the educated, there are in Great Britain local peculiarities, known as dialects, based on the earliest stages of the language.[21] These old forms have been preserved in various ways so that the differences in the British Isles are quite marked. Each

---

[20] See C. C. Fries, *The Teaching of the English Language* (New York, Thomas Nelson and Sons, 1927), "The Rules as Measures," pp. 1–31.

[21] See W. W. Skeat, *English Dialects from the Eighth Century to the Present Day* (Cambridge, University Press), 1911; Joseph Wright, *English Dialect Dictionary*, 6 vols. (London, Henry Frowde), 1898–1905; William Matthews, *Cockney Past and Present: A Short History of the Dialect of London* (London, G. Routledge & Sons, Ltd.), 1938; Eugen Dieth, "A Survery of English Dialects," *Essays and Studies* (Vol. XXXII, 1947), pp. 74–104; Harold Orton and Eugen Dieth, "The New Survey of Dialectal English," *English Studies Today* (Oxford, Clarendon Press, 1951), pp. 63–73; Angus McIntosh, *An Introduction to a Survey of Scottish Dialects* (Edinburgh, *University of Edinburgh, Linguistic Survey of Scotland*, Monographs, No. 1), 1952 (complementary work to Craigie's *Dictionary of the Older Scottish Tongue* and Grant and Murison's *Scottish National Dictionary*). A *Linguistic Atlas of England* has been started under the direction of Harold Orton of the University of Leeds who had the help of the late Professor Eugen Dieth of Zurich and one of Scotland has been begun under Angus McIntosh and Kenneth Jackson of Edinburgh.

county has its own local forms and the speech of the North is very different from that of the South. The speech of southern Scotland, that used by Robert Burns in his immortal poetry, is an example of a dialect, as may be illustrated from one stanza of his *To a Mouse:*

> Wee, sleekit, cowrin, tim'rous beastie,
> O, what a panic's in thy breastie!
> Thou need na start awa sae hasty
>   Wi' bickering brattle!
> I wad be laith to rin an' chase thee,
>   Wi' murdering pattle!

Here one observes the difference of pronunciation in such words as *na, sae, wad, laith,* and *rin* as well as old words no longer heard in Standard English: *sleekit* for "sleek," *bickering brattle* for "hurrying scamper," and *pattle* for "paddle."

5.24 American English   Each colony or land where English has been introduced has developed its own individual characteristics.[22] An example is the language spoken in America. The very title of Professor George P. Krapp's study, *The English Language in America,* showed that the English brought to America in the seventeenth century by the colonists, the English of Shakespeare and Milton, had developed a reasonable degree of uniformity on this side of the Atlantic. The point of view that American English is different and separate from British English has been held from the time of the American Revolution when a definite national consciousness was established. After the signing of the Declaration of Independence, the person who did most in furthering the idea of a separate American language was Noah Webster [23] with his spelling book, grammar, reader, treatment of questions on language, and finally with his *American Dictionary of the English Language* (1828). In the preface to this significant work he says:

"It is not only important, but, in a degree necessary, that the people of this country, should have an *American Dictionary* of the English language;

[22] See Eric Partridge and John W. Clark, *British and American English Since 1900* (London, Andrew Dakers, Ltd.), 1951, for varieties of English today.

[23] See Harry R. Warfel, *Noah Webster, Schoolmaster to America* (New York, The Macmillan Company), 1936.

for, although the body of the language is the same as in England, and it is desirable to perpetuate that sameness, yet some differences must exist. Language is the expression of ideas; and if the people of our country cannot preserve an identity of ideas, they cannot retain an identity of language. Now an identity of ideas depends materially upon a sameness of things or objects with which the people of the two countries are conversant. But in no two portions of the earth, remote from each other, can such identity be found. Even physical objects must be different. But the principal differences between the people of this country and of all others, arise from different forms of government, different laws, institutions and customs. . . . No person in this country will be satisfied with the English definitions of the words *congress, senate* and *assembly, court,* &c. for although these are words used in England, yet they are applied in this country to express ideas which they do not express in that country."

This idea of separate idiom, pronunciation, and spelling has been supported, until today we find Sir William A. Craigie writing "An American Language" in the *Saturday Review of Literature;* [24] the publication of *A Dictionary of American English on Historical Principles,* [25] in four volumes, completed in 1944; *A Dictionary of Americanisms on Historical Principles,* [26] in two volumes, published in 1951; and H. L. Mencken publishing his popular work, *The American Language,* the fourth edition of which appeared in 1937 and to which he added *Supplement I* in 1945 and *Supplement II* in 1948. These works of Mencken's treat many aspects of American English and cite many interesting differences between American and British English. [27] The periodical *American Speech,* started in 1925, has continued to publish both technical and popular treatments of American

[24] Vol. VII, No. 31, pp. 614–615 (February 21, 1931).

[25] Edited by Sir William A. Craigie and James R. Hulbert, University of Chicago Press.

[26] The work of Mitford M. Mathews. Earlier dictionaries of Americanisms were John R. Bartlett's *Dictionary of Americanisms,* published in 1848 and enlarged in a second edition in 1859; J. S. Farmer's *Americanisms Old and New* (1889); R. H. Thornton's *An American Glossary* (1912) with 14,000 dated quotations (*Dialect Notes,* Vol. VI, 1931–1939, also contains other material which Thornton had collected). Gilbert M. Tucker's *American English* (1921) was also a valuable contribution.

[27] The study of Americanisms has led to a study of a Briticisms by Allen Walker Read, who now has in his collection for his projected *Dictionary of Briticisms* some 11,000 items.

English. Many word lists as well as other material pertaining to
American English may also be found in the *Publications of the
American Dialect Society*. Harold Wentworth in his *American Dialect Dictionary* (1944) likewise presented much interesting regional
material.

In many ways, however, the most significant of projects under-
taken is the *Linguistic Atlas of the United States and Canada*, set up
in 1930, under the sponsorship of the American Council of Learned
Societies and under the general direction of Hans Kurath, to record
the characteristics of American Speech. America, following the lead
of Europe,[28] in 1931, started field work in New England, the first
region of investigation. From 1939 to 1943, the New England atlas, a
collection of some 600 maps, showing the distribution of language
features in that area, appeared along with a *Handbook of the
Linguistic Geography of New England* (1939), treating the dialect
areas considered, the selection of informants and communities, the
history of the settlements traced, and the various procedural matters.
Investigations and editing of material from other parts of the country have continued and are proceeding.[29] Frequent articles appear

[28] Linguistic geography began in Europe in the latter decades of the nineteenth century. Jules Gillieron's *Atlas linguistique de la France* (1902–1910)
followed soon after Georg Wenker's *Sprachatlas des deutschen Reichs* of Germany and Karl Jaberg and Jakob Jud's *Sprach— und Sachatlas Italiens und der
Südschweiz* appeared from 1928 to 1940. The most recent survey and exhaustive treatment of linguistic geography is that of Sever Pop: *La dialectologie:
aperçu historique et methodes d'enquêtes linguistiques*, 2 vols. (Louvain, Uni-
versité de Louvain, 1950).

[29] The investigation of the Middle and South Atlantic States has been completed, begun in 1933 by Guy S. Lowman, Jr., and finished by Raven I. Mc-
David, Jr., in 1949. The field word for the atlas of the North Central States,
under the direction of Albert H. Marckwardt was completed in 1956, mainly
by Frederic G. Cassidy, A. L. Davis, and Raven I. McDavid, Jr. In 1957, the
field work for the atlas of the Upper Midwest, directed by Harold B. Allen, was
finished. Based on the investigation done in the two last-mentioned regions,
Virginia G. McDavid brought out *A Survey of Verb Forms in the North-Central
States and the Upper Midwest* (University of Minnesota dissertation, 1956,
Publication No. 20,525). Jean Malmstrom also made use of the atlas material in
her dissertation *A Study of the Validity of Textbook Statements About Certain
Controversial Grammatical Items in the Light of Evidence from the Linguistic
Atlas* (University of Minnesota, 1958, Microfilm 58–7012). The study in the
Rocky Mountain area began in 1950 with Marjorie M. Kimmerle as director and
T. M. Pearce as associate director. Colorado and Utah have been completed. A
significant beginning has been made on the Pacific Coast with David Reed of

in addition to the four summary volumes, three of which have been published by the University of Michigan Press: Kurath's *Word Geography of the Eastern United States* (1949), E. Bagby Atwood's *Survey of Verb Forms in the Eastern United States* (1953), and Kurath and R. I. McDavid's *The Pronunciation of English in the Atlantic States* (1961), and two by the American Dialect Society: Thomas Wetmore's *Low Back and Low Central Vowels in the English of the Eastern United States* (Publication XXXII, 1960) and Clyde T. Hankey's *A Colorado Word Geography* (Number 34, November, 1960). The work on the *Linguistic Atlas* has furnished a valid basis for the many variations in American speech as may be seen, for example, from the figures below showing the speech areas of the Eastern States and the record of the geographic dissemination of the different words *to, of,* and *till* in telling time.

Nevertheless, there is much greater uniformity in American speech than in British. Although there are sectional differences in New England, the South, the Middle West, and the Far West, the dialects are not so distinctive as those in England. This is true, no doubt, because of better communication in the United States and the tendency of the American people to move from one section to another. An Englishman may have difficulty understanding an American and vice versa, but it should be said that the differences are much more marked in the spoken than in the written language.

5.25 English as an International Language More important than the relation of American to British English is the question of English as an international tongue. It is not probable that English will replace local dialects throughout the world, but the language bids fair to become the most important for international relations. Commerce and colonization of those who speak English have spread the language throughout the world so that it is used or understood in

---

California and Carroll Reed of Washington as co-directors. Surveys are also under way in Texas and the Gulf States under the direction of E. Bagby Atwood of Texas and C. M. Wise of Louisiana. In Canada work has been started in the Maritime Provinces by Henry Alexander, in Nova Scotia by Rex Wilson, and in eastern Ontario by the Rev. Brother Pius. In addition, Frederic G. Cassidy has made a study of Jamaica speech. Linguistic geography serves as a bridge between synchronics and diachronics, for it studies the spoken language rather than the written, but deals with relic areas as well as with "advanced" areas of speech.

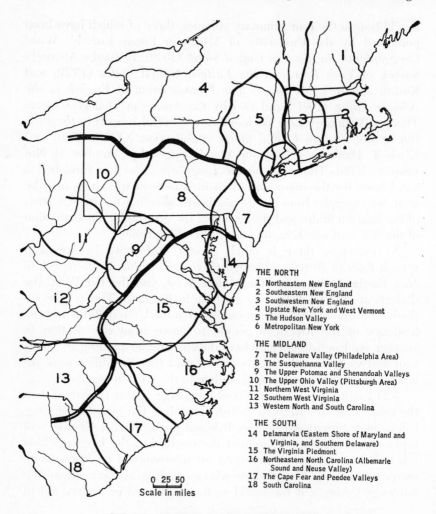

THE NORTH
1 Northeastern New England
2 Southeastern New England
3 Southwestern New England
4 Upstate New York and West Vermont
5 The Hudson Valley
6 Metropolitan New York

THE MIDLAND
7 The Delaware Valley (Philadelphia Area)
8 The Susquehanna Valley
9 The Upper Potomac and Shenandoah Valleys
10 The Upper Ohio Valley (Pittsburgh Area)
11 Northern West Virginia
12 Southern West Virginia
13 Western North and South Carolina

THE SOUTH
14 Delamarvia (Eastern Shore of Maryland and
   Virginia, and Southern Delaware)
15 The Virginia Piedmont
16 Northeastern North Carolina (Albemarle
   Sound and Neuse Valley)
17 The Cape Fear and Peedee Valleys
18 South Carolina

0 25 50
Scale in miles

THE SPEECH AREAS OF THE EASTERN STATES

From Hans Kurath, *A Word Geography of the Eastern United States*, Ann Arbor, University of Michigan Press, 1949.

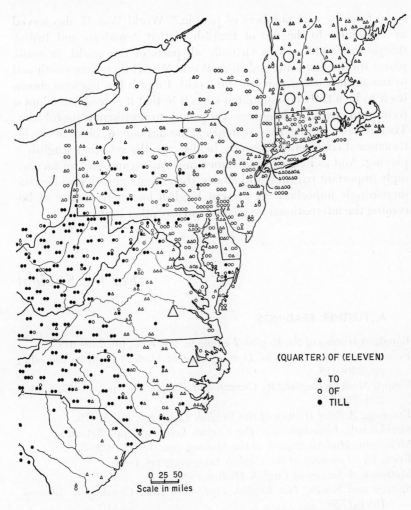

VARIOUS WAYS OF EXPRESSING TIME IN THE EASTERN STATES

From Hans Kurath: *A Word Geography of the Eastern United States*, Figure 44.
Ann Arbor: University of Michigan Press, 1949.

some form by vast numbers of people.[30] World War II also served as a stimulus to the use of English in that American and British troops were stationed in virtually all parts of the world, in many places for the first time, and since World War II they have continued to remain in various parts of the world. English has likewise shown itself to be a truly cosmopolitan speech in that it is ready to adopt a term from any other language if it proves to represent a useful idea. Then it has a simple, easy structure. One has only to observe the international conferences recently held to see the role that English is playing. And as long as Englishmen and Americans play an increasingly important part in world affairs, their language will also become increasingly important. At present English has more chance of becoming the international language than any other tongue.

For the Student

A. FURTHER READINGS

Baugh, *A History of the English Language*, 2nd edit., pp. 240–465.

Robertson and Cassidy, *The Development of Modern English*, 2nd edit., pp. 326–418.

Krapp, *Modern English, Its Growth and Present Use*, pp. 35–43; 83–94; 233–250.

Emerson, *A Brief History of the English Language*, pp. 51–79.

Marckwardt, *Introduction to the English Language*, pp. 204–238.

McKnight, *Modern English in the Making*, pp. 86–416; 460–558.

Fries, *The Teaching of the English Language*, pp. 1–31.

Mathews, *A Survey of English Dictionaries.*

Starnes and Noyes, *The English Dictionary from Cawdrey to Johnson, 1604–1755.*

Hulbert, *Dictionaries British and American.*

Krapp, *The English Language in America.*

Mencken, *The American Language; Supplement I; Supplement II.*

Jespersen, *An International Language.*

Shenton, Sapir, and Jespersen, *International Communication: A Symposium on the Language Problem.*

[30] Estimated at 284 million. See *World Almanac* (1961).

Macaulay, *Interlanguage,* Society for Pure English, Tract No. XXXIV, Oxford, Clarendon Press, 1930.

Marckwardt, *American English.*

Pyles, *Words and Ways of American English.*

Laird, *The Miracle of Language,* pp. 152–291, *passim.*

Sheard, *The Words We Use,* pp. 129–330.

McDavid, "The Dialects of American English," *The Structure of American English,* pp. 480–543.

Kurath (ed.), *et al., Linguistic Atlas of New England.*

Kurath, *A Word Geography of the Eastern United States.*

Kurath and McDavid, *The Pronunciation of English in the Atlantic States.*

B. FOR CLASS DISCUSSION

1. What is meant by the Modern English period? What divisions would you make in this period? Why?
2. What were some of the principal movements in the Renaissance period that affected the English language? Illustrate. (See Baugh, *A History of the English Language,* 2nd edit., Chapter 8, and Sheard, pp. 241–264.)
3. In the Renaissance period what language was universally used for communication? Can you account for the shift from this language to another?
4. What are inkhorn terms? Illustrate. How did they affect the English language?
5. How have colonization and commerce affected the English language? Illustrate. (See Sheard, pp. 265–290.)
6. What were some of the main characteristics of the prose of the sixteenth century?
7. Compare a page of John Lyly's *Euphues* with a page of modern prose and note down the differences.
8. How can one account for the simplicity of the language of the Bible?
9. In describing Modern English as a language of lost inflections, is that an exact description? Illustrate your answer.
10. What is meant by functional shift? How did it affect the English language?
11. What was the attitude toward the English language in the eighteenth century? How did it differ from the Renaissance attitude?
12. Account for the interest in dictionaries and grammars in the eighteenth century.
13. What is the importance of the date 1755 in the history of the English language?

14. Do you think it would have been a good thing for the English language if an English Academy similar to the French Academy had been established? Give reasons for your answer.

15. Compare the attitudes of the eighteenth and nineteenth centuries toward loan words.

16. What effect have scientific discoveries and inventions had upon the language? Illustrate. (See Baugh, 2nd edit., *A History of the English Language*, Chapter 10.)

17. Select a particular invention and see how many words you can list that have been introduced through it. List new words and words with new meanings.

18. What are some of the more important dictionaries which have been published in recent years?

19. What should be the function of a dictionary? Do you think dictionaries fulfil that function? Give reasons for your answer.

20. Why is a dictionary out of date when it comes out?

21. What is the significance of the *Oxford English Dictionary?* See Baugh, 2nd edit., pp. 395–400. Look up a word and note down the various types of information you find.

22. Compare the 450,000 words of the *OED* with the number in other leading dictionaries, including French, German, etc.

23. Can you account for the great respect Americans have for dictionaries?

24. What are some of the dialects in Modern English?

25. Do you consider American English a separate language? Give reasons for your answer.

26. Look up *A Dictionary of American English*. Compare it with the *OED*. In what ways are they similar? How do they differ?

27. Look up *A Dictionary of Americanisms*. Compare it with *A Dictionary of American English*. In what ways are they similar? How do they differ?

28. What is the importance of the Linguistic Atlas?

29. Do you think English has a chance to become the international language? Give reasons for your answer.

30. Do you think an artificially simplified form of English, such as "Basic English" (see par. 21.15) or some other simplified form, would be better for the international language? For information on Basic English, see C. K. Ogden, *Basic English* (London, Kegan Paul, 1930) and *The System of Basic English* (New York, Harcourt, Brace, 1934).

C. SUGGESTIONS FOR RESEARCH PAPERS

1. The Importance of George Pettie, Richard Mulcaster, Sir John Cheke (or any other scholar mentioned in the chapter) in the History of the English Language.
2. The Latin, Greek, or French Influence in the Renaissance Period (or any other period).
3. A Study of the Prose of John Lyly or Sir Philip Sidney.
4. The Bible in the Renaissance Period.
5. Dr. Johnson (Noah Webster, or any other dictionary maker) as a Lexicographer.
6. Swift and the English Academy.
7. Lindley Murray (or any other grammarian) as a Grammarian.
8. A Comparison of American and British English.
9. A Comparison of Two Dialects (American or British).
10. English as a World Language.

II

The Speech Sound
and the Letter:

UNITS OF ORAL AND WRITTEN ENGLISH

II

6

The Speech Organs

6.1 Language and Speech Having considered the heritage of Modern English, we turn now to the study of English sounds. If a person stops to become aware of how he makes the sounds that pour out when he is talking, he is already a long way toward understanding the changes in his language throughout the centuries. Language is primarily oral, and the sound is its basic unit. All written communications are symbols or representations of actual speech. Speech may be defined as communication in oral language. In the following chapters, which are comparatively short in order to insure clarity, we shall consider first the physical basis of speech, then the nature of the thirty-seven individual sounds of English, and finally the history of these sounds as they have developed from Old to Modern English.

6.2 Range of Speech Sounds The human vocal mechanism is capable of producing sounds of a very wide range and variety; perhaps the extremes might be represented by a scream and a groan. For example, a child's scream is at first a reflex action and is not primarily uttered for the purpose of conveying anything to others.

It, therefore, cannot properly be called speech, but is an involuntary, irresistible consequence of the fact that something is not right. Others that one may mention are sighing, panting, sobbing; the yawn, gasp, sneer, moan, hiccough; the murmur of disgust or ridicule.[1] Most of such nonspeech sounds are difficult to fit into the relatively restricted area of our phonetic alphabet. Anyone who has tried to represent with letter symbols the various noises that are not speech, whether made by people or by animals, knows how restricted the area of speech sounds is, compared to the range of noises that the vocal mechanism is capable of making.

6.3 Region of Voice Production   What is this vocal mechanism out of which sounds are drawn, and how does it operate in the production of speech? It is not one thing but many, and it is not simple but tremendously intricate and obscure, so much so that many of its workings are not clear to us even yet. It comprises in general that central region of the body reaching up from the diaphragm to the roof of the nasal cavity, and it is shown in cross section in the accompanying diagram.

6.4 Lungs and Diaphragm   The importance of the breathing process to vocal music is well established, but its importance in speech is less well understood, because talking ordinarily uses up little breath energy. Yet any physical explanation of the nature of speech must begin with the inward and outward alternations of breath, the latter of which carries speech. While meaningful sounds may be made with intaking breath (sniff, sob, etc.), no English speech sounds utilize this impulsion of breath.[2] The reason is that sounds seem to be made with less effort on breath expulsion. Control and modification are more easily possible with the outgoing breath than with the incoming; and speech requires very minute and subtle controls.

6.5 Simplest Speech Sound   We begin, then, with the air which is being pumped out of the lungs and into the windpipe, from which it is normally expelled through the nasal passage. Commonly this expulsion is not accompanied by any perceptible sound, and so the

---

[1] See Kenneth L. Pike, *Phonetics* (Ann Arbor, University of Michigan Press, 1943), "Nonspeech Sounds," pp. 32–41.

[2] A few sounds are made by drawing in the breath. The "clicks" of Zulu are the standard examples.

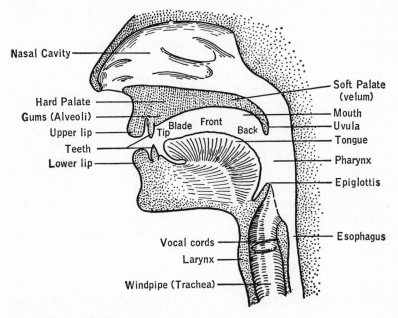

DIAGRAM A A CROSS-SECTION OF SPEECH ORGANS

first necessity for audible speech is to invest the air current with sound. The simplest means of doing this is to give it sufficient force to make its passage heard. This may be done by merely breathing out forcibly, in which case the friction of the outgoing air is audible. Or it may be done by manipulation of the soft palate so as to close the nasal passage and open the buccal or mouth cavity or passage; in this event the resulting sound, which the Greeks called simply "rough breathing," is the one we symbolize by the letter *h*.

6.6 The Vocal Cords   At the upper end of the windpipe, through which breath is expelled, is an enlargement or "bunch," called the glottis. Within this glottis lie the vocal cords, which resemble a pair of lips on opposite sides of the chamber. In normal breathing these cords or lips are separated, but at the will of the individual they may be drawn together to make a narrower passage for the air. In this event the air passing through them causes an audible vibration which we call voice. In whispering the vocal cords are held half extended, producing a murmur rather than full voice. The vocal cords are not active in all speech sounds. Out of the thirty-seven which are readily distinguishable in Modern English, nine are voiceless, that is, formed without vocal-cord vibration, while the others all involve such vibration.

6.7 The Nasal Passage As was said, ordinarily the outgoing breath passes from the body through the nasal passage, the soft palate being adjusted to open this passage and close off the buccal passage. It is possible, moreover, to form various sounds as air passes through the nose, the mouth then acting as a resonance chamber to modify the sounds. Modern English has three sounds, *m, n,* and *ng,* which are produced in this fashion; all three involve vocal-cord vibration. The nasal passage may also act in its turn as a resonance chamber for sounds which are formed with air passing through the mouth, and may be kept open in making vowel sounds. The French language contains several of these nasalized vowels, though they are frowned upon in English.

6.8 Mouth Machinery for Sound Production Within the mouth lie several of the means of sound modification. The lips, the teeth, the tongue, the alveoli or gums, the hard palate, and the soft palate all play their parts in the production of sounds of various sorts. The tongue is probably the most important factor, as the use of the word *tongue* to mean *language* or *speech* would indicate. One speaks a certain tongue, and a person who cannot articulate distinctly is called tongue-tied. The tongue acts to alter the shape of the resonance chamber which the mouth itself forms, and these alterations may be the source of the vocal differences among the vowels, sounds whose formation is still not altogether clearly understood. The tongue may close off the air current altogether, or modify it in any desired fashion for the purpose of sound production. The details of the work of this and the other buccal factors in sound production had best be left to subsequent chapters.

6.9 Delimitation of Parts of Mouth It is worth pointing out that only an imaginary line separates the gums or alveoli from the hard palate and this hard palate from the soft palate toward the back of the mouth. As any part of the roof of the mouth may enter into sound, these terms must naturally be approximate rather than exact. The same thing applies to the naming of the parts of the tongue. We shall distinguish four regions called, respectively, from front to back of the mouth, the point, the blade, the front, and the back. The point is simply what its name implies; the blade and front take up about a quarter of the tongue's surface each, and the remaining half is called the back. Naturally the back, being less mobile than the other parts, is less useful in speech.

For the Student

A. FURTHER READINGS

Kantner and West, *Phonetics*, rev. edit., pp. 40–53; 207–208.
Gray and Wise, *The Bases of Speech*, 3rd edit., Chapter III.
Judson and Weaver, *Voice Science*, Chapters IX, X, XI.
Curry, *The Mechanism of the Human Voice*, Chapters II, IV, V.
Thomas, *An Introduction to the Phonetics of American English*, 2nd edit., pp. 13–31.
Graff, *Language and Languages*, pp. 10–17.
Krapp, *Modern English, Its Growth and Present Use*, pp. 99–106.
Sapir, *Language*, pp. 43–51.
Kenyon, *American Pronunciation*, 10th edit., § 28.
Krapp, *The Pronunciation of Standard English in America*, §§ 1–4; 16–17.
Robertson and Cassidy, *The Development of Modern English*, 2nd edit., pp. 55–58.
Jones, *The Pronunciation of English*, 4th edit., §§ 12–29.
Jones, *An Outline of English Phonetics*, 8th edit., §§ 65–95.
Sweet, *A Handbook of Phonetics*, pp. 1–8, 54–55.
Pike, *Phonetics*, pp. 32–41.
Heffner, *General Phonetics*, pp. 9–41.
Gleason, *An Introduction to Descriptive Linguistics*, rev. ed., pp. 187–204.

B. FOR CLASS DISCUSSION

1. This chapter should be used as the basis for verification and experimentation in determining the functions of the speech organs in sound production. All the students in the class should check carefully each statement made, so far as this is possible. A mirror may be used to verify the character and location of the speech organs which are visible by this means. Each student should make a list of the organs of

speech, following Diagram A, and should understand fully the functions of each of these.

2. Do you know of any sounds in foreign languages which are not present in English? Do you think that such sounds are intrinsically more difficult to produce?

3. If your answer to the last part of Question 2 is "No," how do you explain the difficulty of learning to pronounce a foreign language? (Sapir's discussion may be helpful.)

4. Try to isolate and study individual speech sounds such as *ng* by pronouncing them first in familiar combinations and then separately and in unfamiliar patterns.

5. Can you explain any defects or eccentricities of sound formation in terms of the speech organs?

6. Compare the accounts of the organs of speech given by the authorities mentioned in Part A or by any other available authors treating this subject. Can you now amplify the account given here?

7. Do you think that the Greek method of representing "rough breathing" has any advantages over the English method?

8. If it is true that there is no vibration of the vocal cords in whispering, words like *pat, bad, pad,* and *bat* should be indistinguishable when whispered. Test this statement by constructing whispered sentences in which these words are substituted for one another, and see if hearers notice the substitution.

9. What other peculiarities of whispered speech can you observe?

10. Make the three nasals, *m, n,* and *ng,* without voice by pronouncing *h* before each. Are these sounds harder to make than the voiced values?

C. SUGGESTIONS FOR RESEARCH PAPERS

1. The Use of Incoming Breath in Nonspeech (and Speech) Sounds.
2. Nonspeech Sounds Formed with Outgoing Breath.
3. What Is Whisper?
4. Sounds of Foreign Languages Not in English.

7

Sound Categories: I

7.1 Classifying Sounds Before the thirty-seven speech sounds of English are described, it is necessary to understand the various categories, groups, or types into which they fall, and to learn how to apply these categories to individual sounds. And before sound groups can be properly understood, it is necessary to describe the general nature of sound and its relationships in the sequence of sounds which is speech.

7.2 Speech a Continuity of Sound It must be emphasized that in actual speech there are none of the artificial divisions between sounds, letters, and words which appear on a page of print, or in a phonetic transcription. Speech is a continuous outflow of air shaped and occasionally interrupted for an instant by the action of the vocal organs, particularly the tongue. Everyone has noticed, for instance, that *ice cream* and *I scream* are pronounced in much the same fashion unless one is at pains to distinguish them. And the same thing is true of *at all* and *a tall, is he* and *Izzy,* and even *don't you* and *don't chew.* The identity in the last pair is based on a sound change, from that represented by the *y* of *you*, to *ch*. This alteration will become understandable as we proceed.

7.3 Vowels and Consonants   The sound category with which everyone is most familiar is the division into consonants and vowels. *A, e, i, o, u,* and sometimes *y* are the vowel letters; the others are the consonants. So we glibly say. But this statement, based as it is upon spelling rather than the more fundamental matter of sound, requires much modification and explanation. So far as the ordinary names of these letters are concerned, *a, i,* and *o* are diphthongs, *e* is a vowel, and *u* a consonant-vowel combination, while *y* combines a consonant (*w*) with a diphthong. Indeed the alphabet names of the letters are useless in phonetic study, and it is necessary to discard them in favor of the sounds themselves. Thus the phonetic value of *f* is not *eff*, the name of the letter, but the first sound in *fan*, while the phonetic value of *g* is not *gee* but the first sound in *get*. From now on the student should call sounds phonetically and not by their alphabet names.

7.4 Phonetic Names of Sounds   This calling of sounds by their phonetic names means, of course, that any letter may have more than one name. Thus the *s* of *is* will be called differently from the *s* of *sat*, and the *a* of *father* from the *a* of *cat*. This fact makes necessary a phonetic alphabet which will include names for all the thirty-seven sounds in English, since our twenty-six letters will not cover the sounds we use. It is this phonetic alphabet which the student is about to learn.

7.5 Sequence of Sounds   There are several possible ways of constructing a phonetic alphabet. We may adhere as closely as possible to the arbitrary sequence now followed in the dictionaries; this is done, for example, in the phonetic dictionary of Daniel Jones.[1] Or we may consider consonants and vowels in two separate lists, with different subdivisions for each; this is perhaps the usual method. Or, finally, we may arrange the speech sounds in a continuous and logical series on the basis of their formation in the mouth, consonants and vowels mingled. This is, with some modifications, the plan followed in this book.

7.6 No Clear Dividing Line   The distinction between consonants and vowels is largely arbitrary and becomes obscured in the so-

[1] *Everyman's English Pronouncing Dictionary,* 11th edit. (New York, E. P. Dutton & Company, 1956).

called semivowels, or the consonants which may carry a syllable. The term *consonant* is by derivation "sounded-with," reflecting the notion that a consonant must be sounded with a vowel in order to make a syllable, while a vowel can make a syllable by itself as *a* in the word *about* (the word *vowel* is by derivation simply "voice"). But the semivowels *l, n,* and *r* seem often to be sounded as syllables in such words as *little, button,* and *dinner.* In general, however, the two are fairly easy to distinguish physically, as may be demonstrated by standing before a mirror and pronouncing very slowly and clearly the words *Ann's calm voice.* It is apparent that in the continuous flow of air the consonants represent a catch, an obstruction, or even a momentary stoppage of the air current, while the vowels are made with relatively open and unimpeded positions of the mouth organs.

7.7 Consonants, the Backbone of Speech It might be said that consonants are the backbone of speech, for one usually recognizes a word by its consonant pattern. Take, for example, the sentence *Abraham Lincoln was a great president.* Without the vowels, it becomes *-br-h-m L-nc-ln w-s - gr--t pr-s-d-nt,* which is readily comprehensible to anyone familiar with American history. But without the consonants (*A--a-a- -i--o-- -a- a --ea- --e-i-e--*) it is a meaningless series of letters. That is why children in spelling by ear rarely omit the sounded consonants, although they may omit the vowels, as *britl* for *brittle.*

In ancient times, too, the vowels were apparently held to be of little importance. In Egyptian hieroglyphics and in the early Semitic alphabets, vowels were completely missing, and even Sanskrit has few symbols that originally designated vowels.

7.8 What Is a Consonant? Since consonants have always played a significant role in the language, one may ask what consonants are. In their formation the current of air passing out of the lungs is radically affected by the lips, the tongue, or other speech organs. Typically, therefore, consonants are sharply differentiated from each other, while vowels are often very difficult to distinguish from one another by definition.

> *A consonant is a sound made with comparatively greater effort or obstruction of the air current.*

7.9 The Nature of the Vowel It is customary to say merely that a vowel sound is one formed with a comparatively open or unobstructed passage of the breath; but this definition is far too vague. The tongue is regarded as definitive in vowel formation, but it is by no means certain that this is the fact, since the same vowel may be made with the tongue in more than one position. Possibly the shape of the throat may have something to do with vowel sound.

A vowel is a speech sound shaped by a comparatively open mouth and throat cavity.

By the very nature of their formation, they can shade into one another. For example, a singer may sing "ah-o-u" or "ee-ay-ah," but not "p-t-k" without making new breath impulses with each consonant. It is for this reason that substitutions are found in the use of consonants (*heb'm* for *heaven*), whereas vowels change gradually, approximating the near-by sounds.

In recording these sounds our modern alphabets are equipped with vowels, but it is interesting to observe that the number of them is far smaller than the variety of sounds to be represented, the result being that each vowel must play at least two, and usually several, roles. For instance, the *a* in *gather* is not sounded like the *a* in *father*, the *a* in *all*, or the *a* in *able*. Oddly enough, and perhaps because of this very burden placed on them, the vowels command the chief attention of modern philologists, who are inclined to take the unexciting consonants very much for granted.

Even if early linguistic records lacked vowel symbols, as was stated in par. 7.7, it is certain that vowels were used in speech. Years ago the assumption was general that such vowels must have been employed sparingly, but the weight of authority today leans to the conclusion that there was considerable variety in the vowel pattern, possibly as much as in present-day languages.

7.10 The Consonant-Vowel Category English recognizes fourteen vowel sounds and twenty-three consonant sounds. These figures are indefinitely expansible if we recognize more minute differences such as that between the *k*'s of *keen* and *calm*. It is probable that, in English, consonant sounds are more frequent than those of vowels, whereas in a largely vocalic language, such as Hawaiian, the contrary is the fact. This consonantal character of English is one of the considerations which have led the Danish linguist Otto Jespersen to call English a "masculine" language. Among the consonants frequently used in English are *s, t, n, l,* and *sh.* The most frequent vowel sounds are the unstressed vowels, such as the *a* in *about* and the *a* in *cottage.*

7.11 Voiced and Voiceless Sounds After the category of vowels and consonants, the next broad distinction in English phonetics is that between sounds made with, or without, action of the vocal cords (par. 6.6). The first group, consisting of twenty-eight, is called voiced; the second, containing nine, is called voiceless. The dictinction is not generally applied to vowels, since these are all voiced.

To get the distinction between voiceless and voiced firmly in mind, the student should practice with several of the sound pairs, such as the voiceless [s], made with the glottis or vocal lips open, and the voiced [z], made with the vocal lips or glottis partly closed. The experiment should be continued with [p] voiceless and [b] voiced, [k] voiceless and [g] voiced, and [f] voiceless and [v] voiced. If you cannot grasp the distinction by hearing alone, try placing a finger against the position of the outside of the throat known as the Adam's apple. You will feel vibrations only when the voiced sounds are made. Another test is to put your hands over your ears in making the two sets of sounds. With the voiceless, you will hear nothing except possibly the rush of air, but with the voiced you will hear the vibration of the vocal lips.

7.12 Reason for Tendency to Voice The comparisons suggested above will illustrate another fact concerning the categories of voiced and voiceless—namely, that voiced sounds are actually easier to make than voiceless, even though it might at first glance seem that the opposite would be true. The reason is that in voiced sounds the vocal cords carry the effort, while in voiceless sounds the breath must be expelled with considerably more force so as to make an audible sound. The greater effort involved in, for example, *p* as compared to *b* is sometimes indicated in a statement that there is an intrusive *h* pronounced with *p,* thus, *pʰat.* In colloquial speech, also, *city* is sometimes heard as *sidy* [sɪdɪ] and *committee* as *commidi* [kəmɪdɪ], or even *gommidi* [gəmɪdɪ]. Also if a person is fatigued or relaxed he will tend to voice his sounds. He may say *dop of the dable* for a clear sharp *top of the table.* Certainly the tendency away from voiceless sounds and toward voiced is one evidence of a drift toward ease in speech.

7.13 Stop and Continuant Consonants   Another broad category applying to consonants only is that of stop and continuant. In forming the stop consonants, the breath is entirely cut off momentarily before being released. This means that the sound cannot be prolonged, but only repeated, as for example *t-t-t-t*. If a speaker attempts to prolong a *t-* sound, he simply gets red in the face as if he were very angry. In the continuants, on the other hand, the sound is continuous and prolongable—*m----*. The continuants share with vowels the possibility of being lengthened indefinitely. The stops are the less frequent type of consonant sound in English. There are only six of them as against seventeen continuants, besides the vowels, which are all continuant in character.

7.14 Subdivisions of Continuants   The six stops of English consist of three voiceless-voiced pairs, *p - b, t - d,* and *k - g,* which are made with the lips, the tongue tip, and the tongue back, respectively, along with a complete momentary stoppage of the breath. Continuants are divided by various authorities into numerous types, most important of which are the fricatives, sometimes called spirants. They only partly constrict the breath, producing an audible effect of hissing or buzzing. Then there are the nasals characterized by the breath going out through the nasal cavity and the lateral, *l,* where the breath escapes freely over one or both sides of the tongue.

7.15 Alternative Terms   The terminology of phonetics is becoming somewhat more uniform, although in the past the study has been hampered by the use of diverse terms, and often identical terms were applied to different things. For example, voiced consonants were formerly called sonants, and voiceless consonants, surds. The student may also encounter the term *breath* or *breathed* instead of *voiceless.* The stop consonants are sometimes called plosives or explosives, and the semivowels, glides. For the terms front-back as applied to vowels there is a wide diversity of names such as palatal-velar, open-close, and bright-dark. The student must learn to find his way about in this divergent terminology where he encounters it in books on phonetics.

7.16 Summary   The three categories treated in this lesson, namely, consonant-vowel, voiced-voiceless, and stop-continuant, are applicable to every English speech sound, even though the second and third are usually applied to consonants only. They form distinctions relatively easy for the student to perceive and should be made the basis of laboratory practice which will serve to fix them firmly in mind.

For the Student

A. FURTHER READINGS

Graff, *Language and Languages*, pp. 17–24; 30–31.
Aiken, *Why English Sounds Change*, pp. 1–6.
Krapp, *Modern English, Its Growth and Present Use*, pp. 106–109; 113–115.
Kenyon, *American Pronunciation*, 10th edit., §§ 29–79.
Robertson and Cassidy, *The Development of Modern English*, 2nd edit., pp. 58–70.
Krapp, *The Pronunciation of Standard English in America*, §§ 5, 12–15.
Sapir, *Language*, pp. 51–53.
Wyld, *A Short History of English*, §§ 20–22.
Jones, *An Outline of English Phonetics*, 8th edit., §§ 96–103; 121–188.
Aiken, *English Present and Past*, pp. 22–24; definitions in "Glossary," pp. 272 ff.
Jespersen, *Growth and Structure of the English Language*, 9th edit., pp. 1–16.

B. FOR CLASS DISCUSSION

1. A scientific definition of a consonant sound might be: "the effect produced upon the ear by sound waves originating either by the vibration of the vocal cords or within the mouth or nose, but in either case obstructed by action of the vocal organs and modified by the shape of the nasal or buccal resonance chambers so as to produce a somewhat harsh effect which is generally mitigated by an accompanying, less obstructed sound called a vowel." Compare this definition or explanation with those you find in dictionaries and other textbooks of phonetics, and from all these construct your own definition.
2. In the same way, compare the definitions of a vowel and construct one that satisfies you.

3. Examine each letter of the alphabet to determine the relation between the name of the letter and its usual sound, and generalize concerning the relation of the alphabet as a whole to phonetics.
4. Apply the three categories mentioned in this chapter to as many non-speech sounds as you can list—yawn, sob, sniff, chuckle, scream, etc. Can you tell which part of the vocal mechanism is active in the formation of any of these sounds?
5. Apply the same three categories to all speech sounds.
6. For each of the books listed in the bibliography and treating the subject, study the explanations of the different natures of consonants and vowels, together with the other two distinctions treated in this chapter. Add any pertinent details you can to the present treatment or weigh any divergences of opinion.
7. In the first chapter of Jespersen's *Growth and Structure of the English Language,* you will find the discussion of English as a "masculine" language. Study this discussion in full and analyze your reasons for agreement or disagreement.
8. Test by experimentation the statements made in this chapter as you did with those in Chapter 6—e.g., the comparative ease of producing voiced and voiceless sounds.
9. Comment on the relative importance of vowels and consonants in forming the pattern of a word. Can you explain why some ancient languages had no orthographic symbols for vowels?

C. SUGGESTIONS FOR RESEARCH PAPERS

1. Phonetic Terms Corresponding to Stop and Continuant.
2. Frequency of Consonant Sounds (your own analysis of the division into consonants and vowels of the sounds in a given passage).
3. Consonants and Vowels in Nonspeech Sounds.
4. Relative Ease of Consonant and Vowel Sounds.

8

Sound Categories: II

8.1 Other Sound Categories This chapter considers the remaining categories or divisions of English speech sounds, namely, *lip-to-back, high-to-low, tense-slack,* and *rounded-unrounded.* Then we shall be ready to apply these classifications to the actual sounds of English. Each one of the seven sets of distinctions explained in this and the preceding chapters is applicable to any speech sound, although some of them are in practice applied in a more limited way. For instance, the terms *tense* and *slack* are not used in connection with consonants, whose sounds are sharper and more individual than the sounds of vowels.

8.2 Phonetic Alphabet For any scientific representation of English sounds, the regular alphabet is totally inadequate. It is important to be able to record the distinctive features of sound which are significant in communication. For example, the word *fan* begins with the same sound as *fat, fad, fag,* but has a different ending. On the other hand, it ends with the same sound as *ran, can, man,* but the beginning is different; and in *fun, fin, fen,* the beginning and end are the same but the middle sounds are different. In *fan, fish, fell, furze,* on the other hand, all the words begin with the same sound, but the similarity here is less than in the other groups.

Thus by experimentation we discover the separate units, the distinctive features of a language which are combined for communication. In the word *fan* we find three indivisible units, each of which occurs in other combinations, but cannot be analyzed further by partial resemblances. According to Bloomfield,[1] each of the three is "a minimum unit of distinctive sound-feature, a phoneme." If minor variations of a given sound are not essential to its meaningful use, we consider that only one phoneme is represented by it.[2] For ex-

---

[1] Leonard Bloomfield, *Language* (New York, Henry Holt and Company, 1933), p. 79.

[2] For example, in *fan, fish, fell, furze,* the initial sounds or phone-types, though acoustically and physiologically different, are only varieties of the phoneme /f/ as are the many kinds of *t* sounds, made by placing the tip of the tongue anywhere from behind the lower front teeth to the upper, and as far back on the hard palate as the tongue can reach by curling upwards and backwards, are of the phoneme /t/. For an example of an analysis of the phoneme /t/ in cultivated and uncultivated pronunciations, see Allan F. Hubbell, *The Pronunciation of English in New York City* (1950), pp. 23–27. The symbols *f* and *t* are then general symbols standing for any one of a series of *f* and *t* sounds, respectively. Varieties of the same phoneme (the different phone-types) are called allophones and are said to be in complementary distribution. Each phoneme consists of a family of one or more allophones, which do not contrast with one another structurally (though phonetically they do) and are phonetically similar. Thus since *fan* and *pan* are separate words, /f/ and /p/ are separate phonemes in English, whereas the *p*'s in the words *pan, pet, upper, dipper, step* do not contrast structurally and are thus allophones of the phoneme /p/. In learning the phonemes of a language, one learns the functional patterns, the structure, of sound in that language, the units of meaningful speech-sound. For further detailed information on the phoneme, see Nelson A. Francis, *The Structure of American English* (1958), pp. 119–161; K. L. Pike, *Phonemics: A Technique for Reducing Languages to Writing* (1947), pp. 57–66; H. A. Gleason, Jr., *An Introduction to Descriptive Linguistics* (1955), pp. 158–186; rev. ed., 1960; Charles F. Hockett, *A Course in Modern Linguistics* (1958), pp. 15–32; A. A. Hill, *Introduction to Linguistic Structures* (1958), pp. 47–61; Bernard Bloch and George L. Trager, *Outline of Linguistic Analysis* (1942), pp. 38–52; G. L. Trager and H. L. Smith, *An Outline of English Structure* (1951), pp. 11–52. For other sources, see John B. Carroll, *The Study of Language: A Survey of Linguistics and Related Disciplines in America* (1953), Cambridge, Mass., Harvard University Press, and R. A. Hall, Jr., "American Linguistics, 1925–1950," *Archivum Linguisticum* (Vol. III, 1951), pp. 101–125; (Vol. IV, 1952), pp. 1–16. In recent years, a constant stream of articles and books by American linguists have appeared. Some of the authors not already mentioned are W. Freeman Twaddell, George P. Faust, Martin Joos, Eugene A. Nida, Zellig H. Harris, R. S. Wells, Noam Chomsky.

ample, in some languages there is more than one *l*-sound but in English for practical purposes we recognize only one; it is, therefore, for us a single phoneme, represented by one symbol. There is one symbol for each distinctive feature of the language. Every language has its own phonemes or distinctive features, and the group of symbols which provides one sign for each phoneme is a phonetic alphabet. The phonetic alphabet used in this book will be discussed in some detail in Chapters 9 through 15, but in order to make the present discussion of sounds understandable to the student, it will be reproduced at this point.

Vowels

Phonetic Symbol	Key Word	Transcription
1. ɑ	bar	bɑr
2. æ	rat	ræt
3. e	late	let
4. ε	let	lεt
5. i	need	nid
6. ɪ	sit	sɪt
7. o	note	not
8. ɔ	law	lɔ
9. u	fool	ful
10. ʊ	pull	pʊl
11. ʌ	love	lʌv
12. ə	ablaze	əblez (unaccented syllable)
13. ɝ	heard, burn, learn	hɝd, bɝn, lɝn (accented syllable, *r* coloring)
14. ɚ	baker, Albert	bekɚ; ælbɚt (unaccented syllable, *r* coloring)

Diphthongs

1. ɑɪ	write	rɑɪt
2. ɑʊ	cow	kɑʊ
3. ɔɪ	boy	bɔɪ
4. ɪu	new	nɪu

Consonants

1. b	bat	bæt
2. d	daily	delɪ

Consonants (*Continued*)

Phonetic Symbol	Key Word	Transcription
3. f	fan	fæn
4. g	goat	got
5. h	heat	hit
6. k	club	klʌb
7. l	line	lɑm
8. m	mode	mod
9. n	net	nɛt
10. ŋ	hang	hæŋ
11. p	pole	pol
12. r	red	rɛd
13. s	sand	sænd
14. ʃ	ship	ʃɪp
15. t	tin	tɪn
16. θ	thin	θɪn
17. ð	thine	ðɑm
18. v	vain	ven
19. w	wed	wɛd
20. ʍ	wheel	ʍil
21. j	yeast	jist
22. z	zoom	zum
23. ʒ	pleasure	plɛʒɚ
24. tʃ	child	tʃɑɪld
25. dʒ	jet	dʒɛt

8.3 The Lip-to-Back Series of Consonants   Our first classification of sounds applies somewhat differently to consonants than to vowels, which originate in a more restricted mouth area. Consonants may be made almost wholly with the lips, or they may involve activity mainly in the extreme back of the tongue and even (in some languages) in the glottis. Often, perhaps always, more than one area of the mouth is active in the formation of a given sound; but, according to the place where the chief activity lies, consonant sounds are classified as lip (*p, f*), point of tongue (*t, r*), blade (*sh*), front (the first sound of *yard*), and back (*k, w*).

In watching a person speak, one observes that the most obvious motions are made by the lips. The lips alone or in conjunction with other organs of speech make a number of sounds. For example, the sounds for the phonemes *p* and *b* are made by blowing the lips apart. It will be observed that children learn to make these sounds first, partly because they are able to see how they are formed and partly because lip action is highly developed in nursing.

On the other hand, children have more difficulty with gutturals, sounds made by raising the back part of the tongue toward the back of the roof of the mouth. When trying to learn these sounds, they have a tendency to substitute those made with the point of the tongue, for example, in *Tum to mamma* for *Come to mama,* where the *t* is substituted for the sound of *k.*

Consonant Chart

		LABIAL	LABIO-DENTAL	INTER-DENTAL	ALVEO-LAR	ALVEOLO-PALATAL	PALATAL	VELAR
ops	Voiceless	p			t		k	k
	Voiced	b			d		g	g
ica-	Voiceless		f	θ	s	ʃ		
es	Voiced		v	ð	z	ʒ		
nsals	Voiced	m			n			ŋ
ateral	Voiced				l			
mi- *wels*	Voiced					r	j	w

ricates begin with alveolar stops and immediately change to alveolo-palatal fricatives. The voiceless affricate is thus represented [tʃ] [3] and the voiced affricate [dʒ]. They are alveolo-palatal fricatives.

he sound [h] is a voiceless *fricative,* but is made in various positions.

[3] Square brackets are used to indicate a phonetic symbol, as [t]; phonemic symbols are placed between virgules ("diagonal lines" or "slant-lines"): /t/. Since the transcription in this volume is a "broad," not a "narrow" one, where variants are indicated, the phonetic symbols will be used. There is one symbol for each distinctive feature of the language, for each phoneme in the language.

8.4 The Corresponding Vowels Although the lips are active in the formation of certain vowels, none of them is classified as a lip vowel. Neither the lips nor the point and blade of the tongue are necessary in making vowel sounds, which appear to originate in two regions only: the front and the back. It is apparent that this two-area division is too vague to permit any very exact differentiation among the vowels of either region, and indeed our knowledge of the formation of the vowels is not complete enough to enable us to give very exact descriptions (see pars. 7.6, 7.8, and 7.9). The vowels are commonly described as either "front," "back," or "central" sounds.

8.5 Additional Terms Used Numerous variant terms such as *labial, dental, alveolar, velar,* and even *glottal* are used to express approximations to the lip-to-back series, especially of consonants. Sometimes these terms are synonyms of those used here, occasionally they are useful, and occasionally they are misleading, as for instance to speak of any Modern English consonant as glottal when this extreme low region of the throat is seldom or never important in forming the back speech sounds, whether vowel or consonant. One, of course, may hear a glottal stop in the speech of a particular individual or perhaps in a particular region, but it is not a distinctive feature in Modern English.

8.6 High-to-Low Series The terms *high, mid,* and *low,* with their subdivisions *high-mid* and *low-mid,* are used with reference to the height of the tongue in making certain vowel sounds. If the tongue is close to the roof of the mouth we call the vowel a *high* vowel, but if it is in a low position in the mouth the vowel is called *low.* If the tongue is in a position about midway between its high position and its low position, we call the vowel a *mid* vowel. Thus *a* in *father* [a] is a low vowel while *u* in *humor* [u] is a comparatively high one. Of course these terms apply only to that part of the tongue which is important in forming the sound; thus *i* in *machine* [i] and *u* in *rumor* [u] are both high vowels, but in [i] the blade or front of the tongue is high and in [u] the back. One can observe in pronouncing in order the vowel sounds of the words *mat, mate, meet* that the tongue begins from a position which is somewhat below the roof of the mouth and ends close to the roof. These are the front vowels, made with the front of the tongue. The same thing may be observed in connection with the back vowels in the words *maw,* *mow, moot.* Not only does the tongue go higher in the mouth with each word in this series, but there is an observable upward movement of the jaw as well.

8.7 More Definitions Needed   While it is easy to see that [i] and [u] are high vowels compared to the *a* of *father* [ɑ], it is not so easy to tell whether [e] in *fate* or [ɔ] in *hawk* is the higher sound. There exist in English several vowel sounds which are easily distinguishable by the ear but to which the same descriptive terms are applicable. Evidently the minute differences in tongue height between, say, [ɝ] in *bird* and [ʌ] in *nut* are not measurable. We need some new method of analysis which will help us to chart accurately the comparative height of all the vowels.

8.8 High Sounds Typical   In general, English vowels tend to be high or mid rather than low, and this is true also of the consonants, which are predominantly high. There are twenty-three high or high-mid sounds in English, seven mid, and six low or low-mid, besides [h], which does not admit of exact classification. In the high group also fall all the most frequent speech sounds, so it may be said that English is predominantly a high-tongue language.

8.9 Tense-Slack   Our sixth category, tense-slack or tense-lax, is a somewhat vague one that is used exclusively of vowels.[4] It supplements the long-short distinction of the older phonetics; what used to be called a "long" vowel is now generally called a "tense" one, although certainly the element of length does enter into the distinction. There are, however, two terms employed which relate to the utterance of the consonant: *fortis* and *lenis*. These terms refer to the amount of muscular tension present in the articulatory mechanism and the degree of breath pressure used in producing a consonant. For instance, *p* in *pie* is uttered with tense articulation and strong expiration and is, therefore, described as *fortis*. On the other hand, *p* in *dipper* is uttered with lax articulation and gentle expiration and is described as *lenis*.

8.10 Vowels in Two Groups   The fourteen English vowel sounds split exactly in half, seven falling in the tense category and seven in the slack. When it comes to defining exactly how a tense vowel differs from a slack, however, some difficulty arises. The tongue is

---

[4] For example, if we consider *mate:met, feet:fit, food:good,* in saying the first member of each pair, the tongue is held more firmly than for the second.

higher and more flexed, it is true, but the sound is also usually longer and more stressed, and possibly somewhat higher pitched. As a matter of fact, the tense-slack distinction applied to vowels simply reflects the fact that the two groups of vowels, tense and slack, have behaved differently in their historical development. Where the tense vowels have typically raised or broken, the slack have typically remained stable or even lowered.

8.11 Low Vowels Less Distinct   The low vowels, especially the low-back, exhibit no great difference between tense and slack. In Old as in Modern English tense and slack [ɑ] were much the same sound; both were like the vowel sound in *calm*. In Modern English the sound [æ] (the vowel of *cat*) is approximately the same whether "long" (*paths*) or "short" (*path*); [5] and long and short [ɔ] the vowel of *law* and *long*, respectively) and long and short [o] (the vowel of *note* and *obey*, respectively) are not as different as [i] and [ɪ], [e] and [ɛ], [u] and [ʊ]. For example, consider the words *seat* [sit] and *sit* [sɪt], *beat* [bit] and *bit* [bɪt], *gate* [get] and *get* [gɛt], *bate* [bet] and *bet* [bɛt], *boot* [but] and *book* [bʊk], *root* [rut] and *rook* [rʊk].

8.12 Lips Alter Sounds   In par. 8.3 it was stated that certain consonants, such as *p*, are made almost wholly with the lips. But it must now be added that the lips may and do play a part in shaping other sounds. Try sounding the vowel of *meet* with your lips rounded, and you will find that it has changed and is perhaps nearer to the vowel of *mute* but still distinguishable from it. It is like the German long *ü* in *grün* (*green*). The vowel sound you have just made, [i] with lip-rounding, was a part of Old English phonology, where the symbol *ȳ* was used, e.g., *fȳr*, Mod.E. *fire*. Other examples are *brȳd*, Mod.E. *bride*; *hȳrling*, Mod.E. *hireling*; *hwȳ*, Mod.E. *why*. Another high front round vowel which was frequent in Old English was the sound represented by *y* and pronounced like the short *ü* in the German word *Mütter* (*mothers*). The vowel of *Mütter* may be made by pronouncing the vowel of *mill* with the lips rounded. Old English examples are *synn*, Mod.E. *sin; cyning*, Mod.E. *king; wynsum*, Mod.E. *winsome; hrycg*, Mod.E. *ridge; dysig*, Mod.E. *dizzy; dyde*, Mod.E. *did; hlystan*, Mod.E. *listen*. The front round vowels do not occur in Modern English.

[5] See George Philip Krapp, *The Pronunciation of Standard English in America* (New York, Oxford University Press, 1919), p. 65.

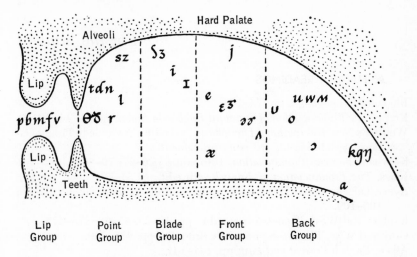

Lip Group | Point Group | Blade Group | Front Group | Back Group

DIAGRAM B THE THIRTY-SEVEN SOUNDS OF ENGLISH

NOTE: *h* has been omitted since it cannot be localized.

8.13 Modern English Roundings In our present speech, a few of both vowels and consonants are pronounced with lip rounding. All the sounds where rounding is used are back sounds; among consonants, there are [w] (*wear*) and [ʍ] (*where*). Among vowels, there are [u] in *moon*, [o] in *boat*, and [ɔ] in *law*. One can observe the difference in rounding in pronouncing the series *maw, mow, moot*. The high back vowel of *moot* is more rounded than the mid back vowel of *mow*, and the latter is more rounded than the low back vowel of *maw*; in fact, *maw* as pronounced by some speakers has very little rounding, if any at all. At the other extreme from these rounded sounds is one like [æ] of *cat*, which is usually accompanied by a flattening of the lips if emphasized. The lack of rounding can be observed in the series of vowel sounds heard in *mat, mate, meet*.

For the Student

A. FURTHER READINGS

Bloomfield, *Language*, pp. 74–108.

Krapp, *The Pronunciation of Standard English in America*, §§ 9–11; 20; 50.

Webster's *New International Dictionary*, 2nd edit., "A Guide to Pronunciation," §§ 31–34; 43; 3rd edit., pp. 34a–46a.

Kenyon, *American Pronunciation*, 10th edit., §§ 6–27; 79–80.

Jones, *The Pronunciation of English*, 4th edit., §§ 31–56.

Avery, Dorsey, and Sickels, *First Principles of Speech Training*, pp. 84–86; 105–109.

Kantner and West, *Phonetics*, rev. edit., pp. 18–25; 57–66; 273–275.

Gray and Wise, *The Bases of Speech*, 3rd edit., pp. 235–320.

Aiken, *English Present and Past*, pp. 141–147.

Graff, *Language and Languages*, pp. 25–29.

Francis, *The Structure of American English*, pp. 50–161.

Gleason, *An Introduction to Descriptive Linguistics*, rev. edit., pp. 14–39; 257–285; 221–250.

Hill, *Introduction to Linguistic Structures*, pp. 31–67.

Lloyd and Warfel, *American English in Its Cultural Setting*, pp. 294–318.

Heffner, *General Phonetics*, pp. 87–162.

B. FOR CLASS DISCUSSION

1. List all seven categories into which speech sounds may fall, and review the explanation of each.
2. Take each letter of the alphabet and list its usual sound or sounds. For each, try applying the sound categories described in this chapter. Which are easy to apply? Which are hard? Check your results with the diagram, p. 131.
3. Pronounce the Old English word *wyrm, yfel* (pronounce *f* like *v*), *cynn, cyning* (Mod.E. *king*), *fȳr, brȳd* (Mod.E. *bride*), *ȳs* (Mod.E. *ice*).
4. By experimentation discover the effect of an abnormal position of the lips or the tongue on various sounds, and discuss the importance of these organs in speech.
5. Does the expression "a long vowel" mean the same thing in English that it does in Latin and Greek? Does this suggest any reason why the terms "tense" and "slack" may be preferable to "long" and "short" in describing English vowel sounds?

6. Test the statement in par. 8.11 that the distinction between tense and slack is less noticeable in low than in high vowels by practicing pairs of words like *paths, path; law, long; note, obey; keen, kin; bait, bet; boon, bull.*
7. The vowels in the pairs of words *led, let; bed, bet; said, set; sad, sat* are all classified as short. When you pronounce these words, do you find that the vowels differ at all in length?
8. Try to pronounce both the sounds [u] and [i] with the lips first rounded and then unrounded. Do the same for the pairs [o] and [e], [ɔ] and [æ]. What happens?

C. SUGGESTIONS FOR RESEARCH PAPERS

1. A Scientific Order of Speech Sounds.
2. A Scientific Classification of Speech Sounds.
3. Rounding in Vowels and Consonants.
4. Tensity and Length as Terms to Describe Vowels.
5. English as a High-Tongue Language.
6. A Comparison of Phonemes in English and German (or any other language).

9

The Lip Consonants and H

9.1 Diagram of Sounds We are now ready to consider English speech sounds in detail, in a logical order, proceeding from the sound made farthest front in the mouth to the one made farthest back. On a broad count, which is sufficient for our purposes, we shall need to recognize only thirty-seven different sounds. These are set forth in Diagram B and will now be described in detail.

9.2 Audible Breathing One sound, so weak as scarcely to be counted at all, has been left out of Diagram B and will be described here although it is not one of the lip sounds. The first item in our phonetic sequence must be what the Greeks called "rough breathing"—breathing so energetic as to be audible. The sound [h] is very unstable and may disappear in nearly any unstressed position. *Sweetheart* regularly becomes *sweetart, him* becomes *'im,* and *he, 'e,* unless the speaker makes a conscious effort to preserve his *h*'s and such an effort leads to artificial enunciation. Since it is audible only in initial position and even there it is often elided in unstressed words, can anyone wonder that the Greeks did not include it in their alphabet?

9.3 Cockney Not the Standard   On the other hand, one must drop one's *h*'s naturally and not as the Cockney, who does not drop them so much as get them mixed up. In the sentence *How have his high hopes of Arthur fallen!* the Cockney might say *'ow, 'ave, 'iz, 'igh, 'opes,* and *Harthur,* while the standard speaker, talking informally, would say *how, have, 'is, high, hopes,* and *Arthur.* The words *have, high,* and *hopes* preserve their *h*'s because they are emphatic. The initial word *how* naturally retains the *h*.

9.4 H Not Glottal   The sound [h] is sometimes called a glottal fricative, which means a sound made in the glottis (see Diagram A) and produced with audible friction localized there; but this is true so rarely as to be negligible. A few very exceptional speakers, mainly foreign, do produce a "gargled" *h;* but for most people *h* is better described as "a puff of breath." This can be observed in pronouncing a series like *heat, hate, hat, heart, haul, hole, hood,* where the lips and tongue assume the position for the following vowel in each word, but do not have a set form for [h]. It may be described as a *voiceless fricative* made in various positions.

9.5 An Infantile Group   The next three consonants on our list, *p, b, m,* are early sounds, if not the earliest, made by babies. They appear to be made naturally without conscious imitation or instruction, probably because in infancy the lips are used actively in taking food, and in these three sounds the tongue is inactive and only the lips are necessary.[1] As lips are less important in eating and drinking in later life, they are not as active in making adult sounds and therefore these consonants are not among those most frequently used; but it is interesting to see how many baby words follow the pattern of *mama, papa,* and *baby,* in beginning with these lip sounds. These baby words, along with *da-da,* also indicate the fact that [ɑ] is the easiest vowel sound for the pre-speech period.

9.6 The Bilabial Stop   First in the lip group comes logically the consonant *p,* which is called a stop or plosive of the voiceless type, using both lips and therefore bilabial. Phoneticians frequently call unfavorable attention to an emphatic or aspirated [p] which they write as (*p'*), *p*ʰ (*p*ʰ*at*); this is rare in ordinary speech and does not require a separate phonemic symbol. In the formation of [p] the

[1] Otto Jespersen, *Language* (New York, Henry Holt and Company, 1933), pp. 105–106.

passage of air through the mouth is momentarily stopped by closing
the lips, and then released, as in *pin, put, upper, uplift.* In final position the stoppage may be held, e.g., *cup, lip, hop.* It is a *voiceless
bilabial stop.*

9.7 Force of Breath in [*p*]   It is a significant fact that the voiceless sound [p] must be made with greater force, and therefore
greater effort, than the voiced sound [b]. It is a general rule that
where voice is lacking, greater effort is required; and this may explain why a number of sounds thought by some Old English scholars
to be voiceless (*hn, hl, hr*) have disappeared between Old and Modern English. For example, we find O.E. *hnecca,* Mod.E. *neck;* O.E.
hnutu, Mod.E. *nut;* O.E. *hnitu,* Mod.E. *nit,* the egg of a louse; O.E.
hlædel, Mod.E. *ladle;* O.E. *hlæder,* Mod.E. *ladder;* O.E. *hlæne,*
Mod.E. *lean;* O.E. *hlanc,* Mod.E. *lank;* O.E. *hlid,* Mod.E. *lid;* O.E.
hræfn, Mod.E. *raven;* O.E. *hrēod,* Mod.E. *reed;* O.E. *hriddel,*
Mod.E. *riddle;* O.E. *hring,* Mod.E. *ring;* O.E. *hrung,* Mod.E. *rung*
(of a ladder). One other voiceless sound which has become voiced
in Standard Southern (British) English is *hw,* now pronounced
[w], as *wat* for *what* or *wim* for *whim.* A separate phoneme for *wh*
no longer exists here. This voiced sound is also heard in the speech
of some in the United States. For instance, O.E. *hwēol* is Mod.E.
wheel, pronounced [wil] and [ʍil]. O.E. *hwīt* is Mod.E. *white,* pronounced [waɪt] and [ʍaɪt]. In all languages voiceless sounds show
a tendency to yield ground in favor of the less arduous sounds.

9.8 Omission of [*p*]   The sound [p] may be omitted in unstressed positions, especially when medial between consonants as in
assumption [ə'sʌmʃən], *consumption* [kən'sʌmʃən]. In conjunction
with [b] it may also disappear as in *cupboard* [kʌbəˑd], *clapboard*
[klæbəˑd]. In general, the sound [p] gives little trouble to speakers of
English, and it is somewhat odd that our most famous tongue-twister,
"Peter Piper picked a peck of pickled peppers," should turn on this
easy sound when the sibilants offer so much more real difficulty. Although relatively infrequent, [p] is one of the easiest English sounds
to use correctly.

9.9 Voiced Equivalent   In all ways [b] is the counterpart of [p]
save that voice is present. As a result of such contrasts as *bet:pet,
bit:pit, bane:pane,* and many others, we must, however, consider
them as different phonemes. It is the *voiced bilabial stop.* The sound

[b], like [p], is also easy to handle correctly. No release of the breath occurs in words like *rubdown,* where [b] is followed by another stop. In final position the stoppage of air involved in [b] is not released and the sound approximates [p], giving *Jacop* ['dʒekəp] for *Jacob* ['dʒekəb]. On the other hand, [bm] is at times substituted for [vn], as in the word *seven,* which becomes *seb'm* (['sɛbm̩] and in *heaven* which becomes *heb'm* ['hɛbm̩] in some dialects. It would seem that in end positions the lip sounds are easier than the lip-teeth-point combination, and perhaps give more of an impression of finality. The pronunciations *seb'm* ['sɛbm̩] and *heb'm* ['hɛbm̩] are informal.

9.10 The Lip Nasal When the mouth passage is closed so that air, the basic material of speech, must pass through the nose, the resulting sound is called nasal. As we have seen, both [p] and [b] also have a stoppage of the mouth passage; but the quick release of the air current keeps them out of the category of nasals. In [m] the breath is held perceptibly longer, and voice is always present even in final position. The use of the nose is apparent from the fact that when the nose is "stopped up" [p] and [b] may still be made, but [m] becomes impossible and [b] is substituted for it, "my, my" [mɑɪ, mɑɪ] becoming "by, by" [bɑɪ, bɑɪ]. When one has a cold the voiced stops tend to replace the corresponding nasals: [b] for [m], [d] for [n], and [g] for [ŋ]. The stoppage of the nasal passages transforms what should be nasals into stopped oral sounds and one says [sprɪg] instead of [sprɪŋ] and [bɑɪ dɛk] instead of [mɑɪ nɛk].

9.11 [m] an Easy Sound Like [p] and [b], [m], a *voiced bilabial nasal,* offers no great difficulty to the speaker. Occasionally [m] tends to be substituted for [n], especially by children, who may say opm [opm] for *open* ['opən], *cupmsaucer* ['kʌpm'sɔsɚ] for *cup and saucer* ['kʌp ænd 'sɔsɚ],[2] and *bime-by* [bɑɪmbɑɪ] for *by and by* [bɑɪ ænd bɑɪ],[2] but this substitution is not very frequent.

9.12 Lips and Teeth Combined Like [m], the other two lip sounds are continuants rather than stops; but unlike [m], this voiceless-voiced pair uses only one of the lips in its production. No sound in all the thirty-seven of English is more peculiarly formed than are [f] and [v]. In each of them the lower lip is brought very near to the

[2] Stressed form with each word pronounced.

upper teeth, and the air is permitted to escape through the resulting aperture with audible friction. Try pronouncing a series of words like *fine, vine, fain, vain, five, revive, knife, knives, wife, wives, fan, van, fault, vault, fail, veil.* The technical name for each of these sounds is *labiodental fricative.* (See Consonant Chart on page 127.)

9.13 Voiceless-Voiced Alternation The pair of sounds [f] and [v] illustrate the general rule that "stress tends to voiceless, lack of stress to voice." Thus the preposition *of,* which presumably at one time had the unvoiced value of the consonant, has come to be universally pronounced with a *v,* because of its lack of stress. And on the contrary, when the word *have* [hæv] is stressed it may tend to become *haf* [hæf]. The substitutions thus illustrated do not hold for [f] and [v] only; they are paralleled in all consonantal voiceless-voiced pairs.

9.14 Influence of Other Sounds The word *have* comes to be pronounced with [f] when it is followed by a voiceless consonant and a schwa, as in *I have to go* [ɑɪ hæftə go]. Compare *I have two shoes* [ɑɪ hæv tu ʃuz]. There is another alternation between [f] and [v] in such pairs as *wife, wives; knife, knives.* This is not a result of stress or unstress, but of the influence of neighboring vowels on the *f* in the plural.

For the Student

A. FURTHER READINGS

Krapp, *The Pronunciation of Standard English in America,* §§ 13; 28–29; 235–246; 254–258; 281–283; 298–300; 357; 364.

Kenyon, *American Pronunciation,* 10th edit., §§ 151–154; 175–182; 199–206; 212.

Jones, *An Outline of English Phonetics,* 8th edit., §§ 496–510; 639–643; 682–694; 776–787.

Kantner and West, *Phonetics,* rev. edit., pp. 109–112; 143–145; 156–160; 180–182.

Webster's *New International Dictionary,* 2nd edit., "A Guide to Pronunciation," §§ 44 (10); 55 (1); 97–99; 137; 149–150; 171–173; 205–208; 254; 3rd edit., pp. 34a–46a, *passim.*

Aiken, *English Present and Past,* pp. 148–150; and Table I, pp. 142–143.
Robertson and Cassidy, *The Development of Modern English,* 2nd edit.,
    pp. 61–64.

B. FOR CLASS DISCUSSION

1. Describe the action of the speech organs in producing the consonants
   mentioned in this chapter: [h], [p], [b], [m], [f], [v].
2. Make up test sentences with numerous *h*'s, such as *Harry knew who he
   hoped had seen him,* and read them first slowly and artificially, then
   rapidly and naturally. What words lose the initial *h?* Include all the
   h words mentioned by Krapp, §§ 254–258. Amplify Krapp's statements from other sources if possible.
3. Make a list of words containing the letter *h* and generalize concerning
   the proportion of sounded and silent *h*'s.
4. Does the [h] sound occur in any possible position (initial, medial, final)
   in a word? Illustrate.
5. Make up sentences containing the five lip sounds treated in this lesson
   and practice reading them as you did with the sentences in Question 2.
6. Make a list of "baby" words utilizing *p, b,* and *m.*
7. Practice the three sentences:
   The word is *cup.*
   The word is *cub.*
   The word is *come.*
   and analyze the difference in the final consonants. What is it that dis-
   tinguishes [b] and [m]? [b] and [p]? Add:
   The word is *cuff.*
   The word is *cuv.*
8. Learn the two rules:
   (a) voiceless sounds take more effort than voiced.
   (b) stress tends to voiceless, lack of stress to voiced.
   Illustrate them with the consonants in this chapter.
9. Account for the Mod.E. spelling *empty* from O.E. *æmetig.* What letter
   has intruded itself? Explain.
10. Hold your nose tightly closed and try to pronounce *m.* What happens?
    Imitate the speech of a person with a cold in the head. Is it scientifically
    correct to say that such a person is "talking through his nose"? Explain.
11. What consonant is often heard after the [m] in such words as *some-
    thing* and *warmth?* Explain.
12. Look up the derivation of *number, slumber, tremble, bramble, grum-
    ble, thimble,* and account for the Modern English spelling and pro-
    nunciation.

13. In some dialects the form *heb'm* is used for *heaven*. Account for the pronunciation.
14. By what means do we distinguish the noun *grief* from the verb *grieve?* Give other similar pairs.
15. Describe what happens in forming the plural of such words as *calf, life, leaf, shelf, thief, wolf.* Add others.
16. The preposition *of* and the adverb *off* were originally the same word (O.E. *of*). Explain what has happened and tell why it has happened. (See par. 13.)
17. To each of the six sounds covered in this chapter, apply all seven of the categories given in Chapters 7 and 8, and start a table or list of all speech sounds on this basis. When complete it may be checked with the table in Aiken's *English Present and Past*, pp. 142–143, or with similar tables or descriptions in other books of phonetics.

C. SUGGESTIONS FOR RESEARCH PAPERS

1. Prespeech Sounds of Infants.
2. Is [h] a Glottal Sound?
3. The *f-v* Plurals in Old English and Modern English.
4. The Intrusive Sounds [p] and [b].

10

The Point Consonants

10.1 Largest Single Group The point consonants are nine in number, or twelve if we include three which were present in Old English but have since disappeared; in frequency they cover roughly two-thirds of all spoken English consonant sounds. In all of them the air current is obstructed or modified by the tip or point of the tongue. Thus they are generally easy to make and to use. Their only difficulty arises from the fact that, being so close together, they either merge neatly (*tr, sn, st, sl* as initial sounds, as in *train, track; snail, snow; storm, static; slow, slide; ld, nd, ns* as end sounds, as in *child, mild; bind, find; guns, chins*) or else they get in each other's way as *t, th,* and *s* do in the tongue-twister, "six thick thistle sticks," which is almost impossible to say fast and at the same time correctly. Also this group includes the sound [r], which is a subject of much discussion by phoneticians since it affects the quality of neighboring vowels and is itself affected by the quality of neighboring vowels and consonants. Because of this fact [r] causes more disagreement than any other sound in English.

10.2 Variety in Classification The tongue tip is used in very different ways in the formation of the point consonants. Of the nine which survive in Modern English we find two stops, seven continuants; three voiceless, six voiced; three so weak as scarcely to be called consonantal (often called liquids and semivowels), six strongly marked by consonantal qualities.

10.3 Useful in Inflections   This point group includes practically all the sounds that have been employed in forming inflections. Thus the plural uses [s] (*rats* [ræts]), [z] (*rafters* [ræftɚz]), and rarely [n] (*oxen* ['ɑksn̩]). The past uses [d] (*answered* ['ænsɚd]) and [t] (*looked* [lʊkt]). The comparative and superlative use [r] (*faster* [fæstɚ]), [s] (*less* [lɛs]), *and* [t] (*least* [list] and *fastest* [fæstɪst]); and the adverb-forming element uses [l] (*badly* [bædlɪ]). Only the present participle ending -*ing* falls outside this group, and it is very frequently pronounced [ɪn] or [ən], with the point nasal instead of the back nasal, a substitution incorrectly described as "dropping *g's.*" One may say *makin'* [mekɪn] instead of *making* [mekɪŋ].

10.4 One Spelling, Two Sounds   The first two of these point consonants are sometimes called the dental fricatives, but the term dental is misleading if it implies that only the teeth are used. What happens is that the tongue tip is placed between the upper and lower teeth without quite touching either, and air (with or without voice) is blown through the aperture. Both the voiced and the voiceless values of this sound are spelled *th.* The one, [θ], a *voiceless interdental fricative*, is heard in *thin, thick, thigh, tooth, wreath;* the *other,* [ð], a voiced *interdental fricative*, in *the, then, this, thy, wreaths.*

10.5 Substitutions for [θ] and [ð]   Foreigners whose native languages do not have these sounds often find them difficult and are likely to substitute [s] and [z], saying *ze sing, zat sing, zis sing* instead of *the thing, that thing, this thing.* Uneducated native speakers of English occasionally are found to make a different substitution, [t] and [d], *de ting, dat ting, dis ting.* Both of these errors can be corrected if the speaker observes how [θ] and [ð] are formed, and practices with them. The phonemic contrast between them can be clearly heard in pronouncing words like *breathe* (v.):*breath* (n.), *teethe* (v.):*teeth* (n.), *wreathe* (v.):*wreath* (n.). In informal speech these sounds are now and then omitted, as in *clothes* [kloz], *asthma* [æzmə], *oaths* [oz], and *close the door* [klozədor].

10.6 *S* a Misleading Letter The fact that *s* is so much the most frequent initial letter in English, taking up roughly one-twelfth or 8 per cent of the pages in Webster's *New International Dictionary*, might lead one to conclude that the sound was more frequent than it actually is. In fact, spelling is no guide. Many of the *s*-letters do not indicate the *s*-sound (*she, sure, dogs*), while the sound [s] occurs often where no letter *s* is found (*box, peace, quartz*). The voiced counterpart of [s], namely [z], is only less misrepresented by spelling. In these two sounds, the grooved tongue is held near but not touching the gums and the air is forced out over the tip. These two sibilants are called disagreeable sounds by many teachers of speech, and [s] is used to express audience displeasure, the sound being called a hiss. Many speech defects involve a nonstandard formation of [s], the *voiceless alveolar fricative*, and [z], the *voiced alveolar fricative*.

10.7 Many Terms for *S* The word *sibilant*, applied to *s* [s], *z* [z], *sh* [ʃ], and *zh* [ʒ], is standard; and the term *alveolar* is also fairly general for these and for *t* [t], *d* [d], *n* [n], and *l* [l]. Other terms sometimes found are tongue-gum, postdental, supradental, teeth ridge, and gum ridge. The sound [s] is the voiceless sibilant, [z] the voiced, as can be seen from such contrasts as *fuzz:fuss, zeal: seal*. Many tongue-twisters involve sibilants, for example, the well-known "She sells sea shells by the sea shore."

10.8 First Pair of Point Stops The four sounds described in the foregoing paragraphs are all continuants, but in the voiceless-voiced pair [t] and [d] we have stops; the tongue first stops the air, and then the point falls from its position against the center of the gums, to let out the breath. The sound [t] is frequently unpronounced, as in *thistle, jostle,* and it is substituted for [d] in *dressed, tapped, walked,* etc. In general, however, [t], the *voiceless alveolar stop,* and [d], the *voiced alveolar stop,* accord with their spelling and offer few difficulties to speakers of English.

10.9 The Point Nasal The sound [n], a *voiced alveolar nasal,* is related to [t] and [d] exactly as [m] is related to [p] and [b] (see Chapter 9). This sound becomes [d] when the nasal passages are obstructed: *id* is substituted for *in* and *nose* becomes *dose.*[1] In [n]

---

[1] See par. 9.10.

the air current is cut off by placing the tongue against the gums, thus forming a resonance chamber different from the one used in the production of [m].

10.10 No Longer Used in Inflection   In Old English *n* was a very common inflectional element for nouns, verbs, and adjectives. In Middle English it yielded to *s,* and today it survives only in a few plural forms, *oxen, brethren;* some past participles, *taken, spoken;* and in two possessive pronouns (predicative forms), *mine, thine.* The sound of *n* is lost in words like *hymn* and *autumn,* but the letter may be pronounced before an added syllable (*hymnal, autumnal*).

10.11 The Lateral Continuant   Like the five foregoing sounds, [l] is alveolar, and with *n* and *r* it is sometimes called a semivowel, because its pronunciation is often weak. It is the only English consonant called a lateral, and this name is used because in its formation the air escapes on either side of the tongue tip, which is pressed against the gums. The sound has been lost, though the letter is still retained, in many words such as *walk, talk, calm, calf,* where *l* precedes *k, m,* or *f.* The body of the tongue is held lower in *l* than in other alveolar consonants. If one, however, contrasts the sounds in *leaf:loaf, leap:loop,* a difference is evident, based on the different positions of the tongue. These are sometimes called the "clear" *l* and the "dark" *l,* but they are not phonemically different. The *l* is a *voiced alveolar lateral.*

10.12 Old English R   No consonant has changed more in the development of English than has *r.* In the early days it was a trill, [R], made in either the point or the glottal region of the mouth. From this it weakened until today it is called a retracted or inverted sound because there is just a vestige of the trill left in that the tongue tip is drawn in or curled slightly back. In Modern English the sound has the phonetic symbol [r]. In Old English *l* and *r* had positional variants after [x]: [l] and [R], as in *hlāf (loaf)* and *hring (ring).*[2]

10.13 Divided Usage in [r]   A great number of sounds are represented by the symbol *r,* a semivowel, variously described as "trilled," "semitrilled," "rolled," "burred," "vocalic," "glide," and "lost," but these variations are non-phonemic. No other symbol pre-

2 See par. 16.3 for description of positional variant.

sents so much variety and so much difficulty. In different words it stands for sounds that range from one formed in the back of the mouth by the tapping of the uvula (the "Northumbrian burr") to one that scarcely has any consonantal quality at all because of the lack of friction. Note the difference of the [r] in *rod* and in *forest* or in *run* and *over*. For the pronunciation of present-day American English, we shall distinguish between the more energetic and distinct *r* that is used initially as in *rob*, preceded by a consonant as in *drop*, or between vowels, as in *foreign*, and the fainter sound, which may not be described as a consonant at all, the one heard in such words as *bird* and *ever*. In the last-mentioned examples the tongue merely rises toward the gums and we have an "*r*-colored" vowel. In *bird* we find the accented "*r*-colored" vowel which will be represented by [ɝ], but in *ever* we have the unaccented "*r*-colored" vowel which we shall represent by [ɚ], the neutral vowel to which a wing of the *r* is attached to show the "*r*-coloring." Thus we have the following representations of the sounds of the two words: [bɝd] and [ɛvɚ]; the first is the accented form and the second is the unaccented. If, however, the *r* is so weakened as to disappear as is ordinarily true in southern England, New England, and the southern part of the United States, then the "*r*-coloring" is omitted as in [ɛvə], *jar* [dʒɑ:],[3] *bard* [bɑ:d], and the preceding vowel, if not already long, is lengthened. The Americans of the Middle West and the North Central states, on the other hand, have a hard palatal or back *r*. These same words would be represented in their speech thus: [ɛvər], [dʒɑr], [bɑrd].[4] These numerous variations, however, are not phonemic and are thus represented by one symbol.

10.14 Intrusive and Omitted [*r*] Especially in New England, an *r* is likely to be inserted between a word ending with a low vowel and another word beginning with a vowel (*idea-r-of, saw-r-(h)im*). But more often the *r* is omitted. Even speakers of the Middle West and the North Central states tend to omit weakened *r*'s in rapid speech.

---

[3] The diacritical mark [:] indicates length in the preceding sound.
[4] See John S. Kenyon and Thomas A. Knott, *A Pronouncing Dictionary of American English* (Springfield, Mass., G. & C. Merriam Company, 1953), "Introduction," pp. xix–xxii.

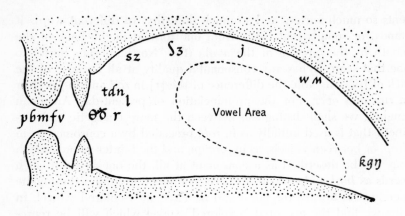

DIAGRAM C CONSONANTS

NOTE: *h* is not shown as it is not localized.

For the Student

A. FURTHER READINGS

Krapp, *The Pronunciation of Standard English in America*, §§ 30–36; 39–
47; 239–246; 273–280; 284–288; 301–325; 336–356.

Kenyon, *American Pronunciation*, 10th edit., §§ 155–166; 183–192; 213–
216; 220–222; 234–243; 3rd edit., pp. 34a–46a, *passim*.

Webster's *New International Dictionary*, 2nd edit., "A Guide to Pronunciation," §§ 44 (4–6, 9); 53 (3); 111; 166–170; 174–175; 211–214; 217–
224; 230–236; 265–266.

Avery, Dorsey, and Sickels, *First Principles of Speech Training*, pp. 94–96;
98–102.

Jones, *An Outline of English Phonetics*, 8th edit., §§ 511–531; 644–649a;
659–678; 695–725; 744–775.

Kantner and West, *Phonetics*, rev. edit., 145–151; 161–164; 168–178; 182–
183.

Aiken, *English Present and Past*, pp. 150–153.

Robertson and Cassidy, *The Development of Modern English*, 2nd edit.,
pp. 64–69, *passim*.

B. FOR CLASS DISCUSSION

1. Describe the action of the speech organs in producing the consonants discussed in this chapter: [t], [d], [s], [z], [n], [l], [θ], [ð], [r].
2. Continue classroom exercise 17 in Chapter 9 to include the nine point consonants discussed in this chapter.
3. Count all the consonant sounds (not letters) in a page of reading matter. What proportion belongs to the point group?
4. Account for the substitutions in the phrase *id by sog* for *in my song*.
5. Look up the derivation of the word *hemp* and explain its Modern English form. Do the same for the word *ant*.
6. Why is [t] substituted for [d] in *dressed, capped, tapped*, etc.? Can you make a general statement about the pronunciation of verb forms of this kind?
7. Is it phonetically correct to say that the plural of nouns is formed by adding [s]? Make a correct rule to cover the following plurals: *bats, logs, bees, mobs, roses*.
8. Can you name some dialect pronoun forms using [n] inflectionally?
9. Give a detailed description of what happens in the pronunciation [fɛnts] for the word *fence*.
10. Account for the omission of [t] in the pronunciation of *listen*. Do the same for the word *often*. Is the [t] always omitted? If not, how do you account for the variation?
11. Account for the intrusion of [d] in *thunder*.
12. Why should an excrescent [t] at times occur in words like *oncet* (*once*), *acrost* (*across*), *wisht* (*wish*)?
13. Look up the derivations of *amongst, amidst, against, betwixt, tapestry, whilst*, and analyze the [t] in each.
14. Do you distinguish in pronunciation between *maw* and *more; poke* and *pork; firs, furs, furze*, and *fuzz*? Make rules governing your own pronunciation of [r].
15. By what means do we distinguish the noun from the verb in such words as *use, house, cloth(e), mouth, abuse*? List other words of this kind.
16. What is the phonetic difference between *advice* and *advise*? Grammatically, what does the difference show? Give other examples.

C. SUGGESTIONS FOR RESEARCH PAPERS

1. Consonant Frequencies in Modern English.
2. Atlas of the Sounded *R*.
3. What Is Lisp?
4. Use of Point Consonants in Old and Modern English Inflections.
5. The Omission of Point Consonants in Modern English Words.

11

The Blade and
Front Consonants

11.1 Blade Consonants Number Only Two The blade of the tongue, that region just behind the point, figures in the formation of only two English consonants, *sh* [ʃ] as in *short, fish, chauffeur* and *zh* [ʒ] as in *treasure, confusion, usual* (this sound is generally confined to medial positions). Neither of these has a single spelling symbol, and this is probably because they do not go back to the early stages of Old English. The older of the two [ʃ], entered our language in the late Old English period, but the more recent did not appear until the Middle English period. In Old English [ʃ] was spelled *sc* (O.E. *scip*, Mod.E. *ship*), but in Modern English the two sounds are represented by a wide variety of spellings.

11.2 The Blade Sibilants With [s] and [z], [ʃ], *a voiceless alveolo-palatal fricative*, and [ʒ], a *voiced alveolo-palatal fricative*, are classed as sibilants, and they complete the list of sibilants in English. In making [ʃ] the tongue blade is raised almost to the gums and the air current is forced through with a noise somewhat less hissing than [s]. Except for the addition of voice, the formation of [ʒ] is the same.

At times [ʃ] and [ʒ] are substituted for [s] and [z], respectively, especially if the speaker has had too much alcohol. In a state of inebriation the muscles are not so well controlled and the speech organs for the sounds [ʃ] and [ʒ] are in a more relaxed position than they are in making the sounds [s] and [z]. For example, one may hear a sailor, who has just arrived in port and is having his first night out, say to his companion, "Sham, pleazhe pash the shalad, old boy. I need to eat a good shupper." for "Sam, please pass the salad, old boy. I need to eat a good supper."

11.3 Spelling Confusion Regarding [ʃ] and [ʒ] Krapp in *The Pronunciation of Standard English in America* (pp. 124–130) lists fifteen spellings for the sound [ʃ], among them *s* (*sugar*), *sh* (*ship*), *ch* (*chef*), *sch* (*schottische*), *ce* (*ocean*), *sci* (*conscious*), *si* (*mansion*), *se* (*nausea*), *ssi* (*mission*), *ssu* (*tissue*), *ti* (*ration*), *ci* (*social*), *x* (*anxious*), *te* (*righteous*), *tu* (*actual*). There are nearly as many spellings for [ʒ], among these *j* (*join*), *g* (*margarine*), *si* (*derision*), *zi* (*glazier*), *su* (*leisure*), *zu* (*azure*), *di* (*soldier*), *du* (*schedule*), *ti* (*equation*).

To understand this variety of spellings, pronounce rapidly, for example, the word *nurse you*. One can scarcely avoid saying [nɝ·ʃu], for the position of the tongue for the initial sound of *you* [j], a *palatal semivowel*, is immediately behind that for [ʃ] so that in changing from [s] to [j], the tip of the tongue remains at the alveolar ridge but allows the blade of the tongue to be raised. In the transference the particular formation necessary for producing the sound [ʃ] is made.

Such words as *social* and *ration*, to take two, were originally pronounced as three syllables with the greatest stress on the last syllable to conform to the pattern of the French, the language from which they were borrowed. In the anglicization of the words the stress shifted to the first syllable, thus neutralizing the last vowel, giving ['sosiəl] and ['rɑsiən]. Then the [ɪ] before a lightly stressed vowel became [j], making the original three syllables into two. Then the combination of [s] and [j] developed into [ʃ] as described in the rapidly pronounced combination of words *nurse you*. That is, [s] plus [ɪ] plus [ə] becomes [s] plus [j] plus [ə] which becomes [ʃə]. In the same way the sound [ʒ] was made except that it was formed from the combination of the voiced sound [z] with [j], instead of with the voiceless [s]. That is, [z] plus [ɪ] plus [ə] becomes [z] plus

[j] plus [ə] which becomes [ʒə], as in *derision* and *Is your paper ready?*

11.4 Substitutions for *[j]*   The blade sibilants [ʃ] and [ʒ] are occasionally substituted for the front consonant *y* [j] in words like *tune* [tjun], and *duty* ['djutɪ], giving the pronunciations *choon* [tʃun] and *juty* ['dʒutɪ]. The reason appears to be that the tongue passes more easily from the point positions for [t] and [d] to the blade positions [ʃ] and[ʒ] than to the front position for [j]. Both [t] and [d] and [ʃ] and [ʒ] are high sounds, whereas [j] is a high-mid sound. See Diagrams B and C.

Just as the sound [ʃ] was developed from an earlier combination of [s] and [j], so [tʃ] was developed from a combination of [t] and [j] as can be readily understood from saying rapidly two words like *don't you,* which sounds like *don't chew* [dontʃu]. In transferring the tongue from the alveolar position necessary to make the sound [t] to the position for a [j], the configuration required for producing [tʃ] is formed. Consider, for example, the word *creature* which was borrowed from the French and originally had three syllables with heavy stress on the first and last syllables, pronounced ['krɪtɪ'ur]. First in conforming to the English pattern the stress on the last syllable was lost, giving two syllables only ['krɪtɚ]. Then the [ɪ] became [j], as ['krɪtjɚ]. Finally the combining of [t] and [j] produced [tʃ], giving the pronunciation ['krɪtʃɚ]. Thus [t] plus [j] plus [ə] or [ɚ] give [tʃə] or [tʃɚ], respectively. In the same way the combining of [d] with [j] gives [dʒ]. That is, [d] plus [j] plus [ə] or [ɚ] give [dʒə] or [dʒɚ], respectively.

11.5 Consonantal Diphthongs   The pre-palatal fricatives, or the blade sibilants, [ʃ] and [ʒ], are frequently combined with the alveolar stops [t] and [d] to form the affricates, *alveolo-palatal fricatives.* The spellings in these combinations are *ch* [tʃ] as in *church, chew, chance* and *j* [dʒ] as in *judge, jail, jar.* Some phoneticians regard these combinations as single sounds; they are of frequent occurrence in English. In fact, the second, [dʒ], is frequently substituted for [ʒ] in words like *rouge, garage, massage,* originally pronounced [ruʒ], [gə'raʒ], [mə'saʒ], but often sounded as [rudʒ], [gə'radʒ], [mə'sadʒ]. The popular tendency is to sound the final consonants of these words like those of *message* and *courage.* The sound [ʒ] never occurs finally in native words and hence is resisted in imported words.

11.6 *Blade* a Misleading Term To speak of the blade of the tongue is perhaps slightly inaccurate, since the tongue is a semioval which may or may not elongate itself into a tip. In the blade sounds the tongue simply does not extend itself so far as it does when a "point" is being made. It would be wrong to think of blade and point as regions rather than elongations of the tongue, however frequently phonetic explanations may imply or express the former notion.

11.7 "Front," the Tongue Center Behind the "blade" of the tongue lies the region called the "front." When the tongue is not elongated into a point at all, this term might serve, but for most phonetic situations it is inaccurate in the extreme. It came into use for vowels, to designate one of the two vowel groups, and it is not properly applicable to consonants, most of which are actually farther front than the part of the tongue generally designated as "front." The term *center* is logically preferable; but since *front* is well established in phonetics it will be used here.

11.8 One Front Consonant The letter *y*, when consonantal, usually represents a voiced, weakly fricative, continuant sound whose phonetic symbol is [j] as in *yard* [jɑrd], *yawl* [jɔl], *you* [ju], *yam* [jæm], *yacht* [jɑt]. In making it, the central, uppermost portion of the tongue is lifted until it nearly touches the roof of the mouth, and air is emitted through the aperture. Thus [j] is the highest English sound, a *voiced palatal semivowel*.

11.9 Consonant-Vowel Diphthong The sound [j] is often present in pronunciation when the spelling gives no hint of it, particularly before the vowel *u*, as in *argue* ['ɑrgjʊ], *few* [fju], *spurious* ['spjʊriəs], *beauty* ['bjutɪ], *mule* [mjul], *tulip* ['tjuləp], *value* ['væljʊ], *view* [vju], *cure* [kjʊr]. Words spelled with initial *u* really begin with [j] when the vowel is long: *use* [jus], *union* ['junjən], *usual* ['juʒʊəl], *usurer* ['juʒərə·]. This occasional value of the letter *u* as a consonant-vowel combination has led to the recognition of [ju] as a consonant-vowel diphthong by some authorities. It occurs most frequently as an initial sound or after [m], [b], [f], [sp], [k], and occasionally after [d], [t], [θ], [n], [s]. Examples are *music* ['mjuzɪk], *rebuke* [rɪ'bjuk], *fury* ['fjurɪ], *spew* [spju], *cube* [kjub], *duty* ['djutɪ], *tune* [tjun], *enthusiasm* ['inθjuzɪˌæzəm], *news* [njuz].

11.10 [j] and [tʃ] Substitution Sounds The high-front semivowel [j] and the consonantal combination [tʃ] are regularly substituted

for the back consonants [g] and [k] where these become high and
fronted sounds (see Chapter 12). This substitution has given us many
Modern English words spelled with *y* where Old English had *g* [j],
for example, *geard* (Mod.E. *yard*), *gist* (Mod.E. *yeast*), *gearn* (Mod.E.
yarn), *gēar* (Mod.E. *year*), *geolu* (Mod.E. *yellow*), *gieldan* (Mod.E.
yield), and words with *ch* [tʃ] where Old English had *c* [k], as in
cinn (Mod.E. *chin*), *cirice* (Mod.E. *church*), *cild* (Mod.E. *child*), *ceaf*
(Mod.E. *chaff*), *cealc* (Mod.E. *chalk*), *cēse* (Mod.E. *cheese*). It should
be noted that Old English *g* before front vowels was pronounced [j].

11.11 Use of [j] Decreasing   The height of [j] is probably the
reason for its decreasing use in English. Often it is simply omitted,
as in *news, duke, tube, student, Tuesday, due*, these words being
pronounced with the sound [u] as in words like *rule, rude, fruit,
rubric, ruble, ruby*. After the labials, however, [ju] is usually pronounced, as in *mule, few, view*. Substitutions are made for it in combination with another sound as [tʃ] in *Tuesday* and *tune*. Hence the
prescriptive teacher of speech, even while advising its retention in
words where its use is standard, often fails to recognize [ju] as a unit
of English speech. [tʃ] and [dʒ] are universally recognized as units.

For the Student

A. FURTHER READINGS

Krapp, *The Pronunciation of Standard English in America*, §§ 229–234;
    259–262; 327–335.

Kenyon, *American Pronunciation*, 10th edit., §§ 193–198; 207–211; 229–
    233; 341–351.

Webster's *New International Dictionary*, 2nd edit., "A Guide to Pronuncia-
    tion," §§ 43(6–9); 45; 58; 100; 104–107; 159–161; 227–228; 237;
    264; and *passim;* 3rd edit., pp. 34a–46a, *passim*.

Kantner and West, *Phonetics*, rev. edit., pp. 151–154; 187–189; 191–193.

Jones, *An Outline of English Phonetics*, 8th edit., §§ 591–616; 726–743;
    813–819.

Aiken, *English Present and Past*, pp. 153–154; see also Table XI, p. 204,
    for list of spellings for [ʃ] and [ʒ].

Robertson and Cassidy, *The Development of Modern English,* 2nd edit., pp. 65–66.

Avery, Dorsey, and Sickels, *First Principles of Speech Training,* pp. 102–103.

B. FOR CLASS DISCUSSION

1. Describe the action of the speech organs in producing the consonants [ʃ] and [ʒ].
2. Continue your tabular analysis of consonants according to the categories in Chapters 7 and 8.
3. Why should the tongue blade and center be poor in consonantal sounds but rich in vowels?
4. Why should [ʃ] and [ʒ] have so many spelling representations?
5. Which of the sounds mentioned in this chapter does not occur initially in Modern English? Can you give a reason?
6. Look up the words *nauseous* and *vitiate* and trace the various stages in their development which resulted in the Modern English pronunciation.
7. Pronounce quickly the words *nurse you* and explain what happens.
8. The words *special* and *vision* were once pronounced as three syllables: [ˌspɛsɪ'ɑl] and [ˌvɪzɪ'uːn]. Trace the numerous stages in their development which resulted in the Modern English pronunciation.
9. Account for the use of [ʃ] in the words *sure, chivalry, ocean, ancient, conscious, transient, noxious, sensual, confession, tissue, nation,* and *fortune,* with reference to the derivation of these words.
10. Account for the use of [ʒ] in the words *occasion, usual, grandeur, camouflage,* and *cordial,* with reference to the derivation of these words.
11. What are the chief sound substitutions in lisping?
12. On the radio or elsewhere, have you heard more than one pronunciation for such words as *nature, education, interesting, literature, appreciate?* If so, analyze them phonetically. Which pronunciation do you prefer and why?

C. SUGGESTIONS FOR RESEARCH PAPERS

1. Is There a Consonant-Vowel Diphthong?
2. Can [tʃ] and [dʒ] Be Called Diphthongs?
3. Spelling and Sound of [ʃ].
4. Spelling and Sound of [ʒ].

12

The Back Consonants

12.1 Fewer Now Than in Old English The back consonants of English now number five, of which one (voiceless *w*) is largely disused in the speech of southern England. But if we count sounds current in former periods we may add two more, making this group the most numerous save for the point consonants. In spelling, the back sounds are *w, wh, k, g,* and *ng.* The two which have been entirely lost are the Old English velar sounds, which were spelled *h* [χ] and *g* [ɣ], as in *niht* [nɪχt], Mod.E. *night* and *lagu* [lɑɣʊ], Mod.E. *law.*

12.2 W Almost like U The first of the back consonants, [w], is a high, rounded semivowel. Because of the lip rounding involved in its formation, it is sometimes called a lip sound. Actually the sound is derived from the entire shape of the mouth cavity, which is determined not only by the lips but by the tongue raising. Calling *w* a lip sound disregards both the tongue height and the likeness of *w* to *u,* with which it has many affinities. It seems to be distinguished from *u* only by being a little farther back. It is a *voiced velar semivowel.*

12.3 U and W The position for the consonant [w] and the vowel [u] are practically identical, as may be seen by practicing with the word *woo* and the nonsense syllable *oow*. In both may be observed the slight lifting of the tongue for the consonant, although there is more friction in the latter. In the former the tongue is somewhat higher and the lips closer than in the latter. When [w] is being taught to students lacking the sound in their native speech, [u] is substituted for it, and as the student learns to say, for example, *u-ater* [uɑtɚ], he naturally comes to pronounce *water* as in Standard English.

12.4 V and W The foreign substitution of [v] for [w], as in *ven, vy,* for *when* and *why,* links [w] again with lip sounds but is really a substitution rather than an approximation, as [v] and [w] have no such intrinsic similarity in their formation as have [w] and [u]. The foreign substitution is also probably due in part to spelling confusion.

12.5 W in Spelling A [w] is sometimes pronounced without appearing in spelling, as in *one, persuade,* etc. There is an intrusive [w] which may appear between a word ending with a rounded vowel sound and another word beginning with a vowel, for instance, *to-w-eat, toe-w-and-heel.* And, on the other hand, orthographic (i.e., unpronounced) *w* appears in *sword, sow, who, two,* etc. An examination of these words along with *wind, wrong, always, now, grow, knew, law, bow, cow, yawl* will reveal that *w* is pronounced only initially and medially before vowels—that is, it must be in a prevocalic position.

12.6 The Combination *qu* It is a testimonial to the unscientific character of the spelling of English that the combination *qu* is entirely superfluous when our alphabet has *k* and *w* to represent its component sounds. For instance, *quell* can as well be spelled *kwell* and *quartz, kwartz,* without any loss of clarity. In Old English *cw* was used instead of *qu* (*cwic,* Mod.E. *quick; cwealm,* Mod.E. *qualm; cwēn,* Mod.E. *queen*). These spellings with *qu* developed when the letter *q* was brought into English from French in the Middle English period.

12.7 The Sound [ʍ] The sound usually spelled *wh* in Modern English (in Old English *hw*), which differentiates such pairs as *wail* and *whale, witch* and *which,* has the phonetic symbol [ʍ]. It is sometimes defined as a voiceless *w* since it is voiceless at the outset when the tongue and lips are in the high back round position. Voice is soon introduced, however, for this sound is really a combination of [h] (see par. 9.4) with the labiovelar opening of the [w]. It is essentially [w] with an initial increase in stress. Like all voiceless sounds (see par. 9.7), even though voice is later introduced, it requires more energy to pronounce than does [w] itself. For this reason speakers tend to substitute [w] for [ʍ]. That is, *wheat* is pronounced [wit] instead of [ʍit] and *while* is pronounced [waɪl] instead of [ʍaɪl]. This pronunciation is the standard practice in southern England and is heard occasionally in the United States.

12.8 "Low" Sounds Not Always Low According to the chart, Diagram B (p. 131), there is a wide gap between the high back consonant [w] and the low back group which includes [k] and [g]. But this is ostensible rather than real, since [k] and [g] may be high as well as low sounds. Compare the [k] of *keep, keen, keel* with that of *cold, call, caught.* In the same manner, compare the g of *geese* and *gear, give, get, gain* with that of *goat, gobbler, gaunt, got, gun, goose.* [k] may be a *palatal* or *velar voiceless stop* and [g] a *palatal* or *velar voiced stop.* What happens in the formation of these stop consonants is that the tongue naturally accommodates itself to its surrounding sounds. When these pull the [k] or [g] high or forward, it may become almost a [j]. The tongue strikes the hard palate at any point in the rear portion of the mouth, cutting off the breath for a moment; and according to the place of this stoppage one may recognize a high, a mid, or a low [k] or [g]. The variations, however, are not phonemic. Pronounced by themselves, [k] and [g] are low sounds, *velar stops.*

12.9 Results of Instability The instability of the sounds [k] and [g] has been the source of much linguistic change, not only in English but in both related and unrelated languages. Indeed, one grouping of the Indo-European languages divides them into *centum* and *satem* tongues according to the words for *hundred* in Latin and Avestan, respectively. In Latin, which retained the more primitive pronunciation of the word, the *c* is pronounced as a [k]; in Avestan the [k] has raised and fronted until it has turned into [s]. To the *centum* group belong the Hellenic, Italic, Teutonic, and Celtic branches, including Tocharian, whereas the *satem* group comprises Indian, Iranian, Armenian, Balto-Slavic, and Albanian. One can see that a line running roughly from Scandinavia to Greece separates the two, suggesting the dissemination eastward and westward.[1]

12.10 *Centum-Satem* in English In the history of English the high fronted [k] has turned, not into [s], but into *ch* [tʃ]. This may be seen in our words *chin, chaffinch, cheek, cheap,* and *birch,* which in Old English were *cinn, ceaffinc, cēace, cēap,* and *birce.* Not all the occurrences of *ch* in Modern English, but a good proportion of them, derive from a raised and fronted [k].

12.11 Similar Development from G Just as a raised and fronted [k] has turned into [tʃ], so a raised and fronted [g] has given [j]. The change occurred when the sounds adjacent to O.E. [g] were front in character. Our word *year* from O.E. *gēar* is an example. In the same manner our verb *yell* comes from O.E. *giellan* and *yearn* from O.E. *geornian.*

12.12 The Third Pair of Stops The consonants [k] and [g] form the third voiceless-voiced pair of stops in English, the other two being [p]-[b] (lip) and [t]-[d] (point). These three pairs have undergone many changes in past centuries, and some of these changes are grouped in the collections of changes known as Grimm's and Verner's Laws, which show how English and its sister languages differ from the language families of Latin, Greek, etc.[2]

12.13 The Low Back Nasal Just as the two other pairs of stop consonants have a corresponding nasal sound, so the nasal [ŋ] corresponds to [k] and [g]. It is made with the air shut off at the back of the mouth and forced through the nose, and its usual spelling is *ng,* as in *long, wring, rang.* It is the only back sound which is used in an inflection—the present participle ending *-ing,* as in *talking, writing, speaking.*

12.14 The Back Nasal in Spelling Although the *voiced velar nasal* [ŋ] is not a frequent English sound, it is probably more frequent than its spelling would indicate, since it is regularly substituted for [n] before [k] and sometimes before [g], as in *sink* [sɪŋk], *drunk* [drʌŋk], *lank* [læŋk], *sank* [sæŋk], *single* ['sɪŋgl̩], *bangle* ['bæŋgl̩], *wrangle* ['ræŋgl̩], etc. On the other hand, the final *ng* of

[1] Professor E. H. Sturtevant has criticized the *centum-satem* hypothesis. See "On the Position of Hittite Among the Indo-European Languages," *Language* (Vol. II, 1926), pp. 25–34.

[2] See Chapter 2.

the participle is frequently turned into [n], giving *singin'* for *singing,* *readin'* for *reading, speakin'* for *speaking.* Both these substitutions illustrate the accord or assimilation of sounds, since [ŋ] fits with [k] better than does [n], and [n] is a more usual and an easier end sound than [ŋ] in unstressed syllables. In words like *syncopate, finger,* we find still other sound patterns.

12.15 Not Found Initially   The back nasal [ŋ] is not used as an initial sound in English. This is a matter of linguistic habit. This sound was a positional variant of *n* in Old English, occurring only before [k] and [g], as, for example, in *finger,* pronounced *fing-ger.* The combination of letters *ng* was pronounced [ŋg]. In Modern English this sound continues to be attracted by [k] and [g], as in *ink* and *dangle.* The sound is formed by pushing the back of the tongue up against the soft palate, as in *long* and *wrong.* In each case there is a closure of the oral cavity.

12.16 Consonants Completed   We have now finished our sketch of the twenty-three consonant sounds of English. Their study is obscured by an unphonetic alphabet and spelling. It is possible, however, to trace their formation and relations with accuracy if we hold to phonetic principles.

For the Student

A. FURTHER READINGS

Krapp, *The Pronunciation of Standard English in America,* §§ 21–22; 26–27; 247–253; 263–272; 289–297; 365–373.

Kenyon, *American Pronunciation,* 10th edit., §§ 167–174; 217–219; 223–227.

Webster's *New International Dictionary,* 2nd edit., "A Guide to Pronunciation," §§ 43(10); 44(8); 101; 107; 138; 164; 177; 210; 255–258; and *passim;* 3rd edit., pp. 37a–46a, *passim.*

Jones, *An Outline of English Phonetics,* 8th edit., §§ 532–551; 650–658; 802–812.

Avery, Dorsey, and Sickels, *First Principles of Speech Training,* pp. 93–94; 96–97.

Kantner and West, *Phonetics,* rev. edit., pp. 164–168; 184–185; 205–206.

Aiken, *Why English Sounds Change,* pp. 76–78.

Robertson and Cassidy, *The Development of Modern English*, 2nd edit.,
pp. 63–64; 67; 69–70.
Aiken, *English Present and Past*, pp. 155–156.

B. FOR CLASS DISCUSSION

1. Describe the action of the speech organs in producing the consonants mentioned in this chapter: [w], [k], [g], [ŋ].
2. Complete your table of the twenty-three English consonants classified under the categories mentioned. Add any descriptive words you like, such as *sibilant* or *fricative*.
3. Look up *w* in several manuals to determine whether it is classed as a lip or a back sound. Where do you think it belongs?
4. Have you a voiceless *w* in your speech? Would it be good or bad for English to lose this sound completely? List as many pairs of words as you can which would become indistinguishable in pronunciation without it. Does the sounding alike of such pairs often lead to a *real* speech confusion?
5. Does the [w] sound occur in any possible position (initial, medial, final) in a word? Illustrate.
6. In an unstressed position, as in *That's why I went,* what tends to happen to the sound [ʍ]?
7. Practice with [k] and [g] followed by [i] (front), [ɑ] (low back), and [u] (high back). How many varieties of these consonants can you find?
8. What is the difference in the sound of [k] in such pairs of words as *keel* and *call, key* and *coo;* of [g] in *geese* and *gall?* Select other pairs of words showing the same differences.
9. It is not uncommon for many speakers to insert the sound [k] into the pronunciation of the word *length.* Explain phonetically the intrusion of [k].
10. Analyze the phonetic elements in the group of words *sin, sing, sink,* and explain each. Can you think of similar groups of words?
11. Analyze the examples *syncopate, finger,* in par. 14. How can you explain them?
12. Can the [ŋ] sound occur in any possible position (initial, medial, final) in a word? Illustrate.
13. What sound does the letter *n* represent in such words as *function, donkey, instinct?* Explain the process phonetically. What is the process called?
14. A speaker is often accused of "dropping his *g*'s" when he says *cryin'* instead of *crying.* Is this a correct statement of what takes place? If not, describe what happens.

C. SUGGESTIONS FOR RESEARCH PAPERS

1. Spelling the Back Nasal.
2. The English Consonants.
3. The Pronunciation of the Word *Pumpkin*.
4. Look up *centum* and *satem* in a dictionary or encyclopedia and write an account of them.

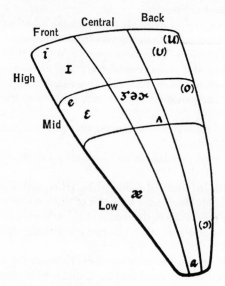

DIAGRAM D   VOWELS

NOTE: Parentheses show the rounded vowels.

13

The Blade and
Front Vowels

13.1 Many Comparisons Many writers have commented on what they call the "vowel triangle" of English. This triangle may be roughly traced on Diagram B by drawing lines to connect [i], [u], and [ɑ]. It is divided into three sections, front, back, and central, as shown in detail in Diagram D. A more fanciful, but in some ways a more revealing, analysis would liken the whole range of vowels to the wheels of a bicycle, the front wheel revolving in a direction opposite to that of the back.

13.2 Paucity of Symbols The fourteen vowels of English have only five letters for their representation. Look at the list of the following words, in each of which the letter *a* has a different sound value: *awe, art, about, may, many, that.* How mystified a foreign student of English must be when he meets such inconsistency! The older phoneticians devised elaborate series of markings, which they called diacritical marks, to show which sound a given vowel letter represented. The diacritical marks failed to solve the problem, because they did not express in a clear and simple manner the actual sounds of English vowels. Thus the sound of the unaccented vowel

in *account* in a recent standard work has a different marking from
the unaccented vowel in *sofa*, although the two have the same value.
The pronunciation of the *a* in *account* is marked ă, and that at the
end of *sofa* is à, whereas both have the unaccented vowel ə. Finally
the alphabet of the International Phonetic Association improved on
the diacritical markings, and while, as will be seen, this alphabet is
not perfect, still it is a great advance over former methods of denoting sounds.

13.3 The Tense Blade Vowel   The tense vowel [i], the first
vowel sound in *meet* [mit] and *deify* [dɪɪfɑɪ] and the last vowel in
trustee [trʌs'ti], is formed so far toward the front of the mouth that
it should be called a blade rather than a front sound. This statement
may be verified experimentally by pronouncing the word *she* [ʃi]
and noting that the same portion of the tongue is active in both of
the sounds of the word. This tense vowel is probably the most frequent of the tense vowel sounds of English and is used for innumerable homonyms, such as *beer* and *bier, meat* and *meet, feet* and *feat,
deer* and *dear*.

13.4 Present in Old English   The tense vowel [i] was present in
Old English but not in the same words where we find it today. Old
English words such as *īs, wīs,* and *mīn,* where this sound occurred,
were altered with respect to their vowel quality. The front [i:] in
Old English, already in the highest position, split and introduced the
low sound [ɑ] before the blade vowel, giving [ɑɪ] instead of [i] and
making the words *ice* [ɑɪs], *wise* [wɑɪz], *mine* [mɑɪn]. Our present
sound [i] as a long sound derives mainly from words which in Old
English had [e:] or [æ:]. For instance, O.E. *hē* [he:] has become
Mod.E. *he* [hi]; O.E. *sǣd* [sæ:d] has become Mod.E. *seed* [sid];
O.E. *wē* [we:] has become Mod.E. *we* [wi]; O.E. *wǣd* [wæ:d] has
become Mod.E. *weed* [wid].

Occasionally the vowel has developed regularly and then has
been shortened as in Mod.E. *deaf*, which came from O.E. *dēaf*. If
this word followed the regular pattern, it would be pronounced
[dif] to rhyme with *sheaf* and *reef*. It once was, as the persistence
of [dif] among old-fashioned people and among the uneducated
shows. Formerly [dif] was in good use among the educated and the
uneducated.

Pronunciations of earlier times can be determined with a reasonable degree of accuracy not only by noting the pronunciations of the old-fashioned and the uneducated, who are more conservative and less likely to accept innovations, but by observing the rhymes of poets,[1] the use of sounds in puns and word play,[2] and the spellings in old records, and by comparing English sounds with those of related languages where pronunciation has been relatively stable.

For example, from the poetry of the eighteenth century one can be reasonably certain that some of the sounds which we pronounce as [i] today were still [e] then. This can be observed in Pope's couplet[3]

> Here thou, great Anna! whom three realms obey,
> Dost sometimes counsel take—and sometimes tea.

where *tea* must have been pronounced [te] to rhyme with *obey*. This conclusion is substantiated by comparing this pronunciation with that of French and German as well as with dialectal forms of English—Irish and Scotch, for example—which have the vowel [e], not [i].

13.5 The Slack Blade Vowel The slack counterpart of [i] is [ɪ]. This sound has persisted unchanged since Old English times; O.E. *sittan*, Mod.E. *sit;* O.E. *him;* O.E. *disc*, Mod.E. *dish*. It is extremely frequent and is often substituted for some other vowel in an unstressed syllable, as in *cottage* ['kɑtɪdʒ], *women* ['wɪmɪn], *lettuce* ['lɛtɪs], *horses* ['hɔrsɪz]. It is also properly used to represent the *y* of such words as *woody* and *lovely*, because the sound here is short and does not have the tense value [i].

13.6 Mid-High Front Tense Next in the front vowel series is a tense vowel, the vowel sound of *eight* [et]. Many phoneticians call this, along with all the other so-called "long vowels," a diphthong rather than a pure vowel, transcribing [eɪt] instead of [et]. It is true that these words may be pronounced with a diphthong, but in General American the pure vowel is probably more frequent and is to be considered standard.

---

[1] See H. C. Wyld, *Studies in English Rhymes from Surrey to Pope* (New York, E. P. Dutton), 1924.

[2] See Helge Kökeritz, "Five Shakespeare Notes," *Review of English Studies* (Vol. XXIII, October, 1947), pp. 312–313.

[3] *Rape of the Lock*, Canto III, ll. 7–8.

13.7 History of [e]   Old English had the sound [e], but again it was not in the same words where it is found in Modern English. The words with O.E. [e], such as *grēne, swēte, cēne, grētan, dēman, fēdan,* and *dēop,* have mostly come to have [i] today—*green, sweet, keen, greet, deem, feed,* and *deep.* Our present words which have [i] have come from a variety of sources, foreign as well as native. For example, from Old French come *cedar, cease, feat, feast, lease, leash, legion, people, preach, reason;* from Latin, *genius, genial, median, mediate, medieval, paean;* from Old Norse, *meek;* from Dutch, *keel;* from Spanish, *Negro, peak, peon.*

13.8 History of [ε]   Just as the tense [i] has its slack, and slightly lower, counterpart in [ɪ], so the tense [e] has its slack [ε], as in *men* and *get.* As is true of [ɪ], this value has remained unchanged from Old English, which had *menn, bed, fen, betera, ende, meltan, sendan,* and *gettan* as ancestors of our forms *men, bed, fen, better, end, melt, send,* and *get.* In [ε] the tongue is lower than in [e], in a position somewhat lower than mid but higher than in the next tense vowel, [æ].

13.9 Low Front Tense Vowel   This next sound is that of the *a* in *cat.* It may be long or short. In Old English both values existed, the long perhaps more nearly equivalent to [ε] than to [æ], though the spelling was *ǣ.* Words spelled with O.E. *ǣ—mǣnan, hǣlan, mǣl, hǣðen, grǣdig,* etc.—regularly have [i] in Modern English— *mean, heal, meal, heathen, greedy.*

13.10 A Disagreeable Sound?   In the formation of [æ] the lips are flatter than for any other English sound, and this fact may contribute to its effect of disagreeability. But the short value at least is in such exceedingly common use that people do not notice any unpleasant effect. One can even compose a sentence with no other vowel sound in the principal words: *Cats and rats ran and laughed.*[4] [kæts ən ræts ræn ən læft] (the unstressed form). Such a sentence does not call attention to itself by reason of its unpleasant vowel sounds. One must prolong and emphasize [æ] considerably to get any unpleasant effect, though it is true that the pure sound by itself,

---

[4] All the authority of the American school system, exercised half a century ago, failed to make *laugh* [læf] into *laugh* [laf]. Evidently the average speaker does not see [æ] as fatally disagreeable.

like the pure sound [s], is occasionally used to convey a sense of dislike or disgust.

13.11 Short [æ] Unchanged While opinions on the subject differ, it is at least possible that the short [æ] of Old English, as in *æt, æfter, æcs* ("axe"), *æppel* ("apple"), *æsc* ("ash"), *bæþ* ("bath"), has remained without change to the present time.[5] Occasionally, as in O.E. *ræst,* this vowel has raised to [ɛ], *rest.* Also many Modern English occurrences of [æ] are in words spelled with *a* in Old English: *can, hand, land, and, sand; a* is the usual letter to represent [æ] now, the ligature *æ* having disappeared from the alphabet at the end of the Old English period.

13.12 Placing of Front Vowels The student will notice that little has been said about the exact tongue position of the five vowels described in this chapter. The reason is that such descriptions have little value. There is no uniformity in the tongue positions held for a given vowel by different speakers or even in different words by the same speaker. Moreover, it is by no means certain that tongue position is determinative in the formation of all vowel sounds; various experimental studies, such as those of G. Oscar Russell[6] and Sir Richard Paget,[6] have cast doubt on the importance of the tongue factor. The quality of vowel sounds, however, depends upon the modification of the resonance chamber, which change seems to be made by the movement of the jaw, the placing of the tongue, and the configuration of the lips. For example, in uttering in succession the sounds [æ], [e], [i], one will notice that the jaw, and with it the tongue, has a lower position for [æ] than for [e], and that it is raised again for the pronunciation of [i]. These positions we may call "low," "mid," "high" in describing the vowel.

[5] Wyld and other authorities believe O. E. [æ] to have retracted to [a] and then fronted again in Modern English. Jespersen, however, doubts this theory. See *A Modern English Grammar,* 3rd edit. (Heidelberg, Carl Winter, 1922), Part I, § 8.63.

[6] See reading suggestions at end of chapter and Ralph K. Potter, George A. Kopp and Harriet C. Green, *Visible Speech* (New York, D. Van Nostrand, 1947) (an experiment conducted at the Bell Telephone Laboratories); Lee Edward Travis, *Handbook of Speech Pathology* (New York, Appleton-Century-Crofts, 1957); Charles Van Riper and John V. Irwin, *Voice and Articulation* (Englewood Cliffs, New Jersey, Prentice-Hall, 1958) with an excellent bibliography, pp. 497–536.

13.13 Disagreement General   Moreover, there is a cleavage between speech experts and students of historical English, regarding their view of vowel phonology. The speech authorities tend to recognize more diphthongs and fewer pure vowels. They attempt to record and to codify minute differences which often are individual variations, or accommodations to neighboring sounds. It is the linguist's contention that such minutiae tend to represent our knowledge as more certain than it actually is, and that they tend to obscure rather than to clarify the historical facts of the development of English. In this book the solution has been in line with the linguist's attitude. Only thirty-seven Modern English sounds are recognized, twenty-three consonants and fourteen vowels, with eight diphthongs. This makes for what is called a very broad count, suitable for students on the college level.

For the Student

A. FURTHER READINGS

For general attitudes and theories see:

Krapp, *The Pronunciation of Standard English in America,* "Preface," pp. iii–vii.

Kenyon, *American Pronunciation,* 10th edit., §§ 64–77; 244–285.

Aiken, *English Present and Past,* pp. 137–140.

Robertson and Cassidy, *The Development of Modern English,* 2nd edit., pp. 87–93; 99–108, *passim.*

Avery, Dorsey, and Sickels, *First Principles of Speech Training,* pp. 73–80; 105–106; 110–112.

Kantner and West, *Phonetics,* rev. edit., pp. 78–83.

Paget, *Human Speech, passim,* especially Chapters 1–5 (a technical discussion of experiments).

Russell, *The Vowel, Some X-Ray and Photolaryngoperiskopik Evidence, passim,* especially Chapters 1, 4, 10, 12–14 (also technical, with many illustrations of the vocal organs).

For specific discussions of vowels see:

Krapp, *The Pronunciation of Standard English in America,* §§ 50–56; 58; 124–145; 161–175.

Kenyon, *American Pronunciation,* 10th edit., §§ 73–76; 244–270.

Webster's *New International Dictionary*, 2nd edit., "A Guide to Pronuncia-
  tion," §§ 28–35; 76 ff.; 115 ff.; 152 ff.; 3rd edit., pp. 32a–42a, *passim.*
Avery, Dorsey, and Sickels, *First Principles of Speech Training*, pp. 113 ff.
Jones, *The Pronunciation of English*, 4th edit., §§ 70–90.
Jones, *An Outline of English Phonetics*, 8th edit., §§ 246–283.
Robertson and Cassidy, *The Development of Modern English*, 2nd edit.,
  pp. 70–74 (discussion of other vowels included).

B. FOR CLASS DISCUSSION

1. Compare the attitudes toward phonetics shown in the readings mentioned in the first section of Part A. Krapp, Kenyon, Aiken, and Robertson and Cassidy express the linguists' attitude; Avery, Dorsey, and
   Sickels and Kantner and West, the speech experts'; and Paget, Russell,
   and Bell Telephone Laboratories, the experimentalists' theories and
   findings.
2. Try to apply the categories mentioned in Chapters 7 and 8 to the vowels,
   making a table similar to the one you have for the consonants. Is this
   table more or less specific? Which categories apply here?
3. Experiment with the five vowel sounds discussed in this chapter to determine as exactly as possible how you form them and what gives them
   their character. Describe the position of the speech organs in making the
   front vowels.
4. Can you frame other sentences confined to one vowel sound, like the one
   in par. 10, but using another vowel?
5. Practice the vowel sounds in sequence, beginning with the lowest unrounded vowel and proceeding to the highest. Select a word to illustrate
   each sound.
6. Do you pronounce *been, Ben, breeches, peaches, creek, clique, sleek*
   with the same vowel? Have you heard different pronunciations for any
   of these words? Are specific sections or different strata of society suggested by the variant pronunciations?
7. What do the following rhymes of Pope show concerning the history of
   vowel sounds?

> Dreading e'en fools; by flatterers besieg'd,
> And so obliging that he ne'er oblig'd.
> —*Epistle to Dr. Arbuthnot*, ll. 207–208.

> Hear thou, great Anna! whom three realms obey,
> Dost sometimes counsel take—and sometimes tea.
> —*The Rape of the Lock*, Canto III, ll. 7–8.

Have you ever heard similar pronunciations in any present-day dialect?
8. From William Cowper's lines:

> God moves in a mysterious way . . .
> He plants his footsteps in the sea . . .
>   *—Light Shining out of Darkness*, Stanza **I.**

and

> I am monarch of all I survey . . .
> From the center all round to the sea . . .
>   *—Verses Supposed to Be Written*
>   *by Alexander Selkirk*, Stanza I.

what do you conclude as to the time when the word *sea* received its present value?
9. Study the diacritical marks used by various dictionaries to represent the front vowel sounds and comment on their adequacy and consistency.

C. SUGGESTIONS FOR RESEARCH PAPERS

1. What Determines the Character of a Vowel Sound?
2. Broad or Narrow Count?
3. Front Vowels in Different Sections of the United States.
4. The Front Vowels in Milton's Rhymes.
5. The Pronunciation of the Front Vowels in the Eighteenth Century (choose an eighteenth-century poet for special study).
6. The Pronunciation of the Front Vowels in the Nineteenth Century (choose a nineteenth-century poet for special study).

14

The Back and Central Vowels

14.1 High to Low   As with the front vowels, the study of the back vowels of English will begin with the highest and proceed from there to the lowest. The tongue is consistently lower in this series than in the front series, since the back of the tongue is not so mobile as the front, and the throat opening enables the lowest back sound to be lower than the lowest front sound. But all these differences are minor.

14.2 Counterpart of W   Slightly lower than the voiced semivowel [w], but in other respects a nearly exact copy of it, is the crooning vowel [u]. Normally this is a long vowel (*you, moon, tune, June*) and always it is tense. It differs from [w] in that there is no release or puff of breath after the pure continuant sound. The lips are rounded and the breath is shaped by a long, slender, even aperture extending from lips to glottis.

14.3 History of [u]   This long tense sound was present in Old English, but the words containing it (*ūre, hūs, ūt*) are usually found in Modern English with the diphthong [ɑʊ] (*our, house, out*). Words which now have [u], if they are not from foreign sources, usually had [oː] in Old English. Thus *mōna* gives Mod.E. *moon; cōl, cool; bōt, boot; hrōf, roof;* and *dōm, doom.* This sound is also found in the Modern English diphthong [ɪu] as in *fuse* [fɪuz] and *fugue* [fɪug].

14.4 The Slack *U*   The slack vowel corresponding to [u] and usually taken as its short value in Old English is lower than the sound we have just been describing. What the difference is, otherwise, is difficult to say. It is usually said that the tongue is held slack instead of tense in forming the sound, but this statement calls for further verification and experiment.

14.5 Occurrence of Slack *U*   It is probable that words such as *ful (full), wulf (wolf), bulluc (bullock)* had [ʊ] in the Old English period and still have it. But many words now containing this sound, but spelled with *oo,* had in Old English the spelling *ō* [oː] and should regularly have [u] today, as is true in the north of England. Examples are O.E. *gōd (good); bōc (book).* For most speakers of English these have been shortened to [gʊd] and [bʊk]. Several words vary in sound between [ʊ] and [u], for example, *room, roof, hoof,* which may be heard as [rum] or [rʊm], [ruf] or [rʊf], [huf] or [hʊf], depending upon the locality from which the speaker comes. For instance, the pronunciation [hʊf] prevails in the northern, eastern, and southern parts of the United States. One or two words spelled with *oo* may be heard with the still more slack vowel [ʌ]; *soot* is pronounced in three ways, [sut], [sʊt], and [sʌt], the last primarily in the South.

14.6 The Central Vowels   The symbol [ʌ] is used to denote the vowel sound in *nut, bud, but.* It is not listed as existing in Old English, and today it is used exclusively to mark this sound in accented syllables. The sound, however, of final [ə] at the end of such words as *sofa* and *china* is lowered almost to the position for [ʌ]. Its formation is exceedingly obscure. One writer calls it a "half-low, middle, lax sound," and describes the tongue as raised only slightly. It is a common vowel sound and includes a few well-known homonyms such as *son* and *sun.* In Modern English [ə], [ɚ], [ʌ], and [ɝ] are called central vowels.

14.7 The Neutral Vowel   One might suppose that tongue slackness could go no farther than with [ʌ], and indeed it is hard to perceive much distinction in sound between this vowel, [ʌ], and the next, [ə]. But such a distinction is made by practically every phonetician and expressed by saying that in [ʌ] the tongue is slightly lower and farther back than in [ə]. If this distinction appears unreal to you, as it may to some, you can still keep the two symbols apart by remembering that [ə] occurs exclusively in unaccented syllables.

14.8 The Most Frequent Vowel The neutral vowel [ə], often called *schwa* or the *schwa* vowel, is the most frequent English vowel sound, since it may substitute for any other vowel in unaccented position. A few phoneticians describe [ɪ], which has the same tendency, as equally frequent. Often [ə] and [ɪ] may alternate in unaccented position, as, for example, in *tortoise* ['tɔrtəs] or ['tɔrtɪs]; *chocolate* ['tʃɔklət] or ['tʃɔklɪt]; *orange* ['ɔrəndʒ] or ['ɔrɪndʒ]; and many others. It is perhaps worth noting that while the slack *u*, [ʌ], and the neutral vowel, [ə], have different symbols, as in *but* [bʌt] and *about* [əbɑʊt], slack *i*, [ɪ], and neutral [ɪ] have the same symbol, as in *sit* [sɪt] and *basket* [bæskɪt]. If these two are the same or near enough to be denoted by the same symbol, it seems wasteful to have varying symbols for [ʌ] and [ə]. The vowel [ə] is so tenuous that it may often seem to disappear altogether, as in *evaporable* [ɪ'væpərəbl̩], *irreparable* [ɪ'rɛpərəbl̩], and ['læbərə͵tɔrɪ] and in other unaccented syllables in long words.

14.9 No Separate Neutral Vowel in Old English Linguists listing the sounds of Old English include neither [ʌ] nor [ə] as a separate symbol for a vowel. Only as the second element of some diphthongs is [ə] found, as *ea* [æə], *ēa* [ɛ:ə].[1] Today these two sounds, [ʌ] and [ə], are extremely frequent.

14.10 The *r*-Vowel Only one vowel of the mid-central group remains to be described, and this is a peculiar one. It appears that the consonant *r* in the combination vowel-plus-*r*-plus-consonant (*first, murk, earth*, etc.) came to have a decided effect upon the vowel preceding it, turning it into a sound which is represented by [ɜ] with the wing of the letter *r* attached: [ɝ] (see par. 10.13). The only vowel unaffected by this peculiarity of *r* is Mod.E. [ɑ] as in *harp, heart*. This vowel, [ɝ], is probably of fairly late development in English, since the various spellings of the words containing the *r*-vowel would indicate that other sounds had maintained themselves before *r* for some time. It is placed at about mid height and somewhat

---

[1] Marjorie Anderson and Blanche Colton Williams, *Old English Handbook* (New York, Houghton Mifflin Company, 1935), p. 11.

farther back than [i] and [e]. It is a tense vowel. The unaccented form is the neutral vowel affected by the "*r*-coloring" and is represented by the symbol [ɚ]. In representing the speech of one who pronounced his *r*'s, a word like *further* would show the *r*-coloring thus: ['fɝˑðɚ]; whereas one who dropped his *r*'s would say ['fɛðə].

Some words with the [ɝ] vowel interchange with the [ɑ] sound as *clerk, Berkeley,* and *Derby,* which in England are pronounced [klɑrk], ['bɑrklɪ], and ['dɑrbɪ]. In American speech one always hears [klɝk], and usually ['bɝˑklɪ] and [dɝˑbɪ]. The pronunciation of *clerk* has changed the spelling when the word is used as a proper name to *Clark* or *Clarke.* We have two spellings of *person: person* and *parson,* the latter having developed a specialized meaning. Other words have changed their spelling to agree with the pronunciation, among them *dark* from O.E. *deorc, bark* from O.E. *beorcan, hark* from M.E. *herken* from O.E. *hercnian. Sergeant,* on the other hand, has changed in pronunciation but has retained its earlier spelling. In all of these words the [ɑ] sound is a later development. The same holds true in *hearth.* The older pronunciation [hɝˑθ] can still be heard in the United States. It once was standard English as can be seen from the rhyme in the following lines of Milton's *Il Penseroso:*

> Far from all resort of mirth
> Save the cricket on the hearth.[2]

14.11 Mid-Back Tense The five vowels just described have taken us from the upper back corner of the vowel triangle (par. 13.1) to its center, rather than directly along its side (see also Diagram B). Returning to the direct line of tongue height between [u] and [ɑ], we find next a tense vowel [o]. This sound is rounded and usually long. Examples are found in *oath, bone, whole.*

14.12 History of [oː] As a long vowel, [oː] existed in Old English, and between that period and today it has been regularly raised to [u], as explained in par. 3. Our Modern English native words containing [o] derive from Old English words in [ɑː] (*bone* from *bān* and *oath* from *āþ*) as is explained in par. 17. The process of altering from [ɑː] to [oː] and from [oː] to [uː] (*boot* from *bōt* and *doom* from *dōm*) is called tense vowel raising and is illustrated in both

2 Ll. 81–82.

front and back vowels. This shift, which has taken place since the fourteenth century, is termed by Jespersen "the great vowel shift." [3]

14.13 History of *o*. Old English spelling included a short value as well as a long of *o*. This short *o* is supposed to have been pronounced [ɔ] and to have fluctuated in its history, sometimes remaining [ɔ], and sometimes lowering to [ɑ]. Examples are some British and American pronunciations of *cot, hog,* and *fox.* Often these are [ɑ]: [kat, hag, faks]. So-called "short *o*," then, is usually not [o] at all but the lower sound [ɔ].

14.14 Low-Mid Tense Next below [o] in the tense vowel series comes the vowel [ɔ], in its long value, as in *law* [ɔ]. This sound has never had alphabetic representation in English, but it is assumed to have existed in Old English, as stated in the preceding paragraph. The tongue in its formation is said to be arched and farther forward than for [o]. Unlike [ʌ] and [ə], but like [o] and [u], [ɔ] is rounded.

14.15 History of [ɔ] The long value of [ɔ] is fairly common in Modern English and has arisen from a variety of sources, such as the vocalization of certain consonants: O.E. *brōhte,* Mod.E. *brought* [brɔt]. The short value is supposedly the survivor of Old English "short *o*." Some phoneticians object to the sound, particularly when prolonged, as in the facetious spellings *dawg* [dɔg] and *hawg* [hɔg].

14.16 Pure Vowel If the mouth is opened and audible breath is emitted, with a deliberate effort to modify the voice so as to produce a low back sound, the resultant sound will be either [ɑ] if the vocal cords vibrate or [h] if they do not. Doctors sometimes tell patients to say [ɑ] so as to get the throat open. This sound can scarcely be said to depend upon the tongue, which may lie neutral or take any of various positions; it is pure voice. The lips are not rounded in its formation. It is hard to see how it can be called a tense vowel, and indeed it is occasionally described by phoneticians as slack. It has both a long and a short value in Modern English.

14.17 History of [a:] This long vowel existed as one of the common vowels of Old English, occurring in such words as *bāt, wā, bān.* Later the vowel was raised, first to [ɔ] and later to [o], so that today we have *boat, woe, bone.* Modern English words with [ɑ] have come from a variety of sources, mainly foreign. It is interesting to compare

[3] See *A Modern English Grammar,* Part I, § 8.11.

the development of O.E. [ɑ:] with that of the same sound in Scottish, where the vowel followed the front sequence, becoming first [ɛ:] and then [e:], Sc. *wae, bane.* Evidently in the north O.E. [ɑ:] must have been pronounced more like [æ:].

14.18 History of [*a*]   A common sound in Old English, so-called "short *a*," has today for the most part assimilated with Modern English words in [æ]. Whether this latter group first retracted to [ɑ] and then moved forward again, as some linguists assert, is problematical. The contrary view appears in Aiken, *Why English Sounds Change* (p. 93) and in Jespersen (see par. 13.11). Compare Wyld, *A Short History of English* (p. 103).

For the Student

A. FURTHER READINGS

Krapp, *The Pronunciation of Standard English in America,* §§ 57; 59–69; 110–123; 146–160; 176–206.

Kenyon, *American Pronunciation,* 10th edit., §§ 176; 286–326.

Webster's *New International Dictionary,* 2nd edit., "A Guide to Pronunciation," §§ 120; 158; 179 ff.; 239 ff.; 245 (The sections assigned in Chapter 13 should also be reviewed.); 3rd edit., pp. 34a–46a, *passim.*

Avery, Dorsey, and Sickels, *First Principles of Speech Training,* pp. 118–127.

Kantner and West, *Phonetics,* rev. edit., pp. 74–78; 83–89; 92–96.

Jones, *An Outline of English Phonetics,* 8th edit., §§ 284–376.

Jones, *The Pronunciation of English,* 4th edit., §§ 92–159.

Krapp, *Modern English, Its Growth and Present Use,* pp. 165–166.

B. FOR CLASS DISCUSSION

1. Try to apply the six categories of Chapters 7 and 8 to the back vowels. Which categories apply?
2. Experiment with the vowel sounds described in this chapter to determine as exactly as possible how you form them and what gives them their character. Describe the position of the speech organs in making the back vowels.

3. Practice the vowel sounds in sequence, beginning with the lowest rounded vowel and proceeding to the highest. Select a word to illustrate each sound.
4. Why does a doctor in examining a throat ask the patient to say [ɑ]?
5. Do you pronounce *groom, hoof, hoop, roof, room, root* with the same vowel? Have you heard different pronunciations for any of these vowels? Are specific sections or different strata of society suggested by the variant pronunciations?
6. Apply Question 5 to *bond, borrow, box, doll, hog, hot.* Add other words.
7. Apply Question 5 to *wallet, wampum, wash, watch, water.* Add other words.
8. Do you use the same vowel in the following pairs of words: *hoarse* and *horse; born* and *borne?* List other pairs which illustrate the same point.
9. How do you pronounce *brooch, Bolingbroke, Cowper, route, wound?* What is meant by the term *spelling pronunciation?*
10. Describe the different vowel sounds in the following words: *blood, good, book, soon, soot, moon, flood.* In Old English all these words had the same vowel sound. Can you account for the present differences?
11. Look up the etymology of *person* and *parson* in the *Oxford Dictionary.* Which is the earlier form? Do you know other pairs similar to this?
12. What does Milton's rhyme,

> "Far from all resort of mirth
> Save the cricket on the hearth . . ."
> —*Il Penseroso,* ll. 81–82.

show? Have you ever heard this pronunciation? Can you account for it?
13. Can you detect any differences in sound or in the position of the tongue in pronouncing the unstressed vowels in *scarlet, fountain, around, lettuce, besides, character, endless, knowledge, noses, porous, parallel, negligent?*
14. Have you ever heard speakers or radio announcers try to use the full value of vowels in unstressed syllables where the neutral vowel would be used in ordinary conversation, as in [gʌvɝ·nmɛnt], *government?* Do you consider this practice desirable?
15. How do you pronounce the word *constable?* Have you ever heard another pronunciation?
16. Bring in a list of words of various spellings for the sound [ʌ].
17. How do you pronounce *forgo, forego, forehead, forward, toward?* Are there variant pronunciations for any of these words?

18. How do you pronounce the following words: *after, basket, bath, chance, dance, half, path?* List other words of this kind. Are specific sections or different strata of society suggested by the variant pronunciations?

C. SUGGESTIONS FOR RESEARCH PAPERS

1. Are [ə] and [ʌ] the Same Sound?
2. [ɪ] and [ə] in Unstressed Syllables.
3. The Use of the Back Vowels in Two Regions or in Southern England and a Region of the United States.
4. A Study of the Dialect of a Particular Regional Author.

15

Diphthongs

15.1 Definition A diphthong is a combination of two vowel sounds within a single syllable, made with the tongue beginning in one position and gliding to another before the sound closes. The two sounds pronounced in juxtaposition are made with one breath impulse but with a change of the resonance chamber in the process. There are eight diphthongs in English, two consonantal, five vocalic, and one a consonant-vowel combination. Many phoneticians do not include the consonantal among diphthongs, and many recognize a far greater number of vocalic; but on a broad count, such as we are using here, eight seems the proper number.

15.2 The Consonantal Diphthongs The two consonantal diphthongs [tʃ] as in *chicken, chide,* and *chief,* and [dʒ] as in *judge, juggle,* and *julep,* are the voiceless-voiced equivalents of each other. They are described in Chapter 11, along with [ju], as in *usufruct, usurp,* and *utilitarian,* the combination of consonantal semivowel sound or glide-sound and vowel which constitutes the alphabet name of the letter *u.*

15.3 Rising, Falling, and Level The consonantal diphthongs [tʃ] and [dʒ] may be classified as level diphthongs, since neither component is emphasized more than the other. [ju] (see par. 11.9) is called a rising diphthong,[1] because the second element is more strongly emphasized or stressed. On the other hand, [aɪ], as in [raɪt], is called a falling diphthong, in that the heaviest stress is placed on the first element.

15.4 Low-High Tense   The first personal pronoun *I* echoes the name of the first vocalic diphthong, [aɪ], a tense unrounded pair of sounds, which is fairly frequent in accented position. This diphthong has existed in English for at least three centuries, but did not exist in Old English. It is used today mainly in the words which in Old English had the vowel [y:] or [i:]: O.E. *fȳr*, Mod.E. *fire;* O.E. *wīf*, Mod.E. *wife;* O.E. *mīl*, Mod.E. *mile;* O.E. *mȳs*, Mod.E. *mice;* O.E. *līf*, Mod.E. *life.*

15.5 One Step More   It is a significant fact linguistically that in the southern United States the diphthong [aɪ] sometimes becomes [a], so that *time* becomes *tahm* [tɑm], *my* becomes *mah* [mɑ], and *I* becomes *ah* [a]. Parallel to [aɪ] is the back tense diphthong [aʊ], which has appeared in Modern English as the successor of O.E. [u:]: O.E. *scūr*, Mod.E. *shower;* O.E. *nū*, Mod.E. *now;* O.E. *hū*, Mod.E. *how;* O.E. *ūt*, Mod.E. *out.* While in some sections there is a tendency to substitute [ɑ] for the diphthong, as, for example, in the pronunciation *shahr* [ʃɑr] for [ʃaʊr], this is not so well marked or so general as the tendency described in connection with [aɪ].

15.6 Third Vocalic Diphthong   The third vocalic diphthong, a combination dating from the Middle English period, is [ɔɪ]. It is the vowel sound of *boy, oil, voice,* etc., and it is interesting in that it is one of the English diphthongs which combine a back with a front vowel. Although tense, it does not figure in the vowel cycles just described. Its history is not of special interest, as the sound was derived mainly from foreign sources. But there is a peculiar usage of this diphthong in one New York City dialect that is often commented on. That is the custom of applying it where it does not belong and failing to apply it to words that should have it. Thus, in this dialect, according to humorous accounts, *girl, bird, third,* and *thirty* become

---

[1] Another use of the terms *rising* and *falling* is to indicate the tongue rising or falling between the two elements of a diphthong. This use of the term is in connection with speech rather than grammar.

[gɔɪl], [bɔɪd], [θɔɪd], [θɔɪtɪ] and *oil, boil, voice,* and *choice* become [ɜˑl], [bɜˑl], [vɜˑs], [tʃɜˑs]. This presentation is, of course, somewhat exaggerated, for very mixed patterns occur in the pronunciation of these words. What has happened is that the [r] in a word like *girl* has been lost and a glide-vowel has taken its place, creating a diphthong with the preceding vowel. The sound is more like [ɜɪ] or [ʌɪ] than like [ɔɪ]. This usage does not belong to uncultivated speakers only but is employed by cultivated speakers as well. To them, however, *earl* and *oil,* for example, are not homonyms; nor *curl* and *coil.* The pronunciation of [ɜɪ] or [ʌɪ] for [ɜˑ] is not limited to New York City, but may be heard in parts of the South and even in the Southwest.[2]

This is an odd confusion of sounds, but no odder than the Cockney English predilection for dropping the [h] from words that should have it while tacking it on to words that should not. This New York dialect sometimes puzzles a person not familiar with it. Thus, when a waitress in a New York restaurant told a newcomer to the city that the [bɜˑld ʌnjənz] were particularly good, he ordered them, thinking he was getting a new dish, but was surprised to discover that his order was actually for boiled onions.

15.7 Diphthongal [e]   In Chapter 13 the vowel [e] was given as a pure tense sound, and no doubt this is its usual value in General American English. In southern British English, however, and in some localities of the United States, as well as in end position in all dialects, this vowel tends to break into two sounds, becoming [eɪ], as in *play* [pleɪ] and *way* [weɪ]. Some phoneticians recommend the use of this diphthong in preference to the pure vowel (see par 13.6).

15.8 Diphthongal [o]   Precisely the same pattern and explanation are to be given to the tense back diphthong [oʊ], which appears in General American English chiefly at the end of words, as in *go* [goʊ], *row* [roʊ]. It indicates the rising tendency in the tense vowels, which underlies most of the changes in this group between Old and Modern English.

15.9 Other Diphthongs   For an account of numerous other English diphthongs, even triphthongs, the student is referred to various manuals of phonetics, such as Jones, *The Pronunciation of English.*

2 See Allan F. Hubbell, *Pronunciation of English in New York City* (New York, King's Crown Press, 1950), §§ 9.4, 9.5.

Many of these sounds arise out of the elimination of final *r*, or *r* before a consonant. It does not appear essential to include any of them in a broad analysis of English sounds from the historical aspect, such as is attempted here.

For the Student

A. FURTHER READINGS

Krapp, *The Pronunciation of Standard English in America*, §§ 70–79; 207–228.

Webster's *New International Dictionary*, 2nd edit., "A Guide to Pronunciation," §§ 36–39; 45; 159; and *passim*, under the individual vowels; 3rd edit., pp. 37a–43a, *passim*.

Kenyon, *American Pronunciation*, 10th edit., §§ 327–376.

Jones, *An Outline of English Phonetics*, 8th edit., §§ 219–233; 378; 466x.

Avery, Dorsey, and Sickels, *First Principles of Speech Training*, pp. 127–135.

Jones, *The Pronunciation of English*, 4th edit., §§ 160–219g.

B. FOR CLASS DISCUSSION

1. What is a diphthong? Do you think [tʃ] and [dӡ] should be included?
2. Make a list of words including falling diphthongs.
3. Make a list of words including rising diphthongs.
4. What do the eighteenth-century rhymes *design: join; wild: spoil'd; joined: find* indicate?
5. Have you ever heard the *oi* spelling pronounced with the diphthong [ɑɪ]? Explain how this pronunciation might arise.
6. What has happened to the diphthong [ɑɪ] as suggested by such spellings as *toime, moind* for *time, mind?* Explain phonetically.
7. Is there another spelling for *roil?* If there is, which do you use?
8. Is the second element in front diphthongs [ɪ] or [i]? Discuss.
9. List additional diphthongs given in speech manuals and discuss their validity.
10. Have you ever heard the pronunciation of [ɔɪ] or [ʌɪ] for [ɝ]? From what region did the speaker come? Do you know any regional writers who make use of this pronunciation? How is it represented?

C. SUGGESTIONS FOR RESEARCH PAPERS

1. Phonetician versus Linguist concerning Diphthongs.
2. A Study of the Diphthongs of New York City.
3. A Study of the Diphthongs of Any Particular Region (specify the region).
4. The Diphthong in a Particular Dialect (specify one).
5. A Study of the Diphthongs at a Particular Time (specify it).
6. Authors' Representation of Diphthongs in Dialect Writing (select specific authors).
7. Diphthongs and the Tense Vowel Cycle.

16

Consonants of
Former Periods

16.1 Historical Background Here and there in other chapters, facts about the history of English sounds have been given. No one can fully understand the phonology of Modern English without some knowledge of its history, and although many details will be omitted in this presentation, enough will be given to form a fairly clear idea. In this chapter there will be completed the picture of the historical background of the Modern English consonants.

16.2 Consonants Stable Sounds The word *consonant* implies that a consonant is an adjunct or appendage to some other sound, but this is not true. The consonant forms the framework of speech. It is the vowels which are "sounded with" consonants. Not only are the consonants the strong sounds, but they are the stable ones, altering little from century to century in the history of a language.

16.3 Modern Consonants in Old English Of the twenty-three consonant sounds we have today, all had appeared before the close of the Old English period with the exception of [ʒ] (see par. 8). It should be said, however, that [ŋ], [v], [z], and [ð] were positional variants of [n], [f], [s], and [θ], respectively, and were not significant sounds in themselves. These sounds appeared in certain positions. As is pointed out in par. 12.15, [ŋ] appeared before [g] and [k]. [f], [s], and [θ] become voiced between two vowels or between a vowel and a voiced consonant (see pars. 4, 5, 6). In addition to these, there were five consonant sounds present then which have since been lost. The English of the year 1000 thus had twenty-nine consonant sounds. The five lost consonants, which are explained in this chapter, are [n̥], [l̥], [R̥], [χ], and [ɤ].

16.4 Lip Consonants in Old English All our five lip consonants, [p], [b], [m], [f], and [v], were present in the year 1000, except that [v] was not represented in spelling. The spelling *f* between two vowels had the value of [v], as in *ofer, over,* and *sife, sieve.* This fact explains the dozen *v*-plurals in Modern English, such as *loaf, loaves.* Since the plural of *hlāf* was *hlāfas,* with the [v] sound for the letter *f,* it is natural that this sound should survive in Mod.E. *loaves,* as well as in *wives, thieves, wolves,* etc.

16.5 Point Consonants—*th* There were in the year 1000 two symbols, called the "thorn," *þ,* and the "eth," *ð* (see par. 3.15), to denote the sounds [θ] and [ð], but they were used interchangeably. The sounds themselves were probably used in the same words where they appear today. Thus O.E. *þis* or *ðis* is Mod.E. *this* [ðis], and O.E. *þrītig* or *ðrītig* is Mod.E. *thirty* ['θɝtɪ]. The two symbols *þ* and *ð* disappeared in the Middle English period.

16.6 The Point Sibilants The pair [s] and [z] were treated in Old English just as [f] and [v] were. There was no symbol for [z], but the letter *s* between vowels had this value. The same tendency exists in Modern English, for example, in *Susan* ['suzn̩], *wise* [wɑɪz], though it is not followed without exception. The final *e* of the last example is silent now but was once sounded. It was present, for example, in the nominative and accusative plural masculine forms in Old English (*wīse* [wiːzɛ]), and in Middle English was the regular plural form for the weak adjective, as well as the plural form for the strong adjective (*wīse* [wiːzə]).

16.7 Other Point Consonants The sounds [t] and [d] were spelled and pronounced in the year 1000 as they are now. So were [n] and [l], except that they had positional variants after *h* [x], spelled *hn* and *hl,* which have since disappeared. The symbols used for these are [n̥] and [l̥]. The consonant *r* (see par. 10.12) was a much stronger trill, [R], possibly with a weakened counterpart corresponding to the pair [r] and [ɹ]. This consonant also had a positional variant after *h* [x]: [R]. Examples of these variant point consonants are O.E. *hlūd,* Mod.E. *loud;* O.E. *hlot,* Mod.E. *lot;* O.E. *hræfn,* Mod.E. *raven;* O.E. *hnutu,* Mod.E. *nut.*

Why these positional variants disappeared is not known. Bloomfield in *Language* [1] states: "The general direction of a great deal of sound-change is toward a simplification of the movements which make up the utterance of any given linguistic form. Thus, consonant-groups are often simplified. The Old English initial clusters *hr, hl, hn* . . . have lost their initial consonants. . . . The loss of the *h* in these groups occurred in the late Middle Ages . . . we do not know what new factor intervened . . . to destroy the clusters which for many centuries had been spoken without change. The [h-] clusters are still spoken in Icelandic." He does not venture to give an explanation.

16.8 Blade and Front Consonants   By the year 1000 the sound [ʃ] had undoubtedly entered English; it was spelled *sc,* as in *scip,* Mod.E. *ship.* The sound [ʒ] was not present unless it may have been a part of the consonantal diphthong [dʒ] in such words as *ecg* [ɛdʒ], Mod.E. *edge,* and *brycg* [brydʒ], Mod.E. *bridge.* The consonantal diphthong *ch* [tʃ] may have been present in O.E. *cild* [tʃɪld]. As for the front semivowel [j], that sound was used in such words as O.E. *ge* [je], Mod.E. *ye;* O.E. *to-dæg* [todæj], Mod.E. *today;* O.E. *gielpan* [jɪəlpɑn], Mod.E. *yelp,* where the *g* preceded or followed a front vowel or diphthong.

16.9 The Back Semivowels and Stops   The sounds [w] and [ʍ], spelled *w* and *hw,* respectively, were present and sounded in Old English very much as they are today, as in *web,* Mod.E. *web,* and *hwī,* Mod.E. *why.* The symbol for [k] was *c,* as in *cynn,* Mod.E. *kin,* and *cyning,* Mod.E. *king,* but the sound was used as it is today, except when fronted to [tʃ], as in *cīdan* (Mod.E. *chide*) and *ceorl* (Mod.E. *churl*), where it may have been present at that time, or in combinations, as indicated in the preceding paragraph. The sound [g] was also present and represented by the letter *g* as in *gōs* [gos], Mod.E. *goose,* although the letter *g* had other values also (see below).

[1] New York, Henry Holt and Company, 1933, p. 370.

16.10 The Old English Velars Lower than [k] and [g], and with no letters to represent them exclusively, were the Old English velar continuant consonants, the back-open voiceless-voiced pair [χ] and [ɣ], which were pronounced with an effect of gargling or clearing the throat. The voiceless [χ] was similar in sound to the German *ch* in *ich* and the voiced [ɣ] to the *g* in North German *sagen*. Scottish retained the voiceless velar in such a word as *loch* until fairly recent times, but it now seems to be weakening. Old English usually spelled [χ] as *h*, as in *niht* (Mod.E. *night*), *sōhte* (Mod.E. *sought*), *seah* (Mod.E. *saw*, past tense of *see*). The voiced [ɣ], on the other hand, was generally spelled with a *g* as in *āgan* (Mod.E. *own*) and *sagu* (Mod.E. *saw*, "saying").

16.11 Development of Consonants The history of these twenty-nine Old English consonants is simple. The four sounds [n], [l], [ʀ], and [ʍ] were lost, the first three entirely, the last partially. The two velar continuants [χ] and [ɣ] disappeared, leaving their mark on the spelling and pronunciation of words like *night, bought,* and *law.* A few spelling symbols were introduced (*v, z, j, q*), and a couple were lost (*þ, ð*). Otherwise English consonants are substantially the same that they were a millennium ago.

For the Student

A. FURTHER READINGS

Robertson and Cassidy, *The Development of Modern English,* 2nd edit., pp. 93–99.

Aiken, *Why English Sounds Change,* pp. 65–84.

Emerson, *A Brief History of the English Language,* pp. 127–135.

Wyld, *A Short History of English,* §§ 80; 85–93; 153; 275–280.

Aiken, *English Present and Past,* pp. 168–175.

Moore and Knott, *The Elements of Old English,* 8th edit., §§ 16; 20–33.

Moore, *Historical Outlines of English Sounds and Inflections,* rev. by Marckwardt, pp. 20–21.

Marckwardt, *Introduction to the English Language,* pp. 313–315 (a phonetic transcription of an Old English passage: *Matthew* 6:9–16, 28).

B. FOR CLASS DISCUSSION

1. Pronounce the following Old English words and tell what words they became in Modern English: *cēosan, cēas, heofon, lufian, seofon, frēosan, hæfen, hefig, rīsan, wulfas*. What changes in consonants do they illustrate?
2. Make a list of words that form their plurals by changing *f* to *v* and adding *-es*. Look up the etymology of each one to find out the original Old English word from which it is derived. What change has taken place?
3. Pronounce the following Old English words and tell what words they became in Modern English: *hlāford, hlǣder, hlædel, hlǣne, hlǣnnes, hlǣst, hlanc, hleahtor, hlēapan, hlid, hlinc, hlūdnes, hlystan*. What changes do these words illustrate from Old English to Modern English?
4. Pronounce the following Old English words and tell what words they became in Modern English: *hnacod, hnappian, hnappung, hnecca, hrace, hrēod, hrēol, hriddel, hring, hrōc, hrōf, hrōst, hrycg*. What changes do these words illustrate from Old English to Modern English?
5. Pronounce the following Old English words and trace them into Modern English: *cealf, ceaf, cealc, ceorl, ceorlisc, cildisc, wecg, secg, lǣce, sceacan, sceadd, scēaf, sceaft, scēap, scearp, scēað, scēotan, scield, sciell, scilling, scīr, scō, scortnes, scrīn, scrūd, riht, sōhte, brōhte, fliht, mihtig, līoht, geard, cēowan, geolu, geong, gieldan, giellan, cwic, scip, ðanc, ðing, ðrēo, āð, bæþ, hǣðen, þē, norþ, forþ, brōþor*. What changes do these words illustrate from Old English to Modern English?
6. Can you explain why English has lost its guttural sounds?
7. Of the alphabetic changes mentioned in this chapter, which were gains and which were losses?
8. Relate the material on *c* in this lesson to the *satem-centum* material in Chapter 12. Characterize various modern European languages, including English, as *satem* or *centum*.
9. Bring in several words (other than plurals, possessives, or verbs in third person singular) where Mod.E. *s* has the value [z].

C. SUGGESTIONS FOR RESEARCH PAPERS

1. Signs of Weakening in Modern Voiceless Consonants.
2. The Story of Our Plurals in *v* (*Wife, Wives*).
3. Origin of Modern Words in *sk* and *sh*.
4. The Study of Certain Consonants (name them) in Middle English (base study on a particular text or texts).

17

Old English Vowels
and Diphthongs

17.1 Intricate Picture The history of the Old English vowels, while fairly simple in its main outlines, is very much more complicated than the story of the consonants. It is moreover obscured by a mass of exceptions and individual developments, so that the student must not generalize too much from the partial history presented here. A full discussion belongs to the study of historical linguistics.

17.2 Tense-Slack Puzzle The matter most difficult of explanation is why the tense vowels should have had a development differing from that of the slack vowels. In general, the tense vowels have moved upward (that is, tongue height has become progressively greater) until diphthongization has taken place. But the slack vowels have remained at the same height or even lowered between Old and Modern English.

17.3 Number of Vowels in Old English If the judgments of linguists are well founded, Old English had thirteen vowels. Modern English, on the other hand, has fourteen. Our vowels [ɝ] as in *bird* and [ʌ] as in *but* have supposedly appeared since the year 1000. On the other hand, Old English had two blade vowels, [y:] as in *lȳs,*

Mod.E. *lice,* and *brȳd,* Mod.E. *bride,* and [y], as in *fyllen,* Mod.E. *fill,* and *cyssan,* Mod.E. *kiss,* which do not enter modern speech.

17.4 Old English Blade Vowels Instead of our two high front vowels, Old English had four. The sounds [y:] and [y] were formed like [i] and [ɪ] except that the lips were rounded. In the course of time this lip rounding disappeared, and [y:] and [y] were merged with [i:] and [ɪ], respectively. Thus *hȳdan* [hy:dan] became Mod.E. *hide* [haɪd], and *synn* [syn] became *sin* [sɪn]. The slack vowels remained the same, while the tense diphthongized (see par. 13.4).

17.5 Front Vowels The tense sounds [e:] and [æ:] of 1000 may have been the same as in Modern English, or the second may have been somewhat higher, [ɛ:]. These two vowels were both raised and in the Modern English period came together as the sound [i]. Thus O.E. *he* [he:] became our *he* [hi], and O.E. *hǣlan* [hɛ:lan] became our *heal* [hil]. There were many exceptions to this development. The slack vowels [ɛ] and [æ] either both remained stable, or else the latter retracted to [ɑ], later to front to [æ] again (see par. 13.11): O.E. *menn* [mɛn], Mod.E. *men* [mɛn]; O.E. *fæst* [fæst], Mod.E. *fast* [fæst].

17.6 Back Vowels The tense high back vowel [u] was present in Old English, with its slack value [ʊ], as were also tense [o], tense [ɔ], and tense and slack [ɑ]. Their history was glanced at in Chapter 14. The tense vowels moved upward or diphthongized, while the slack stayed stable or lowered. Slack [ɑ] moved forward to become [æ]: O.E. *ganot* [gɑnɔt], Mod.E. *gannet* [gænɪt].

17.7 Falling Diphthongs In addition to the thirteen vowels just listed, Old English had four diphthongs, besides several minor diphthongs occurring in dialects. These diphthongs indicate a frequent drawling tendency on the part of the early speakers of English. They are ordinarily falling diphthongs; that is, the first element was always accented, the second being much obscured.

17.8 First Element Determinative The two tense Old English diphthongs are *ēa* and *ēo,* pronounced probably [ɛ:ə] and [e:o]. Following the Old English period the second element disappeared and the two developed to Mod.E. [i] as did O.E. *ē.* Some indication of the sound background of the modern descendants of these sounds may be found in the spelling. Words spelled with *ee* are likely to derive from *ē* or *ēo:* O.E. *sēcan* [se:kɑn], Mod.E. *seek* [sik]; O.E. *dēop* [de:op], Mod.E. *deep* [dip]. Words spelled with *ea* today are likely to derive from *ǣ* or *ēa: rǣran* [Rɛ:ran], Mod.E. *rear* [rir]; O.E. *tēar* [tɛ:ər], Mod.E. *tear* [tir]. There are numerous exceptions, such as *great* (O.E. *grēat*), *deaf* (O.E. *dēaf*), and *dead* (O.E. *dēad*), where the development to [i] did not take place; but in general the diphthongs *ēa* and *ēo* follow the regular rising to [i].

17.9 The Slack Diphthongs The other two important Old English diphthongs, *ea* [æə] and *eo* [ɛo], seem to have had a variety of developments, though in general they follow the tendency of the slack vowels not to change, and the rule that Old English diphthongs tend to simplify on the first element, as in O.E. *ceaf* [tʃæəf], Mod.E. *chaff* [tʃæf], and O.E. *heofon* [hɛovɔn], Mod.E. *heaven* ['hɛvən].

17.10 Account Incomplete The foregoing sketch of Old English phonology is visualized in Diagram E, which charts the probable sounds of the year 1000, or the late Old English period. It disregards dialect and exceptional developments for the most part, but should assist in giving the student some degree of historical background for Modern English phonology. It should be supplemented if possible by the further study suggested in the references below.

For the Student

A. FURTHER READINGS

Anderson and Williams, *Old English Handbook*, pp. 10–11; 24–31.

Moore and Knott, *The Elements of Old English*, 8th edit., §§ 17–19.

Moore, *Historical Outlines of English Sounds and Inflections*, rev. by Marckwardt, pp. 19; 24–35.

Robertson and Cassidy, *The Development of Modern English*, 2nd edit., pp. 99–108.

Emerson, *A Brief History of the English Language*, pp. 136–146.

Aiken, *English Present and Past*, pp. 176–188.

Wyld, *A Short History of English*, §§ 81–84; 201; 271, for lists of vowels and vowel changes; sections discussing these changes more fully are referred to in the text.

	LIP	POINT	BLADE	FRONT	BACK
High		tdnnll ˘˘ θð sz	ʃ3	j	
High-mid	pbmfv	RrR̥	i y: ɪ y		uwʌ ʊ
Mid				e ɛ	o ə
Low-mid				æ	ɔkgŋ
Low					ɑ χɤ

DIAGRAM E   **SOUNDS OF OLD ENGLISH**

NOTE: *h* is omitted as in Diagrams B and C. It is of course impossible to be dogmatic about the exact character of Old English sounds.

The phonetic transcription in Marckwardt, *Introduction to the English Language,* pp. 313–315, should also be reviewed in connection with this lesson.

B. FOR CLASS DISCUSSION

1. What vowels and diphthongs do we have in Modern English that were not present in Old English?
2. Are all the Old English vowels and diphthongs present in Modern English? If not, list those that belonged to Old English in particular.
3. Make a list of the Old English vowels and diphthongs. Give three words using each and show what these words have become in Modern English.

4. Give three sources of Mod.E. [i] with an Old English word to illustrate each.

5. Give two sources of Mod.E. [ɪ] and [ɑɪ], with an Old English word to illustrate each.

6. Pronounce the following Old English words and tell what Modern English word developed from each: *wē, hēl, scīnan, wīr, wērig, mȳs, tūn, hām, mǣnan, cū, spēdan, ðūsend, grǣdig, drēorig, lȳs, mōd, sōna, ēast, ēare, gāst, āc, drēam, gēar, rād, fūl, bī, mīn, nā, bān, hālig, Crīst, mūð, fōt, frēondscipe*. Where has the change occurred in each word? Why?

7. Pronounce the following Old English words and tell what Modern English word developed from each: *cwic, helpan, eorðe, oxa, sunne, standan, cyning, cribb, ende, willan, bringan, glæd, heard, ðæt, cyssan, settan, sittan, leornung, spendan, sendan, dyde, swellan*. Have these words changed much? What kind of vowel or diphthong is in each?

8. Give ten more examples of Old English words from which we get words now in good usage. Explain each.

9. In a small dictionary, such as *Webster's New Collegiate, Webster's New World, American College,* or *New College Standard,* run through all the words beginning with the letter *c*. Explain the changes in those which have come from Old English.

10. A rustic pronunciation for the word *deaf* is [dif]. Relate this to the history of the word. Do the same for the British pronunciation of the word *been*.

11. Sketch a short history of each of the following words, using the *Oxford Dictionary* as your source: *such, which, also, either, through*.

12. Give three compound words where the vowels have not slackened and three where slackening of one or more vowels has taken place.

13. Take two pages at random from Clark Hall's *A Concise Anglo-Saxon Dictionary* and see how many words you can trace into Modern English. Bring the words to class.

14. Give several examples of peculiar rhymes in Shakespeare and, if possible, account for them.

C. SUGGESTIONS FOR RESEARCH PAPERS

1. Survivals of Old English Vowels and Diphthongs in the Scottish Dialect (or some other dialect).

2. Diphthongs in Old English and Modern English.

3. Surviving Old English Sounds in Milton.

4. Surviving Old English Sounds in Shakespeare.

18

Middle and Early Modern English Phonology

18.1 Foreign Influence It may seem out of order to consider Middle English last, after the beginning and the end of English sounds have both been described; but there is some justification for the *a-c-b* order followed. During the Middle English period the language was, so to speak, taken apart and put together again. It went into eclipse and emerged in many ways a different tongue. There is no doubt that one impulsion for change lay in the foreign influences of Danish and French upon English, even though we do not find these influences embodied in the language until long after the conquests which caused them. There is always a cultural lag before a structure so basic to a people as language is can be altered.

18.2 Cause of Vowel Cycle Even so, the actual cause of the phonetic alterations which saw such rapid progress in the Middle English period, and particularly the cause of the dual cycles of the rising and breaking of tense vowels (see pars. 15.5, 15.6, 17.2), are not fully explained by referring them to so vague a thing as a foreign conquest. Why should foreign conquest cause tense vowels to rise and diphthongize? That it should cause changes in vocabulary, inflections, even syntax, is readily understandable. But why this particular sort of change in the tense vowels?

Climate, social class distinctions, change of occupation have all been advanced as the answer to the questions posed in the previous paragraph. Then there is the accord theory, set forth in *Why English Sounds Change,* by Janet Rankin Aiken. It is based upon the principle of sound assimilation and suggests that the tense vowels rose because they were influenced by neighboring consonants, which would in general be higher than the vowels themselves, and that the diphthongization resulted from the entrance of pure voice, in the form of the sound [ɑ], before the high tense vowel. This intrusive [ɑ], inserted to maintain the vowel character of the sound, would then tend to swallow up the vowel sound following it, and the whole cycle would begin over again. The slack vowels failed to rise because of their unstressed character. None of these answers seems adequate.

18.3 Time of Changes   It is impossible to pin down a linguistic change to a particular century, but the linguist Zachrisson is of the opinion that the tense vowel changes of English extended in the main from the fifteenth to the eighteenth century, that is, approximately from 1400 to 1700. Wyld agrees regarding the beginning but would place the end somewhat later. This makes these changes fall chiefly in the Early Modern English period. But there is ample evidence that vowels, both tense and slack, had altered before 1400.

18.4 French Influence   Many Middle English vowels owe something to French phonetic influence. Thus while O.E. [i:] remained fairly stable in Middle English, and O.E. [y:] merged with [i:], the French tense *u*, a sound much like [y:], entered in words like *fruit* and *suit*. Though the rounding of this French sound affiliated it with back vowels finally, still it retained an *i* in spelling, indicating its likeness to [y:]. Old French [ɑ:], as in *dame, fame,* came in and later began to rise, not in the back sequence, but in the front, to [ɛ:] and finally to [e] or [eɪ], as it is today. French *j* entered as in *juge,* Mod.E. *judge,* and assimilated to English [dʒ], giving us the modern spelling *j* as well as *dg* for this sound. Two varieties of the spellings *e* and *o*, pronounced [e] and [ɛ], [o] and [ɔ], respectively, were used side by side.

18.5 Testimony of Rhyme   It is from misspellings, from rhymes,

and, after about 1600, from the testimony of grammarians and phoneticians that we get our evidence regarding Middle English sounds.
The poet Chaucer, for example, avoids rhymes such as *meat* and
sweet, showing that the vowel values of O.E. *ē* and O.E. *æ* were different in his time—a difference which persisted in Standard English
until late in the eighteenth century and which still persists in the
Irish dialect.

18.6 New Diphthongs The Old English diphthongs (pars. 17.7
ff.) were lost by 1100, the beginning of the Middle English period;
but a whole crop of new ones had risen to take their place. Wyld
lists eight such diphthongs, which are rather like our present ones in
that they end with either [ɪ] or [ʊ], indicating a tendency of the
vowel to rise in tongue height and prophesying the actual rises which
did take place.

18.7 Chaucer and Shakespeare Chaucer, near the end of the
Middle English period, and Shakespeare, equally near the beginning
of Modern English, offer excellent material for study of the phonology of their times. In reading Chaucer, one may still use the Old
English values. In reading Shakespeare, one finds that most of the
modern sounds have entered, so that there is relatively little difference between his sound values and ours. Shakespeare no doubt
spoke with what would seem to us an Irish brogue in pronouncing
leap, meat, reap, and similar words. He could still pun on *Rome* and
room, the latter word not yet having its full [u] sound.[1] It must also
be said that for many cultivated speakers *room* has never achieved
a full [u] sound but has stopped at [ʊ].

18.8 Chaucer's Final *E* One of the peculiarities of Chaucer's
English was the vestigial suffix -*e,* which was all that he had left of
Old English inflectional endings in -*a,* -*u,* etc. This final *e* was pronounced like our neutral vowel [ə], and it had disappeared as a
sound by Shakespeare's time. Because it usually followed a syllable
containing a tense vowel, and because it remained in spelling, it
came to be known as "the sign of a long vowel." Actually it is the
unsounded remnant of a dead inflection, which happens to serve a
somewhat useful purpose in determining modern pronunciation.

[1] See Helge Kökeritz, *Shakespeare's Pronunciation* (New Haven, Yale University Press, 1953) for a thorough study.

18.9 Table of Middle English Sounds For the student who wishes to study Middle English phonology more particularly, the following table of vowel sounds may be helpful.

	Middle English Phonology			*Modern English Phonology*		
a	drank	[a]	[draŋk]	drank	[æ]	[dræŋk]
	shape	[a:]	[ʃa:pə]	shape	[e]	[ʃep]
aa	caas	[a:]	[ka:s]	case	[e]	[kes]
e	lest	[ɛ]	[lɛst]	lest	[ɛ]	[lɛst]
	depe	[e:]	[de:pə]	deep	[i]	[dip]
	clene	[æ:]	[klæ:nə]	clean	[i]	[klin]
ee	meel	[ɛ:]	[mɛ:l]	meal	[i]	[mil]
	feend	[e:]	[fe:nd]	fiend	[i]	[find]*
i	milk	[ɪ]	[mɪlk]	milk	[ɪ]	[mɪlk]
	tide	[i:]	[ti:də]	tide	[aɪ]	[taɪd]
ii	wiis	[i:]	[wi:s]	wise	[aɪ]	[waɪz]
o	god	[ɔ]	[gɔd]	god	[a,ɔ]	[gad, gɔd]
	over	[ɔ:]	[ɔ:vər]	over	[o]	[ovɚ]
	dom	[o:]	[do:m]	doom	[u]	[dum]
	good	[o:]	[go:d]	good	[ʊ]	[gʊd]
	coppe	[ʊ]	[kʊp:ə]	cup	[ʌ]	[kʌp]
	wolf	[ʊ]	[wʊlf]	wolf	[ʊ]	[wʊlf]
	rode	[ɔ:]	[rɔ:də]	road	[o]	[rod]
oo	hoom	[ɔ:]	[hɔ:m]	home	[o]	[hom]
	hood	[o:]	[ho:d]	hood	[ʊ]	[hʊd]
	food	[o:]	[fo:d]	food	[u]	[fud]
u	us	[ʊ]	[ʊs]	us	[ʌ]	[ʌs]
	put	[ʊ]	[pʊt]	put	[ʊ]	[pʊt]
	entuned	[ju]	[ɛntjunəd]	entuned	[ju, u]	[ɪntjund, ɪntund]
y	tyl	[ɪ]	[tɪl]	till	[ɪ]	[tɪl]
	swyn	[ɪ:]	[swɪ:n]	swine	[aɪ]	[swaɪn]
ai, ay	dai, day	[æɪ]	[dæɪ]	day	[e]	[de]
au, aw	sauce, sawce	[aʊ]	[saʊsə]	sauce	[ɔ]	[sɔs]
ei, ey	wei, wey	[æɪ]	[wæɪ]	way	[e]	[we]
eu, ew	deu, dew	[ju]	[dju]	dew	[ju, u]	[dju, du]

* M.E. [e:], [æ:], and [ɛ:] all developed into Mod.E. [i]. In general, words with M.E. [æ:] or [ɛ:] are spelled in Modern English with *ea*, as in *clean* and *meal*, and those with M.E. [e:] are spelled with *ee, e,* or *ie*, as in *deep, me,* and *fiend*.

	Middle English Phonology			Modern English Phonology		
iu, iw	*Tiuesnight, Tiwesnigkt*	[ju]	[Tjuəsnɪχt]	*Tuesday night*	[ju, u]	[Tjuz(dɪ), Tuz(dɪ) nɑɪt]
ou, ow	*oure, owre*	[uː]	[uːrə]	*our*	[ɑʊ]	[ɑʊr]
	oune, owne	[ɔːʊ]	[ɔːʊnə]	*own*	[o]	[on]
	sought	[ɔʊ]	[sɔʊχt]	*sought*	[ɔ]	[sɔt]
oi, oy	*coine, coyne*	[ɔɪ]	[kɔɪnə]	*coin*	[ɔɪ]	[kɔɪn]
er	*service*	[er]	[servisə]	*service*	[ɝ]	[sɝvɪs]
ir	*first*	[ɪr]	[fɪrst]	*first*	[ɝ]	[fɝst]
or	*word*	[ɔr]	[wɔrd]	*word*	[ɝ]	[wɝd]
ur	*hurt*	[ʊr]	[hurt]	*hurt*	[ɝ]	[hɝt]

For the Student

A. FURTHER READINGS

Marckwardt, *An Introduction to the English Language*, pp. 228–231; 263–266 (phonetic transcriptions of selections from Middle English and Early Modern English: Shakespeare's *Hamlet*, I, ii, 129–156; II, iii, 1–9; Chaucer's *Prologue*, A 118–150).

Moore, *Historical Outlines of English Sounds and Inflections*, rev. by Marckwardt, pp. 36–50; 64–78; 110–140.

Emerson, *A Middle English Reader*, "Introduction," pp. xx–xxii; xxv–lxxvii.

J. and E. M. Wright, *An Elementary Middle English Grammar*, 2nd edit., pp. 5–132.

Aiken, *Why English Sounds Change*, pp. 85–110.

Wyld, *A Short History of English*, §§ 146–148; 208–213; and *passim* throughout Chapters 6 and 7 for detailed discussion of individual vowels.

Baugh, *A History of the English Language*, 2nd edit., pp. 282–289.

Robinson (ed.), *The Works of Geoffrey Chaucer*, 2nd edit.

Kökeritz, *Shakespeare's Pronunciation*.

B. FOR CLASS DISCUSSION

1. What are the three divisions of the English language? Give approximate dates.

2. Make a list of the stressed vowels and diphthongs which are found in Modern English but are not present in Middle English.

3. Make a list of the stressed vowels and diphthongs present in Middle English but not in Modern English.
4. What sounds in Middle English developed into Modern English [i]? Illustrate.
5. In Early Modern English such words as *tear* [tir], *hear* [hir], and *dreary* [driri] were pronounced [ter], [her], and [dreri]. Do you know of any present-day dialect words in which the [e] is used instead of the Standard English [i]? What does this show about the dialect pronunciations in general?
6. Do all the words containing the sound [i] in Modern English have the same spelling for it? If not, can you account for some of the spellings you find?
7. What Middle English sounds developed into Modern English [e]? Illustrate.
8. Give some of the Middle English sources of Modern English [o]. Give examples.
9. Give some Middle English sources of Modern English [u]. Of [ʊ]. Of [ʌ]. Give examples.
10. From what Middle English sound is Modern English [aɪ] developed? Illustrate.
11. From what Middle English sound is Modern English [aʊ] developed? Illustrate.
12. From what Middle English spellings did the Modern English [ɝ] develop?
13. Middle English *smert* [smɛrt] and *ferthing* [fɛrðɪŋg] have become *smart* and *farthing* in Modern English. Can you list any other words in which the same change has occurred? Can you account for the eighteenth-century spellings of *sarvents, Jarmany, sartainly,* etc., and the dialect forms *sartin* and *larn?*
14. Give some Middle English sources of Modern English [ɔ]. Illustrate.
15. Can you explain phonetically the dialect pronunciations of [sʌt] and [tʌk] for *soot* and *took?*
16. In Middle English what was the spelling of the sound [χ]? Is this sound present in Modern English? Does the Middle English spelling occur? What does this show about Modern English spelling?
17. Pronounce the following Middle English words and tell what Modern English word developed from each: *smyling, ooth, she, divyne, lippes, amiable, been, reverence, wolde, houndes, herte, preest, gerner, reyn, sheep, dayerye, hoolly, heeth, wrighte, knight, enclyne, wyves, bisyde, housbondrye, deel, deyntee, yerd, chirche, toun, clerk, mayde, word, preye, lerned.*

18. *Veyne, engendred, vertu, tendre, chambres, condicioun, chivalrye, batailles, sovereyn* are words used by Chaucer in the beginning of the *Prologue* to the *Canterbury Tales.* What modern English words developed from them? Consult the *Oxford Dictionary* to determine the source of these words. When were they first introduced into the English language? What does this evidence show about the English of Chaucer's time?

19. Make a list of all the nouns in the first hundred lines of the *Prologue* to the *Canterbury Tales* which have changed their method of forming the plural since the time of Chaucer. Which inflection has been adopted mainly?

20. If a facsimile folio or quarto or other edition of Shakespeare retaining the original spelling is available, study the use of the final -*e* in some one play. Is it pronounced? Does it appear consistently in any particular form of the word?

21. In the same play, make a list of the words for which you find variant spellings. Do any of these spellings help to show the pronunciation of the words in Shakespeare's time?

C. SUGGESTIONS FOR RESEARCH PAPERS

1. A Comparison of the Pronunciation of the *er* Words in Chaucer with That of Shakespeare in His *Sonnets.*
2. Chaucer's Use of the Final *e.*
3. Chaucer's Spelling.
4. Extent of Inflection in Middle English.
5. Comparison of Inflection in Middle English with That of Old English or Modern English.
6. The Verb in Middle English (or any other part of speech).
7. The Forming of Plurals in Middle English.
8. Elements of French Phonology in Chaucer.

NOTE: The preceding subjects are all very broad and suitable for extended research projects such as the M.A. or Ph.D. thesis. For a beginning class they may be limited to a short selection in Chaucer or any other Middle English writer.

9. Shakespeare's Pronunciation of *ea* and *ee* from a Study of the Rhymes in the *Sonnets.*
10. Shakespeare's Use of Dialect in *Merry Wives of Windsor* (Evans and Caius) and *Henry V* (Fluellen).

19

Review of Phonology

19.1 General Tendency of Sounds The history of English sounds has exemplified the general tendency in all language for the area of sound production to become ever more restricted and for superfluous sounds to fall away. The desire for ease, generally unconscious, has made phonetic history in its broad outlines an approach toward a more compact system of sounds, made with greater ease, usually with the mobile tip of the tongue (consonants) assisted by vocalic glides (vowels) which smooth the transitions from consonant to consonant. In English, ease has been well served by the loss of two velar sounds, three voiceless sounds, and two difficult rounded front vowels.

19.2 Probable Future Losses While the voiceless value of [w], namely [ʍ], has not yet been dropped from General American, it seems quite probable that it may come to be, and possible that other voiceless sounds might follow. Otherwise the unstable sounds are those at the fringes of the vowel area, since English could be made more compact by their loss. However, we must remember that such changes take place very slowly and might be delayed for centuries or even millenniums.

19.3 Development of Consonants   Where consonants have altered, the changes have generally been in the direction of ease and the elimination of superfluous sounds. Voiced sounds have replaced voiceless, and back sounds have been fronted to point or blade positions. However, changes have been few, since consonants are stable sounds and alter, if at all, only at a glacial rate.

19.4 The Slack Vowels   The relatively unstressed and therefore indeterminate character of the slack vowels tends to keep them stable; and when fully unaccented they tend to level under [ə]. Eventually many such unstressed syllables will no doubt disappear from the language, so that we may confidently expect present English words to shorten with the passage of time, though new longer words may enter to keep the balance even.

19.5 The Tense Vowel Shift   The broad historical changes in the tense vowels may best be summarized in a diagram, such as the one that follows:

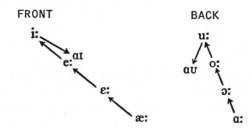

DIAGRAM F   **THE TENSE VOWELS**

Examples of Old English words with their Modern English equivalents will illustrate the shift.

*[æ:] > [ɛ]	*ǣr, ere; pǣr, there; hwǣr, where.*
*[æ:] > [e]	*grǣg, gray; wǣn, wain; hwǣg, whey.*
[æ:] > [i]	*dǣd, deed; wǣd, weed; mǣl, meal.*
[e:] > [i]	*mē, me; tēð, teeth; cwēn, queen.*
[i:] > [ɑɪ]	*mīl, mile; līf, life; glīdan, glide.*
*[ɑ:] > [ɔ]	*brād, broad; āht, aught; tāhte, taught.*
[ɑ:] > [o]	*hām, home; gā, go; rād, road.*
[o:] > [u]	*bōt, boot; tōð, tooth; dōn, do.*
[u:] > [ɑʊ]	*mūs, mouse; hū, how; mūð, mouth.*

* Examples marked with asterisk show irregular or exceptional development.

19.6 Transcriptions and Dialects In considering the actual phonology of present-day English, we need not remind ourselves that there is no such thing as an absolute standard. Speakers of good English differ in the sounds they use, by reason of age, sex, race, locality, and education. Even occupation may make a difference in the sounds one uses. Instead of speaking of English phonology as one thing, therefore, or even as two things which may broadly be called General American and Southern British, in the United States and England, respectively, we are forced to confine ourselves to studying specifically how we ourselves talk, how our friends talk, and what speech we hear on the radio, from the platform, and elsewhere.

19.7 How to Review It is important that the student master completely the thirty-seven English pure sounds together with the diphthongs, the seven categories into which they may be put, and the significance of any changes in their place of formation.[1] When, for example, he reads the title of a "funny book" by Milt Gross of some years back, *Nize Baby* [nɑɪz bɛbɪ], he should be able to explain at once that in the first word the [s] of Standard English has become voiced, and that in the second word (though this is not

[1] In addition to reviewing readings given in previous chapters, among the many other studies that may be examined are: Argus Tresidder, "The Speech of the Shenandoah Valley," *American Speech* (Vol. XII, 1937), pp. 284–288; "Notes on Virginia Speech," *ibid.* (Vol. XVI, 1941), pp. 112–120; "The Sounds of Virginia Speech," *ibid.* (Vol. XVIII, 1943), pp. 261–272; Lester V. Berrey, "Southern Mountain Dialect," *ibid.* (Vol. XV, 1940), pp. 45–54; A. H. Marckwardt," Folk Speech in Indiana and Adjacent States," *Indiana History Bulletin* (Vol. XVII, 1940), pp. 120–140; "Middle English ō in the American English of the Great Lakes Area," *Papers of the Michigan Academy* (Vol. XXVI, 1941), pp. 561–571; R. I. McDavid, Jr., "Low-back Vowels in the South Carolina Piedmont," *American Speech* (Vol XV, 1940), pp. 144–148; "Post-vocalic /-r/ in South Carolina: A Social Analysis," *ibid.* (Vol. XXIII, 1949), pp. 194–203; "Derivatives of Middle English [oː] in the South Atlantic Area," *Quarterly Journal of Speech* (Vol. XXXV, 1949), pp. 496–504; (with V. G. McDavid) "h Before Semivowels in the Eastern United States," *Language* (Vol. XXVIII, 1952), pp. 41–62; "The Position of the Charleston Dialect," *Publications of the American Dialect Society* (Vol. XXIII, 1955), pp. 35–49; E. F. Shewmake, "Distinctive Virginia Pronunciation," *American Speech* (Vol. XVIII, 1943), pp. 33–38; E. Bagby Atwood, "*Grease and Greasy*—A Study of Geographical Variation," *Texas Studies in English* (Vol. XXIX, 1950), pp. 249–260; Katherine E. Wheatley and Oma Stanley, "Three Generations of East Texas Speech," *American Speech* (Vol. XXXIV, 1959), pp. 83–94.

represented in the spelling) the usual [e] or [eɪ] has dropped and slackened to [ɛ]. He should practice with dialect material until he understands readily such modification as [ɑɪ] for [ɔɪ] in *bile* for the standard *boil,* or [ɝ] for [ɔɪ] in the occasional New York pronunciation of *voice.* If he hears a speaker pronounce *poor* as if it were spelled *po* [po], he should be able to state the two changes involved, the total dropping of [r] and the lowering of the vowel from [ʊ] to [o].

19.8 Practice Necessary   Such ability does not come without a good deal of practice, and this practice may be based on hearing or reading of dialect material. In reading one must be careful to differentiate between real dialect and phonetic spellings such as *wuz* and *sez* for *was* and *says.* Occasionally misspellings will give a clue to dialect; an example is the spelling *esk* and *equeduct* in the papers of students in Greater New York. Here the variation is a matter of raising [æ] to [ɛ].

19.9 Start With Yourself   When you have mastered the theory contained in the foregoing lessons, particularly Chapters 6 to 15, the next step is to analyze carefully your own speech and to determine its differences from the speech of those about you. Then go on, as suggested in the exercises for this chapter, to use phonetic transcription until you know how to handle it. If you find that the broad count given here will not suffice for your purposes, study a narrower count of sounds such as will be found in any speech manual.

For the Student

A. FURTHER READINGS

Thomas, *An Introduction to the Phonetics of American English,* 2nd edit., pp. 191–252 (with transcriptions).

Krapp, *The Pronunciation of Standard English in America,* "Preface," pp. iii–xi; §§ 99–101; 109; transcriptions, pp. 151 ff.

Kenyon, *American Pronunciation,* 10th edit., pp. 8–17.

Schlauch, *The Gift of Language,* pp. 19–32.

Aiken, *Why English Sounds Change,* pp. 22–38.

Wyld, *A Short History of English,* §§ 60–74.
Jones, *An Outline of English Phonetics,* 8th edit., §§ 54–64.
Jones, *The Pronunciation of English,* 4th edit., transcriptions, pp. 179 ff.
Hall, *The Phonetics of Great Smoky Mountain Speech.*
Stanley, *The Speech of East Texas.*
Kurath (dir. and ed.), *Linguistic Atlas of New England.*

B. FOR CLASS DISCUSSION

1. Pronounce the following: [ʃʌn, ʃon, ʃin, ʃɑɪn], [tʃɝn, tʃɪn, tʃoz, tʃuz, tʃɑʊ], [dʒʌst, dʒɔɪst, dʒɛst, dʒɑʊl, dʒel, dʒɛl], [jɛt, jir, jor, jul, jʌŋ], [lɔ, le, lo, lɑɪ], [kɪŋ, kɑɪnd, kip, kɪn, kʌm].

2. How would you explain the pronunciation [rɪŋɪŋ] for *ringing* in place of [rɪŋɪn] or [rɪɲɪŋg]?

3. List other variations from standard pronunciation and explain them phonetically.

4. How would you explain phonetically the process of whistling to someone who does not know how to whistle?

5. Write a letter in your own speech, using phonetic instead of alphabetic symbols. List the sounds in which it differs from standard speech. Are there any differences too minute to be expressed in symbols? If so, describe them phonetically.

6. Transcribe the speech of one of your classmates and analyze it. Then describe it phonetically.

7. Listen to a speaker over the radio and transcribe his speech. Then describe it phonetically.

8. Various issues of *American Speech* (1933–1945) devoted several pages to phonetic transcriptions. Select the transcriptions of two different persons and analyze the speech of each. Describe phonetically the differences. See also Jane D. Zimmerman (ed.), *Phonetic Transcriptions from American Speech,* rev. ed. (New York, Columbia University Press, 1939).

9. Study some of the phonetic transcriptions given by Krapp and Jones and comment on any individual or regional peculiarities that you find recorded there.

10. List the sounds substituted for the "correct" ones by some particular child learning to talk. Classify them and explain phonetically the substitutions.

11. List sounds which give trouble to a foreigner talking English. Explain phonetically his difficulty. Compare the sounds of his language with those of the English language.

12. Select a foreign language that you know and pick out the sounds not represented in English and those that are slightly different. Explain their nature phonetically.

13. Transcribe several sentences spoken by a very tired, angry, or somewhat intoxicated person. Explain phonetically what happens to the standard sounds.

14. Joel Chandler Harris' Uncle Remus stories (southern), Bret Harte's short stories (western), and James Russell Lowell's *Biglow Papers* (New England) all give dialects current in the United States less than a century ago. How have they altered since then? Make an analysis of any one about which you have sufficient knowledge.

15. Choose any writer who has made an attempt to represent dialect (e.g., Leonard Q. Ross in *The Education of Hyman Kaplan,* Streeter in the *Dere Mable* stories of the World War I era, George Ade in *Fables in Slang,* the writings of Ring Lardner, and John Steinbeck in *The Grapes of Wrath*), make an analysis of the speech represented, and comment on the adequacy of the method used by the author. If you have available any phonograph records in the particular dialect or know any individuals from the region discussed, make a comparison to see whether the author of the dialect material has represented the speech correctly. Describe phonetically the sounds represented.

16. Examine Dr. Joseph S. Hall's *The Phonetics of Great Smoky Mountain Speech* and bring to class a list of words representative of that speech. Describe phonetically each sound represented.

17. Examine the *Linguistic Atlas of New England* and bring to class a number of words representative of certain sections. Describe phonetically each sound represented.

18. Do you say *skillet, frying pan,* or *spider?* By asking your friends try to make some statements about the regional distribution of these three words.

19. Do you think English sounds will change in the future as they have in the past? Why?

C. SUGGESTIONS FOR RESEARCH PAPERS

1. Where Are You from?
2. A Study of the Speech of Certain Sections or of Certain Individuals (be specific).
3. The Use of Dialect in the Comic Strips.
4. Consonant Substitutions in American Dialects.
5. The Influence of the Stage and the Radio on American Pronunciation.
6. The Tendency of Unstressed Syllables to Disappear.

20

Background of the Alphabet

20.1 Symbols and Sounds Speech, as has been suggested, is language; but it is just as true that we know speech very largely through the medium of writing; and therefore the method for representing speech is of great importance. Even the study of phonology must be reduced to symbols. Letters, therefore, as symbols for sounds, become of an importance comparable to that of sounds themselves.

20.2 No Common Source Some 250 alphabets are known to scholars; in England alone during the past fifteen centuries there have been three. These many various alphabets have often influenced each other, but it is certain that they do not reflect a common origin but fall into groups originated independently within various countries. The Chinese ideograms are by origin separate from the Mayan symbols of Central America and Mexico; and our English alphabet, while allied ancestrally to very many others, including the Arabian and Hebrew, is in some respects independent of them all.

20.3 A Common Idea If the alphabets used today and in the past have no common source, they do nevertheless have an idea in common—the idea of a picture. *Symbol* is not a good word to describe the earliest letters of any people; they were pictures. For example, a pictured sun figures largely in the primitive writing of American Indians and by a natural transference of idea came to mean "day" oftener than "sun." This development by which a picture was given a different yet related meaning is another step in alphabet formation and turns into rebuses or picture puzzles certain communication systems, like those of the Indians, in which the picture itself regularly stood for some associated or easily inferable idea which would not lend itself so well to pictorial representation.

20.4 The Early American Type It is easy to see what a field this picture-plus-idea concept opens up to human ingenuity; and the result has a tremendous advantage when, as seems to have been the case with the American Indians, there was no common language but a vast complexity of hundreds of separate tribal idioms differing widely from one another. This sort of picture rebus-writing can be understood by anyone with the necessary training or ingenuity, whether his word for *sun* is or is not the same as the writer's. America before the white men came may be regarded, therefore, as a vast heterogeneous network of tribal units with differing speech but a common written language, which can still be read by students unfamiliar with the words it represented to the writers.[1]

20.5 Ojibwa Hunting Expedition[2] Below is a communication written by the Ojibwa Indians, one of the Algonquian tribes. It is a record of a hunting expedition. The two lines represent a wave-tossed river, on which floats a bark canoe, steered by the owner, who is sitting in the back. In the front is a piece of birch bark which forms a shield for a fire of pine knots used to light the course for the man in the canoe. By means of the light, game, as it comes to the water to drink, can be observed by the hunter. In front of the canoe are two deer, and following is a circle representing a lake from which appear the head and horns of a third deer. To the right of the lake a doe appears, and beyond her the two wigwams of the hunter. The four animals, no doubt, represent the game secured.

---

[1] The Mayans seem to have added some use of phonetic symbols. See Edward Clodd, *The Story of the Alphabet* (New York, D. Appleton-Century Company, 1938), pp. 72–74.

[2] *Ibid.*, p. 57. Reprinted by permission of D. Appleton-Century Company.

DIAGRAM G   OJIBWA HUNTING EXPEDITION

Redrawn from E. Clodd, *Story of the Alphabet.* Copyright 1938 by D. Appleton and Company.

20.6 The Oriental Type   In a very crude state, this Indian rebus idea is the same as that developed by the Chinese for a civilization somewhat similar in that many dialects existed, making it impossible for people in different parts of the country to understand one another orally. The Chinese early modified the pure pictorial concept (which would have required a new picture for every separate word) by an ingenious system of "strokes," which lessened the labor of learning separate and ever more complicated "pictures." Even so, the difficulty of learning to handle the Chinese pictographs is tremendous and has always kept literacy at a low level until within the present century.

20.7 Sound Plus Picture   The great difference between the forms of writing just described and that which we use is that the Indian and Oriental types are not phonetic. They do not use pictures to represent sounds. Whether one race only, or several, had the ingenuity to take this step is uncertain; we know only that it was done, and that it gave us our present alphabet. It seems to have been done in two ways, the first syllabic and the second truly phonetic. The syllabic method is as though one should make a picture of a toe and then use it to form words related in sound but not in idea, such as *total, toga, token.* In the second, the picture stood not for the entire word but for a single sound, usually the initial sound of the word naming the picture, as the picture of a dog might stand for *d* and that of a sun for *s.*

20.8 The Egyptian Writing   The syllabic form of symbolizing was used by the ancient Assyrians and by them given to the Babylonians and others who made use of the cuneiform or wedge-shaped type of writing, possibly as early as 6000 B.C. But this system has not survived to modern times. The earliest writing to utilize the phonetic principle based upon single sounds, the principle which we employ today, was the writing of Ancient Egypt; and we can even see the three progressive steps or stages by which the development took place. The Egyptians had not one but three forms of writing: the hieroglyphic, the earliest picture writing, with its later development, the hieratic, an abridged form of hieroglyphic writing assuming a cursive character, which came to be reserved for religious writings; and the demotic, a simplified kind of hieratic writing, which was used by the people generally after the sixth or seventh century before Christ. According to Flinders Petrie, the hieroglyphic writing was invented before 4777 B.C.; our earliest specimen of hieratic dates from 3500 B.C.

20.9 Birth of the Alphabet   The phonetic principle by no means sprang into full being in the Egyptian writing of over six millenniums ago. It struggled into existence bit by bit, and the Egyptians never entirely discarded the pictorial type, which survived to the end in inscriptions, particularly for writing royal names. About 400 varied symbols appear to have been devised and used or abandoned, finally reducing themselves to a basic set of twenty-five phonetic symbols which were used side by side with nonphonetic elements, much as in some of our modern rebuses in which words and pictures are combined. It was left to other races to discard and adapt.

20.10 Phoenician and Hebrew   Despite some differences concerning details, there seems to be general agreement that a Semitic people, the Phoenicians, borrowed and refashioned the Egyptian system of writing at some time prior to the earliest Greek records, that is, at some time between the fall of Mycenae and the civilization of Crete, about 1150 B.C., and the rise of the Homeric Greek culture, about 800 B.C.

20.11 Greeks Receive Alphabet   These Phoenicians traded with the Egyptians and readily adopted their simple and labor-saving script. Some signs they altered; for example, the second letter, which corresponds to our *B*, appeared in Egyptian as both a leg and a crane, but the Phoenicians borrowed this symbol only as a crane, and it later appears as *beth*, a house, in the Hebrew script. The picture, though not the sound, had been changed. During the three centuries of their prominence, the Phoenicians, a trading people whose home was a narrow strip of territory along the western seacoast of Palestine, transmitted their improved and rejuvenated phonetic system of writing to both the Hebrews and the Greeks. By this theory the Greek and Hebrew alphabets are related through being derived from a common source. This close connection is shown in our present word *alphabet,* composed of the first two letters of the Greek alphabet, *alpha* and *beta,* which are *aleph* and *beth* in Hebrew.

20.12 Greek Improvements Whether it was the semimythical king Cadmus or another who imported the Phoenician alphabet into Greece, the Greeks made several improvements in the new tool they had acquired. Perhaps the chief of these was the introduction of vowel sounds. Neither the Egyptian nor the Semitic alphabets recorded the vowels with any completeness, but the Greeks added full representation of their vowels. Moreover, they made the letters run from left to right, as in Modern English, instead of in the opposite direction. Over four or five centuries the Greek alphabet was in process of improvement, until finally it was a fit instrument for the great ideas it was to embody.

For the Student

A. FURTHER READINGS

Clodd, *The Story of the Alphabet,* pp. 1–178, particularly the "Foreword," pp. 1–9, by George H. McKnight.

Atkinson, "Alphabet," in *Encyclopaedia Britannica* (1959), Vol. I, pp. 677–685.

Giles, "Alphabet," in *Encyclopaedia Britannica,* 11th edit., Vol. I, pp. 723–732.

Moorhouse, *Writing and the Alphabet,* pp. 20–36.

Pedersen, *Linguistic Science in the Nineteenth Century,* pp. 143; 166–188; 203–215.

Schlauch, *The Gift of Language,* pp. 35–41.

Robertson and Cassidy, *The Development of Modern English,* 2nd edit., pp. 9–13.

Bradley, *On the Relations Between Spoken and Written Language with Special Reference to English,* p. 10.

Taylor, *The Alphabet,* 2 vols., *passim.*

Roberts, *Understanding English,* pp. 48–65.

Sturtevant, *An Introduction to Linguistic Science,* Chapter III.
Laird, *The Miracle of Language,* pp. 211-217.

B. FOR CLASS DISCUSSION

1. Look up a few nonalphabetical systems of writing, describe each, and illustrate each.
2. Of what importance is the Rosetta Stone?
3. When did drawing become writing?
4. Does any modern system of writing omit vowels? Could English be written in this way?
5. Look up the etymology and the definition of the following words: *alphabet, rune, write, pen, papyrus, cuneiform, hieroglyphic, ideogram, pictogram, phonogram, syllabary, acrophonetic.* What have you learned concerning the earlier forms of writing?
6. What is the advantage of an alphabet over a syllabary or over ideographs?
7. Is the Greek alphabet an improvement over the Semitic? If so, how?
8. In what way does the Roman alphabet differ from the Greek?
9. Look up the runic alphabet. How does it differ from the one we use today?
10. We know that Cynewulf is the author of certain Old English poems because of his spelling his name out in the poem by means of runes. Bring to class his name written in runes.
11. It is usually assumed that the function of writing is to represent the sounds of language. See Bradley's argument in *On the Relations Between Spoken and Written Language, with Special Reference to English,* p. 10. Do you agree with him? Formulate your own answer.

C. SUGGESTIONS FOR RESEARCH PAPERS

1. A Comparison of the Semitic Alphabet with Ours.
2. The Origin of the Greek Alphabet.
3. Contributions to the Knowledge of the Alphabet Made by Alan H. Gardiner, Flinders Petrie, E. S. Roberts, and Sir Arthur Evans.

21

Development of the English Alphabet

21.1 Efficiency Appreciated Although it is the modern era, and particularly the American culture, that is supposed to have deified Efficiency, there is plenty of evidence that the ancients, too, were glad to adopt an idea that worked well, and one bit of this evidence is the way that the Phoenician modification of the Egyptian alphabet spread to almost all corners of the world. It was the introduction of this system into Greece, reputedly by Cadmus, that provided the direct ancestry for written English, but it is interesting to note, in passing, that in one form or another this alphabet became the possession of such diverse peoples as the Hebrews, Syrians, Arabs, Armenian, and Georgians in the area of Mesopotamia and Iraq, and spread eastward to the Burmans, Siamese, Javanese, and Singalese, as well as to the Tibetans, Kashmiri, Bengali, and Malayans. In fact, apart from the Chinese ideograms, it became the chief alphabet of the vast territory of Asia. It was, of course, through the Greek that the Russian, Coptic, and Latin alphabets, including the one we use today in writing English, developed.

21.2 Fundamental Unity There are differences in the individual letters of the alphabets enumerated above, but there can be little doubt as to the fundamental identity of origin. Scholars may, if they wish, continue to argue that certain literary forms, such as the ballad, could have been created spontaneously in several parts of the world, but it is too much to believe that peoples who were hundreds, or thousands, of miles apart, with no direct means of communication, could have devised similar symbols for similar sounds, independently of one another.

21.3 For Experts Only   It is true, of course, that the similarities between certain letters in English, say, and corresponding ones in Javanese, or even Russian, are not discernible to a layman. Only an expert in comparative philology can trace and identify all the ramifications of individual letters. Such a study is beyond the scope of this book; it will suffice here to point out that there was such a common origin for a large number of the existing alphabets in the world.

21.4 In Unrelated Languages   This original likeness is all the more striking in view of the fact that this Phoenician version of the Egyptian alphabet came to be used regardless of the language system to which a particular tongue belonged, and the only plausible reason for such general adoption is that the early peoples, wherever located, recognized the efficiency of this "new" way to make written records. Looking again at the classification of language systems set forth in Chapter 1, the student will notice how the alphabet disregarded linguistic barriers in its development over the centuries. This alphabet proved as useful for other language systems as for the Indo-European.

21.5 Ionian the Greek Standard   The important Greek alphabet was at first modified in various ways to suit the preferences of the little Greek city-states, and it is said that there were at one time forty more or less divergent forms of it used among the Greeks; but in 483 B.C. the Ionian was agreed upon as the Athenian standard. From this Ionian Greek alphabet were later borrowed the Coptic alphabet (early in the Christian era) and the Cyrillic or Slavonic (before the tenth century), in which Russian is now written. Another Greek alphabet, the Chalcidian, was the basis for Roman borrowing.

21.6 Roman Borrowing Foremost   Just as the Romans have given us many of the grammatical terms originated by the Greeks and borrowed by their western neighbors of Italy, so it is the form of the Greek alphabet used in Rome which has spread today to all quarters of the globe as the medium for writing most of the languages of Europe, Australia, and North and South America. The date of its appearance in Italy may be as early as 700 B.C., and while, as in Greece, there were at first various local forms—Umbrian, Oscan, Etruscan, and others—the political ascendancy of Rome soon assured the parallel ascendancy of the Roman alphabet.

21.7 Three English Alphabets The Roman method of writing accompanied the Romans to England on their early voyages of conquest, beginning in 55 B.C., and remained there until the last Roman legion was withdrawn in A.D. 410. Many Roman inscriptions still remain. But after 410 there came a hiatus lasting nearly two centuries, and during this time two alphabets, which may or may not have had a Roman origin, were used. These are the ogams (also spelled oghams) and the runes.

21.8 Series of Notches The ogam characters in their primitive form were apparently sets of notches on the edge of a stone or squared stick. Later they were written on a flat surface either above, below, or through a central horizontal line, something like modern systems of shorthand. Thus, one perpendicular line hanging from the central horizontal line represented the sound *b;* two such notches stood for *l,* and three denoted *f.* There were twenty symbols in all, arranged in four groups of five each. One group had its notches below the horizontal line, another above it, a third through it, and a fourth through it diagonally.

Some 300 inscriptions in this alphabet have been discovered, the majority of them in the southwest of Ireland, particularly the counties of Kerry and Cork. About twenty-two have turned up in Scotland, thirty in England and Wales, and two on the Isle of Man. The generally accepted theory is that the system was first worked out in the southwest of Ireland by some scholar or scholars familiar with the Latin alphabet. Some of these inscriptions go back to the fifth century of the Christian era, and perhaps even earlier. Nothing in the ogams represents in any way the letters of the alphabets we know, and they may have been devised for secret messages, as tradition has it. There is no diversity in the form of the notches, as the meaning is obtained solely from the number of them and their position with regard to the central line.

21.9 Runes Alphabetical   The runes, however, have a recognizable source and presumably were developed by the ancient Goths after contact with the classical Greek and Latin alphabets. The runes constitute the earliest form of Germanic writing and were prevalent in Scandinavia as early as the third century of the Christian era. In some of the isolated districts of Sweden their use persisted almost down to the present time. The runic alphabet took various forms, but usually contained twenty-four symbols, some of them strikingly similar to modern letters, notably the *f*. The rune *ð*, *eth*, survives in the present-day phonetic alphabet and was long an integral part of Old English, as was another rune *þ*, the *thorn*, misrepresented nowadays in such pseudo-ancient phrases as "Ye Olde Gifte Shoppe." The *þ* in *þe (the)* was misread and thought to be a *y*.

21.10 Teutonic Heritage   The runic alphabet was being used by several of the Teutonic tribes of Britain at the time that the Christian missionaries brought over the Roman alphabet from the Continent and from Ireland. Runes had spread over a wide area from the Danube valley to the Orkney Islands, and the earliest of such inscriptions is about a thousand years older than the latest ones. During this long period constant development went on, and the result was that runes of different countries and of different periods presented many variations. Some scholars have divided the runes into three main types, the Gothic, the Anglican, and the Scandinavian.

21.11 Mysterious Connotations   The name "rune" is supposed to be derived from *Rún,* a Teutonic term for the mystery of writing, and "runa" meant "a whisper." As late as the thirteenth century, a moral ode said, with regard to the Deity:

> Elche rune he ihurð & he wot alle dede.
> [Each whisper he hears, and he knows all deeds.]

In the course of time runes came to be associated with mysteries, magic, and even witchcraft. Many superstitions grew up around this heathen way of writing, in the centuries just after the seventh, when the Roman alphabet began to gain the ascendancy along with Christianity. Runes are found on gravestones, church crosses, bells, fonts, amulets, rings, bracelets, brooches, etc., as late as the eleventh century. Because of the idolatrous veneration given runes by the

heathen, they were an especial object of attack by the Christian missionaries.

21.12 Bypaths in Linguistics Interesting as the ogams and
runes are as illustrations of the curious bypaths taken by the human
mind in arriving at a system of writing, they are of little practical
value to students of English. With the exception of the *eth* and the
thorn noted above as runic contributions, it was the Roman alphabet
that came into universal use for the writing of Old English.

21.13 More Sounds Than Symbols This Roman alphabet had
twenty-three characters denoting sounds. There were, however,
more sounds than symbols. As has been pointed out, all seven vowel
letters had at least two values apiece, which may or may not be
marked. The letters *f*, *s*, *þ*, *ð*, *h*, *c*, and *g* had at least two values
each, depending upon the surrounding sounds. Three symbols, *æ*, *þ*,
and *ð*, not present in Modern English, were included, while four,
j, *q*, *v*, and *z*, were lacking. The letter *k* was rarely used.

But if in the alphabet of Old English some letters carry more
than one sound, it is well-nigh perfection compared to the alphabet
we use today, whose letters and letter combinations express on an
average five sounds apiece. It is even worse if we consider the
sounds of English and try to count the letters and combinations of
letters which may represent them. For instance, one may cite a number of possible sounds with the spelling *ea*: h*ea*rth [ɑ], gr*ea*t [e],
br*ea*st [ɛ], chang*ea*ble [ə], *ea*rth [ɝ], l*ea*p [i], guin*ea* [ɪ]. Even more
striking, perhaps, is the variety of sounds associated with the weirdly
unphonetic group of letters -*ough*, as in b*ough*, c*ough*, th*ough*,
thr*ough*, and r*ough*. Another example is the possible spellings of the
sound [ʃ]: *ch*aperon, o*ce*an, mousta*che*, fu*chs*ia, musi*c*ian, *sch*wa,
con*sci*ence, nau*se*a, *sh*ould, fa*sh*ion, man*si*on, pre*ss*ure, pa*ss*ion, initi-
ate, ra*ti*on, comple*xi*on, an*xi*ous. Notice that the italicized letters in
the last list of words always denote the single sound [ʃ] and do not
include the consonantal diphthtong [tʃ]. These three examples are
sufficient to prove the disparity between the English alphabet and
the sounds of English.

21.14 Added and Dropped Letters To glance at the alphabetic
changes in English, some of which have already been mentioned, we
see that *æ*, *þ*, and *ð* were lost to English during its middle period,
probably because they did not correspond to any letter in the French

alphabet. The symbols *z*, *q*, and *v* were added to correspond to French letters. An elongated *i*, now called *j*, was developed to differentiate between the vowel and consonant values of Early Modern English *i*, as in *iudgement*, which now is spelled *judg(e)ment*. Finally *u* and *v*, which were used interchangeably until into the seventeenth century, were unscrambled and confined, *u* to vowel, and *v* to consonant uses. Even today one sometimes sees a *V* for *U* on an engraved inscription.

21.15 Transcription Necessary So complete is the unphonetic character of Modern English as to call for a new alphabet of thirty-seven symbols (see Chapters 9 to 15). It might seem that we would do well to use such an alphabet to replace entirely our twenty-six-letter one, but there would be some disadvantages in such a course. In the first place, thirty-seven letters would be more difficult than twenty-six to handle in typing, printing, and writing. And, second, since every individual pronunciation differs to some extent from every other, one of two plans would have to be followed. Either everyone would have to write as he talked, which would lead to a mild sort of spelling anarchy; or else everyone would have to adopt some sort of uniform spelling, which would still leave many persons' spelling unphonetic.

But the weightiest argument of all against the general adoption of the phonetic alphabet for everyday use is that such a step would immediately make obsolescent, if not obsolete, the whole body of existing writings in the English language. Not only our literature, but our laws, our business contracts, and all the records of our English and American culture would acquire an antiquarian and unreal flavor and would be incomprehensible to a new generation schooled only in the phonetic alphabet. A modern culture, unlike primitive ones, is based almost entirely on writings of one sort or another. The task of translating even a tiny portion of this written record into the new symbols would be such as to stagger the imaginations of even the doughtiest reformers. Therefore, it would seem to be necessary to leave our spelling pretty much as it is, using the phonetic alphabet as a scholarly device for transcription purposes among students of the language.

It is unfortunate that our orthography bears so little relation to our phonology, not only because of the time wasted throughout the lives of each one of us to make the effort to spell correctly, but particularly because this circumstance is the one great and unsurmountable barrier to the adoption of some form of English as an international auxiliary language. The relative simplicity of English grammar, the flexibility of its sentence structure, the copiousness of its vocabulary, and the richness of its idioms would all seem to mark it as excellent material for development into an international *lingua franca*—as has, indeed, been proposed many times; but the world as a whole can never be made to learn to associate the sounds of English with the wholly capricious and illogical spelling that afflicts the language and must, unfortunately, continue to afflict it for the reasons set forth above.

Regardless, therefore, of the many claims put forward on behalf of Basic English—a proposed world language with a fundamental vocabulary of only 850 or so words—the inescapable fact seems to be that neither Basic nor Standard English can become the universal language, except possibly by slow expansion during the centuries to come, or by fiat imposed after a conquest.

21.16 Spelling a Problem Perhaps the worst feature of our present unphonetic alphabet is the burden it places upon generation after generation of school children in learning to spell. Certainly a moderate reform which would eliminate some of the spelling hurdles for the young would seem to be worth while.

But various simplified spelling projects in the last half century have been unable to make any lasting impress on the language, except that in some areas *thru* and *tho* are accepted for *through* and *though*. Also *catalog* has replaced *catalogue* and *program* does duty for the older *programme*. But the other simplified spelling device of *-t* for *-ed* in the past tense, as *drest* for *dressed,* is hardly ever used now though in the early part of this century it was the "standard" spelling for the defunct *Literary Digest* magazine and scores of newspapers, most of them in the Middle West. Even the redoubtable President Theodore Roosevelt could not convert America to simplified spelling.

Common sense seems to call for such an improvement in the language, but the fundamental stumbling block is the disagreement as to how radical the changes should be. *Thru, catalog,* and *drest* are logical and understandable spellings, but when it comes to dealing with such a word as *rough,* should it merely be changed to *ruff,* thus agreeing in sound and spelling with *cuff,* or should both words drop that final unsounded *-f* to give us *ruf* and *cuf?*

The tinkering with a few spellings like that would not cope with the fundamental discord between sound and spelling. Nothing less than phonetic transcriptions would do for the *-sh* sound of *-ti* in *traditional,* for instance. Simplified spelling, therefore, either must stop short of bringing improvement enough to warrant the bother, or it must go all the way to altering the language by the phonetic alphabet. So, the dilemma of English spelling remains unsolved, aside from what appears to be a growing tendency to look with more tolerance than formerly on misspellings. The standardizing effects of the printing press can be counted on, however, to prevent absolute individuality in orthography.

For the Student

A. FURTHER READINGS

Pedersen, *Linguistic Science in the Nineteenth Century,* pp. 229–239.
Clodd, *The Story of the Alphabet,* pp. 178–204.
Schlauch, *The Gift of Language,* pp. 41–47.
Moorhouse, *Writing and the Alphabet,* pp. 36–54.
Aiken, *English Present and Past,* pp. 191–207.
Robertson and Cassidy, *The Development of Modern English,* 2nd edit.,
    pp. 52–54; 88–93; 330–335; 353–361.
Taylor, *The Alphabet,* Vol. I, pp. 70–82.

B. FOR CLASS DISCUSSION

1. Look up the approximate age, source, etc. of each of the letters in the alphabet.
2. What runes did the Old English scribes use?
3. *Book* and *beech* are from the same root. How does this bear upon the story of the runes in Old English?
4. Is our alphabet a logical one? What suggestions could you make for devising a new one?

5. Old English had a comparatively phonetic orthography. What causes can you give for the chaotic spelling of Modern English?

6. From Old English times can you think of any examples of spelling reform? Were they advantageous?

7. Study the Roman alphabet. From the opening remarks in any good Latin grammar, estimate how nearly phonetic it was.

8. Do you think that the English alphabet has been improved, from the point of view of phonetics, by the loss of some symbols and the gain of others?

9. Would it be possible by means of letters and letter combinations to make English a phonetic language? Explain.

10. In solving the orthographic problem, would it be easier to have the pronunciation of English conform to the spelling or the spelling to the pronunciation?

11. Make a list of letters and letter combinations which have a variety of pronunciations in English and of different spellings used to represent the same sound. Compare your lists with the tables on pp. 198 ff. and 202 ff. in Aiken's *English Present and Past.*

12. What are the advantages of phonetic spelling? Do they outweigh the disadvantages? See Robertson and Cassidy, 2nd edit., pp. 361–373.

C. SUGGESTIONS FOR RESEARCH PAPERS

1. A Comparison of Early Greek Alphabets.
2. Story of the Ogams.
3. Story of the Runes.
4. A Logical Alphabet.

III

Words

22

Origin of Words

22.1 Fascinating Subject Words are the fundamental stuff out of which language, as we understand the term, is made, and in preceding chapters we have studied words in regard to their sounds. In this section it will be our purpose to deal with the origin and meaning of words, the most fascinating and most popular subject in the whole field of linguistics. Trace back almost any of the common English words and you will get a rich and rewarding glimpse of the history, the customs, and even the beliefs of earlier ages.

Take, for instance, *board,* which at the outset meant nothing more than *a piece of timber,* as it still does. Since theatrical stages were made of wood, the phrase *on the boards* became current for *on the stage,* and a further definition as an *extensive surface of wood* is exemplified by chessboard, from which develops the idea of any flat, thin surface, not necessarily of wood, as in *cardboard* and *pasteboard,* where no timber is present at all. Also, derived directly from the first meaning, *board* conveys the idea of a table for food, as in *bed and board* and *the groaning board.* The word likewise becomes attached to the group of persons who customarily hold meetings around a table, such as *Board of Health* and *Board of Aldermen*.[1]

Or consider the word *lozenge,* which nowadays usually has the humble, prosaic meaning of *cough drop* or *small piece of hard candy.* The word comes from Old French *losange,* also spelled *losenge* and *lozenge,* and denoting, first, *flattery* and then *praise.* The Modern French *losange* still has the meaning *praise, commendation,* or *eulogy. Lozenge* broadened in its meaning, however, to denote first the eulogies that appeared as epitaphs on funeral monuments and still later the monuments themselves. But monumental inscriptions usually appeared in diamond-shaped figures; so by a further extension of meaning *lozenge* became the equivalent of such a figure, and thus was used as an architectural term, since many buildings were decorated with *lozenges.* Moreover, other things also took on or already had this diamond-shaped form, especially small confections of sugar, usually medicated. By a final extension of meaning, *lozenge* has come to refer to a cough drop or bit of hard candy, whether or not in the diamond shape.[2]

These are but two examples of word development. Tracing the ramifications of a word can be a most interesting occupation or hobby, but the further back the research goes the more difficult the task becomes, and usually mere speculation must be resorted to.[3]

22.2 No Actual Origins   Indeed, according to the context theory of word beginnings, it is impossible to trace a word to an absolute origin, because human word sounds have not come about through any consciously creative process; they are simply the continuation of animal noises. Neither, according to this theory, did meanings originate at the dawn of human speech; the animal sounds involved defi-

[1] George H. McKnight, *English Words and Their Background* (New York, D. Appleton-Century Company, 1923), p. 211.

[2] *Ibid.*

[3] For interesting studies, see Ivor Brown's *I Give You My Word* (1946), *Say the Word* (1947), *I Break My Word* (1951), *Chosen Words* (1955): (London, Jonathan Cape); *A Word in Your Ear* and *Just Another Word* (1945), *No Idle Words* and *Having the Last Word* (1951): (New York, E. P. Dutton); Ernest Weekley's *Words Ancient and Modern* (1926), *More Words Ancient and Modern* (1927), *Words Ancient and Modern* (1946): (London, John Murray); *Something About Words* (New York, E. P. Dutton, 1936); Owen Barfield, *History in English Words* (London, Methuen & Co., Ltd., 1926).

nite communication, as they still do. What made meaningful sounds into words was the use of them as we employ words—to talk with rather than to react to.[4] *Ouch,* for example, became a word by being talked about, whereas a dog uses his yelp, his *ouch* equivalent, only as a reaction to a situation involving actual or expected pain.

22.3 Root Theory Linguists of the last century used to take account of this prehistoric linguistic period by talking about "primitive roots" of words, which they took to be the prototypes of groups of related modern terms. They looked, for example, at our current verb *drive,* which is obviously the source of the noun *drove* (*a drove of cattle*) and is somewhat less obviously connected with *drift* (*a drift of snow*). There is a similar idea underlying these words, which have long existed in the Germanic as well as other Indo-European dialects; and as a result the older scholars used to talk of the root *dry,* or *drf,* as one of the probable items in the primitive Indo-European speech which, they were sure, once had an individual existence.

22.4 Discouraged? Today linguists talk less about roots and origins. They seem to feel that there is no solution to the problem of the precise nature of primitive speech, and there is a tacit agreement to disregard it in favor of the study of today's English. The old theories [5] with their quaint names (one was called the "bow-wow," another the "ding-dong," as a supposed popular clue to the origin of speech) are seldom mentioned. What has taken their place is a keen preoccupation with theories of meaning and the emotional colorings of words, theories which will be glanced at in Chapter 35. But first the various ways of making English words must be discussed.

22.5 Few "Original" Words Even in the more than half-million entries in a modern unabridged dictionary, there are practically no words made up without some sort of source. The stock example of such an "original" word is *kodak,* which is said to have been manufactured by putting together letters very much as a bench might be made by putting together boards. Perhaps some other advertising or trade names are made in the same way; but if so, they have not entered the dictionary as has *kodak.* Of course there are many trade

---

[4] This context theory was formulated in Janet R. Aiken, *Commonsense Grammar* (New York, Thomas Y. Crowell, 1936), pp. 47 ff.

[5] Gray, *Foundations of Language, op. cit.,* p. 40, gives a brief account of the old theories.

names getting into popular speech, and perhaps into some dictionaries—such as *Victrola* and *Frigidaire,* often written without the
capital letters—but these are adaptations of real words and not the
combination of previously unrelated letters that *kodak* is. There are,
however, telescoped words arbitrarily formed from two distinct
words, such as *cyclotron,* from *cycle* and *electron.* These are called
portmanteau words or blends.

22.6 Borrowing   If the student looks up the "derivation" of a
word in the dictionary, he will almost certainly find it traced back in
English to some particular time, and then listed as derived from
Latin, Greek, French, German, Hebrew, or some other of the thousands of languages spoken on earth. It may, especially if it is a common word, be listed as of Old English origin, with nothing (or perhaps Gothic) before that. It is not assumed that a word either can or
need be traced back more than from one to two thousand years.

22.7 Compounding   Aside from borrowing, probably the greatest source of new words is the compounding or joining together of
old ones. *Buttercup* is a different word from both *butter* and *cup;*
stepchild is not the simple joining together that it seems to be, for
the first syllable is the Old English *stēop* (Modern English *steep*)
that meant *high, projecting* and hence *unprotected.* These are just
two samples of the compounding method of word formation.

22.8 The Various Methods   Chapters 23 through 27 cover various methods of word formation, beginning with a detailed treatment
of borrowings and compounding because of the importance of these
two aspects of the subject. It may be well here to give the complete
list in the order of discussion:

    1. Creation from nothing (negligible)
    2. Borrowings from other languages
    3. Compounding
    4. Formation by affixes
    5. Functional shift
    6. Figures of speech
    7. Back-formation
    8. Initial words
    9. Onomatopoeia (echoic words)
   10. Name words
   11. Portmanteau words or blends (telescoping)

22.9 Word Change   But not only do words enter English; they have a history after their entrance. Words change. They may disappear from use. They drop one meaning or acquire another. Metaphorically (for of course a word is basically merely a meaning which has associated itself with a certain set of sounds) one may compare a word to a person with a career falling within a certain life span. The changes discussed in Chapters 28 through 34 are:

1. Degeneration and elevation
2. Generalization and specialization
3. Exaggeration and understatement
4. Abbreviation and extension
5. Metathesis and folk etymology
6. Shifts in association
7. Radiation of meaning

22.10 Semantic Interplay   And finally, having learned how words are born, change, and die, the student must acquire some idea of their interaction in human society, with their potentialities for good and for harm. This brings up the semantic doctrines and is a fitting approach to the student's further lifelong study of the English language.

For the Student

A. FURTHER READINGS

Jespersen, *Language: Its Nature, Development, and Origin,* pp. 26–29; 61; 413–416.

Jespersen, *Growth and Structure of the English Language,* 9th edit., pp. 149–167.

Robertson and Cassidy, *The Development of Modern English,* 2nd edit., pp. 1–14.

McKnight, *English Words and Their Background,* pp. 163–179.

Greenough and Kittredge, *Words and Their Ways in English Speech,* pp. 1–6; 168–192.

Aiken, *English Present and Past,* pp. 75–90.

Baugh, *A History of the English Language,* 2nd edit., pp. 357–378.

Sheard, *The Words We Use*, pp. 35–93.
Laird, *The Miracle of Language*, pp. 52–98.
Pyles, *Words and Ways of American English*, pp. 3–55.
Graff, *Language and Languages*, pp. 291–318.
Kennedy, *Current English*, pp. 329–335.
Smith, *The English Language*, pp. 109–125.
Emerson, *The History of the English Language*, pp. 113–124.
Schlauch, *The Gift of Language*, pp. 75–108.
Zandvoort, *A Handbook of English Grammar*, 5th edit., pp. 316–363.

B. FOR CLASS DISCUSSION

1. From what did Bentham coin *international;* Huxley, *agnostic* and *agnosticism;* Macaulay, *constituency;* Whewell, *scientist;* Newton, *centrifugal;* Browne, *hallucination, retrogression, incontrovertible, insecurity, electricity, literary, medical;* Browning, *artistry;* Milton, *Pandemonium, Satanic, liturgical;* Shakespeare, *multitudinous;* Johnson, *irascibility;* Burke, *colonization, diplomacy, electioneering;* Coleridge, *pessimism;* Lewis Carroll, *galumphing;* Shaw, *superman;* Eastman, *kodak;* Gamaliel Bradford, *psychography?*

2. Abbott in his *Shakespearian Grammar* points out that "you can *happy* your friend, *malice* or *foot* your enemy, or *fall* an axe on his neck." What does this statement show about the use of words?

3. What is the relationship between the following pairs of words:

cadence : chance	dominion : dungeon
pale : pallid	interlocutor : interrogator
pride : proud	bishop : episcopal
temporal : extemporize	piano : pianoforte
compute : count	treasury : thesaurus
astrology : astronomy	blaspheme : blame

4. Explain the process by which the following words originated:

midday	idealism	gas
watt	Nabisco	cab
tick-tock	radiogram	beg
piecemeal	mob	blitzkrieg
writer	whir	typewriter

5. Look up the derivation of *nostril, hussy, gossip, orchard, Christmas, goodbye.* How were they formed?

6. Examine the headlines of a number of newspapers and see what words are used in the place of others to save space, as *wed* for *marry*. In what way does this substitution in headlines affect the language?
7. Make a list of the names of gems and find out their origins.
8. See how many words you can find that look like new formations. Are they in the dictionary? How were they formed?
9. Consult the *Oxford Dictionary* or Webster's *New International Dictionary* for the sources of the following words: *alligator, mirage, sheriff, vanilla, hatchet, Webster, cockroach, Messiah, tomato, fruit, sassafras, soil, tapioca, gingham, cherub, geyser, studio, pogrom, moccasin, tattoo, mohair, fetish, tulip, silk.*
10. Compose a glossary of words connected with some specific subject, such as dress, sports, food. Are the words chiefly loan words or native compounds?
11. In each of the following words, what changes have taken place in the meanings?

nice	brave
dandelion	holiday
gossamer	candidate
gospel	virtue

12. In how many ways can you use the word *smoke?* What does this fact show? How was it used in the time of Jonathan Swift?

C. SUGGESTIONS FOR RESEARCH PAPERS

1. Language, a Mirror of Progress.
2. Words of World War I (World War II).
3. What the Automobile (Moving Picture, Radio, or any other invention) Has Done for the Language.
4. Word Coinage.
5. Words Coined by Sir Thomas Browne in *Pseudodoxia Epidemica.*

A paper may be written on any one of the eleven points mentioned in par. 8 or on any one of the seven mentioned in par. 9.

23

Borrowings from
Other Languages

23.1 Native Element   The English language may be said to have started its life in the fifth century after Christ (traditionally 449) when the two Saxon chieftains Hengist anod Horsa bore it to its new home from the European country around the mouths of the Elbe and Weser Rivers. The Angles, Saxons, and Jutes were the three groups who migrated to England, taking with them a language not entirely unaffected by any other European speech. (See Chapter 3, pars. 1 and 6.) Even before the removal to England, a few Latin words, *wall, wine, pound, street* among them, had been borrowed. A second slight infiltration of Latin words occurred at the time of England's Christianization.[1] But the tongue of the Germanic invaders, who at that time were without a permanent literature, had enough force and drive to insure its survival.

23.2 Invaders Invaded   The English vocabulary as well as the English people was invaded, during the years following 787, by the Danes, a Scandinavian people who liked the country and visited it,

---

[1] The Roman missionary Augustine arrived in England in 597.

first to plunder and then to stay (see par. 3.7). For nearly three centuries they harried the English, particularly in the north of the island, and Svein, king of Denmark, finally succeeded in seizing the throne in 1014. He died in that same year and was succeeded by his son Cnut, who had to fight three more years to establish his claims to the throne. In 1017 Cnut became king and for the next twenty-five years England was ruled by Danish kings.

23.3 Danish Loan Words As Danish was also a Germanic language and hence like English, it is sometimes hard to tell whether a Modern English word goes back to one or the other. We know certainly, however, that the pronouns *they, their,* and *them* are from the Danish, and these are a great acquisition to English, since without them the plural and singular forms of *he* would sound almost exactly alike. In addition to these pronouns, and the adverb *fro* of the phrase *to and fro,* there are among Danish borrowings in English the nouns *law, sky, keel, bank, window, sister, knife,* and *skirt;* the verbs *give, die, thrive, hit, take, call,* and *want;* and adjectives such as *meek, odd, low, wrong,* and *ugly.* Until recently these Danish borrowings in English have not been fully appreciated, but it is now apparent that they constitute a significant part of the language in that they are primarily familiar, everyday words. Robertson and Cassidy write,[2] "Aside from Greek, Latin, and French, only Scandinavian, the language of the people whom the Anglo-Saxons called "Danes," has made a really substantial contribution to the English vocabulary."

23.4 Final Invasion The next invasion of England, and the last that the English have had to suffer, occurred in 1066 and came from just across the English Channel, in Normandy, where Duke William considered that he had a legitimate claim to the English throne. The Normans were Scandinavians racially but they had adopted the French language a century or so before, so that it was linguistically a French invasion which English now underwent. (See Chapter 4, pars. 4–8.) In the following centuries, French probably contributed more words to English than Danish had in the years before the Norman Conquest, but the influence of French was less fundamental, for the added words did not seriously affect the grammar of English.

[2] *Op. cit.,* p. 161.

23.5 English Submerged   The Norman Conquest of 1066 did not instantly result in loan words, but it did make English for over a century an obscure language, with almost no literature. At first all offices of trust were filled with Normans, and the result was that Norman French was the language of the court and the higher official life. For generations the two languages went on existing side by side, English losing a good deal of its old vocabulary and only gradually acquiring new French words to take the place of the words lost. Not until the time of Chaucer (1340–1400) did the English use of French words reach its height.[3] But by this time English had reasserted itself as the main speech of the island, and the danger of its permanent effacement was over.

23.6 Character of Borrowings   Words connected with law, government, the army, the church, various trades, and matters of general conduct and conventions seem to have been the chief groups of borrowings from French, but there were also many words of very common use (see par. 4.31). Words for the parts of the body are still English or Danish, but *face* is French. Words for the most intimate relationships are English or Danish, but *uncle, aunt, cousin,* and *grandparent* are all French. Also the names of the common animals— *ox, calf, sheep, swine*—are English, but names for the dainty meats served at the table—*beef, veal, mutton, pork*—are French.

23.7 Latin Active   During all this time, and for long afterward, Latin words continued to enter English in immense quantities. Perhaps the sixteenth century saw the peak of the borrowing. If we include the many Latin words entering English through French, an offshoot of Latin, a majority of the entries in the English dictionary are from Latin sources. This does not mean that most English words used are of Latin origin. The nine most frequently used English words, *and, be, have, it, of, the, to, will,* and *you,* are all of native origin, and the percentage of Latin words used by various great authors varies from about 6 to 30 per cent, according to various statistical studies.

23.8 Greek for Science   Most of the English borrowings from Greek have taken place since the fifteenth century. In number the words borrowed are not very large, but in importance they rank

[3] Krapp, *Modern English, Its Growth and Present Use, op. cit.,* p. 226.

high, because they include many scientific terms and form the basis for such compounds as *telephone* and *diagram*. One of the latest of these is *geriatrics,* the science of aged persons, and of relatively recent entrance into the language are *psychoanalysis* and *psychiatry.* Terms of rhetoric, medicine, and many other modern sciences come very largely from the Greek.

23.9 Other Sources Besides the sources mentioned, English has enjoyed a trickle of words from Flemish, such as *spool, stripe,* and *tub,* and others said to have been brought in during the fourteenth century by the workmen imported under Edward III. During modern times Low German or Dutch sources have made many contributions, including *trek* and *veld* (South Africa), *monsoon* (Arabic via Dutch), *cockatoo* (Malayan via Dutch . During the modern period also have come musical terms from Italy, geologic terms from Germany, Spanish words of romance and adventure, and at least a few words from every corner of the world, for some native idea or specialty. Even Chinese, which is not a major source, has contributed *tea, pongee, mandarin, ginseng, typhoon,* and of course *chop suey* and *foo-yong.* The dictionary is a monument to the world-wide sources of the English vocabulary, the most cosmopolitan and international speech on earth.

For the Student

A. FURTHER READINGS

Jespersen, *Growth and Structure of the English Language,* 9th edit., pp. 55–148.

McKnight, *English Words and Their Backgrounds,* pp. 99–162.

Krapp, *Modern English, Its Growth and Present Use,* pp. 211–285.

Sheard, *The Words We Use,* pp. 168–330.

Robertson and Cassidy, *The Development of Modern English,* 2nd edit., pp. 146–184.

Baugh, *A History of the English Language,* 2nd edit., 83–126; 200–216; 222–227; 267–275; 364–365.

Bradley, *The Making of English,* pp. 80–110.

Mencken, *The American Language,* 4th edit., pp. 104–121.

Greenough and Kittredge, *Words and Their Ways in English Speech,* pp. 93–109; 128–146; 159–167.

Smith, *The English Language,* pp. 33–62; 154–211, *passim.*

Skeat, *Principles of English Etymology,* Vol. I, pp. 432–442; 453–490.

Emerson, *The History of the English Language,* pp. 125–179.

Johnson, *English Words,* pp. 56–112.

Bloomfield, *Language,* pp. 444–475.

Kennedy, *Current English,* pp. 366–385; 395.

Bentley, *Dictionary of Spanish Terms in English.*

Bense, *A Dictionary of the Low-Dutch Element in the English Vocabulary.*

Carr, Charles T., *The German Influence on the English Vocabulary,* S.P.E. Tract No. XLII (Oxford, Clarendon Press), 1934.

Clark, G. N., *The Dutch Influence on the English Vocabulary,* S.P.E. Tract No. XLIV (Oxford, Clarendon Press), 1935.

Daryush, A. A., *Persian Words in English,* S.P.E. Tract No. XLI (Oxford, Clarendon Press), 1934.

Taylor, Walt, *Arabic Words in English,* S.P.E. Tract No. XXXVIII (Oxford, Clarendon Press), 1933.

Turner, *Africanisms in the Gullah Dialect.*

B. FOR CLASS DISCUSSION

1. What is the origin of the word *English?* Look up its derivation and give its history.
2. From what source come the words most often used? What sources furnish the greatest number of borrowed words?
3. Select a page of modern prose or a column of the newspaper and estimate the proportion of native words to foreign. Count each word every time it occurs.
4. Do the same for fourteen lines of Spenser, of the King James version of the Bible, of Shakespeare, of Milton, of Dr. Johnson, of De Quincey, of Tennyson. Compare the results.
5. What language furnishes the source for most scientific terms? Illustrate.
6. Select ten scientific terms and show how they are made up.
7. Examine the use of classical compounds in the vocabulary of one of the sciences or of philosophy. In the one that you select, what language is used most often? You may be able to secure special word lists, such as *A Glossary for Photography* by Frank Fenner, Jr., and *Source Book of Biological Terms,* by A. L. Melander.

8. Select ten grammatical terms and show from what language they are derived.
9. Select words from the Danish illustrating as many parts of speech as possible.
10. Do the same for Latin and French.
11. When did the English language borrow most from the French? From the Latin?
12. Which of the pronouns come from another language? What is the advantage of these word borrowings?
13. What effect did the Norman Conquest have upon the table? Illustrate. Why are modern menus often written in French?
14. Select ten uncommon words and look up their origins.
15. In a dictionary turn to the supplementary pages which include the very recent words. Classify fifty or more, giving the proportion which falls under each language as a source.
16. Select from your reading five words about which you are uncertain and look up their sources.
17. Make a study of the technical words connected with one of the fine arts. What other languages have been drawn upon?
18. Do you know of any English words that have been borrowed by other languages? What types are they? Have they been changed in any way?
19. Do you know any authors whose extensive use of loan words gives the effect of snobbishness or artificiality?
20. In your community do you know of the use of any borrowed words? From what source do they come? (See M. M. Mathews, *Some Sources of Southernisms,* University, Ala., University of Alabama Press, 1948.)
21. Select ten words connected with fashion and show from what language they are derived.
22. In a page of prose eliminate all loan words and restate with words of Anglo-Saxon origin. Compare the result with the original. What is your conclusion?
23. What is the profit of word borrowing? Is there a loss? (See Sheard, pp. 320–330 and Krapp, pp. 275–285.)

C. SUGGESTIONS FOR RESEARCH PAPERS

1. Malayan (or any other language) Loan Words.
2. Loan Words of Today.
3. Scientific Loan Words.
4. Loan Words in Music (or Art).
5. Select some trade or profession and find the source of the principal words connected with it.

24

Compounding

24.1 Loans Consolidated   Often in studying an English word it is not enough to give the source of the whole or its parts. One must ask further, were these parts put together before or after being borrowed? For example, the word *delicatessen* was a German compound before coming into English, and, on the other hand, *telegraph* consists of two Greek elements put together in English. There is even a term, *mongrel words,* to describe those which, like *television* (Greek and Latin), are put together from diverse languages and hence lack a pure ancestry. A sizable proportion of the foreign borrowings of English consists of word parts rather than words themselves, hybrid combinations, a native root with borrowed affix, as in *graceful, grateful, merciful, outcry, outdistance,* where the foreign word has been combined with the native suffix *-ful* and the native prefix *out-,* or in *dislike, reborn, superhighway,* where the foreign prefixes *dis-, re-,* and *super-* have been joined to the native words *like, born,* and *highway,* respectively.

24.2 Juxtaposition   The foregoing paragraph illustrates one aspect of a method of word formation which is undoubtedly the most common of all methods now in use. It consists merely in putting two or more parts together to make something with an entity of its own, different from its parts. Simple juxtaposition is, and no doubt has been in all ages, the easiest and therefore the most widely used means of word formation. If the student will keep track of the words and phrases he finds coined in current newspapers or in the radio, he will find that the great majority consist of juxtapositions like *check-off, kick-back, frame-up,* and *knock-out,* which has its full form now in the meaning *triumph,* and an initialed form *k-o* (often spelled *kayo*) in its relation to the boxing arena.

24.3 Products of War Many new compoundings entered the language during World War II, beginning with the English adoption of the German term *Blitzkrieg,* often shortened to *blitz,* and continuing on through the onomatopoetic but terrible *buzz-bomb* in the later stages of it. An airplane that flew low in special military operations was a *hedge-hopper,* and one that swooped down to fire a machine gun at troops or civilians along the roads was engaged in *ground-strafing,* this being a mongrel combination of an English with a German word. Fixed fortifications played but a minor role in the conflict, but the most effective of the stationary defenses was the *pillbox,* which usually was a protective covering for a single big gun.

24.4 More War Terms The World War II term *G.I.* came to be accepted in general usage in referring to an enlisted man. An odd compound was *Seabee,* to denote a member of the United States Navy's Construction Battalion. This compound was formed by spelling out the initials C. B. (Construction Battalion). Perhaps the most unusual, and certainly the most illogical, of the wartime compounds was *near-miss,* to describe a bomb that came close to its intended target but did not strike it. Actually, it was a *near-hit,* but the word goes into the language as *near-miss,* regardless of logic.

24.5 Flights of Fancy Some really fanciful compounds are the creations of the postwar aviation industry in America. It had become a tradition of American transportation that de luxe forms of travel should have de luxe names. The railroads glorified their crack trains in this way, many such names being compounds such as *Pacemaker* and *Trail-blazer.* The *airlines* (a shortening of *airplane lines*) have made some striking additions to this technique. One company called all its big planes *flagships,* although in nautical terminology

there is only one flagship in a fleet. Another aviation concern called
its craft *mainliners,* since it advertised that its route is the "main
line" straight across the continent. Still another firm called its passen-
ger planes *skycruisers* and its freight planes *skyfreighters.* A fourth
company named the first commercial plane to span the Pacific Ocean
the *China Clipper* and the first to span the Atlantic the *Yankee
Clipper* and now calls all of its planes the *Clipper Ships.* Craft that
ascend into the stratosphere, or what earthlings choose to regard as
the stratosphere, were called *strato-liners* or *strato-cruisers,* but are
now called *jet planes* because of the method of propulsion (more
often shortened to *jets*), so named by Sir Frank Whittle. Since jets
have been introduced, we now have the *Jet Clipper Ship,* the *Jet
Liner,* the *El Dorado Superjet,* the *Jet Mainliner,* and the *Astrojet.*
These coined terms exemplify the American zest for the picturesque,
a zest that has been characteristic of usage in this country from earliest times.

24.6 Examples from Railroading   For instance, the portion of
the front of a railroad locomotive that is designed to prevent objects
from getting under the wheels is prosaically called a *plough* by the
British because that is what it looks like, but the Americans call it
by an imaginative compound word *cowcatcher.* Compounding is not
necessarily an imaginative device; sometimes the reverse is true, as,
for example, when the staid British term *crossing-plate* becomes the
more pungent single word *frog* in American railroading. Occasionally, however, the British too concoct a picturesque term, as when
their overseas airline calls its planes *speedbirds.* No involved explanations are needed to account for the graphic American compounds *bobby soxer* and the somewhat more sedate *teen-ager,* terms
that have advanced from "slanguage" to language. They are now
listed in one of the standard dictionaries without even the label
colloquial. Most of the compoundings are self-explanatory unless
they involve a word from a foreign language, as a couple of the wartime terms did, but sometimes a compounding changes markedly
the meaning of the separate terms out of which it has been formed.
Thus, a *brickyard,* a place where bricks are made, is quite different
from a *brick yard,* meaning a yard paved with bricks.

24.7 One Mysterious Compound   Even when a compound is
used in a figurative sense, it is almost always possible to comprehend

the meaning intended and the way that the meaning came about. But the newspaper business uses a term that has baffled even such a pundit as Henry L. Mencken, longtime newspaperman and author of *The American Language* and *The American Language, Supplement One* and *Supplement Two*. The term is the compound *bulldog* to refer to the early (sometimes a predated) edition of a newspaper. Nobody seems to know exactly why such an edition should be so designated, but the theory sometimes advanced is that in the early 1900's a couple of the more sensational New York newspapers were engaged in bitter battle for circulation, and the circulation crews of the papers "fought like bulldogs" to be the first to get the earliest edition of their respective sheets on the newsstands. Some other possibilities are discussed in the "Shop Talk at Thirty" column of *Editor & Publisher* for April 17, 1947, but the matter remains obscure; certainly there is nothing in these early editions themselves that suggests a bulldog.

24.8 Longer Compounds One thing that students of English can be thankful for is that compounding in this language has not gone to the extremes that it has in German, where a single word may be a whole definition, as the World War I term *Maschinengewehrkampfwagen,* literally "machine gun armored car," to which its British inventors of the weapon gave the beautifully simple name *tank*. But once in a while a writer, particularly an American one, will bestow upon the language such a compound as *five-starrer*,[1] to denote our highest ranking generals; or *wide-open-spacer* for one who wants to avoid that shut-in feeling;[1] or a term like *kick-out-behinder*[2] to describe a person who dances in other than the approved ballroom manner. Words like these are exceptional and it is doubtful that they will become permanent parts of the language. As Mencken observes, a compound term often is used in the United States by way of disparagement, as *bonehead, roughneck, killjoy, do-gooder,* and *cheapskate*.[3] There is a fascination in compounds, especially in the carefree manner in which they are created by American colloquial speech,

[1] Allen Walker Read, "The Word Harvest of '45," *The Saturday Review of Literature* (June 29, 1946), p. 41.

[2] Niven Busch, *Duel in the Sun* (Popular Library, Paper Cover Edition, 4th Printing), p. 80.

[3] Henry L. Mencken, *The American Language* (New York, Alfred A. Knopf, 1936), p. 187.

but the important thing for the student to remember is the linguistic principle that underlies the forming of such words.

24.9 Use of Hyphen   One aspect of compounds that is bound to plague any writer of the language is the uncertainty whether to use a hyphen or run the two or more parts together as one word. No instructions can be laid down that would be valid in every case. The old rule of thumb guide is to omit the hyphen when the compound has only two syllables, as *bedroom,* but to insert the hyphen when the word formed contains more than two syllables. But large numbers of the words already in established usage disregard any such rule. For many compound terms, the form to be used depends on individual idiosyncrasy, and even a particular writer may not always be consistent. He might employ the form *living-room* on one occasion, *living room* on another, and even *livingroom* on still a third. This last-named, run-in style along the lines of the German is particularly popular with the author John Dos Passos,[4] who in the course of a few pages of his novel *Number One* offers to his readers such words as *dinnerparties, musclerelaxing, potatopeelin',* *wafflemakin', noaccount, cigarettecase,* and *sourlooking.* This does not, however, appear to be a specific trend in English. Many readers may feel that such a procedure, while it gets rid of the vexatious hyphen question, is a drawback to quick comprehension because of the unfamiliar appearance of the words. The unabridged dictionaries are still the best guide as to what form to use, even though there may be some disagreement among the lexicographers themselves in a particular instance.

24.10 In Old English   The juxtaposition type of compounding to form new words has been common in all periods of English, and has given us many of our shortest and simplest appearing words—*barn, also, alone, window, York, lord, lady, steward,* and *daisy.* Indeed, it is probable that if we could trace back into prehistoric times all present-day monosyllables, it would be found that a majority of them sprang from combinations of words. So far back as we can see, and in all probability from the very dawn of language, men have been making two words into one and then reducing the resulting com-

---

[4] John Dos Passos, *Number One* (Boston, Houghton Mifflin, 1943).

pound into a monosyllable again. It is the basic method of linguistic growth. To take at random one of the examples just given, the word *barn* was a compound of O.E. *bere, barley,* with *ærn, building,* and meant a storage place, or building, for barley—a derivation with agricultural and sociological bearings as well as linguistic. A modern compound of precisely the same sort is *suitcase.*

24.11 Grammar of Compounds It may be of interest to ask, what is the grammar of English compounds? These new formations appear to reflect the general distribution of the parts of speech; nouns are much the most frequent, as they are in the dictionary itself; connectives and adverbs have been numerous in the development of the subordinating and complex principles in English; only verbs have lagged behind, as not lending themselves to the compounding process to the same extent as other parts of speech. Such a verb compound as *We weekended at the Browns'* is a functionally shifted noun, and actual compound verbs such as *to outpoint* are not very frequent. Occasionally one hears a new one coined, as *Can you interuse the tickets on rail and bus?* but this is not frequent.

24.12 Verbs Are Compounded But if conservative linguistic habits do not often originate compounds that function as verbs, it is noticeable that verbs figure in very many compounds, from the child's *tattletale* to the adult's *telltale, livelong,* and *safeguard.* A very common current type is the noun compound formed of the parts of a merged verb, such as *pay-off, kick-back, lock-out, hold-up.*[5] A three-part process is shown in *sit down,* which was first a merged verb, then an adjective with *strike,* and finally a noun in its own right. And a new coinage of this type would be readily understood, as, for instance, *She doesn't discard her clothes but keeps a collection of used-ups and worn-outs.* Notice the plural inflection on the end, indicating the unit character of the compounds.

[5] See A. G. Kennedy, *The Modern English Verb–Adverb Combination* (Stanford, University Press, 1920); Edwin R. Hunter, "Verb + Adverb = Noun," *American Speech* (Vol. XXII, April, 1947), pp. 115–119. For verbs derived from a verb plus a noun, as *air-condition* or *brain-wash,* see Robert A. Hall, Jr., "How We Noun-Incorporate in English," *American Speech* (Vol. XXXI, May, 1956), pp. 83–88. See also Hans Marchand, "Compound and Pseudo-Compound Verbs in Present-Day English," *ibid.* (Vol. XXXII, May, 1957), pp. 83–94.

24.13 Classification It is possible to make an ordered list of compounds on the basis of their grammar as follows, though not all possible combinations would be present.

1. Noun plus noun equals noun: *barn, inkpot, railroad, typewriter, shotgun.*
2. Adjective plus noun equals noun: *blackberry, highway, hothouse, liveoak, bluegrass.* These are very common.
3. Verb plus noun equals noun: *breakfast, scarecrow, makeweight, cookbook, whirlwind.*
4. Verb plus adverb equals noun: examples given in preceding paragraph; also *touchdown, throwback, walkover, runaround, tieup.*
5. Adverb plus verb equals noun: *income, downpour, output, upkeep, undertow, upsurge, undersigned.* These are less modern than the reversed type, but are still actively produced.
6. Noun plus adjective equals adjective: *snow-white, penny-wise, stone-cold, watertight, war-weary.*
7. Adjective plus noun equals adjective: *all-time, all-American, long-time, new-style.*
8. Adverb plus adjective equals adjective: *ever-new, evergreen* (also noun), *worldly wise, outright.*
9. Connective and particle compounds: *into, upon, alongside, notwithstanding, insofar, inasmuch.*
10. Phrase oddities: *hand-me-down, hand-to-mouth, dryasdust, Johnny-come-lately, dead-alive, out-of-date.*

24.14 Compound-Conscious The student who wishes to keep in touch with current progress and get some idea of what is happening in the language at the same time can do nothing better than to keep track of the compounds he reads and hears, analyzing and classifying them in some such way as that suggested above, and recording their manner of use. Such a study will keep him abreast of the newest developments in English, exercise his mind, and offer the possibility of material rewards.

For the Student

A. FURTHER READINGS

Skeat, *Principles of English Etymology*, Vol. I, pp. 414–431.
Bradley, *The Making of English*, pp. 111–128; 133–142.
Krapp, *Modern English, Its Growth and Present Use*, pp. 187–191.
Kennedy, *Current English*, pp. 346–351; 386–388.
Robertson and Cassidy, *The Development of Modern English*, 2nd edit., 191–194; 210–211.
Sheard, *The Words We Use*, pp. 61–69.
Baugh, *A History of the English Language*, 2nd edit., 75–77; 221; 365; 401–403.
Smith, *The English Language*, pp. 81–85.
Hatcher, *Modern English Word-Formation and Neo-Latin, passim.*
Zandvoort, *A Handbook of English Grammar*, 5th edit., pp. 316–328.

B. FOR CLASS DISCUSSION

1. What parts of speech did Keats use in forming *tight-rooted, deep-delved, spectre-thin, leaden-eyed, soft-lifted, soft-dying, palsy-twitched, far-heard, deep-damasked, dew-dabbled, full-throated?* Analyze Tennyson's compounds: *evil-starred, green-glimmering, fire-crowned, many-towered, silken-sailed, thick-jewelled, saddle-leather, white-breasted.*
2. Name six compound words, such as *delicatessen,* taken bodily from other languages. Show how they were formed.
3. What departments of modern life frequently need new words? Illustrate.
4. Name ten brands of commercial products that use compound words to describe them. What parts of speech are they likely to use?
5. Bring in three more illustrations for each class in par. 13 and analyze them.
6. Can you find compound words to illustrate all possible combinations of parts of speech, such as verb + verb = adjective, as in *wishy-washy?* Make as many classifications as you can to supplement those in par. 13.
7. Read an article in a current magazine and see how many compound words you find. From what parts of speech are they formed?

8. Examine the advertisements in a magazine and see how many make use of compound words. Analyze each.

9. Can you figure out what words originally formed the following place names? *Indianapolis, Stanton, San Francisco, Middleton, Northfield, Nashville, Washington, Portland, Charleston.* Can you think of additional examples using other languages?

10. Collect examples of the compounding of words in *Thomas Hardy's The Dynasts* and analyze each.

11. Analyze *forget-me-nots, manhole, would-be, armchair, four-in-hand, rosebush, merry-go-round.*

12. If you need more practice in compounds, select any reading matter about you and find the compounds and then analyze them.

C. SUGGESTIONS FOR RESEARCH PAPERS

1. Compoundings in Old (Middle, Modern) English.
2. Consolidated Loan Words (such as *delicatessen*, par. 1).
3. Monosyllables from Compounds.
4. Compound Verbs.
5. Compounds in Advertising (or any other trade or profession).
6. Scientific Compounds.
7. A study may be made of any one of the ten classifications mentioned in par. 13.

25

Formation by Affixes

25.1 Dictionary Practice It is the plan of all good modern dictionaries to list not only words but also those parts of words to which linguists have given the names *sememe* (*meaning unit*) and *lexeme* (*dictionary unit*). Thus you will find in the dictionary not only *able* but *-able*, the latter being the suffix which appears in *debatable, practicable, countable,* etc. You will also find prefixes such as the *dis-* of *dislike, distaste, disfavor.* This *dis-* has a clear meaning of *the absence of,* and *-able* means much the same as *able* itself.

25.2 Formed Words The examples just given illustrate what is probably next to compounding the most common method of making new words—the addition of one or more affixes, with a consequent change in meaning or function or both. The process of making formed words is not unlike inflection; it covers the *-ly* which turns an adjective into an adverb (*new, newly*) and may be added to some adjectives such as *good* and *kind* (*goodly, kindly*) without any change in function.

25.3 Other Extreme But if at one extreme formed words are like inflected words, at the other extreme they are almost indis-

tinguishable from compounds. Is the *out-* of *outnumber* a word or a
formative element? There are a great many prefixes (*out-, in-, over-,
ever-,* etc.) which are in form exactly like words; and to determine
whether *incapable, overbearing,* and *everlasting* are or are not compounds is a hard problem.

25.4 History of Formatives   Many formative affixes have worn
down to their present state from full words. This is true of *-ly,* which
even as late as Old English had status as the word *like,* and indeed
is the forerunner of our present word *like,* which is used in compounds such as *lifelike* very much as it was in Old English. The
suffix *-dom* (*kingdom, freedom*) was in Old English a full word
dōm, from which comes our Modern English word *doom.* There is
every similarity, from the historical aspect, between the compounding and the forming of words.

25.5 Living Affixes   Two words with affixes that are very much
in use are *prenatal* and *postnatal.* They are employed with reference
to the care given to mothers before and after the birth of a child.
We also speak of *preschool* age, *precollege, premedical, prelaw,
prevocational, prewar.* Interestingly enough, however, the pre-Civil
War era is often given the Latin designation *ante-bellum.* As we
freely employ *pre-,* in the same way we use *post-* in such words as
postwar, postimpressionists in art, *postoperative, post-Renaissance,
postconvention.* We may likewise buy a car from a *supersalesman,*
ride on a *superhighway,* and park in a *superlot,* trade at a *super-
market,* or look forward to a trip in a *supersonic plane.* We *defrost* a
refrigerator, *de-ice* the wings of a plane, or *deflate* the currency. We
may have a *subdean,* a *subprincipal,* a *subchairman,* or a *subdebu-
tante.* We may be a *co-actor,* a *co-equal,* a *co-executor,* a *co-heir,* a
co-chairman, make use of a *coaxial cable,* or *coexist.*

Not all English affixes are today living, in the sense that they can
be freely applied to new words. Thus the suffix *-hood* (*hardihood,
manhood, childhood*) could scarcely be attached to a recent word
such as *draftee.* The prefix *pre-* (*before*) is living in that it may be
attached to words so as to make novelties like *pre-Pearl Harbor* and
pre-social security. Among living prefixes may be mentioned *un-,
post-, pre-, anti-, co-, sub-, super-, de-, quasi-,* and *re-;* among living
suffixes, *-ist, -ism, -ize, -ness, -by,* and perhaps *-ish* and *-y.*

25.6 A Diminutive   The last example is interesting because it is one of the few remaining English diminutives. Jespersen calls attention to the English lack of diminutives as compared to Russian, German, and other languages,[1] and he uses the fact to reinforce his thesis that English is a masculine language, since it scorns the "little words" of tenderness and dalliance which appear so freely in the Slavic dialects, for instance. A few diminutives such as *-el* in *kernel* (*little corn*), *-ette* in *cigarette* (*little cigar*) and *luncheonette* (*little lunch*), and *-kin* in *manikin* and *lambkin* survive in English, but diminutives in general are not encouraged. Even *-y* has only a restricted use in Modern English, and many a child who endures being called *Jacky* or *Johnny* in early life insists on *Jack* or *John* later on.

25.7 Classical Formatives   As with compounds (par. 24.1) formed words may be originated within English (*pro-British, pro-Axis*) or they may be taken over from some other language as loan words. Thus *profane*, which looks somewhat like the examples just given, is really very different in meaning and in origin, having had its parts joined together while it was still a Latin word. Very many of our English formed words derive thus from Latin, affix and all. Examples are *generator, transfusion, transition, procurator, reciprocate, recede, prosecutor, subsist.*

25.8 Accommodation   The classical derivatives, as well as formations originating in English, often show a change in sound, spelling, or both, designed to accommodate the affix to the main part of the word. It is a study in itself to understand the phonology of *impossible, affix, annex, irresistible, wholly, companion,* and other similar combinations, and such a study will help to constitute a review of the second part of this textbook for any student who needs it. To analyze just one of the examples given, the *m* of *im-* obviously fits better with the *p* of *possible* than would *n*, since *n* is a point nasal while *m* and *p* are both lip sounds; and this accommodation has accordingly taken place not only in *impossible* but in *impatient, impair, impress,* and other words.

25.9 Formative Groups   The number of formative affixes, living and dead, native and foreign, which are to be found in English words, is very large; Nesfield lists 52 prefixes besides a number of disguised ones, 56 noun-forming, 33 adjective-forming, and 6 verb-

[1] Otto Jespersen, *Growth and Structure of the English Language,* 8th edit. (Leipzig, B. G. Teubner, 1935), p. 9.

forming suffixes from the Romanic languages alone.[2] And this fact has brought it about that English contains large groups or families of words all coming from a single root idea but differentiated by the addition of one or more formative affixes. One of the more interesting of these is the family built on the Latin verb *portō, portāre, portāvī, portātum,* meaning *I carry. Porter* is an obvious and simple derivative, as is *portable,* now used as a noun to name a typewriter which can be carried easily. *Portfolio* is more a compound than a formed word, used to name a case to carry *(port)* leaves *(folio)* of paper. But then we have *import, export, deport,* with all their changes such as *deportable, deportation, undeported,* and even a possible *anti-deportationist* to join no fewer than five affixes to the original *portō.* Altogether several dozen formations could be counted, traceable to this single Latin verb.

For the Student

A. FURTHER READINGS

Sheard, *The Words We Use,* pp. 51–61.

Robertson and Cassidy, *The Development of Modern English,* 2nd edit., pp. 194–202.

Baugh, *A History of the English Language,* 2nd edit., 74–77; 218–221; 366–367.

Bradley, *The Making of English,* pp. 133–141.

McKnight, *English Words and Their Background,* pp. 171–176.

Kennedy, *Current English,* pp. 335–346.

Greenough and Kittredge, *Words and Their Ways in English Speech,* pp. 185–192.

Jespersen, *Growth and Structure of the English Language,* 9th edit., 151–152.

Krapp, *Modern English, Its Growth and Present Use,* pp. 191–193.

Mencken, *American Language,* 4th edit., pp. 176–181.

Zandvoort, *A Handbook of English Grammar,* pp. 329–361.

[2] J. C. Nesfield, *English Grammar Past and Present* (London, Macmillan & Company, Ltd., 1924), pp. 391–408.

B. FOR CLASS DISCUSSION

1. What is meant by a sememe and a lexeme?
2. Look up in Webster or in the *Oxford Dictionary* the meanings of the following prefixes and suffixes. Then form two words from each of them and tell what part or parts of speech the result is.

PREFIXES

arch-	for-	retro-
by-	fore-	subter-
circum-	omni-	tri-
counter-	on-	ultra-

SUFFIXES

-age	-fold	-most
-ance	-ice	-ory
-craft	-let	-ship
-ee	-ment	-y

3. List a dozen other prefixes and a dozen other suffixes besides those mentioned in the chapter or in Question 2. Form two words with each.
4. Name a dozen living affixes. Form two words with each one and use each word in a sentence.
5. How many diminutives can you list in English? Illustrate each one.
6. List a dozen words in which the affix has accommodated itself to the main part of the word. Explain what has happened in each case.
7. By adding prefixes and suffixes, build up as many derivatives as you can from the following head-words. It will frequently be necessary to change the vowel of a stem, as in *exemplify* from *example,* and a consonant as in *derision* from *deride.* Try to think of nouns, verbs, adjectives, and adverbs.

pathos	critic	act
slave	decide	compare
modern	civil	prefer
lucid	long	facile
repair	heart	authentic

8. Make verbs from the following words by adding a suffix:

material	ample
code	captive
satire	person

9. Make adjectives from the following words by adding a suffix:

tragedy	ethics	fascism
norm	poet	luxury
elegy	autumn	monogamy
nucleus	tyranny	tempest

10. By adding suffixes, make nouns from the following words, denoting "one who."

auction	object	royal
machine	claim	medieval
profit	oppose	drunk
drug	audit	antique

11. In the following words, point out each affix and give the meaning of it. Verify by the dictionary.

inaudible	congregation
revolutionary	supernatural
irrelevant	nonnegotiable
intramural	introspection
unequivocal	hypersensitive

12. Form the negative from the following words by adding a prefix:

legal	symmetric
obey	sincere
constitutional	content

13. Form two words containing the following. Look up the meaning and source of each.

anthropo-	mono-
auto-	neo-
bene-	omni-
gram-	phil-
graph-	poly-
log-	pseudo-
mal-	semi-

14. From the following roots form as many words as you can by adding affixes:

cred- (to believe)   fid- (to trust)
tract- (to draw)   fin- (boundary)
cord- (heart)   mort- (death)
nomin- (name)   spec- (to look)

15. What did Carlyle do in creating such words as *croakery, Bedlamism, grumbly, dandiacal, gigmanity;* Browning in making *crumblement, garnishry, darlingness;* Scott in coining *outcome?*
16. Analyze all the derived forms occurring in an editorial in your daily newspaper. Select all the prefixes and suffixes and show how the word was formed.
17. What are some of the recent suffixes that have been used? Give illustrations. See Mencken, *American Language,* 4th edit., pp. 176–181.

C. SUGGESTIONS FOR RESEARCH PAPERS

1. A Study of *pre-* (or any prefix or suffix).
2. Verbs (or any other part of speech) Formed by Prefixes.
3. History of the Living Affixes (or any others).
4. Diminutives in English.
5. Accommodation of Affixes to the Main Part of the Word.

26

Imagery and
Functional Shift

26.1 Language Is Poetry   In their classic work, *Words and Their Ways in English Speech,* Greenough and Kittredge devote a chapter to proving that language is poetry; and in a later work by Mc-Knight, *English Words and Their Background,* the statement of Emerson that words are fossilized poetry is quoted. What these statements mean is that under the surface of the most commonplace-appearing word will often shine some flash of imagery, some bold metaphor, which is of the nature of the poetic art. Images, figures of speech, are of the very stuff of poetry; and word-creation is rich in these.

26.2 Different Approach   In speaking of imagery as a source of words, however, one is approaching the general question from a new angle, since poetic creation may result in compounds, formed words, or simple monosyllables. Here the *why* rather than the *how* of creation is considered. Thus when the phrase *the day's eye* became the simple modern word *daisy,* it was a compound to be sure, and it was also a poetic creation. The image in *daisy* is now fossilized; it was plain to Chaucer, who nearly six centuries ago took delight in this common flower.

26.3 Often Fossilized Poetic imagery in a word is often obscured by the passage of time. This is true of the formed word *recalcitrant,* whose meaning, *balky* or *stubborn,* does not suggest the bold metaphor the word originally held. It derives first from the Latin *calx,* meaning *heel,* a word which developed a verb form *calcitro, I kick.* Adding the prefix *re-* (*back* or *again*) and the adjective ending (present participle) *-ant,* the word *recalcitrant* was formed. Its basic meaning is thus the same as the slang word *kick* in such a sentence as *You've got no kick coming.* Yet *recalcitrant* is not slang but a good literary word.

26.4 Metaphors Common Such metaphors are exceedingly common and can be seen in the creation of a sizable portion of the English vocabulary. Later abstract ideas have developed out of earlier concrete and vivid ones. *Daisy* is only one of a whole group of flower names of this sort, and in some of them—*bleeding-heart, Jack-in-the-pulpit, Indian pipe, lady's slipper, maiden-hair*—we may still see this figure clearly stated. Sometimes a word may retain both the literal and the figurative meaning, as in *ship* (literally, *any large seagoing vessel*), which has taken on a symbolical meaning referring to "one's fortune or affairs," as when "one's ship comes in," a common expression.

War exemplifies the poetic power of a language and the vivid imagery that is called into play by fertile minds. In World War II aircraft carriers, devoid of almost all superstructure to provide landing areas for planes, soon acquired the nickname *flattop,* and a small aircraft carrier became a *baby flattop.* Destroyers, which are the most unstable of surface ships, became known as *tin cans,* and torpedoes, for obvious reasons, as *tin fish.* A battleship was often referred to, a bit grandiloquently, as a *battle-wagon,* though no one could explain what a *wagon* would be doing at sea.

26.5 Slang Is Poetry One of the unappreciated uses of linguistic imagery is the creation of slang,[1] which is ordinarily a bold and met-

---

[1] A few of the many sources for slang may be mentioned. Numerous articles dealing with the conversation of the prisoner, the racketeer, the soldier, the student, etc., as well as with American slang in general, may be found in *American Speech,* the *Publications of the American Dialect Society,* and in *Dialect Notes.* Larger collections are: John S. Farmer and W. E. Henley, *Dictionary of Slang and Colloquial English,* abridged from the 7-vol. work *Slang and Its Analogues* (New York, E. P. Dutton, 1905; 1 vol. edit., 1929); Godfrey Irwin, *American Tramp and Underworld Slang* (New York, Oxford University Press,

aphoric presentation of an idea in which there is a marked contrast
between the literal and figurative meanings of the word. Such an
expression as *beat it,* current some years ago, and raised into re-
spectability as the noun *beat,* the territory of a policeman, brings up
a clear picture of feet pounding against stone. Then came the usage
of *beat* in *beat generation, beatnik,* etc. There is no lack of poetry in
slang; the difficulty is that the poetry is ephemeral; the slang expression is created, circulates feverishly for a time, and then goes completely out of fashion. Slang is overused and then underused; its
transitory character is its chief limitation.

26.6 Poetic Language   In contrast to slang, poetry is not only
conservative but might almost be called reactionary, in that it tends
to preserve archaisms such as *thou, o'er, orb,* and *maiden.* Modern
poetry, to be sure, has to a degree avoided the archaic, but it has
fallen into a practice of using current words with outworn meanings.
Examples given by Margaret Schlauch in *The Gift of Language* include *express* as meaning *to press out, conjugate* as *to put a yoke on,*
and *intent* to indicate something taut and stretched for action. It may
be questioned whether this use of words tends to make poetry more
universal or democratic or to convert it into a sort of linguistic rebus
which one must study in order to find the key.

26.7 Functional Shift   A happier expedient than the use of discarded meanings by modern writers would appear to be functional
shift (see pars. 38.7–8), which also figures largely in the creation of
words and has been a source of fine poetic effects in the work of our
greatest poets, including Shakespeare and Keats. Since poetry may
frequently be called "double talk," that is, saying one thing in terms
of another, a poetic image, the change in word usage which is called
functional shift would appear to have its merits.

26.8 Nouns from Adjectives   But our subject is word formation
rather than poetics; and just as it was shown in par. 24.13 how adjec-

---

1931); H. N. Rose, *A Thesaurus of Slang* (New York, Macmillan Company,
1934; Maurice H. Weseen, *Dictionary of American Slang* (New York, Thomas
Y. Crowell Company, 1934); Eric Partridge, *A Dictionary of Slang and Uncon-
ventional English* (New York, Macmillan Company, 1937); Lester V. Berrey
and Melvin Van den Bark, *The American Thesaurus of Slang* (New York,
Thomas Y. Crowell Company, 1942); Harold Wentworth and Stuart Berg
Flexner, *Dictionary of American Slang* (New York, Thomas Y. Crowell Company, 1960).

tives might be compounded to form nouns, so now it will be shown how adjectives, through being used as nouns, acquire noun standing and noun meaning, thus becoming virtually new English words. A first example may be *blue,* which has not only become a noun in the singular to name the heavens, but in the plural is the name for a popular mood (formerly *the blue devils*) as well as a popular type of music. This versatile adjective has quadrupled itself through adding three noun meanings to its own.

26.9 Other Examples   Many other new nouns have been formed from adjectives by functional shift. A *green* is a spot on a golf course or in a village, while the noun *pink* is used in some localities to name a flower. *Pink,* with a capital, is used in political slang—usually preceded by the word *Parlor*—to denote a rather insipid radical, as contrasted with a *Red,* a radical of the violent or militant type. Then there is *white,* as in the *whites* of the eye. The *main* is well established as a name for the ocean and for certain pipes, while a *natural,* which used to indicate a simpleton, is now a slang term of strong admiration, denoting a successful production or a person with a special gift. The word *editorial* has so long been accepted as a noun that most people have forgotten the former purist demand that *editorial article* be used instead. British usage, however, does not include *editorial* in this sense. A British *editorial* is called a *leader.*

26.10 Other Shifts   Nouns have also been made out of verbs through functional shift;[2] an easy instance is the British *lift,* corresponding to the American *elevator.* The word *rule* is well accepted as a noun meaning *sway,* which itself is also derived from a verb; and *rule* for a measuring stick is probably as common as *ruler.* The *yield* or *produce* of a field is an equivalent for its *crop,* also a verbnoun of earlier date.

From these illustrations it becomes manifest that language is much less rigid than students realize when they study the pigeonholes called parts of speech, into which words are usually put so neatly. Functional shift plays an important role in the fluidity of our mother tongue.

[2] For uses of nouns as verbs, see Manuel Prenner, "The Current Tendency Toward Denominative Verbs," *American Speech* (Vol. XIII, 1938), pp. 193–196.

For the Student

A. FURTHER READINGS

Krapp, *Modern English, Its Growth and Present Use,* pp. 193–211.
Robertson and Cassidy, *The Development of Modern English,* 2nd edit., pp. 205–211.
Kennedy, Current English, pp. 119; 301; 313; 316–322; 357–359; 426–428; 612.
Greenough and Kittredge, *Words and Their Ways in English Speech,* pp. 7–18; 55–79.
Jespersen, *Growth and Structure of the English Language,* 9th edit., pp. 152–159.
Weekley, *The Romance of Words,* 4th edit., pp. 105–112.
Schlauch, *The Gift of Language,* pp. 230–235; 251–252.
Johnson, *English Words,* pp. 118–122; 127–128.
Baugh, *A History of the English Language,* 2nd edit., pp. 376–378.
Lee, *Functional Change in Early English.*
Zandvoort, *A Handbook of English Grammar,* 5th edit., pp. 302–315.

B. FOR CLASS DISCUSSION

1. Analyze the following adjectives. From what parts of speech are they formed?

battered-up	wearing-down (process)
broken-down	long-drawn-out
closing-out (sale)	played-out
coming-out (party)	

2. Make a list of your own and analyze each one.
3. Analyze the following nouns. From what parts of speech are they formed?

cleanup	writeup	income
dugout	thinning-out	downfall
gadabout	popovers	intake
holdup	leftovers	outlet
Passover	runabouts	upturn
send-off	hangers-on	thoroughfare
offset	overthrow	two-year-olds
hand-me-downs	smashup	washout
turnout	output	

4. Make a list of others and analyze each one.
5. Can you make two sentences of the following: (1) in which adverbs become verbs; (2) in which adverbs become nouns; (3) in which prepositions become adjectives; (4) in which adverbs become adjectives; (5) in which adjectives become verbs; (6) in which nouns become verbs; (7) in which verbs become nouns; (8) in which adjectives become nouns; (9) in which nouns become adjectives?
6. Can you explain the poetry of these slang expressions: *bird, peach, off his nut, cracked, fire, bounce, grafter, chiseler?* Make a list of your own and explain the poetry of each expression.
7. What functional shift is found in the following poetic phrases: Shakespeare's "sicklied o'er with the pale cast of thought"; "violenteth in a sense as strong"; "Lord Angelo dukes it well"; Tennyson's "diamond me no diamonds"; Keats' "Lethewards had sunk"; Joyce's "hitherand-thithering waters"; Cummings' "the feline she"; Masefield's "wash-deck buckets"; Pound's "ivory-sandaled"; "the lights . . . are pearled"; Lindsay's "bronze-brown wing"; Frost's "harp-like morning-glory strings"; Hardy's "all-enacting Might"; "thy too-forced pleasantry."
8. Collect ten examples of functional shift from Keats and from Shakespeare.
9. Read a poem in a current magazine and see how many instances of functional shift you can find.
10. Can you name other metaphors used for the names of things, similar to the ones mentioned in par. 4? Analyze each one.

C. SUGGESTIONS FOR RESEARCH PAPERS

1. Imagery as a Source of Words in Shakespeare (or any other author).
2. Metaphors in Tennyson (or any other author).
3. The Poetry of Slang.
4. Archaisms in Poetry.
5. Functional Shift in Keats (or any other author).
6. Adjectives as Nouns.
7. Nouns as Verbs.
8. Verbs as Nouns.

27

Formation by
Other Methods

27.1 Back-Formation A process the reverse of the use of formative elements has given us a handful of new words. The peculiarity of this method, named by Sir James Murray *back-formation*, is that the source words must look as if they carried inflections or formative elements. A stock example is *editor*, which is not *edit* with *-or* added, though it looks so. From *editor* has been formed the verb *to edit*, which after a slight struggle was accepted in the English language. Then there is *enthusiasm*, which has given rise to the verb *enthuse*, a verb which has had a harder struggle than *edit*; in fact, some writers avoid it today.

27.2 Mistaken for Plural Most English back-formations come from words ending with *s* which were singular but have been mistaken for plurals, or from words ending with what looked like the agent-suffix *-er*. *Edit* from *editor* is an example of the second, as are *beg* from *beggar*, *rove* from *rover*, *hawk* from *hawker*, and the sometimes heard *butch*, *burgle*, and *buttle* from *butcher*, *burglar*, and *butler*. An example of the plural error is *sherry*, which to Shake-

speare's Falstaff was *sherris sack;* when the second word was
dropped, *sherris* looked like a plural and so the *s* was dropped, giving *sherry*.[1] Other like instances are *asset, cherry, pea, bridle, riddle.*
And other words formed by the same method are *swashbuckle,
peeve, grovel, to sunburn, vamp, jell, launder,* and *to henpeck.* Notice
that some of these such as *vamp* are really new words, while others
such as *cherry* are merely changed forms of old words.

27.3 Words from Initials A source of new words of very minor
but perhaps growing importance consists of the initials or initial syllables of words. This was probably first used in connection with
commercial trade names, many of which are formed on this plan, as
Socony for Standard Oil Company of New York. But in World War I
people in England began to speak of the Defense of the Realm Act
as *DORA,* and of soldiers of the Australian and New Zealand Army
Corps as *Anzacs.* Later, in this country, *NIRA* enjoyed a brief existence as the name of the National Industrial Recovery Act, enforced
by the better known NRA, the National Recovery Administration.
Likewise there seems to be some use of *Ascap* to designate the American Society of Composers, Authors, and Publishers, and *Aftera* to
refer to the American Federation of Television and Radio Artists.
Also, the Government took care, in forming women's groups in the
armed forces, to have abbreviations that could be used as words:
WAC, WAVE, SPAR. Then there is *SHAEF* (Supreme Headquarters
of Allied Expeditionary Force) and *FIDO* (Fog Investigation Dis-
persal Operation), a British device for clearing fog from airfields by
burning large quantities of oil. Another interesting word that has
been made is the one designating the Cooperative Agency for the
Relief of Europe—*CARE.* Probably the most famous of these initial
words is *Gestapo* (*Geheime Staats-Polizei*) originating with the German secret police, but now applying to a secret police in any dic-
tatorship. Three other words that have become a part of the language are *radar, loran,* and *shoran. Radar* was coined in the United
States from "radio direction and ranging." [2] It has come into general
use even in England, where it was first called "radio location." Simi-

---

[1] It should be remarked also that the French pronunciation of *sherris* would
not sound the *s.*

[2] *Encyclopaedia Britannica's Book of the Year,* 1946, pp. 617–618.

larly, *loran* was made from the words "long range navigation" and *shoran* from "short range navigation." Loran and shoran are used to determine the geographical position of a ship or aircraft.

The "alphabet agencies" were one of the outstanding features of the New Deal under President Franklin D. Roosevelt though there were such prior to his administration, notably the *ICC* (Interstate Commerce Commission) and the *RFC* (Reconstruction Finance Corporation). But the idea proliferated so rapidly in the early 1930's that often one set of initials stood for two or more things: for example, *CCC* meant Civilian Conservation Corps and also Commodity Credit Corporation, another governmental bureau, and *AAA* could refer to either the Agricultural Adjustment Act or to the private motor club known as the American Automobile Association. And millions of Americans never did learn the distinction between *PWA* (Public Works Administration) and *WPA* (Works Progress, later renamed Projects, Administration). These combinations of initials do not, of course, make words, but *CAB* (Civil Aeronautics Board) does.

Perhaps the most interesting aspect of this discussion of initials, however, is its relationhip to the United Nations. Originally, the press used the abbreviation *UNO,* on the assumption that the formal name of the world body was United Nations Organization. Later the word went forth officially that the actual name was United Nations, only that and nothing more. The press then had to make its abbreviation UN, an awkward situation, to say the least. Even though UN is a prefix in English that is negative in its implications, as in *UNsuccessful, UNfortunate, UNjust, UNfriendly,* nevertheless, it is UN, despite the fact that UNO would look more like a real word and, symbolically, could be regarded as a form of the Latin *unus,* meaning *one,* thus conveying the idea of One World, an inspiring acronym.

Another reason for preferring UNO was advanced in the *American Esperantist* for September-October, 1946, which observed (p. 104) that UNO would be the proper form in Esperanto, since all nouns end in *-o* and since "in all probability in another generation or two the vast majority of the people of the world will speak Esperanto and refer to the United Nations as UNO." This, however, was mere wishful thinking. According to most linguists, little hope exists for the general adoption of Esperanto or any other artificial world language in the predictable future.

An interesting combination of letters that has already become a household byword is *DDT*. It is a chemical discovered by the Army Chemical Corps called dichloro-diphenyl-trichloroethane.

Military exigencies gave birth to many odd combinations of initials in World War II (*ETO* for European Theater of Operations, for instance, as one of the simplest), but it is doubtful that many of them were pronounced as words, and most of them have passed into discard or will soon. However, one bit of Army slang that showed the service man's derisive cynicism toward military inefficiency in general may be found in the acronymic word *SNAFU*, said to be an abbreviation of Situation Normal, All Fouled Up.

The Navy deliberately set out to make words that could be pronounced, so as to save time in speaking, as well as in writing. For instance, *CINCLANT* stands for Commander in Chief, United States Atlantic Fleet. One jaw-breaker which the Navy coined was *COMPHIBTRALANT*, standing for Commander Amphibious Training Command, United States Atlantic Fleet. These words are formed from first or significant letters or syllables. It is needless to say that these words were current only in official Navy circles.

Probably the best known example of all is *OK*, sometimes phonetically respelled *okay*, standing for "Oll Korrect" or "Old Kinderhook." [3]

27.4 Words by Onomatopoeia If initial words are few and recent, the next group to be considered is old and extensive, yet still being augmented by new creations. These are, as the Greek term says, *onomatopoetic* or "name-making," that is, "self-made" words; an alternative name in recent writings is *echoic*, because they echo the sound they name. Among their very large number are *hiss, fizz, sizzle, giggle, burn, cock-a-doodle-doo, bow-wow, slip-slop.* Such imitative words are always vivid and expressive, and the process is responsible for a great many dictionary listings.

[3] See M. M. Mathew's *Dictionary of Americanisms* (Chicago, University of Chicago Press, 1951) and the references to Allen Walker Read's research on this question. For the latest evidence on this word, Favoring "Oll Korrect," see Ralph T. Eubanks, "The Basic Derivation of 'O.K.,'" *American Speech* (Vol. XXXV, October, 1960), pp. 188–192.

Armed combat gives rise to many such "echoic" words which are thought of as representing certain battle sounds or conditions. From the Boer War comes *pom-pom,* which took a new lease on life when naval vessels in World War II installed *pom-pom* guns to stave off attacks by aircraft. In World War I, *whizz-bang* was supposed to "echo" the sound made by a particular type of shell, and World War II produced *ack-ack,* presumably portraying the sounds of anti-aircraft guns, which became known as *ack-ack* guns.

27.5 People and Places   Poetic transference of ideas is notice-able in the next group of words to be considered, the small but inter-esting number of words which have been made from the names of people or places. From saying *He is like Napoleon* or *That is China ware,* people get to using the term direct: *He is a Napoleon of in-dustry,* or *These dishes are china.* One of the most common words in this industrial age, *sandwich,* was named for no less a personage than John Montagu, the Fourth Earl of Sandwich, who enjoyed this type of snack in the eighteenth century. Note also the names of sci-entists used later as common nouns of measuring units in electricity: *ampere* from the French scientist, A. M. Ampere; *watt* from James Watt, the English scientist. This method of making words out of names is of long standing as can be seen from *simony,*[4] which harks back to Middle English as a term for the purchase of church employ-ment, and *palace,* which is a faint echo of the Palatine Hill in an-cient Rome, with its stately buildings. Others in this group are *to hector, pander, dunce, meander, babel, maudlin, tawdry.*

27.6 The Portmanteau   This term as a humorous description of a humorous group, originated not with a linguist but with the mathe-matician-poet Lewis Carroll, who explained in *Through the Look-ing-Glass* that he had created words such as *chortle* and *galumph* by fitting words into one as clothes are fitted into a portmanteau or traveling bag. *Chortle,* from *chuckle* and *snort,* is in general use and bids fair to be a permanent part of humorous English. And then there are *slanguage* (*slang-language*), *insinuendo* (*insinuate-innu-*

---

[4] The word is derived from the name of a Samaritan sorcerer (Simon Magus) who was converted by Philip (see *Acts* 8:9–24) and was severely re-buked by Peter for offering money to purchase the power of giving the Holy Ghost.

endo), brunch (breakfast-lunch), and numerous others, originally for comic effect and hence limited in their general usefulness. The gossip columnists of newspapers are particularly fertile in this sort of word coining, notably Walter Winchell with *infanticipate* for *expect a baby* and *Renovate* for *obtain a divorce in Reno, Nevada*. Earl Wilson, writer for the *New York Post*, cynically suggested that useless talk be called *Congressation (Congress* and *conversation*). One of the most amusing of portmanteau words is *globaloney (global* and *baloney)* used derisively by former Representative Clare Boothe Luce to ridicule the "one world" concept of international affairs in the postwar world, held by Henry A. Wallace, vice president at the time, and others opposed to isolationism in the United States.[5]

27.7 Blends   Instead of *portmanteau words*, linguists call many of these words which have been telescoped into one blends.[6] Examples are *twirl, slide, flurry, flush, electrocute, dumbfound, scurry, splatter, flounder* (verb), *boost, blurt, flaunt, foist, grumble, squash. Travelogue* is given as a recent example. Probably the best plan is to keep serious blends of this sort separate from the portmanteau words, which are witticisms.

Mencken, in his *Supplement One*,[7] lists several blends, including *Hobohemia (hobo* and *Bohemia), Aframerican (Africa* and *American)* to designate a Negro, *Hoovercrat* (a democrat who voted for Hoover in the 1928 presidential election), *refugew (refugee and Jew), sneet (snow* and *sleet), sportcast (sport* and *broadcast),* and *radiotrician (radio* and *electrician)*.

In this connection could likewise be cited the instance found in the *New York Herald Tribune* supplement, "Books," for May 18, 1947, page 7: the word *nucleonics*. Since the discovery of the atomic bomb, the world has reverberated with explanations of the *nucleus* of the atom. Also, developments in advanced electricity have been generally referred to as *electronics*. *Nucleonics* is a word coinage from *nucleus* and *electronics* to designate developments in the field

[5] For other examples, see Robert Withington, "More 'Portmanteau' Coinages," *American Speech* (Vol. VII, February, 1932), pp. 200–203.

[6] See Louise Pound, *Blends: Their Relation to English Word Formation* (Heidelberg, Carl Winter, 1914).

[7] Henry L. Mencken, *The American Language, Supplement I* (New York, Alfred A. Knopf, 1945), p. 326.

of nuclear science.[8] It has become a part of scientific terminology, referring to that branch of physical science which deals with all phenomena of the nucleus. This field has produced a host of new words. Other recent blends are *astronaut, audiophile, cosmonaut, heliport, simulcast, teleprompter, telethon* and *transistor*, among the many that may be mentioned.

27.8 Dictionary Citations   In addition to these varied processes by which new words come into being, there are now and then individual word creations by individual men and women. Mainly these are scientific, such as the blend *nucleonics* cited, and *periodicity*, coined on a French model by the astronomer Herschel in 1833. Sometimes they are the invention of a well-known person, as George Eastman's *kodak* and Bernard Shaw's *superman*. But most often such new words are formed by a man unknown to fame as, for example, *cyclone*, introduced in 1848 by H. Piddington.[9] To have even one entry in the dictionary to their credit is an honor few men have achieved, although without doubt such creations have been made by numberless individuals whose contribution was never recorded. The periodical *American Speech* has a regular department conducted by I. Willis Russell, entitled "Among New Words" and an annual list appears in the *Britannia Book of the Year*.

For the Student

A. FURTHER READINGS

Robertson and Cassidy, *The Development of Modern English*, 2nd edit., pp. 186–189; 202–204; 211–215.
McKnight, *English Words and Their Background*, pp. 163–166; 177–178.
Sheard, *The Words We Use*, pp. 41–45; 69–90.
Kennedy, *Current English*, pp. 351–356.

[8] For other expressions and coinages in the field, see E. N. Lockard, "Fertile Virgins and Fissile Breeders: Nuclear Neologisms," *American Speech* (Vol. XXV, February, 1950), pp. 23–27.

[9] See G. H. McKnight, *English Words and Their Background, op. cit.*, p. 179.

Greenough and Kittredge, *Words and Their Ways in English Speech*, pp. 16; 155; 372–389.

Bradley, *The Making of English*, pp. 142–147.

Baugh, *A History of the English Language*, 2nd edit., pp. 367–370.

Schlauch, *The Gift of Language*, pp. 103–104.

Pound, "Word Coinage and Modern Trade Names," *Dialect Notes* (January, 1914).

Wentworth, *Blend-Words in English* (abstract of Cornell thesis), Ithaca, New York (1933).

Jespersen, *Language*, pp. 312–314.

Krapp, *Modern English, Its Growth and Present Use*, p. 185.

Johnson, *English Words*, pp. 123–126.

Bloomfield, *Language*, pp. 156–157.

Weekley, *The Romance of Words*, 4th edit., pp. 39–53.

Zandvoort, *A Handbook of English Grammar*, 5th edit., pp. 323–324; 327; 362–363.

B. FOR CLASS DISCUSSION

1. What process of word formation can be seen at work in the erroneous use of *specie* or *serie* as the singular of *species* and *series*, or *Chinee* for *Chinese*, and in the definition of *jeopardy* as "an act committed by a jeopard"? Explain its operation.

2. Look up the origin of the following words and explain how they were formed. From what parts of speech are the verbs derived?

laze	quince	bodice
marquee	peddle	darkle
scavenge	greed	frivol
resurrect	reminisce	burial

3. Are the words mentioned in Question 2 all in good standing at present? Can you think of other back-formations whose status is questionable; of others which are universally accepted? See Zandvoort, pp. 323–324.

4. List all the words you can think of which are composed of initials, like those in par. 3. Do you think the tendency to form words in this way is more active at present than it has been in the past? Discuss.

5. Is there more than one type of onomatopoetic words? Explain. (See McKnight's *English Words and Their Background*, pp. 164 ff., and Bradley's *The Making of English*, pp. 155 ff.)

6. Why is *echoic* preferable to *imitative* as a description of the type of onomatopoetic words which attempt to represent directly the cries of animals, etc.? How closely do such words approximate the actual sounds? (Compare, for example, such popular names of birds as *bobolink* and *whippoorwill* with the calls of these birds.)

7. Make a list of onomatopoetic words and divide them into groups according to the particular kinds of effects that they produce. Do you find that certain sounds or groups of sounds are consistently associated with particular ideas?

8. Do you know of any echoic words which are used by some family or group but are not in general use? What can you predict as to their future standing?

9. Go through the words listed under *bl* in *Webster's New Collegiate Dictionary* or some other dictionary of similar size and count those marked *imitative* or *onomatopoetic*. What is the percentage? How many of these words are directly imitative and how many depend on a conventionalized relation between sound and idea?

10. Look up the words mentioned at the end of par. 5 and study their history. Do the same with the following words:

epicurean	canary	italic
slave	jeremiad	damask
morocco	calico	champagne

11. Make a list of words of more recent origin than those in Question 10 which are derived from the names of actual persons or places. How many of these words are still capitalized? What does the loss of the capital indicate?

12. How many words can you think of that are derived from the names of characters in fiction?

13. How many trade names can you think of that are derived from the names of people? What is peculiar about a name like *Ediphone?*

14. Read the poem "Jabberwocky" in Lewis Carroll's *Through the Looking-Glass,* and Humpty Dumpty's explanation of the first stanza. See how many of the other words in the poem you can dissect. How many of them are still in use?

15. Examine a copy of *Time* magazine and pick out any blend words that occur. What effect is produced by the use of such coinages? How many of them would you say were likely to remain in the language?

16. How does a blend differ from an amalgamated compound word such as *daisy?* (See Kennedy's *Current English,* p. 351.) What examples of blends can you give?

17. Look up in Webster's *New International Dictionary* the words given as examples of blends by Kennedy and McKnight. How many of these are of certain derivation? What can you say about the origin of the others?
18. What types of blends does Kennedy recognize? (*Current English*, pp. 351–354.) Which ones does he suggest are most likely to remain in the language?
19. Look up the following words in the *Oxford Dictionary* and see what you can find out about their origin and their earliest use in English.

folklore	minimize
altruism	municipality
dynamite	centripetal
decadent	

Can you find any other words which can be traced back to some particular person?
20. Why is it difficult, even with the help of *Oxford Dictionary* citations, to be sure that a scientific term originated with the person who first used it in writing or with the person who made it popular?
21. What is the attitude of the general public toward experiment and innovation in the coinage of words? How have experiments such as those of James Joyce, Gertrude Stein, and e. e. cummings been received? In your opinion, how valuable is the contribution made to the language by such writers?

C. SUGGESTIONS FOR RESEARCH PAPERS

1. A Study of Blends in American Place Names.
2. The Contribution of Classical Mythology (or the Bible) to the English Vocabulary.
3. The Use of Initials (or Blends) in Making Trade Names (or, Words of Governmental Administration).
4. Onomatopoetic Words in Tennyson (or some other poet).
5. Onomatopoeia in the Comic Strips.
6. Onomatopoeia in the Names of Birds and Animals.
7. Names of Textiles (or Foods) as Reflections of History and Geography.
8. Scientific Terms Derived from Proper Names.
9. James Joyce as a Creator of Words.
10. The Influence of Migration and Colonization on Word Formation.
11. Select a dozen or more words from Gelett Burgess' *Burgess Unabridged* and analyze them. How have they been formed?

28

Degeneration and Elevation

28.1 Word Biography The previous chapters have dealt with the origination, creation, or birth of new English words; and now it remains to consider their vicissitudes in the course of their longer or shorter careers. Such words as *birth, biography,* and *career* are obviously used metaphorically, as words have no objective existence. What actually happens when a word is "born" is that a certain notion becomes attached to a particular cluster of sounds. Other notions (meanings) may then add to, fall away from, or replace the original one, until perhaps in time no meaning at all remains, and the sound-cluster is no more a word because no one sees any meaning in it. But these accurate abstract terms for the history of words are hard to handle; metaphor is the easiest way to speak of these impalpabilities and hence it is the way taken here.

28.2 Vicissitudes In the course of a word's career, then, many changes occur, a few of which will now be traced. One of the most obvious as well as the most interesting is the change called elevation or amelioration on the one hand, and degeneration or pejoration on the other. These two tendencies apply especially to certain sorts of words—those denoting time, social status, intelligence, religion, and relative maturity, among others.

28.3 Example Perhaps the best word to use as a first example is one which has itself gone in not one but several directions. The word *person*, which came into English about 1225 from the Latin via French, is basically a colorless, neutral term for a human being. Yet as used by someone—*Oh! You mean that person!*—it may be a term of distaste; while used by someone else—*He's quite a person*—it may convey a sense of admiration. In short, *person* is what the user chooses to make it. It is bad, good, or indifferent, as its use may require.

28.4 Farmers and Servants But the story is far different with those words which originally named workers on the soil, or servants to a master. Farm work is not conducive to grace and daintiness; [1] and servants are seldom fully appreciated by those they serve. So it came about that words originally meaning *farmer* or *servant*—*villain, varlet, knave, churl, boor*—took on their present unsavory meanings. As a group, the meanings represented by these sound patterns have deteriorated radically.

An example of pejoration that has taken place recently is the word *collaborator*. This was long a word of dignity. College professors were glad to be collaborators in the writing of important textbooks, and scientists were proud to be known as collaborators in some new technique or discovery, but because of those who assisted the Nazis in their brief conquest of Europe, the collaborators, the word is now used chiefly for reproach or denunciation. Whether this derogatory meaning of *collaborator* will become the dominant one, or whether it is a temporary aberration in the language, only time will tell.

28.5 Contrary Instances But there are other words for which the meanings have improved. Many of our most esteemed occupations bear names which are of very lowly origin. *Minister* itself was originally no better than *servant*. *Marshal* was a boy who held horses. *Chamberlain* still shows its original connection with menial labor through the first two syllables, *chamber*. Even *merchant* was at one time far less respected than now. Perhaps the most interesting ex-

---

[1] See Harold B. Allen, "Pejorative Terms for Midwest Farmers," *American Speech* (Vol. XXXIII, December, 1958), pp. 260–265.

ample is *pioneer,* which a few centuries ago named a very low grade of soldier, a foot-soldier, and today is one of the proudest titles of the scientist, philosopher, or settler.

28.6 Opprobrious Nomenclature   If to these instances are added the names which have been applied to political and religious groups by their detractors, we shall find a like story of rehabilitation. On many occasions down the centuries, organized groups have accepted derisive or opprobrious names and have made them respected. Examples are *Quaker, Shaker, Tory, Whig, Yankee, Hoosier, Puritan.* Indeed there are few instances of such names going in any other direction but up, in the scale of social respect. *Assassin,* which originally named a Mohammedan secret order, is an exception to the usual trend.

28.7 The Late English Words   Perhaps it is not a very desperate failing of humanity that it tends to procrastinate; however that may be, adverbs meaning *now—presently, directly, soon, anon—*have come to mean *in a little while.* The phrase *by and by,* which in Chaucer's time meant *side by side,* came to mean *immediately* [2] as to time; but it too has procrastinated. To be sure, *now* has held its own through the centuries from Old English to the present instant. Adjectives and nouns also have been unaffected.

28.8 Distrust of Brains   With some reason, perhaps, the English language reflects a definite distrust of human intelligence, as shown in the history of various words indicating mental quickness and power. While *wise* (O.E. *wīs*) has held firmly to its good meaning except in certain phrases such as *worldly wise,* other terms—*sly, cunning, crafty, knowing—*have come to indicate unscrupulous use of knowledge or skill. A later amusing parallel is furnished by the group of presidential advisers to Franklin D. Roosevelt, who were given, in jest or earnest, the title of the *Brain Trust.* It was soon apparent that the name was not one of respect, and the group itself had but a brief existence. Rather, one sees words like *egghead* applied to the intellectual. On the other hand, the word *smart,* which now means *admirable* in appearance as well as intellect, has advanced from an earlier meaning connected with pain to its present standing.

28.9 Hypocrisy Detected   Side by side with the elevation of

---

[2] The idea of adjacent place was transferred to time in the immediate future.

names of religious sects such as the Quakers (par. 6) has gone a lowering of such words as *pious, sanctimonious, saint, holy, fanatic, zealot, proselyte,* and *propaganda.* Hypocrisy and self-interest have too often defaced such words, and English mirrors the fact while still retaining good meanings in connection with *saint, holy,* and other religious words unsmirched by less admirable qualities. *Religion* itself, for example, has not been lowered.

28.10 A Juvenile Word Our modern term *negative,* which today is rather overworked to cover matters not conducive to social or individual progress, is almost exactly paralleled by a word of the Elizabethan era, the word *naught* and its related *naughty,* which at that time meant *bad* or *wicked.* During the nearly four centuries intervening, *naughty* took a curious path. It became juvenile. Today it is entirely a child word, and seems to be disappearing in favor of the colorless *bad.*

28.11 Weakened Intensives A feature of word deterioration which has rhetorical significance is the weakening or loss of intensives—*so, extremely, awfully,* etc. Such words have appeared and vanished frequently in past centuries, as the story of *swiðe, sore, full, well, monstrous, passing,* and *vastly* will prove. The writer of Modern English will be well advised to avoid intensives where possible, and this avoidance will help to preserve his writing from becoming dated.

For the Student

A. FURTHER READINGS

Greenough and Kittredge, *Words and Their Ways in English Speech,* pp. 284–299.
Bloomfield, *Language,* p. 427.
Sturtevant, *Linguistic Change,* Chapter IV.
Schlauch, *The Gift of Language,* pp. 117–120; 127.
Bradley, *The Making of English,* pp. 190–195.
Robertson and Cassidy, *The Development of Modern English,* 2nd edit., pp. 241–245.

McKnight, *English Words and Their Background,* pp. 280–292.
Kennedy, *Current English,* pp. 562–566.
Weekley, *The Romance of Words,* 4th edit., pp. 80–85.
Weekley, *Etymological Dictionary of Modern English.*
Schreuder, *Perjorative Sense Development in English.*
Van Dongen, *Amelioratives in English.*

B. FOR CLASS DISCUSSION

1. Compare the development of the words *fellow* and *companion* to that of *person* cited in par. 3. Make sentences to illustrate your meanings.
2. Look up the words *engineer, broker, ambassador.* Show how these words have risen in dignity.
3. Look up the words *keen, sharp, clever, cute* and compare the change in meaning to that of the word *smart.*
4. Look up the history of the word *radical.* What has happened to that word?
5. Trace the changes in meaning that have taken place in the following words, and, in the case of each, determine whether the development has been in the direction of elevation or degeneration.

respectable	rash	sophist
vile	counterfeit	wench
revel	devotee	idiot
erring	silly	regard
nimble	bishop	lady
paradise	asylum	fond

6. Comment on the use of *wise* in the slang expression *wise guy.* Can you think of other uses of *wise* in Modern English which show that its connotation is not entirely favorable?
7. Can you find other words besides *naughty* which have followed the course described in par. 10 and become juvenile?
8. In student compositions study the effect of intensive words like *such, very, extremely.* Do they strengthen or weaken the effect? What in general can you say about the value of such words and their probable fate?
9. Comment on the suggestion of Robertson and Cassidy (p. 243) that social forces such as the institution of chivalry or the romantic movement have changed the status of whole groups of words. Give examples.

10. Can you think of other epithets besides those mentioned in par. 6 which have acquired an honorable standing? Are there any which are at present in process of change?
11. Do you think that the tendency of time-adverbs to procrastinate is still in operation? Do such expressions as *immediately, right away, at once* always mean *now* in business and social relations?
12. Can you think of examples of word degeneration caused by snobbishness and prudery? (See Schlauch's *The Gift of Language*, pp. 117 ff.) Is this tendency still in operation?

C. SUGGESTIONS FOR RESEARCH PAPERS

1. Opprobrious Epithets.
2. Why Words Degenerate in Meaning.
3. Elevation of Words.
4. The Loss of Force in Intensives.
5. The Development of Words Meaning *Child.*

29

Generalization
and Specialization

29.1 Generalization As the vocabulary develops, and new words are formed by any of the various methods listed in Chapters 24 to 27, certain of these words take on a more generalized meaning. Class nouns (collectives) enter, and abstract ideas begin to emerge. Finally the language is well provided with words of this kind. Sometimes the new idea is expressed not in a new word but in a new meaning given to an old one; thus the Hebrew *ru'ach*, from meaning *wind, breath*, comes to mean also *spirit*, so that it is used in *Genesis* 1:2 (*the Spirit of God moved upon the face of the waters*) with the latter meaning and in *Genesis* 3:8 (*and they heard the voice of the Lord God walking in the garden in the cool of the day*) with the former, *the cool of the day* being the "breeze" of the day. Typically the progress of language is from such concrete to such abstract meanings. Thus in English the verb *throw*, from O.E. *ðrāwan*, originally meaning *to turn, to twist*, and especially applied to torture, has lost its special meaning, becoming generalized so that no one is any longer conscious of its having any connection with twisting.

29.2 Forerunner Most of the large and generalized words in Modern English have at some past time had a much more specialized meaning out of which they have developed. A striking instance of this is the verb *to be,* which as has been stated is not one verb but a combination of three roots which have amalgamated into one. The first of these roots, which gives us *be, being,* and *been,* comes from a verb meaning *to grow.* The second, giving *was* and *were,* had as its earlier meaning *to dwell;* while the root giving *am, is,* and *are* may have meant *breathe* or *sit*—no one knows exactly but everyone is sure that the meaning was something less general than *be.* Thus the copula of Modern English shows a widening of three amalgamated narrower meanings. Other examples are *hazard,* a name of a dicing game, which came to mean *risk* in general; *arrive,* from Lat. *ripa* (*shore*), originally applying to the end of a voyage, but now generalized to apply to the end of any journey.

29.3 Other Form Words The other form words of English, like *to be,* go back to more specialized earlier forms. *Do* originally had a physical meaning of *put* or *place. Shall* went back to a meaning *to owe,* and *will* had the varied meanings of *wish, choose,* and later *intend.* As for the prepositions, some like *to* and *of* are so wrapped in antiquity that they cannot be traced, but *among* goes back to an Old English meaning *in the crowd,* being related to the verb *gemengan, to mingle. Across* and *beside* carry their derivations on their surfaces.

29.4 Specialization But if one reasoned from these examples to the conclusion that generalization is the rule in English word changes, one would be mistaken. Far more frequent than the changes of the sort illustrated are those of an opposite sort. A little reflection will show the logic of the fact. The vast scientific vocabulary of Modern English is all minutely specialized and subdivided; many of the terms represent less specialized predecessors. To be sure, a word may undergo both widening and narrowing, and very many do. But of the two processes the latter is the more common.

29.5 Instances A typical example is the Old English verb *steorfan, to perish, die.* There are many ways to die, and all of them were included in the meaning of this verb as they are today in its Modern German cousin *sterben.* But Middle English specialized *steorfan* into *to die with hunger.* In the North of England the meaning *die* *by cold* was associated with *steorfan,* and this is still a dialectical usage for our current word *starve* in that region.

29.6 Other Narrowings To give more examples it is necessary only to pick at random from any list of Old English words. *Wedd* meant *pledge* and the word appeared in the compound *wedlāc,* the second element meaning *an offering.* The modern word *wedlock* has narrowed itself to one particular sort of pledge. Another Old English word, *gāst,* has given us the word *ghost,* which originally had the broad meaning *spirit,* surviving in *Holy Ghost,* but has narrowed its meaning in nonecclesiastical matters to *the returning spirit of one who is dead.* One element in the modern compound *bridegroom* was the Old English word *gūma,* which meant *man* in general, whereas the modern *groom* is either a special sort of attendant or a man about to be married—two specializations from the same source.

29.7 Nice Example As a more complicated and instructive example of generalization, the word *nice* will serve. The story begins with a Latin word *nescius,* which had the meaning *ignorant.* It continues with the passage of this word into French, with the spelling *nice,* as now, and the meaning slightly altered to *foolish.* From French *nice* passed to England during the thirteenth century, keeping the meaning of *foolish* but adding that of *fastidious—foolishly fastidious.* Next *nice* dropped all sense of ignorance or folly, and came to mean simply *fastidious* as a personal quality. Up to this point one can scarcely speak of widening or narrowing meaning, since each change has been within this notion of a character attribute. But next the word broadened to mean *precise* as a quality of things as well as persons. This meaning it still possesses in such a phrase as *a nice distinction.* But then, without any apparent reason, the word *nice* expanded to the very limits of human experience to indicate anything or anyone agreeable or satisfying. For some time the purists fought this final shift on the part of *nice,* but their battle is now lost.

29.8 Moral The story of *nice* has an application somewhat broader than this chapter. In the six changes of meaning of the word, we see the normal, natural process of language shifting associations from century to century. In its present meaning, *nice* is a needed word. It is as shortsighted and absurd to say that *nice* must mean *precise* as it would be to say that it must still mean *ignorant.*

For the Student

A. FURTHER READINGS

Greenough and Kittredge, *Words and Their Ways in English Speech*, pp. 234–258.
McKnight, *English Words and Their Background*, pp. 248–264.
Bradley, *The Making of English*, pp. 177–184; 192–194.
Robertson and Cassidy, *The Development of Modern English*, 2nd edit., pp. 236–241.
Baugh, *A History of the English Language*, 2nd edit., pp. 372–376.
Schlauch, *The Gift of Language*, pp. 120–121.
Bloomfield, *Language*, pp. 151–152; 426–434.

B. FOR CLASS DISCUSSION

1. In primitive languages does one find more specialized or more generalized meanings? Give reasons.
2. What accounts for the independent names for different types of the same animal, such as *horse, mare, stallion, foal, colt*? Can you think of other illustrations?
3. Why does one always say *a bay horse, a fallow deer*? Can you think of other similar specializations of color words?
4. Give a dozen words naming ocean-going boats and differentiate them. What does this indicate?
5. What does the word *mammoth* bring to your mind? What is the origin of the word? Has the meaning generalized or specialized?
6. Take a dictionary of Biblical Hebrew, such as that of Feyerabend, and study the combination of literal and figurative meanings given to the nouns. Bring in a list of twelve words illustrating the development of abstractness out of concreteness.
7. Do the same for twelve abstract English words like *peace, justice*.
8. What is the origin of *colossal, butcher, miniature*? Are the present meanings generalized or specialized?
9. Does sport language tend toward specialized or generalized meanings? Illustrate.
10. Look up the history of the words *paraphernalia, circumstances*. Have they generalized or specialized in meaning?
11. What is the early meaning of *do*? How is it preserved in the words *don* and *doff*?

12. What does the adding of adjectives as in *Indian corn, hat box, steam engine,* etc. do toward generalization or specialization? Can you list other examples?

13. How have the following words become specialized in meaning?

salvation	fowl	apparition	estate
room	stare	liquor	virtue
convert	meat	carol	stool
token	spill	persecute	coast

14. How have the following words become generalized in meaning?

copy	paper	proposition
injury	picture	dean
layman	companion	manuscript

15. Take one letter in a Chaucer glossary and divide the words into two groups: (1) those that have developed a broader meaning; (2) those that have developed a specialized meaning. What is the proportion?

16. Do you know any words that are at present becoming specialized in meaning? That are becoming more generalized in meaning?

C. SUGGESTIONS FOR RESEARCH PAPERS

1. How a Modern Science (select one) Gets Its Vocabulary.

2. McKnight in *English Words and Their Background* (p. 158) gives 34 words which make up 50 per cent of spoken or written English. Trace these words to discover the concrete ideas out of which they developed.

3. Select a number of words and study the history of their meanings as to specialization and generalization.

30

Exaggeration and
Understatement

30.1 Extremes   In the changing of English word meanings there may be "too much," that is, hyperbole or exaggeration; and there may be "too little," that is, litotes or understatement on the one hand, and euphemism on the other. Although euphemism is not a true opposite for hyperbole, the two are frequently considered together, and they will be so treated here. An instance of hyperbole is the *Thanks a million* of the would-be polite of a few years ago. Litotes is seen in the *Rather!* of the colloquial Britisher. And euphemism, or the softening of unpleasant expressions, is exemplified by *pass away* or *on, breathe one's last, expire, depart this life, go west,* for the verb *die.*

30.2 Advertising Techniques   In advertising it is necessary to impress the reader, and this means that words must be impressive. Advertising in all periods must employ what is called "ballyhoo," but the proportion of ballyhoo varies with the period and the social group which is being addressed. Today the usual advertising technique is intimacy rather than hyperbole, although the latter lingers in the movies and a few similar fields. Adjectives such as *colossal,* *breathtaking, shattering, supermagnificent* are in fairly general use, although the last-mentioned prefix, *super-*, has been burlesqued in the phrase *superduper,* which shows a healthy general distrust of the merely spectacular.

30.3 Process of Change   Hyperbolic change in the use of words is somewhat similar to the changes in slang. Some word, perhaps *vast* or *awful,* will become popular, run its course, lose its sharpness, and become disused for a time at least. The two examples chanced to become popular in their adverbial form, the one in the eighteenth century, and the other within the memory of people living today, who will recall how purists denounced *awfully pretty* or *awfully nice* at the same time that the fashionable world was overusing such phrases. The turmoil about *awfully* has died down to an occasional grumble; but the objection to hyperbole will persist as long as the thing itself.

30.4 Opposite Extreme   Logically, if there is opposition to saying too much (hyperbole), there should be an equal objection to saying too little (litotes). In answer to *How are you this fine morning?* the answer *Just able to be around,* given as understatement, is just as reprehensible as a *Perfectly great,* which is an exaggeration. Yet, perhaps because litotes is the less common of the two extremes, and perhaps because it usually carries humorous connotations, it has escaped the condemnation of the authorities.

30.5 Typically British?   The tradition of litotes reaches back to Old English, though the word itself was first used in connection with the elaborate rhetorics of the sixteenth and seventeenth centuries. England is supposed to be the home of understatement, as America is supposed to be the home of hyperbole; and no doubt this may have been true in the spread-eagle days of the past. But today one encounters understatement very generally wherever people speak the English language. *Rather,* and *not bad,* typical British understatements, have their cousins in *You don't say* and *it'll do* of rustic speech, particularly in New England. One advantage of understatement is that it does not use up words very fast; *rather* has been in English from the earliest period, although O.E. *hraðe* meant *quick* and *early* rather than *preferred.* Our word *rather* was the comparative of *rathe,* which was used in its earlier meaning well into the Modern English period. From meaning *earlier, rather* naturally shifted to include an idea of preference (cf. *sooner*) and Shakespeare uses it this way in Hamlet's great soliloquy: ". . . And makes us rather bear the ills we have. . . ." Besides this meaning of preference, *rather* as an adverb came to mean *moderately*, and this meaning seems likely to persist.

30.6 Euphemism Closely allied to understatement is the choice of modest words to use in place of terms felt to be shocking, fearful, or for some other reason best avoided. The ideas of certain bodily functions, of death, of terrifying enemies, of certain sorts of disease are all subject to euphemistic replacement. Even the name of God is frequently avoided, particularly among primitive peoples. The Hebrews of the Old Testament and later times, while they cannot be called primitive in their basic religious concepts, were subject to this feeling concerning the name *Jahveh*, or *Yahweh*, which was the real name of their Supreme Being. They adopted the curious expedient of writing the consonants of this name with the vowel points of *Adōnāi* (*my Lord*), which was a less sacred name for God; and this mixture led the translators of the King James Bible to adopt the form *Jehovah*, which is not a Hebrew word but a combination of the consonants of *Yahweh* with the vowel points of *Adōnāi*. Even present-day Jews use *Adōnāi* instead of *Yahweh* in their religious observances.

30.7 Other Euphemisms The word *euphemism* is from the Greek *eu-*, meaning *fair*, and the verb *phemi, to speak*. It was a religious word, in its imperative form a warning to worshipers to use only fitting terms in the temple. As used today it covers such phrases as *pass away* for *die*, *high* for *drunk*, *odor* or even *aroma* for *stink*. *Disease* is itself a euphemism, its early meaning being much the same as *discomfort;* many mild oaths like *gosh* or *darn* are euphemisms for stronger phrases.

30.8 Political Uses During World War II euphemism had rather an astonishing career in the phrases used to describe the activities of Hitler's Germany. The term *concentration camp* is mild and gives small suggestion of what actually occurred in such places. Another term *protective custody* was well calculated to allay the misgivings of outsiders when another country was added to the list of victims; and *liquidate* is a far milder term than *execute* or *murder*. It may be that the uses of understatement in politics are only beginning to be explored.

30.9 Advice In ordinary life the average person probably would do well to avoid both hyperbole and litotes, and stick to the facts in conversation and writing. A certain amount of euphemism is necessary, however, in polite society. When bodily needs become urgent we go to the *smoking room, powder room,* or *rest room,* even though we may have no intention of smoking, powdering, or resting in the conventional meaning of those words. It may seem absurd to an enlightened person to shun use of the word *die,* but he must realize that other persons not so well informed may be shocked or troubled if he does not employ such euphemisms as *pass away.* Common sense should dictate the amount of euphemism that can be resorted to without sounding either insincere or artificial. Occasionally, of course, hyperbole, litotes, or euphemism can be effectively used for humorous purposes, but on the whole rhetorics and grammars do well to point out the dangers from such distortion of facts.

For the Student

A. FURTHER READINGS

McKnight, *English Words and Their Background,* pp. 265–279.

Greenough and Kittredge, *Words and Their Ways in English Speech,* pp. 16–17; 300–329.

Mencken, *American Language,* 4th edit., pp. 284–300.

Robertson and Cassidy, *The Development of Modern English,* 2nd edit., pp. 245–251.

Schlauch, *The Gift of Language,* pp. 121–122; 278–282.

Jespersen, *Growth and Structure of the English Language,* 9th edit., pp. 7–10; 226–231.

Graff, *Language and Languages,* pp. 282–284; 313.

Bloomfield, *Language,* pp. 155; 427.

B. FOR CLASS DISCUSSION

1. What is the derivation of the word *hyperbole?* Is it a good name for the tendency to exaggerate in language? Why?

2. How is exaggeration related to degeneration in meaning? Illustrate with histories of specific words such as *insane, undertaker, stench.*

3. Collect and bring to class ten examples of exaggeration in advertising.

4. Look up the history of *yes, no,* and *not.* Did they originally express simple or strengthened affirmation or negation? What do they express today? What words are now used to show strong affirmation or negation? Do such words show any tendency to weaken in force?

5. What is the literal meaning of *astonished, furious, stunned, enraged, amazed?* What is their meaning in ordinary conversation at present? Discuss their development and give examples of other words which have followed the same course.

6. Do you know the euphemisms for *spittoon, coffin, cemetery, hearse, clerk, janitor, plumber, dirty clothes?* Give other examples of euphemisms.

7. In what respects do euphemism and hyperbole approach each other? How do they differ in origin? (See McKnight's *English Words and Their Background,* p. 273.)

8. Do you know any euphemisms used politically at the present time?

9. Look up *sympathetic magic* in an encyclopedia or in Frazer's *The Golden Bough.* What magical powers were supposed to inhere in the use of names? Do you think any remnants of these beliefs persist among average people today?

10. Look up and compare the words *grammar* and *gramarye.* What is the relation between their meanings?

11. Why did the Greeks call the Furies *Eumenides* (*well-minded-ones*) and the stormy Black Sea *Euxine* (*hospitable*)? Considering modern substitutions for names of diseases and death, do you think the same tendency is still at work?

12. Bring to class a list of euphemistic expressions introduced by modern advertising. How many of these have become common in current speech? Do you consider that their adoption has been a gain to the language? If so, in what way?

13. Study the use of slang in a novel by P. G. Wodehouse. Is the slang used there less extravagant than American slang? Do you think it is typical of British slang in general?

14. Compare one of Dorothy Sayers' mystery stories or John Buchan's stories of adventure with an American novel of the same type. Do you find understatement to be more characteristic of the British writer?

15. What tendency is at work in the substitution of such names as *place, avenue, boulevard, terrace, parkway* for *street?* Give other examples of its operation.

16. Comment on the suggestion made by Robertson (*The Development of Modern English,* p. 449) and McKnight (*English Words and Their*

Background, pp. 273 ff.) that the results of hyperbole and euphemism are not entirely to be deplored. In what way may such practices be beneficial to language?

17. Read a modern translation of *Beowulf* and find examples of litotes, especially in the conversation.

C. SUGGESTIONS FOR RESEARCH PAPERS

1. Magic and Language.
2. Litotes (or Hyperbole) in the Speech of a Particular Region (or in some literary work, such as *Beowulf*).
3. Mark Twain's Use of Exaggeration (or choose some other American humorist).
4. The Political Uses of Euphemism.
5. Hyperbole in Advertising.
6. The History of Litotes in English.
7. The History of *Rather.*
8. A Comparison of Present-Day Advertising Techniques with Those of Fifteen Years Ago.

31

Abbreviation and Extension

31.1 Trend in Length When new words are formed by compounding, the result is of course a longer unit; and it might seem that, since compounding and the adding of formative elements are the chief means of creating new words, the words making up the English language must be getting longer and longer. Just the contrary is the case. Modern English is far more nearly monosyllabic than was Old English; and very many of the short, terse words which we think of as typically Anglo-Saxon were neither so short nor so terse a thousand years ago. The forces tending to lengthen English words are not so active as those ending to shorten them.

31.2 Phonological Change In the first place, it is an observed fact of phonology that unstressed sounds, syllables, even words tend to become obscured and lost. All polysyllables contain some unaccented sounds and hence tend to shorten with the passage of time. There are few Old English words which survive in Modern English without some degree of shortening. The loss of inflectional elements is one evidence of this abbreviation, but only one; scores of words like *hawk, fowl, king, lord,* and *lady* give further evidence to the same conclusion.

31.3 Clipped Words   This phonological change is largely an unconscious process; but words are often shortened by speakers who know what they are doing. It is by no accident that English has *still* from *distillery* or *wig* from *periwig.* Some of these abbreviations, like *mob* from *mobile vulgus,* aroused active opposition in Swift, who more than once wrote in an attempt to counteract what he considered affronts to the English language. In *A Proposal for Correcting, Improving and Ascertaining the English Tongue,* addressed to Robert, Earl of Oxford and Mortimer, Lord High Treasurer of Great Britain (see par. 5.15), he pleaded for help in perfecting and fixing the English language thus: [1]

"My lord, I do here, in the name of all the learned and polite persons of the nation, complain to your lordship, as first minister, that our language is extremely imperfect; that its daily improvements are by no means in proportion to its daily corruptions; that the pretenders to polish and refine it, have chiefly multiplied abuses and absurdities; and that in many instances it offends against every part of grammar." He also pointed out that ". . . if it were once refined to a certain standard, perhaps there might be ways found out to fix it for ever, or at least till we are invaded and made a conquest by some other state. . . ." [2]

It is amusing to note how little good Swift's animadversions accomplished; many of the words he denounced are today good English. In the *Tatler* (No. 230) for September 26, 1710, he acknowledged that he had been fighting a losing battle when he wrote: "I have done my utmost for some years past to stop the progress of *mobb* and *banter,* but have been plainly borne down by numbers, and betrayed by those who promised to assist me." [3] He also wrote of the young readers in the churches:

"In reading the absolution, they are very careful to say '*pardons* and *absolves*'; . . . Then in their sermons they use all the modern terms of art, *sham, banter, mob, bubble, bully, cutting, shuffling,*

[1] *The Prose Works of Jonathan Swift,* edited by Temple Scott (London, George Bell and Sons, 1907), Vol. XI, p. 6.

[2] *Ibid.,* p. 9.

[3] *Ibid.,* Vol. IX, p. 35.

and *palming*, all which, and many more of the like stamp, as I have heard them often in the pulpit from such young sophisters, so I have read them in some of those sermons that have made most noise of late." [4]

Thus one can see that Swift's efforts were in vain.

31.4 Beginning or End Abbreviating may affect the beginning, the middle, the end, or a combination of these, in the words it shortens. Shortening at both ends is unusual. Probably most clipped words have lost sounds at the end, as *curio*, from *curiosity*, when there has been any considerable shortening. Frequently a word will lose a sound or a syllable at the beginning, as *mend* from *amend*, *tend* from *attend*, *cute* from *acute*, etc.

31.5 Slang Clippings Abbreviating English words often makes them slang. A few remain slang, while others go into the language. *Monk* for *monkey*, *butch* for *butcher*, *prof* for *professor*, *doc* for *doctor* are among the first sort, while *piano* for *pianoforte*, *bus* for *omnibus*, *zoo* for *zoological gardens* are now accepted as Standard English. Of the mass of new slang which appears periodically, a part will consist of abbreviations; and this part seems to have a better expectancy of life than the rest. The abbreviation *ad* for *advertisement*, which used to be thought one of the slang group, has been accepted in practice, if not in theory, by the majority of cultivated people.

31.6 Phrase Clippings An earlier paragraph (26.8) mentioned the fact that the term *blues* is by origin *the blue devils*. Similarly, many phrases and even sentences have shortened. One which will come to everyone's mind is *goodbye* from *God be with you (ye)*, and *farewell* was once *fare you (thee) well*. *After all* is said to be the remnant of *after all is said and done*, and *hoax* probably comes from *hocus pocus*. These are only a few of the large number of examples, including the alleged Americanism *fall* for *fall of the leaf*, instead of the British *autumn*.

31.7 Name Words Shortened Many of the English words which derive from names (par. 27.5) are in a shortened form which often prevents the connection from being apparent. Thus *spaniel* is a clipped form of *Espagnol* or *Spanish* (dog). *Copper* is *Cyprium*

[4] *Ibid.*, p. 37.

aes, and *magnet, magnesia,* and *magnesium* are all "Magnesian stone" from the district of Magnesia in Thessaly. *Tawdry,* from *St. Audrey,* the English form of *St. Ethelreda,* came into English first as *St. Audrey's lace,* that is, a lace bought at a fair in honor of this saint.

31.8 Lengthening　Aside from the lengthening treated in the chapters on the creation of words, there has been no great amount of this activity among English words. Once in a while a word takes an extra letter and perhaps an extra sound: *thunder* (from *þunor*); sound (from *soun*). A few inflections have doubled: *hers, lesser, nearer, innermost.* There is a certain amount of simple repetition in English; *meow-meow, fiddle-faddle, bonbon, teeny-weeny.* The echoic word *murmur* is formed by reduplication, and so is *turtle* (from Lat. *turtur*), which named a bird before it named an animal. Many of these reduplicated words are juvenile in nature: *goody-goody, quack-quack, moo-moo.*

31.9 Interaction　As with the other pairs of forces dealt with in former chapters, the lengthening and shortening tendencies interact upon each other to create that equilibrium which is literary expression. Joining word to word means lengthening, but no sooner has the lengthening force spent itself than the shortening begins to operate.

31.10 -al- Words　The syllable -*al*- is a good one to show this interaction of long and short. In popular speech, -*al*- is very often dropped from *accidentally, incidentally,* etc. This shortening is held to be a serious mistake, and students striving to keep the syllable often use it where it does not belong, for example in *apparently* (apparentally), *audibly* (audibally), etc. In this instance mistakes in -*al*- tend to an equilibrium, reflecting the interaction between short and long in language generally. So also, the uninformed use *preventative,* when the word actually is *preventive.*

For the Student

A. FURTHER READINGS

Greenough and Kittredge, *Words and Their Ways in English Speech,* pp. 61–65; 70–72; 252–255; 385.

Bradley, *The Making of English,* pp. 147–154.

Weekley, *The Romance of Words,* 4th edit., pp. 61–71.

Bryant and Aiken, *Psychology of English,* 2nd edit., pp. 117–119; 160–167.

Robertson and Cassidy, *The Development of Modern English,* 2nd edit., pp. 81–85; 204–205.

McKnight, *English Words and Their Background,* pp. 50; 176–177.

Kennedy, *Current English,* pp. 354–356.

Baugh, *A History of the English Language,* 2nd edit., pp. 311–314.

Jespersen, *Growth and Structure of the English Language,* 9th edit., pp. 7; 165–166.

Schlauch, *The Gift of Language,* pp. 100–102; 104.

Jespersen, *Language,* pp. 328–329; 403–406.

Krapp, *Modern English, Its Growth and Present Use,* pp. 152–153.

Zandvoort, *A Handbook of English Grammar,* 5th edit., pp. 326–328.

Wentworth and Flexner, *Dictionary of American Slang.*

Berrey and Van den Bark, *The American Thesaurus of Slang.*

B. FOR CLASS DISCUSSION

1. Look up Swift's *Proposal for Correcting, Improving, and Ascertaining the English Tongue* and his letter to the *Tatler* (No. 230) on September 28, 1710. In these he attacked a number of faults in the language. What does he criticize? How effective were his objections? How many words to which he objected have established themselves in the English language?

2. Look up the etymology of *like, mind, moot, reeve, sight.* What in general has happened to Old English words beginning with *ge-?*

3. Which part or parts of a word are most likely to be affected by the shortening process? Give examples of words which have lost (1) an initial syllable; (2) a final syllable; (3) a medial syllable.

4. Can all clipped forms of words be regarded as new words? When can they be considered to have attained the status of new words? (*See* Bradley's *The Making of English,* pp. 147 ff.) Give examples of clipped words whose status is still questionable and of those which have become established in the language.

5. Make a list of clipped words and phrases used in any scientific or technical vocabulary with which you are familiar (chemistry, photography, printing, etc.). How many of these would be immediately comprehensible to an outsider?

6. What clipped words are popular in modern slang? Which of these, would you say, are most likely to persist?

7. Collect and bring to class as many examples as you can find of shortened Latin words and phrases which are in common use.

8. How do the words in the following pairs differ in meaning at present: *cab, cabriolet; fence, defence; mend, amend; size, assize; tend, attend?* Look up their derivation and comment on their history.

9. In the light of the preceding question and of Greenough and Kittredge's comments (*Words and Their Ways in English Speech*, pp. 252 ff.), what would you say is, in general, the relation between word- and phrase-shortening and the specialization of meaning? Between shortening and funcitonal shift? Give examples.

10. What is the origin of the following words: *alarm, alert, carouse, culprit, patter (to talk glibly), propaganda?* Can you add other words similarly derived?

11. Make a list of all the words of greeting and parting which are shortened phrases.

12. How do you pronounce *geography, interesting, laboratory?* Have you heard variant pronunciations? Give other examples and explain what tendency is at work.

13. Bring to class other examples of clipped name words like those in par. 7 in which the connection with the original person or place has been lost because of the shortening.

14. How do you explain phonetically the adding of a sound to the words mentioned in par. 8 and the intrusion of a sound into such phrases as *the idea-r-of it, lower the-y-awnings, they came to-w-aid him?*

15. How do you account for the incorrect forms *drownded* for *drowned, celestrial* for *celestial, frequentally* for *frequently, Woodses* for *Woods, attackted* for *attacked?*

16. Can you think of other reduplicated words besides those mentioned in par. 8? (See Wentworth and Flexner, "Appendix," pp. 645–646, and Zandvoort, pp. 326–328, §§ 834–837). In what kind of speech are they generally found?

C. SUGGESTIONS FOR RESEARCH PAPERS

1. Slang as a Method of Shortening Words.
2. Shortened Phrases and Sentences.
3. Lengthening in Words.
4. Affection and Disrespect as Factors in the Shortening Process.

32

Metathesis and
Folk Etymology

32.1 Physical Change Of the word changes considered thus far, elevation (amelioration) and degeneration (pejoration), generalization and specialization, hyperbole, litotes, and euphemism are all matters of meaning change. Lengthening and shortening, on the other hand, are matters of physical change; the sounds and not the sense are altered in most of the examples in this chapter, which mentions some of the odd ways in which words alter physically from one century to another.

32.2 Children's Errors There is observable among children a tendency to get sounds mixed up. Children will often call a *wasp* a *waps,* or say *ax (aks)* for *ask. Cinnamon* and *elephant* become *cimmanon* and *heffalump. Library* will get its *r's* mixed up and merged, making the word *li-berry;* and *February* in the same way becomes *Febyuary.* The sounds most susceptible to change are [l], [r], and [s].

32.3 Old Standing What most speakers of English do not know is that such errors are specimens of a tendency existing at all periods and dignified with the name *metathesis,* from the Greek *meta, be-*

yond, over, and *tithemi, to place.* Indeed, the very verb *ask,* mentioned above, had more than one form in Old English. In addition to *ascian,* there was the form *acsian* or *axian,* which would give in Modern English the form *ax* (*aks*) and not *ask.* Incidentally, *ax* (*aks*) is a "show-off" pronunciation among some high school youngsters. Another metathesis of the same sort was *fersc,* which has given Mod.E. *fresh.*

32.4 The *Horse* Group   Not one but several words enter into the story of O.E. *hors,* Mod.E. *horse.* The modern form is not metathesized, but the metathesized form survives in *walrus.* The first syllable is *whale* and the second *horse,* making a lively name for this marine mammal. The name *Rosinante,* familiar to all lovers of *Don Quixote,* enshrines as its first syllable the same word.

32.5 Other Metatheses   The sound [r] is the sound most given to changing its position. It is present in the following modern words showing metathesis: *bird, grass, third, thirty, through, wrought.* The frequent but incorrect modern pronunciations *prespiration, prehaps,* and *perscription* are further examples.

32.6 More Children's Errors   But metathesis is not alone as a child's error of linguistic significance. A child is likely to see relations between words which are hidden from adults. One little girl, for example, talked about *c-gulls* and *e-gulls* (*eagles*); and she wished her friends and relatives would never be *sour-castic.* These are modern instances of the phenomenon known to linguists as *folk,* or *popular, etymology.* The meaning of a word is rationalized (erroneously) in terms of some word or idea to which it is felt to have some resemblance; and this fancied connection leads to a change in the form of one of the words, to bring the two into line.

32.7 Examples   The very modern word *penthouse* is an instance of popular etymology; it is by derivation *apentis,* a sort of shed or lean-to, and as the structure got more pretentious the last syllable was made into *house.* The *English walnut* is a compound word. The syllable *wal* is not *wall* but O.E. *wealh,* meaning *foreign* or *Welsh,* and hence the word means a *foreign nut.* Another phrase with *Welsh, Welsh rabbit* (compare *Hudson seal* and *Arabian lynx*), has been etymologized into *Welsh rarebit,* perhaps to enhance its flavor.

32.8 More Instances   It may be that *teetotal* and *teetotaler* were more popular words in former generations than they are today; they have been taken as if they had something to do with *tea*, whereas they hold just a reduplication or repetition of the opening of *total*. At an important temperance meeting in Preston, England, in 1833, an enthusiast, Richard Turner, who stammered over his *t's*, kept repeating that "nothing but t-total abstinence will do." The *t-total* caught the public fancy and thus the name of the great temperance movement *teetotalism* was born and along with it *teetotal, teetotaler, teetotally*. In much the same way, *shamefaced* has nothing to do with one's face; it is *shamefast*, the last syllable meaning *fixed* or *confirmed*. The word meant *modest*, the older sense of *shame* being *modesty*. Thus *shamefast* was a complimentary term, unlike the present *shamefaced,* which includes the pejorative meaning of *shame* and implies *guilt*.

32.9 Pennyroyal Students of herbs, who have wondered about the delightful name *pennyroyal*, will be dashed to discover that it concerns nothing more aristocratic than *fleas* (Lat. *pulex*). The plant's Latin name is *puleium* (or *pulegium*) *regium, flea remedy* (cf. *fleabane*). This Latin name gave first *puliall royal,* which was too odd for English tongues and ears. Although *puliall* and *penny* are not very near in sound, and pennies have no possible connection with the plant, the substitution was made and *pennyroyal* was born.

32.10 Other Plants Indeed, a chapter might be written exclusively on the derivation of names of plants—*dahlia* from an individual name, *daisy* from a figure of speech, and so on. The *Jerusalem artichoke* would fit as another instance of this quaint etymology. The two names come from the Italian, the one the name of a plant called *girasole,* or *turning with the sun,* which resembles an artichoke; the other from *articiocco,* first Anglicized as *artichock,* but now having its last syllable *choke*—not the best possible recommendation for the vegetable itself.

For the Student

A. FURTHER READINGS

Greenough and Kittredge, *Words and Their Ways in English Speech,* pp. 330–344.

McKnight, *English Words and Their Background,* pp. 180–190; 199.
Robertson and Cassidy, *The Development of Modern English,* 2nd edit.,
    pp. 79; 253–356.
Weekley, *The Romance of Words,* 4th edit., pp. 59; 113–138; 181.
Kennedy, *Current English,* pp. 360–366.
Graff, *Language and Language,* pp. 280–282.
Bryant and Aiken, *Psychology of English,* 2nd edit., pp. 198–200.
Sheard, *The Words We Use,* pp. 90–93.
Schlauch, *The Gift of Language,* pp. 103–104.

B. FOR CLASS DISCUSSION

1. What is meant by metathesis? Give examples.
2. Look up the origin of the words mentioned in par. 5 and show what happened to each word. Do you know any other words in addition to the ones mentioned in which metathesis has taken place?
3. Look up the word *trouble* and explain how it derived its present form.
4. Are sounds and letters the only elements of language affected by metathesis? (See McKnight's *English Words and Their Background,* p. 199.) How does McKnight explain word metathesis?
5. Are there other sounds besides [r] which are peculiarly subject to metathesis? Illustrate.
6. What is folk etymology? What is its psychological basis?
7. Give five examples of folk etymology.
8. Look up the derivation of *island, belfry, counterpane, earwig* and explain the operation of popular etymology in these words.
9. How do soldiers' adaptations of foreign place names and other words illustrate folk etymology? Give examples.
10. What is unusual about the following words: *reindeer, saltcellar, greyhound, turtledove?* Can you add other words to the list?

C. SUGGESTIONS FOR RESEARCH PAPERS

1. Metathesized Words.
2. Derivation of the Names of Plants.
3. Folk Etymologies.
4. Infantilism in Language.

33

Shifts in Association

33.1 Word and Thing Ever since language came into being, people have felt that there must exist some sort of relationship between the word and the thing it named. This feeling was manifested philosophically in opposing schools of Greek thought, and romantically in various magical beliefs, such as the one that a person could exert power over another by knowing his name. At present, scholars are sure that there is no necessary connection between word and thing except a more or less temporary one existing in the mind of the speaker. They have learned that a word is immaterial in its very nature and can have no commerce with the world of things. Although one may speak of words as more concrete or less concrete, the terms are misleading if they convey the impression that any word is a concrete entity.

33.2 Strands of Meaning The truth seems to be that a word is an idea-complex made up of an indeterminable number of threads or strands of meaning, all twisted together as a rope or a thread is twisted. One of these may be said to give the primary or basic meaning and the others the associated meanings. A simple example is

the verb *to begin.* The primary meaning is *to start, to set in motion.*
But mingled with this is a large number of other periphery meanings such as *newness, youth, creation, wonder, the dawn* (figurative), *birth,* and perhaps others.

33.3 Meaning Shifts This picture of the word as including not
one but several ideas of varying essentiality is a necessary one if the
student is to understand clearly the history of changes in word
meanings. It is not a matter of discarding one sense and substituting
another. It is a matter of emphasizing a subordinate meaning
(which, however, is already present) to the overshadowing of the
meaning originally felt as stronger. This newly emphasized significa-
tion then becomes the central meaning of the word, until or unless
yet another meaning becomes emphasized and in turn crowds it out.

33.4 An Example Since language is almost infinitely complicated, an easy, unambiguous example is hard to find; but perhaps
the word *ambition* will do. This word is a fairly direct representative
of a Latin word *ambitio.* But *ambitio* did not mean *aspiration.* It sig-
nified quite simply *going about,* much like one colloquial meaning
of the modern verb *circulating.* Now one application of the Latin
ambitio contemplated the going about of a politician to collect votes,
and this secondary meaning strengthened until it grew to be the
central one belonging to the word. Politicians are eager, insistent
gentry, with a keen desire for the aim they pursue; and so the noun
was formed, first specializing the thought of desire in the one who
goes about, and then generalizing to denote this quality of desire as
applied to any struggle, as well as vote-getting. A final shift of
emphasis occurring in *ambition* was ameliorative. To Shakespeare
and Milton it was a bad quality. Today it is regarded as desirable
and even urged on youth by parents who want them to "get on in
the world." Thus we see four shifts or stages in the development of
the word's meaning: (1) a going about; (2) electioneering; (3) evil
desire for place or power; (4) initiative.

33.5 Reversal of Meaning So unpredictable is this transfer of
emphasis in word associations that it may lead to a reversal of a
word's former meaning. The Old English noun *weald* meant *forest,*
but as forests made way for human habitations, the name clung, as
place names do, to the deforested district. And thus our *wold* came
to be used to refer to a district (1) with a forest and (2) without a

forest. By other such alterations *fast* may mean either *fixed* or *rapid;* *alto* means *low* though derived from an Italian word *high* (by abbreviation of *contralto*); a *commencement* ends a college course; and an aiplane *lands* on the sea. Some words get confused regarding time. Thus a *journal* may appear weekly or even monthly or quarterly, in spite of the name's obvious connection with the French *jour, day.* The Old English word *tīd,* meaning *time,* got mixed up with the idea of the ebb and flow of the ocean, and keeps its early meaning only in *Christmastide, Eastertide,* etc. Most persons, however, construe the proverbial "Time and tide wait for no man" as referring to time and the ocean waves. Actually, the phrase was only one of those repetitions found so often in early English and even later, and meaning no more than a single word would. The King James version of the Bible, for example, has many such instances of two nouns doing the work of one, or two verbs, as in "Behold, he that keepeth Israel shall neither slumber nor sleep" (*Psalms* 121:4).

33.6 A Complicated Case   Some words have an extraordinarily long history of shifts in meaning behind them, and the word *lumber* in its American sense of *wood for building* is a good illustration. It was originally *Lombard,* the same word as the Italian district of *Lombardy;* but if one should guess an association with Lombardy poplar and hence wood from Italy, one would be wide of the mark. The story is much more circuitous, going back to the famous bankers or money lenders of Lombardy.

33.7 Original Meaning   The story begins with certain residents of Lombardy with financial acumen and migratory leanings. These Lombards made London a center for their activities, as is evidenced by the name *Lombard Street* for a thoroughfare in the financial districts. Lending money on security, the Lombards became pawnbrokers, and their shops were known as *Lombard shops,* as were other pawnshops whether or not they were operated by one of this group. In the same way the words *victrola* and *frigidaire* are often used of similar appliances bearing other trade names.

33.8 Further Changes   From naming a pawnshop, the word *lombard,* or *lumber,* came to be applied by metonymy to the contents of the shop. These are heterogeneous, as every city dweller knows. They necessitate space for storage; and through this fact, a miscellaneous collection of what Americans would call *junk* has

come to be named in British English *lumber*. A lumber room is a
storage place for the variety of articles called lumber.

33.9 Last Step But there is another place where articles of varying sizes and shapes are assembled, and that is the yard of a dealer in
wood as a building material. And so wood became *lumber* in the
sense of articles diverse in size and shape. This meaning has never
become current in England, where building wood is called *timber*.

33.10 Not Typical The story of *lumber* is unusual not only because of the number of its shifts in association but because of its
fairly unified meaning after each shift. It has not radiated meanings
as have other common English words, developing in not one but several directions simultaneously. This multiple development is much
more nearly the rule in English, and it will be considered in the next
chapter.

For the Student

A. FURTHER READINGS

McKnight, *English Words and Their Background*, pp. 202–247.
Bradley, *The Making of English*, pp. 160–177; 184–214.
Robertson and Cassidy, *The Development of Modern English*, 2nd edit.,
    pp. 232–236; 251–253; 261–262.
Weekley, *The Romance of Words*, 4th edit., pp. 86–104.
Bloomfield, *Language*, pp. 139–154.
Jespersen, *Language: Its Nature, Development, and Origin*, pp. 174–177;
    274–275.
Baugh, *A History of the English Language*, 2nd edit., p. 370.
Laird, *The Miracle of Language*, pp. 54–56.

B. FOR CLASS DISCUSSION

1. Look up the history of *treacle, pencil,* the verb *to lumber*.
2. What other words do you know like *fast* that have opposite meanings?
3. What does *pitted* mean to you? Do you know other words that are
   similar?
4. Select different parts of the body and show how different meaning
   shifts have originated additional meanings for these words.

5. What is the meaning of *quick* in *quicksilver, quicklime, cut to the quick, the quick and the dead?* What shift has taken place in this word?

6. What were the original meanings of *ruminate, brood, cogitate, ponder, reflect, examine?* How were the present meanings of the words derived?

7. What is the relationship between *captain* and *chief?* Look up their sources.

8. Take the names of the animals *dog, horse,* and *cat* and see in how many ways you can use these words and list a few meaning shifts.

9. What other meanings, paradoxical in character, can you think of similar to *Blackberries are red when they are green?* (See McKnight, *English Words and Their Background,* p. 209.) Do proper names (*Walker, Green,* etc.) always fit with the characteristics of their bearers?

10. Look up the words *cardinal, pocketbook,* and *board* and trace their shifts in meaning.

11. What shifts in meaning are evident in the flower names *pansy, aster, anemone?*

12. Can you account for the shift in meaning of *derrick, contrite, career, perplex, exaggerate, distinguish, scruple, error?*

C. SUGGESTIONS FOR RESEARCH PAPERS

1. Frequency Study of the Average Number of Meaning Shifts in the Common English Word.

2. Choose any group of words and study the shifts in meaning.

34

Radiation of Meaning

34.1 Doublets The nature of the word, as consisting of one or more central meanings with a periphery of an indefinite number of fringe meanings, will explain the fact that words multiply. This occurs in either of two ways. A word may split physically into two or more; or it may become a multiple word through acquiring many key meanings so that it may be used in various contexts to denote distinct ideas or things. *Off* and *of* are an example of the first possibility; such words as *pipe, head, key,* and *hand* exemplify the second.

34.2 *Of* and *Off* The differentiation between *of* and *off*, which were both *of* in Old English, is a matter of grammar as well as meaning, and illustrates well the fact of a basic distinction between preposition and adverb. In early Old English this undifferentiated word was regularly a preposition, with a sense of motion or position outward or away from something. An example is *him feollon tēaras of ðǣm ēagum, tears fell from his eyes. Of* corresponded roughly to our modern preposition *from*, and its earliest meaning is still apparent in *He came out of the door*, and *It is a quarter of nine.*

34.3 Stress the Determinant This Old English word *of* was also an adverb with the same meaning as the preposition; and *off* has been remarkably conservative in preserving its original sense to this day. An example of this adverb use in Old English is *þā hē him of dyde īsernbyrnan, then he took off his iron coat of mail.* As is apparent from the examples given, the adverb use is the more emphatic, since the preposition merely paves the way for its object. By the laws of phonology, stress tends to voiceless and lack of stress to voiced consonants. So it was to be expected that the stressed adverb should become [ɔf] while the unstressed preposition remained or rather became [əv], the vowel becoming obscured to [ə] and the consonant voicing to [v]. To show the voiceless character of the consonant in *off*, the letter was doubled; and thus Modern English has two words for what was one.

34.4 Many Doublets This process of making two or more words out of one is by no means rare in English. It applies to *through* and *thorough, grammar* and *glamour, antic* and *antique*, even *shah* and *check* (as a term in chess). If one includes as doublets all the varied forms of proper names such as *Elizabeth,* and also all the English forms of a single Latin word such as *capto, I catch,* one must conclude that words are like guinea pigs in their multiplying propensities.

34.5 Many in One It is not necessary that words themselves multiply to have meaning radiation. A single word may collect dozens of distinct significations, so many that it may be to all intents and purposes that many words. Thus the sentence *They boxed near where the box lay under the box hedge* might as well be given three different words instead of *box—They fought near where the parcel lay under the evergreen hedge.* Such multiplying of meanings is a common thing in English; many words have dozens of dictionary meanings, all developed by association (par. 34.1) out of the same original.

34.6 The Story of *Land* For an illustration of the radiation of meanings in English words one has been selected which is not outstanding in this respect but which is all the more typical of the common English vocabulary. The word *land* occupies eleven columns of space in the *Oxford Dictionary,* where *life* takes up nine and *man,* because of its greater variety of meanings, fifteen columns. For *land* as a noun there are twelve main headings of definitions and for *land* as a verb there are eight. Interjectional uses such as *My land!* or *Land sakes!* are not listed separately, perhaps because such uses are chiefly American.

34.7 Expansible Perhaps the most elementary fact about *land* as a noun is its expansibility, its capacity to name anything from a handful of earth to the great globe itself. Its derivation, from O.E. *land,* presents no difficulties. Another point of interest is its figurative use in the phrase *see how the land lies.* In general its noun uses are two: to point out earth as distinct from air, water, etc., and to express people as well as earth. This use of *land* to mean a country with its people is common in the Bible (*Isaiah* 9:1, . . . *when at the first he lightly afflicted the land of Zebulun and the land of Naphtali* . . .). The verb uses of *land* are more modern and might often be called colloquial. First applied to people coming ashore from a voyage (*We landed at Southampton*), it has expanded to any sort of reaching a destination by sea, rail, or air. It has developed also a transitive use (*We landed the fish in the boat*). As a phrase, *my native land,* it represents an intangible possession.

34.8 More Radiation Many other common words have developed more meanings than *land,* and to the student who has felt the attraction of words there is no richer and more profitable activity than the dictionary practice suggested in the exercises at the end of this chapter. Knowing the English language is an endless occupation, and yet even a little knowledge is no dangerous thing unless it makes the learner conceited or arrogant in the little he knows.

For the Student

A. FURTHER READINGS

Bloomfield, *Language,* pp. 425–443.

Greenough and Kittredge, *Words and Their Ways in English Speech,* pp. 259–271; 345–360.

Kennedy, *Current English,* pp. 402–407.

Robertson and Cassidy, *The Development of Modern English,* 2nd edit., pp. 239–240.

Bryant, "What One Word Can Do," *College English*, December 1941, pp. 284–290.
McKnight, *English Words and Their Background*, pp. 131–134; 152; 167; 388.
Weekley, *The Romance of Words*, 4th edit., pp. 139–154.

B. FOR CLASS DISCUSSION

1. What is meant by radiation of meaning? Illustrate.
2. What accounts for a doublet? Give an illustration and distinguish between the two words.
3. Look up the doublets mentioned in par. 4 and analyze them.
4. What is the relationship between the following pairs of words?

minister : monastery	feeble : foible
frail : fragile	faith : fidelity
regal : royal	legal : loyal
annoy : ennui	gentle : jaunty
warrant : guarantee	reward : regard
poesy : posy	dike : ditch
courtesy : curtsy	fancy : phantasy
taint : tint	tinge : tincture

5. Look up the history of *power, front, pipe, head, key*, and *hand* in the *Oxford Dictionary* and show how they exemplify radiation of meaning.
6. Look up the derivation of each of the following words and explain the relationship between the members of each pair. If both words are borrowed, determine which of the two words was borrowed first.

dignity : dainty	tavern : tabernacle
guest : hostile	arch : arc
shirt : skirt	clench : clinch
guardian : warden	chase (verb) : catch (verb)
domain : demesne	mettle : metal
dungeon : dominion	human : humane

7. Look up *corn* (on the foot) and *corn* (the grain) and *weeds* (plants) and *weeds* (garments). Are they different meanings of the same word or are they from different sources?
8. Look up the derivation and cognate relationship of this group of words: *read, write, pen, style, letter*, and *alphabet*.

9. Look up the derivation of each of the following words and explain the relationship of each group of three words:

gentile	gentle	genteel
molar	molest	emolument
capital	chief	chef

10. Read Margaret M. Bryant, "What One Word Can Do," *College English*, December 1941, pp. 284–290. What do you learn about the meaning of a word? Select another word and look up the various meanings.
11. How many names do you know that are derived from *Elizabeth?* What other names do you know that give rise to many shorter ones?

C. SUGGESTIONS FOR RESEARCH PAPERS

1. Doublets (Triplets) in English.
2. Select a group of words and show the radiation in meaning.

35

Semantics

35.1 A Child's World A child in first learning to talk is taught the names of concrete objects. He learns, for example, what part of the body "leg" refers to and gets an idea of the function of a leg. This knowledge can be transferred without any difficulty to corresponding limbs of other animals. Soon, however, the word is extended in meaning to include new referents, which resemble in some way the original one. The child finds that table and chairs have legs as well as human beings. He may even hear his parents speak of completing the first "leg" of a journey. At this moment he is getting his introduction into the vast metaphoric world in which he is going to live and try to make himself understood.

35.2 Associated Meanings As a word shifts to a new function it accumulates a background of associations, especially emotional associations, which have to be reckoned with each time one hears the word. For instance, if one has known at some time a thoroughly disreputable man by the name of Gordon and has hated or feared him, one often dislikes the name itself throughout life because of the earlier associations which surround the word. No two persons have ever learned the same word under exactly the same circumstances; therefore each word has a special context for each individual. Communication at best is a compromise, for each person talks out of his own private world: his experiences, memories, and impressions.

35.3 Semantics a Recent Study   Despite the fact that two persons can never completely understand each other, it is not until recent years that semantics, one of the most fascinating branches of language, has been explored. The term *semantics* was made popular by Michel Bréal in his great pioneer work *Essai de Sémantique* (1897). It is derived from the Greek, *semaneien*, "to signify." The term, however, was used in 1894 by the late Professor C. R. Lanman of Harvard in an address before the American Philological Association.[1] Bréal's study, a comprehensive treatise on the subject of word meanings, was derived almost exclusively from a study of Sanskrit, Greek, and Latin. He was concerned primarily with historical etymology and could have no knowledge of the many and varied interpretations and applications semantics would assume.

35.4 Popular Interest in Semantics   Obsessed as we in the modern world are with the psychological aspects of life, we have undoubtedly become more aware of the part words play for propaganda purposes. Situations in the world at large also make us realize the necessity for communication and understanding. At present we know that there is little understanding even among those who speak eloquently in the same language. As was pointed out in Chapter 33, the word is not one meaning but a meaning-cluster; and this obvious fact leads to a great deal of trouble with words—shifting, misleading, and all the other elements of what the semanticists call magic. Any good advertising man understands how words may be manipulated to bring about a given result, which in his case is the selling of merchandise. Recent years have seen a great increase in organizations for public relations, publicity, and propaganda in general. For this reason, perhaps, one can understand the popular interest in semantics that has been shown in the last two decades.

---

[1] See *New Evidence on Americanisms*, *s.v.* "Semantics," *American Speech*, Vol. XVII, No. 2, Part 1 (April, 1942), p. 125 (contributed by H. B. Allen). Professor Lanman's statement was: "The doctrine of the principles that underlie the processes of the development of the meanings of words may be called semantics or semasiology."

Modern semantics was greatly influenced by Lady V. Welby's work *Significs and Language*.[2] In her interest in the science of meaning, in significance in all its forms and relations, she dealt with the articulate form of our expressive and interpretative resources, which she held was not a matter of the meaning of words alone but applied to all forms of human energy and expression. Another work which gave impetus to the movement was *Principia Mathematica* by Bertrand Russell and A. N. Whitehead,[3] who in their concern with the foundations of mathematics gave much attention to the analysis of language. Their findings had a vast influence upon the logical positivist school of philosophy, which aided greatly in forwarding semantics by pointing out that an examination of many statements would show them to be about language and not about reality. They also designated the numerous functions of language and the types of utterances that are not worth consideration because of their inability to be proved to be true.

When a motion picture preview, flashed on the screen, informs us that the forthcoming attraction is "supercolossal," we know from sad experience that we must discount heavily such exuberance in adjectives, and the preview does not really mislead us. So too, when we read an advertisement stating that the X Car is "the best car in the low-price field," we realize that this is advertising sales talk and the courts usually are lenient about such boasts.

There is, however, a difference between permissible boasting and a misrepresentation of facts. In the United States, it is the Federal Trade Commission that has jurisdiction over claims in advertisements of a product. If the Z Tobacco Company calls its Zippo cigarettes "the best on the market," that is a subjective statement of opinion hard to prove or disprove. But if it asserts that Zippos contain milder tobacco rival manufacturers can protest to the Federal Trade Commission, and if the Zippo Company cannot prove that its tobacco is milder than that of other leading brands the Commission will forbid the use of such a phrase as either misleading or fraudulent advertising.

[2] Lady V. Welby, *Significs and Language* (London, Macmillan and Co., Ltd., 1911).
[3] Alfred North Whitehead and Bertrand Russell, *Principia Mathematica* (Cambridge, England, The University Press, 1910–13).

The introduction of colorful adjectives is likely to do its real dis-
service, however, in interpretive accounts of news events or of controversial issues in the world at large. We must be constantly on
guard against "bias words" in such material, and we must learn to
tell the difference between a strictly objective description and one
that is slanted for or against a person or idea.

It is hard for the alert, active mind not to take sides on some
crucial issue, and harder still to keep such bias out of writing or
speaking. For a rather obvious example of this kind, consider the
account in a news magazine of the hearing before the Atomic Energy
Committee of the United States Senate on former President Tru-
man's nomination of David Lilienthal to be chairman of the Atomic
Energy Commission. The foremost opponent of this nomination, and
long-time foe of Mr. Lilienthal, was Senator McKellar of Tennessee,
and the news magazine (*Time*, February 24, 1947, p. 23) opened its
account as follows: [4] "For three weeks Tennessee's Senator Kenneth
McKellar, an *ancient* knight on a *spavined* horse, had *roared* accusations at David Lilienthal in Washington. . . . He *bludgeoned* him
with *gossip, crackpot* letters, *unsupported* charges. . . . The whole
thing, it seemed, might subside: McKellar would *clump* off on his
moth-eaten charger and Lilienthal would be confirmed."

Study for a moment the italicized words and you will see how
far they go toward creating an unfavorable impression of Senator
McKellar. As an exercise in semantics, it would be interesting to set
about to create an entirely opposite impression by merely changing
these words in some such fashion as: ". . . An *elderly* knight on a
noble horse *piled up* accusations. . . . He *overwhelmed* him with
testimony of conversations, incriminating letters and *a multitude of*
charges. . . . McKellar would *ride majestically off* on his *sturdy*
steed."

This author has no intention here of taking any part in the
McKellar-Lilienthal controversy, and nothing cited is intended to do
so. It is purely an exercise in semantics to show how the choice of
certain "bias words" can determine the impression to be conveyed.

35.5 Ogden and Richards As the problems of semantics have
been studied, different schools of thought have developed, one of

---

[4] The italics are mine.

which was headed by C. K. Ogden and I. A. Richards, who in 1923 published *The Meaning of Meaning,* in which they pointed out the complexity of the general problem and stimulated interest in it. Richards himself has influenced literary groups through his *Principles of Literary Criticism* (1924), *Interpretation in Teaching* (1938), and *How to Read a Page* (1942) by stressing the accurate explication of texts. Hugh R. Walpole in his *Semantics: The Nature of Words and Their Meanings* (1941) has also helped in creating interest in this field. A popular text explaining the ideas of this school is *Understanding English: An Introduction to Semantics* (1942) by F. A. Philbrick. His thoughts have been especially influential in the legal field. Philbrick includes in his text also the idea of operational definitions and some scientific concepts which he gained from Professor P. W. Bridgman's *Logic of Modern Physics,* who explained for the layman the semantic changes that a specialist in his field makes in employing words like *time* and *space* as used by the average person. These terms mean something quite different to the specialist. After studying this problem he proposed a new technique in definitions called "operationalism." His idea is that one's concepts are synonymous with the operations by which one tests for the concept. He abandons all concepts that he cannot test by operations, for he believes they are meaningless. If one cannot test a concept like "democracy," according to Bridgman, it should be discarded.

35.6 General Semantics   As the problems of semantics have been studied, different schools of thought have developed, one of which was headed by Count Alfred Korzybski, a Polish mathematician and engineer, the author of *Science and Sanity.*[5] Korzybski's formulation is known as "general semantics." In a paper entitled "Psychiatry, Psychotherapy and Prevention," he explains the use of the term thus: [6]

We use the term "general semantics" in preference to the old "semantics" to indicate a fundamental difference between the two. The older difficulties originated because specialists in the "meaning" of words disregarded

[5] Alfred Korzybski, *Science and Sanity* (Lancaster, Pennsylvania, Science Press Printing Company, 1933; 2nd edit., 1941). Another basic book of his is *General Semantics* (Chicago, Institute of General Semantics, 1940).

[6] M. Kendig (ed.), *Papers from the Second American Congress on General Semantics* (Chicago, Institute of General Semantics, 1943), p. 95.

an unavoidable factor; namely, that any linguistic or mathematical theory must begin with undefined terms which cannot be defined any further by words. In principle these *undefined terms* are labels for direct experiences and observations which involve subcortical processes on the *silent (unspeakable) level*. Obviously no amount of verbal definition can convey to the individual first order pain, which he has to evaluate on the silent, organismal level inside of his skin.

It is the intent of this new science, the aim of which is to coordinate and bring together the various other sciences, to be of the utmost practical value in curing not only the linguistic but also the social and many of the individual ills of mankind, to be a guide to sane living through the use of scientific knowledge and method. Basically, the means to this end are the elimination of the biased or emotional element from all language used for factual purposes and the diagnosis of the degree to which any given utterance is an abstraction, so that the thinker may make his thinking progressively more concrete and therefore more effective. Mr. H. R. Huse, the author of *The Illiteracy of the Literate* (1933), in his essay "Reading and Understanding" [7] enthusiastically states that "the work of Korzybski would probably rank as one of the great accomplishments of the century if only for its exposition of the process of abstracting and the dangers of abstractionism."

35.7 Language in General Semantics Language plays a significant role in general semantics in that it is an instrument that man finds helpful in adjusting himself to his environment, to reality. The idea of the general semanticists is that language represents only imperfectly the actualities of the external world; and often there exists no externality to correspond to a given word. Words stand for ideas as well as things, and these ideas are frequently vague and are as frequently colored with the emotional bias which makes them less than impersonal in their rendering of an idea. The general semanticist, therefore, holds that man must realize that words are employed denotatively and connotatively; that words are changing quantities which depend upon their context; that words are not separate and fixed entities, are not things, but are symbols that mean what one

---

[7] *Studies in Language and Literature,* edited by George R. Coffman (Chapel Hill, University of North Carolina Press, 1945), p. 336.

makes them mean in a particular environment; that words are maps of a given territory and that a good map should represent as nearly as possible the territory it is supposed to present; that each individual should endeavor to date and index statements and to discount absolutes, generalizations, the idea of "allness"; and that in so doing he will become better adjusted to the world in which he lives.

35.8 Followers of Korzybski In 1938 Stuart Chase attempted to popularize Korzybski's *Science and Sanity* in the fields of law, government, economics, and sociology in his *Tyranny of Words*. He stressed the necessity of the clarification of definitions and the elimination of meaningless terms that are bandied about. Following him came S. I. Hayakawa and Irving J. Lee, writers of popular texts expounding the principles of "neuro-semantics" for the laymen. Hayakawa's *Language in Action* and Lee's *Language Habits in Human Affairs* both appeared in 1941. In 1949 Hayakawa brought out another volume, *Language in Thought and Action,* a restatement and expansion of his first book, and Lee brought together a collection of essays about language, background readings in semantics (pieces written by linguists, physicists, philosophers, mathematicians, physicians, sociologists, anthropologists): *The Language of Wisdom and Folly.* These two authors combined Korzybski's ideas with a good deal of the propaganda analysis which was current. Hayakawa also became editor in 1943 of a magazine which serves as the organ of the school of general semantics. Its title *Etc.: A Review of General Semantics* illustrates the idea of non-allness of the general semanticist, showing that not everything has been said or ever can be said about any object or event, for language is not exact. Two popular texts that have likewise stimulated a great deal of interest in the subject are Wendell Johnson's *People in Quandaries: A Semantic Approach to Personality Adjustment* (1946), a systematic presentation of the psychologic and physiologic substrata of general semantics, and Anatol Rapaport's *Science and the Goals of Man* (1950).[8]

35.9 Large Claim In *The Gift of Language,* Margaret Schlauch has stressed the need for caution in evaluating semantics in harmony with the enthusiastic claims of its proponents. She has pointed out

---

[8] More recent books of Rapaport are *Operational Philosophy* (New York, Harper & Brothers, 1953) and *Fights, Games and Debates* (Ann Arbor, University of Michigan Press, 1960).

that semantics is not so new or revolutionary as its propaganda would indicate, and has suggested that it may not after all prove to be the panacea for all ills. She grants, however, that the writers of Korzybski's school have made some contributions toward the techniques of definition by exploring some of the psychological aspects hitherto neglected.

35.10 Carnap The third school of semantics is based on *The Logical Syntax of Language* by Rudolf Carnap. In the "Foreword" to his work,[9] he clearly states that his aim is "to provide a system of concepts, a language by the help of which the results of logical analysis will be exactly formulable." He says, *"Philosophy is to be replaced by the logic of science*—that is to say, by the logical analysis of the concepts and sentences of the sciences, for *the logic of science is nothing other than the logical syntax of the language of science."* Following this work came *Introduction to Semantics,* in which he states that in addition to a purely formal analysis of language, an analysis of the signifying function of language—a theory of meaning and interpretation—is needed and that he is attempting to furnish a theory of that kind; that is, to find adequate, exact definitions for the customary semantical concepts [10] and for new concepts related to them and to supply a theory based on these definitions.[11] In his *Formalization of Logic* which followed [12] he then attempts to apply the method of semantics set forth in the *Introduction to Semantics,* and shows the possibility and scope of the formalization of logic, a much discussed problem, especially during the last century, the period of the development of modern logic.

His work, the third volume of the series in "Studies in Semantics," entitled *Meaning and Necessity: A Study in Semantics and Modal Logic* (1947), had as its main purpose the development of a

[9] Rudolf Carnap, *The Logical Syntax of Languages* (New York, Harcourt, Brace and Company, 1937), p. xiii.

[10] He points out some of the concepts employed, not only in science but in everyday life, as, for example, a person's saying that he is using a certain word in a different sense from someone else; or that a certain assertion is true or false; or that a particular statement is analytic, *i.e.,* true for purely logical reasons; or that a second statement follows from the first or contradicts it.

[11] Rudolf Carnap, *Introduction to Semantics* (Cambridge, Mass., Harvard University Press, 1942), "Preface," p. v.

[12] Rudolf Carnap, *Formalization of Logic* (Cambridge, Mass., Harvard University Press, 1943).

new method for analyzing and describing the meanings of linguistic expressions. This method, called "the method of extension and intension," [13] in contradistinction to other semantical methods employed in traditional philosophy and by present-day writers, regards an expression, not as naming something, but as having an intension and an extension. He regards semantics as a tool, as one among the logical instruments needed for the task of getting and systematizing knowledge.

In 1938, a group of "logical empiricists," as they called themselves (Niels Bohr, Rudolf Carnap, John Dewey, Otto Neurath, Bertrand Russell, Charles W. Morris), began the *International Encyclopedia of Unified Science.* They believed that a theory of signs well worked out would furnish the basis for the unification of knowledge. Their purpose was to study the languages of the special sciences and to find the relationships of these languages to each other and then to find the relationships of scientific language to the languages of other fields of human activity. An important contribution in explaining the foundations of a theory of signs was Charles W. Morris's *Signs, Language, and Behavior,* published in 1946. Following came Susanne K. Langer's *Philosophy in a New Key* (1948), another significant work stressing the need of symbolization in our lives.

35.11 Practical Semanticists In speaking of semantics, one should not leave out the practical group including such persons as Stuart Chase (see par. 7); Oliver L. Reiser, author of *The Promise of Scientific Humanism Toward a Unification of Scientific, Religious, Social and Economic Thought,* in which he advocated a new mode of orientation—or semantic reaction—a new culture pattern, termed "global thinking"; Thomas C. Pollock, who wrote an interesting book entitled *The Nature of Literature: Its Relation to Science, Language and Human Experience;* Jerome Frank, who, by applying psychological teachings, examined the whole nature of law and legal thought; and Thurman Arnold, a specialist in law and government who writes about the power of symbols, including words, over us. His thesis that we are ruled by those who manipulate our symbols is evident in *The Symbols of Government* (1935) and in *The Folklore*

---

[13] Rudolf Carnap, *Meaning and Necessity: A Study in Semantics and Modal Logic* (Chicago, University of Chicago Press, 1947), "Preface," p. v.

of Capitalism (1937). He examined law and economics as symbolic thinking and conduct which condition the behavior of men in groups, and not as collections of truths. He considered the ceremonies and the theories of social institutions the symbols of government. Jerome Frank showed that not only social and economic facts should be considered in making legal decisions but also our use of words to convey thought, the limitations of formal logic, and the delusive manner in which an oft-repeated legal fiction becomes an accepted maxim, as well as the fact that we are living in a modern, dynamic, ever-changing world. Mr. Frank felt that justice cannot be meted out unless both the lawyer and the judge are aware of the deficiencies in their own thought processes, are aware of the power of clichés, and know that rules of law are not predictable certainties.

35.12 Understanding of Terms Necessary Whether semantics be regarded as a genuinely modern technique or as merely the new name for an old one, there can be no gainsaying the fact that the writings of the twentieth century on semantics have served admirably to draw attention to the dangers that lie in misconceptions of the meaning of our commonest terms. Take the word *American,* which may mean opposite things to two different persons. National discord and even international friction can be caused by differing interpretations of a word or phrase. As has been indicated in this chapter, semantics has commanded the time and effort of a number of scholars. Allen Walker Read is preparing *A Semantic Guide to Current English,*[14] an interesting and worthwhile project, in which he will deal with several thousand words, based on some 40,000 quotations that he is amassing from various sources, to show the different levels of abstraction in connection with a term. He will include such important terms as *Americanism, foreigner, liberal, loyal, progress, propaganda, socialist,* and *subversive.* If this study achieves its goal, semantics will be able to provide a still more tangible aid to the study of our language than it already has done. Attempts such as those the semanticists have made would seem to be essential as

[14] "The Lexicographer and General Semantics with a Plan for a 'Semantic Guide to Current English,'" reprinted from General Semantics Monographs, Number III, *A Theory of Meaning Analyzed* (Chicago, Institute of General Semantics, 1942).

one of the steps toward promoting that goodwill of which the world is so badly in need today.

For the Student

A. FURTHER READINGS

Bréal, Semantics.

Hayakawa, *Language in Action.*

Hayakawa, *Language in Thought and Action.*

Lee, *Language Habits in Human Affairs.*

Lee (ed.), *The Language of Wisdom and Folly.*

Etc.: *A Review of General Semantics,* Vol. I, No. 1 (August, 1943), to date.

Kendig (ed.), *Papers from the Second American Congress on General Semantics,* Institute of General Semantics, 1943.

Korzybski, *Science and Sanity.*

Johnson, *People in Quandaries: A Semantic Approach to Personality Adjustment.*

Hayawaka (ed.), *Language, Meaning and Maturity* (Review of General Semantics, 1943–1953).

Hayakawa (ed.), *Our Language and Our World* (Review of General Semantics, 1953–1958).

Gray and Wise, *The Bases of Speech,* 3rd edit., Chapter IX.

Rapaport, *Science and the Goals of Man.*

Rapaport, *Operational Philosophy.*

Rapaport, *Fights, Games and Debates.*

Ullmann, *The Principles of Semantics,* 2nd edit.

Huse, *Illiteracy of the Literate.*

Huse, "Reading and Understanding," *Studies in Language and Literature,* edited by George R. Coffman.

Chase, *The Tyranny of Words.*

Schlauch, *The Gift of Language,* pp. 109–132.

Philbrick, *Understanding English.*

Ogden and Richards, *The Meaning of Meaning.*

Richards, *Interpretation in Teaching.*

Walpole, *Semantics: The Nature of Words and Their Meanings.*

Pollock, *The Nature of Literature: Its Relation to Science, Language and Human Experience.*

Arnold, *The Symbols of Government.*

Arnold, *The Folklore of Capitalism.*

Frank, *Law and the Modern Mind.*

Reiser, *The Promise of Scientific Humanism Toward a Unification of Scientific, Religious, Social and Economic Thought.*

Carnap, *The Logical Syntax of Language.*

Morris, *Signs, Language and Behavior.*

Bloomfield, "Language or Ideas?" *Language,* Vol. XII (April, 1936), pp. 89–95.

Firth, "The Technique of Semantics," *Transactions of the Philological Society,* London, 1935, pp. 36–72; also in *Papers in Linguistics 1934–1951.*

Edwards, *Group Leader's Guide to Propaganda Analysis.*

Glicksberg, "General Semantics and the Science of Man," *Scientific Monthly,* Vol. LXII (May, 1946), pp. 440–446.

Bryant, "Semantics Today," *Word Study* (December, 1945), pp. 6–7.

B. FOR CLASS DISCUSSION

1. What does the word *semantics* mean? Look up its origin in the *Oxford Dictionary.*

2. Read an editorial in your daily newspaper and see what means has been used to slant the writing in a certain direction. Can you rewrite the editorial, using the same facts, so as to give a different impression?

3. What is the difference between report writing and editorial writing?

4. Make sentences illustrating numerous areas of meaning from the following words: *fast, free, fight, battle, gas, x, strike.*

5. Hayakawa calls *fourflusher* in *He is a fourflusher* a "snarl-word" and *statesman* in *He is a statesman* a "purr-word." Make a list of twelve such "snarl-words" and "purr-words."

6. Jot down as rapidly as you can the words associated in your mind with *aeroplane, army, eraser, vacation, president, paper.* Compare your lists with those of other students to show the trend of your thinking.

7. What words do you know that take on unpleasant associations in certain contexts, as the word *protective* in certain phrases?

8. Select from your daily newspaper words which cause semantic difficulty and explain the reason.

9. Why do such words as *democracy, personality, liberty, freedom, morality* cause so much difficulty in civil life?

10. Make a list of political terms which need to be clarified. Ask the ordinary person the meaning of the terms. Then look them up in the *Encyclopedia of the Social Sciences* or some similar authoritative source

for explanations. Can you make a simple definition that will render the word semantically innocuous?

11. Read the pages on "Propaganda" in Hitler's *Mein Kampf*. What method did Hitler use in his campaign to dominate the German people?

12. Arrange the following words in order of their abstraction. Begin with the most concrete.

(a) magazine, *Time*, a weekly, channel of public information, a publication, a digest.
(b) Edith Jacobs, girl, blonde, Texan, American, human being, female, teacher.
(c) rain, moisture, cloud, atmosphere, sun, heat, condensation, saturation.

13. From the point of view of position and social status, what is the difference between a roomer and a paying guest; a clerk and a receptionist; a nursemaid and a governess; a drummer and a sales manager; a Pullman porter and an airline hostess; a page and an errand boy?

14. Anlyze the key words and phrases in well-known political speeches of the past. How did the speaker use language to achieve his particular end?

15. Do the same thing with a speech of the present.

16. Familiarize yourself with the work of Clyde Miller, Harvey Cantrell, Violet Edwards, who studied propaganda analysis without using the name *semantics*.

17. Look up Violet Edwards' analysis of propaganda in her *Group Leader's Guide to Propaganda Analysis* and work out some of the suggested group projects. Discuss the semantic aspects of propaganda analysis.

C. SUGGESTIONS FOR RESEARCH PAPERS

1. A Study of "Loaded" Words (words that reveal or arouse feeling).
2. Semantics in Relation to Propaganda Analysis.
3. Semantics as a Tool for Dictators.
4. A History of the Bureau for Propaganda Analysis.
5. The Use of Semantics in Public Relations (Politics).

IV

Grammar and Usage

36

Definitions and Principles

36.1 Familiar Material   After a survey of the heritage of Modern English, a study of the speech sounds, the letter, and the origin and meaning of words, we turn now to the use made of language by the person of normal intelligence, who constantly employs sounds, words, phrases, and sentences in his daily life. To understand the functioning of a language, it is necessary to know its grammar, and that will now be our task with respect to English.

The very word "grammar" has some unfortunate connotations; it reminds the student of his struggles in composition and diction classes, and it also conjures up visions of meaningless, dry-as-dust, hair-splitting scholarship, such as was immortalized wryly by Robert Browning in "A Grammarian's Funeral":

> He settled *Hoti's* business—let it be!—
> Properly based *Oun*—
> Gave us the doctrine of the enclitic *De,*
> Dead from the waist down.[1]

[1] Ll. 95–98.

It is in the Germany of the nineteenth century that the pains-taking but dull linguistic research reached its zenith, and there is the apocryphal story of the philologist who had devoted his whole life to the study of the dative and ablative cases in Tacitus. On his deathbed he said with a sigh that his life had been a failure, but his friends tried to cheer him by pointing to the monumental tomes he had written on his specialty.

"Ah, yes," he replied sadly, "but I fear I dissipated my energies. I could have accomplished so much more if I had confined myself to the dative case alone."

We shall try to avoid the pitfalls of such a deadening, fruitless attitude toward the subject, yet it is only fair to make it clear at the outset that a true understanding of grammar is not easily gained; it requires genuine thinking, and a mere parroting of rules will not suffice. It is, however, a challenge to our intellectual power, just as philosophy and higher mathematics are.

There is the temptation to over-emphasize the subject by claim-ing that training in grammar is absolutely essential to the communi-cation of ideas, but that is not true. Many persons are unaware of the nature and structure of the messages they receive, either by reading or listening, but they understand them thoroughly. They cannot describe or explain them scientifically, even though the com-munications are a necessary part of daily existence. It is this com-monplace everyday communication which grammar raises from the unconscious to the conscious level of thought and examines in an orderly manner. Even so, it is difficult to convince some persons that grammar is essential. One middle-aged parent of the author's ac-quaintance, provoked at her daughter's poor marks in English, re-marked petulantly, "I don't see why they make all that fuss over grammar, as long as a person knows how to speak proper." It would have been too unkind to point out to the woman that she did not know how to speak properly.

36.2 Intricacy of Task   Although grammar deals with the sim-plest and most near-at-hand of human phenomena, this is by no means to say that grammar in itself is simple or easy. The hand-picked sentences of the average elementary textbook misrepresent a subject which is endless and abstruse. The complete analysis of even a brief sentence might easily call for a volume larger than this one.

Thus Edward Sapir in *Language* devoted a chapter to the sentence *The farmer kills the duckling,* and a whole volume could be written on certain sentences, if it dealt really exhaustively with the grammatical aspects of the words included. The student must not delude himself that grammatical analysis stops with the particular answer demanded by a particular exercise. Even the simplest sentence mirrors the cumulative linguistic intelligence of the race and may in a very real sense be called too deep for complete understanding.

36.3 Broadest Concept   The most generalized term which we shall have occasion to use is *communication. A communication is a message originated in one mind and (normally) transferred to another.* Notice that this definition assumes two elements, which may somewhat loosely be named, first, the speaker or writer, and, second, the hearer or reader. Lacking the combination of these two, the communication is incomplete. This fact of the dual character of communication is often disregarded, because the hearer or reader plays a passive part; but it is a real duality nevertheless and should be recognized as such.

36.4 Definition of Language   The term *communication* includes more than the term *language,* because communications may be and often are made by other than linguistic means. Such messages are frequently transmitted by means of facial expression, by gesture, by nonspeech sounds such as whistling, by gifts, by actions, by sirens, and so on. *Language is a systematic scheme of communication in "idea" units which are usually words.* The eminent linguist Sapir defined language [2] as "a purely human and non-instinctive method of communicating ideas, emotions, and desires by means of a system of voluntarily produced symbols."

36.5 Word a Fluctuating Concept   The student will naturally expect to receive next a definition of the term *word,* but this is not an easy task, as all lexicographers and other workers with words know. Is *baseball* one word or two? Is *seventy-five* one word or two? Is *dining room* one word or two? In employing compounds, especially in writing them, there is the eternal problem of writing the different elements as one solid word, or as separate words, or joining them by means of hyphens. Why should one not write *dining room*

[2] Edward Sapir, *Language* (New York, Harcourt, Brace and Company, 1921), p. 7.

as one solid word if *bedroom* is written as one word? Then there are
the shortened or clipped forms of words, such as *ad* for *advertisement* and *gym* for *gymnasium*. Is *ad* to be considered as a separate
word along with *advertisement?* Certainly it conveys to the hearer
or reader as definite an idea as does *advertisement* and is perhaps as
frequently used. Are *dog* and *dogs* two separate words or merely
different forms of the same word? As for the verb, are *walk, walked,
walking,* for instance, separate words or only different forms of the
same word? [3]

36.6 Larger Uses of Word The basis of the definition of the
term *word* is psychological rather than factual and is moreover obscured by the fact that certain arbitrary distinctions enter and tend
to govern our thinking. We are likely to regard a word as being
merely a set of letters printed in a group on a page. But this concept
is inadequate. It should be corrected by the concept, formerly usual
and even now frequent, of a word as any unitary group of linguistic
elements, whether phrase, sentence, or even volume. Such a concept
is reflected in the greeting, "Well, what's the good word?" in the
question, "Have you had any word from John yet?" and in many
Biblical passages such as *Psalms* 68:11: "The Lord gave the word;
great was the company of them that published it." The distinguishing feature of the word is thus unity in communication. The term is
generally confined to the smallest isolable unit of communication,
and it is only the exceptional word (such as *yes, hello, goodbye*)
which is used as a complete communication. But the larger possible
uses of the term should not be wholly disregarded.

36.7 "Idea" Unit One should also remember that there may be
an "idea" unit within a word, that is, subword elements, such as *un-*
and *over-* in *unfortunate* and *overflow;* or the idea may be suggested
not by separate words or parts of words but by word collocations,
illustrated in *cash and carry, get over, get to,* and *get in with.*

---

[3] One of the latest definitions is that of James Sledd. He says that "any free
form which consists of a single base, with or without accompanying prefixes or
suffixes but with a superfix [a stress pattern], is a word." (*A Short Introduction
to English Grammar,* Chicago, Scott, Foresman and Company, 1959, p. 65).
This definition refers to a base like *kind* which can be used as a free form but
can have the prefixes and suffixes *un-, -ness,* and *-es* (only parts of words which
cannot stand alone).

A word is a pattern (oral or represented), a linguistic form, consisting of one or more speech sounds, a base and its stress (a superfix) with or without one or more affixes.

36.8 Two Aspects of Word A word may be considered mechanically and functionally. Mechanically, it is a conglomerate consisting of one or more speech sounds; and functionally, it is a unitary concept, idea, or thought which constitutes or may constitute a communication.

36.9 Grammar The English language, or any language, may be studied as an art, in which case the student is trained to master his linguistic instrument as the violinist or the painter masters his artistic medium, for the purpose of artistic communication. Composition, rhetoric, creative writing, elocution, public speaking, prosody, and poetics are among the various names used for the treatments of the many and varied aspects of English as an art, none of which properly belongs under the head of grammar, even though they may overlap grammar at times. In eliminating the consideration of the English language as an art, we have left English as a science, which calls for a systematic analysis of the complex of patterns which have grown up through the centuries by those using it, the kind the scientist devotes to his subject of investigation. *Grammar is the analysis of communication in words.*[4]

36.10 No Universal Grammar With the possible exception of *word,* the terms we have been defining up to this point are all universal terms. That is to say, they are applicable to every language on earth. *Word* may also be regarded as a universal term if we keep our concept sufficiently flexible. Thus *amo* is one word in Latin while *I love* is two words in English; and in certain dialects of primitive peoples an entire communication may be a single conglomerate word. But aside from these four concepts—communication, language, word, and grammar—there are few terms which will apply to all languages; and this fact indicates that there is no such thing as a universal grammar.

[4] See discussion of *grammar* in its different senses (descriptive, prescriptive, historical, comparative) in Porter G. Perrin, *Writer's Guide and Index to English,* 3rd edit., rev. with assistance of Karl Dykema (Chicago, Scott, Foresman and Company, 1959), pp. 545–546.

36.11 Sentence an Ambiguous Term   The term *sentence*, next to
be defined, may or may not be universal, according to the definition.
It is often described by grammarians as being simply a complete
and independent communication. On this basis it is obviously characteristic of all languages. Since, however, it is the English language
with which we are concerned, the specific definition applicable to
that language will be considered. The term *sentence* is often defined
as a group of words expressing a complete thought. The difficulty
with this definition is that it does not tell us what a complete thought
is. It is entirely subjective. Jespersen, one of the outstanding modern grammarians, expands this definition when he states: "A sentence
is a (relatively) complete and independent human utterance—the
completeness and independence being shown by its standing alone
or its capability of standing alone, i.e., of being uttered by itself." [5]
In this definition he wishes to take in as sentences such utterances
as "Hands down!" "How wonderful!" "What a delicious dinner!"
"Anything on the table?" "Jolly old Jack!" which he considers as
complete as those utterances containing subjects and predicates.

Another definition which one often finds in grammar books is
that a sentence is a group of words containing a subject and a predicate. The definer also adds that the group of words must not be in a
dependent clause. This definition fails to take into account the many
subjectless and verbless expressions, similar to those cited in the
preceding paragraph, which occur in much of our conversation and
to a lesser degree in our writing. Even if ellipsis is assumed, one can
not tell exactly what subject or what verb has been left out, for no
particular subject or verb has been associated with a particular expression.

Many other attempts have been made to define the sentence,
especially by the linguistic scientist.[6] Recently the definitions have
been given in terms of intonation patterns. Because of the many

---

[5] *Philosophy of Grammar,* p. 307.

[6] See Sapir, *Language,* pp. 36–37; Bloomfield, *Language,* pp. 170–177;
Block and Trager, *Outline of Linguistic Analysis,* pp. 71, 75; Henry M. Hoen-
igswald, *Proceedings of the International Congress of Linguists* (1948), p. 160;
Fries, *Structure of English,* pp. 9–28; Whitehall, *Structural Essentials of English,* pp. 29–30; Francis, *The Structure of American English,* pp. 367–373;
Hockett, *A Course in Modern Linguistics,* p. 199; Sledd, *A Short Introduction
to English Grammar,* pp. 166–182; 246–247.

complications involved some linguists are inclined to discard *sentence* as a scientific term.

But for practical purposes for formal, written expository English a specific definition will be given. *A sentence is a communication in words, usually containing at least one independent verb and its subject with end punctuation, representing a final intonation-pause pattern,* as in *The book is on the table* or *The car runs.*

36.12 New Term Required The sentence narrowly defined, as above, is not the only kind of communication in English. There are numerous communications—on buildings, billboards, and windows; on letters, envelopes, and cards; in conversation and even in formal writing—variously called incomplete, partial, fragmentary sentences, verbless sentences, and nonsentences, no term of which is accurate or adequate. The term *nonsentence* is perhaps the best, but one can object to it on the basis that it suggests that the nonsentence is derived from the sentence, whereas it is undoubtedly true that the nonsentence is the primary in the historical development of grammar and the sentence the derivative. *The nonsentence is a communication in other than sentence form.*

36.13 Disagreement General The student must not accept the six foregoing definitions, or indeed any statement made in this book, as certainly true. He must learn at the outset to adopt and maintain a critical attitude toward grammatical authority. No matter how axiomatic or reasonable a statement may sound, it may be, and in all probability has been, contradicted or modified by some other authority. One of the best lessons which the student can learn will grow out of comparing and weighing authorities, testing their divergent views, and coming to his own conclusions about what to accept and what to reject. He will also learn that language is always changing and that grammar changes accordingly.

For the Student

A. FURTHER READINGS

Sapir, *Language*, pp. 1–23; 32–42.
Robertson and Cassidy, *The Development of Modern English*, 2nd edit.,
    pp. 1–14.
Jespersen, *The Philosophy of Grammar*, pp. 45–57; 92–95; 305–312.
Roberts, *Understanding Grammar*, pp. 292–296.
Aiken, *English Present and Past*, pp. 51–74.
Sweet, *A New English Grammar*, Part I, pp. 1–8; 204–211.
Francis, *The Structure of American English*, pp. 200–208; 367–373.
Bloomfield, *Language*, pp. 170–177.
Fries, *Structure of English*, pp. 9–28.
Hockett, *A Course in Modern Linguistics*, pp. 166–176; 199.
Sledd, *A Short Introduction to English Grammar*, pp. 63–68; 166–182;
    246–247.

B. FOR CLASS DISCUSSION

1. From this chapter select five general propositions concerning grammar
   (for example, no universal grammar) and substantiate or refute them
   from your knowledge of English or other languages.
2. The duality of form and function (see par. 8) runs throughout grammar
   and is discussed by many grammarians, among them Jespersen, *The
   Philosophy of Grammar*, Chapter 3. Find and discuss five examples of
   this duality of form and function in grammar.
3. Other dualities mentioned in this chapter are
   (a) speaker and hearer;
   (b) writer and reader;
   (c) art and science;
   (d) speech sounds and nonspeech sounds;
   (e) speech and nonspeech communication;
   (f) sentence and nonsentence.
   Discuss and explain each of these critically with examples and with
   special reference to English grammar.
4. The term *lexeme* has been coined to indicate "idea" units, whether
   words or not, which are included in a lexicon. From your dictionary
   collect ten examples of different kinds of lexemes. See Hockett, pp.
   169–171, § 19.4.
5. In your own conversation or reading, find examples of the nonsentence.

6. Take one or two paragraphs in this or some other textbook and put them into the language of everyday conversation. In what ways does your version differ from the original? Do you think these differences can generally be found in comparing spoken language with written language?
7. After reading the first chapter of Sapir's *Language,* discuss the relation between language and thought. Do you believe that it is possible to think without speech?
8. Study five different definitions of the sentence in the suggestions given for "Further Readings" and then make a definition of your own.

C. SUGGESTIONS FOR RESEARCH PAPERS

1. Write a 1000-word paper on "What Is a Word?" using several dictionary definitions, Chapter 6 in Jespersen's *The Philosophy of Grammar,* Sledd (pp. 63–68), Francis (pp. 200–208), and Hockett (pp. 166–176), together with any other authorities you find helpful.
2. Do the same for the five other words (for example, *sentence*) defined in this chapter. In connection with the definition of *nonsentence,* you may use Chapter 7 of Aiken's *Commonsense Grammar* and the discussions of fragmentary, incomplete and verbless sentences in several composition manuals or grammars of recent date, such as those by Perrin and Dykema, *op. cit.,* pp. 52–54 (subjectless and verbless sentences); pp. 54–56; 73–74; 535 (fragmentary sentences) and Roberts, pp. 298–300.
3. Do the same for four additional terms (for example, *sound*) which are universal in grammar.
4. Select some language other than English and write a sketch of its grammatical differences from English so far as you understand them, stressing as far as possible points covered in this chapter. (For students who know a foreign language.)

37

The Nature of English Grammar

37.1 Best Method of Study To get a clear idea of what the English language is today, it is not enough to look at modern examples. We must compare English grammatically with its past self, measuring its maturity by the yardstick of its adolescence. Only thus can we see how it has developed, and only thus can we get a perspective on matters of present-day grammatical choices, *i.e.*, correctness and incorrectness.

37.2 Many Changes to Be Studied The Greek language has altered less in the course of twenty-five centuries than English has in ten. English has changed almost beyond recognition in its history of little more than a thousand years. The alphabet has changed; sounds have changed; words are different; and even the structure of sentences has undergone considerable alteration. A comparison of the English of nine centuries ago with the English of today will not only show us the extent of the change; it will reveal some interesting facts about the English grammar we now use.

37.3 Historical Passage Selected For the purposes just indicated I have chosen the famous description of William the Con-

queror, written partly in prose and partly in verse, by a contemporary
or a near-contemporary of that king. The extract is based upon Laud
MS #636 of the *Anglo-Saxon Chronicle,* which is now in the Bod-
leian Library of Oxford University. The modern equivalents of all
words not immediately comprehensible are placed just below their
first occurrence.

Character of William the Conqueror

Sē cyng Willelm þe wē embe specað wæs swīðe wīs man ꟻ
this King William that about speak was very wise and

swīðe rīce ꟻ wurðfulre and strengere þonne ǣnig his
great more honored more powerful than any (of) his

foregenga wǣre. Hē wæs milde þām gōdum mannum þe God
predecessors were gentle (to) those good men

lufedon ꟻ ofer eall gemett stearc þam mannum þe wiðcwǣdon his
loved beyond all measure severe resisted

willan. . . . Ēac hē wæs swȳðe wurðful. . . . Swilce hē wæs ēac swȳðe
will also likewise

stearc man ꟻ rǣðe swā þæt man ne dorste nān þing ongēan his willan
stern fierce so that not dared no thing against

dōn. Hē hæfde eorlas on his bendum þe dydon ongēan his willan. Biscopas
do had earls fetters acted bishops

hē sǣtte of heora biscoprīce ꟻ abbodas of heora abbodrīce ꟻ þægnas
removed from their bishoprics abbots abbeys nobles

on cweartern ꟻ æt nēxtan hē ne sparode his āgenne brōðor. . . . Betwyx
prison at last spared own brother among

ōðrum þingum nis nā tō forgytane þæt gōde frið þe hē macode on
other things is be forgotten order established

þisan lande swā þæt ān man þe him sylf āht wǣre mihte faran ofer his
this a himself good might travel

rīce mid his bōsum full goldes ungeradad ꟻ nān man ne dorste
kingdom with bosom (of) gold unmolested

slēan ōðerne man næfde   hē næfre swā micel yfel gedōn wið þone
slay another   had not   never   much evil done to   the
ōðerne. . . .
other

Hē rīxade ofer Englæ land. Ꝺ hit mid his gēapscipe swā þurh
    ruled   England   it   skill   thoroughly

smēade þæt næs   ān hīd landes   innan Englæ lande þæt hē nyste
surveyed   was not   plot (of) land in   knew-not

hwā hēo   hæfde oððe hwæs   hēo wurð wæs. . . . Witodlīce on his
who she (it) had   or   (of) what   value   certainly

tīman hæfdon men mycel geswinc Ꝺ swīðe manige tēonan.
time had   trouble   many sorrows

    Castelas hē lēt   wyrcean
    castles   caused to-be-built

    Ꝺ earme men swīðe swencean
      poor   to labor

    Sē cyng wæs swā swīðe stearc

    Ꝺ benam of   his underþēoddan manig marc
      took from   subjects   marks

    goldes   Ꝺ mā hundred punda seolfres.
    (of) gold   pounds (of) silver

    ðet hē nam be wihte Ꝺ mid mycelan unrihte
      took by weight   much   injustice

    of   his landlēode, for littelre nēode.
    from   citizenry   need

    Hē wæs on gītsunge befeallan
        avarice fallen

    Ꝺ grǣdignesse hē lufode mid   ealle. . . .
      greediness   loved above

    Wālā wā þæt ǣnig man sceolde mōdigan   swā
    alas woe   should become proud

    hine sylf upp āhebban Ꝺ ofer ealle men tellan
    himself   exalt   rule

Sē ælmihtiga God cȳþæ his sāule mildheortnisse
   almighty   show   soul mercy

Ꞁ dō   him his synna forgifenesse.
  grant   sins   forgiveness

37.4 Alphabet Changes A glance at this sample of Old English shows three symbols which we lack today: æ, ð, þ. In addition, there have been other changes, so that it would be difficult for one unacquainted with Old English to read this passage in the original manuscript. Certain letters which we now possess (v, z, j, q) are not represented at all.

37.5 Unstable Spelling As for the spelling in the quoted passage, not only is it different from that of Modern English, but it varies within the passage itself, so that the same word may be spelled in more than one fashion. Frequently the spelling is all that prevents our recognizing a modern word, such as *silver*, in its earlier form. Early orthography is of course complicated by the fact that many of the words have case or other inflectional ending, making it doubly difficult to recognize them for the ancestors of familiar modern words. Examples are *macode* (*made*) and *sceolde* (*should*).

37.6 Phonology Different The pronunciation does not show itself on the printed page, but in general it may be said that the sounds in this passage are according to spelling. Thus the word *his* is pronounced *hiss* rather than *hiz*, as it is today. Our word *who* keeps two of the old letters, but very little of the sounds of the earlier form *hwā*. In general the old vowels had their Continental values rather than those of Modern English, while the consonants and the short vowels usually follow their present values.

37.7 Vocabulary Altered Probably a majority of all the words in this Old English passage have some descendant word still existing in Modern English; but very often the modern word has acquired a different meaning or is used differently from the old. Thus our word *worth* is, in adjective form, *worthy* rather than O.E. *worthful*, and the Latin-derived *predecessors* has replaced *foregenga* or *foregoers*, even though the meaning of the latter word might in context be clear. The word *stark* (O.E. *stearc*) is not in very common use, and its common meaning is no longer *severe* or *stern*. Nevertheless the fact that Old English is actually English is apparent in the ease with which any modern student can get a feeling for the language, and the pleasure involved in tracing the meanings which its words convey.

37.8 Prepositions in Old English   Coming at last to the grammar of this early English, we notice that prepositions are used in what seem to be peculiar ways. The words *of* and *from* are the same word, *of*. The preposition *with* in this passage is used to indicate opposition rather than accompaniment, which latter idea is expressed by *mid;* while the old use of *with,* which survives in such phrases as *to fight with him,* is not general today. Also in the passage studied it is noticeable that a preposition such as *with* or *under* or *for* often combines with another word (usually noun or verb) in a sort of loose compounding, a phenomenon rare in Modern English. It is worth while to study separately the usage of each preposition in this passage, to get an idea of the difference between Old and Modern English.

37.9 Inflections Abundant   Whereas today on the average printed page about one word in six shows inflectional modification, probably the majority of Old English words were inflected. Often the inflection made it unnecessary to use a preposition which would be required today. The letter *n* was as frequent in Old English inflections as *s* is now. Often inflections are repeated in a series of words—*þām gōdum mannum.* Each inflection in the quoted passage should be studied.

37.10 Negative Prominent   Whereas today the double negative is discredited, in Old English it occurred frequently, and the negative letter *n* might also be prefixed to a verb to indicate negation, much as *n't* may be added today: *nis* for *isn't* and *næfde* for *hadn't.* We have today one survival of this in the expression *willy-nilly.*

37.11 Sentence Order Established   The sentence order of this passage is worthy of very careful study. In general it is subject-verb-object as in Modern English, showing that the modern sequence had already become established; but when this order is not followed, the variations are extremely interesting. Occasionally the verb is placed at the end, as often in Modern German—"nothing against his will to do," instead of "do nothing against his will." The student may make a list of all instances in which there is variation from the modern sentence order.

37.12 Rhyme Used in Poetry The student will notice that the poetical passage makes use of rhyme, sometimes between lines and sometimes within the line. This poetical usage is not typical of early Old English verse, which ordinarily was alliterative. The presence of rhyme is one of the indications that this was a piece written after the Norman invasion had made the French technique of rhyming familiar to the English. The fact that the poem was about the Conqueror was probably another incentive for employing the new method of versification that he and his men had brought over.

37.13 Other Grammatical Indications The student may scan the illustrative passage for other grammatical matters such as the use of pronouns, distinctions between the parts of speech, and placing of adjectives in relation to nouns. If necessary an Old English grammar may be consulted to identify the various forms.

For the Student

A. FURTHER READINGS

General

Baugh, *A History of the English Language*, 2nd edit., pp. 59–77.
Bradley, *The Making of English*, pp. 1–13; 35–58.
Emerson, *The History of the English Language*, pp. 286–395.
Krapp, *Modern English, Its Growth and Present Use*, pp. 56–98.
Robertson and Cassidy, *The Development of Modern English*, 2nd edit., pp. 40–44; 115–145.
Jespersen, *Negation in English and Other Languages*.

Works on Old English

Quirk and Wrenn, *An Old English Grammar*.
Moore and Knott, *The Elements of Old English*, 8th edit.
Anderson and Williams, *Old English Handbook*.
Bright, *An Anglo-Saxon Reader*, rev. edit. by Hulbert.
Campbell, *Old English Grammar*.
Clark Hall, *A Concise Anglo-Saxon Dictionary*.

Works on Middle English

Cook, *Literary Middle English Reader.*
Emerson, *A Middle English Reader.*
Mossé, *A Handbook of Middle English,* translated by James A. Walker.
Dickins and Wilson, *Early Middle English Texts.*
Funke, *A Middle English Reader.*
J. and E. M. Wright, *Elementary Middle English Grammar.*
Krapp, *The Rise of English Prose Style.*

B. FOR CLASS DISCUSSION

1. According to the number of students in the class, divide the passage in par. 3 into parts (by sentences, by lines, by parts of speech, or in some other fashion). Each student should make a critical analysis of the letters, sounds, words, and grammar of the part assigned him.
2. Examine other Old English passages, as time permits, from the books mentioned or from any other available Old English reader.
3. Examine also examples of Middle English prose to get an idea of its grammar as compared to that of today. Good sources are the books mentioned.
4. Make a list of all instances in the passage quoted, or in any other passage, in which there is variation from the modern sentence order.
5. Make a list of the personal pronouns in the quoted passage and compare them to their Modern English forms.
6. Look up the paradigms of the third person pronoun in an Old English grammar and compare them to the corresponding forms in Modern English. Note the changes that have occurred.
7. In the quoted passage make a list of the antecedents of the pronouns and determine the gender of each. Consult Clark Hall's *A Concise Anglo-Saxon Dictionary* for those of whose gender you are uncertain. Does Old English, like Latin and German, have grammatical gender or logical gender? Which is characteristic of Modern English?
8. Make a list of the nouns in the quoted passage and point out the different endings. What do you observe about the inflection of nouns in Old English? Compare the inflected forms in Old English with the corresponding forms in Modern English. Consult an Old English grammar. What differences do you note?
9. Note down all the different forms of the article in the quoted passage. Look up the paradigms in an Old English grammar. What change has come about in Modern English? Which forms have been preserved?

10. In the quoted passage, note all the forms of the adjectives. Classify them according to the case, number, and gender of the nouns they modify. Consult an Old English grammar for the declension of adjectives. What changes have taken place from the Old English period to the Modern English period? Consult Emerson's *A Middle English Reader* for the forms in the Middle English period. Are the Middle English forms nearer the Old English forms or the Modern English form?

11. In the quoted passage note down all the forms of the verb *to be* and compare them with the Modern English forms. Consult an Old English grammar for the conjugation of the verb *to be*. What forms have been preserved in Modern English?

12. Make a list of all other verb forms in the quoted passage and classify them according to person, number, tense, and mood. Consult an Old English grammar for the complete conjugations. What changes have taken place from the Old English period to the Modern English period?

13. From the passages which you have studied, make a list of Old English words which have been replaced by Latin-derived words. Make a list of Old English words which, like *stark,* have survived with changed meaning.

C. SUGGESTIONS FOR RESEARCH PAPERS

1. Negation in Old English (consult Jespersen's monograph mentioned in Part A above).
2. *With* and *mid* in Old English and Modern English.
3. Other Prepositions in Old English (specify which).
4. Sentence Order in Old English.
5. Extent of Inflection in Old English.
6. The Old English Subordinate Clause.
7. Placing of Adjectives in Old English.

NOTE   These are all very broad subjects and suitable for extended research projects such as the M.A. or Ph.D. thesis. For a beginning class they may be limited to the passage quoted in this lesson or to another short selection.

38

Form and Function

38.1 Two Main Divisions English grammar is concerned with syntax and the study of inflections, the former being the more important since every word in any communication has syntactical significance. Syntax is the science of words dealing with their relation to one another. Thus in *Children play* we have two words standing in the relation of subject and verb. The second concern, the study of inflections, is variously called accidence and morphology, the latter term being derived from the Greek *morpho*, meaning "form." Accidence is derived from the Latin *accidere*, "to fall together," and refers to the merging of an inflection with its stem. It is immaterial whether *accidence* or *morphology* be used to name this study in English speech and writing.

38.2 The Unit of Accidence It is scarcely accurate to speak, as some do, of the inflection as the unit next larger than the sound, the unit of spoken English, and the letter, the unit of written English, since inflections may themselves be single sounds or single letters, and very many of them are. Neither is it correct to speak of inflections and of form words interchangeably, as the two are not quite the same. An inflection is always part of a word, and in Modern English is a suffix which is added to a word to show time, as in *crossed* (past tense), number, as in *houses* (plural of *house*), or some other grammatical coloring. Form words are those little empty words—auxiliaries and prepositions for the most part—which do the same sort of work in the communication that inflections do. The study of accidence covers all these words or word-parts.

38.3 Grammatical Pattern Just as a word may be regarded as a group of letters arranged in a particular way, or as a configuration of idea elements, so a sentence is a pattern in which words are related to other words and their parts. Any simple sentence, such as *She will leave Friday,* shows a pattern of more or less intricate character. Here the form word *will* invests *Friday* with future meaning (compare the *t* of *left* in *She left Friday*). The pronoun *she* has its nominative or subject form, and the order is a conventional one of subject-verb-adverb. The only other order possible for English would be to put the adverb first (*Friday she will leave*), and this sounds rather unnatural.

38.4 Formula or Free But this is only a start at the analysis of the sentence used as an example in the preceding paragraph. Perhaps the most interesting thing about it grammatically is that it *is* a pattern—a mold into which an indefinite number of other sentences may be put. Suppose I say *I shall depart Tuesday.* Not a single word of the example has been retained, and yet one feels at once that the pattern is the same in every way. *You must go Thursday* varies the pattern through introducing an idea of obligation by the form word *must;* otherwise the pattern, future time and all, is the same. Much of the pattern remains even in *They should have started on Saturday,* although this example introduces several new factors. The preposition *on* is inserted, perhaps unnecessarily, making a phrase adverb instead of a word adverb after the verb. And instead of future intention or obligation we now have past duty unperformed, a desired condition contrary to fact. In short, *She will leave Friday* is a living pattern in English grammar, which may be reproduced or modified indefinitely. The Danish linguist Otto Jespersen gives the name *free expression* to a living pattern of this sort, while its opposite, the idiom or fixed expression not susceptible of change (*How do you do?*), he calls a *formula*.

38.5 Form and Function   To pursue a step further the dissection of the example sentence, it may be noticed that form and function combine and interweave. Thus *she* is formally a word, a pronoun, in the nominative case, feminine gender; *will leave,* a phrase verb in the future tense, third person; and *Friday,* an uninflected noun. Functionally the first word is the subject, the second and third the verb, and the fourth an adverb modifier. It is this duality and unity of form and function which the student must comprehend if he is to master the grammar of the English language. In such a word as *travels* the *-s* termination is perfectly clear as a matter of form; what we do not know is its significance in function—whether it means the plural number (more than one journey) or the third person singular of the present tense. A sentence may make the matter clear through context, and it is context which gives us the key to morphology. Without it no word would be clear in this sentence: *Travels form interesting ventures.*

38.6 Illustrative Diagram   To show further the interrelation of grammatical form and function the following diagram may be helpful.

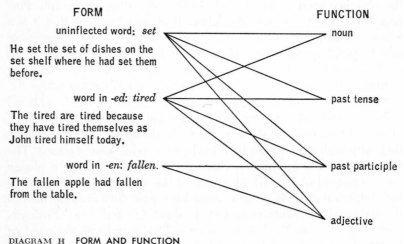

DIAGRAM H   FORM AND FUNCTION

38.7 Functional Shift   The diagram above illustrates one of the basic principles of modern English, that of functional shift, called conversion by the grammarians Henry Sweet, Arthur G. Kennedy, and R. W. Zandvoort. *Functional shift is the tendency to use any English word in any grammatical function instead of limiting it to a single use as any particular part of speech,* as is illustrated by the word *set* in Diagram H, which is employed as a noun, a verb, and an adjective. It does not take a different form for each part of speech (see also pars. 26.7–10). To a small degree functional shift existed in Old English, adjectives and adverbs often having the same form, but it was not nearly so common as it is in Modern English [1] and it bids fair to be even more active in the future. Because of the extent and variety of functional shift in Modern English the parts of speech inherited from Latin grammar may well be questioned and examined.[2]

38.8 Examples Functional shift is most frequent between nouns and adjectives. Almost any word which can be a subject or a complement can also modify another noun, as in *brick wall, steel knife, glass dish, floor mop.* This shift can be observed even in the pronouns, as in the slang phrase *he-man.* Functional shift is not so common between nouns and adverbs, but there are nouns which have an adverbial use, especially nouns of distance, weight, measure, and time as *Sunday* in *She came Sunday, block* in *He ran a block,* and *ounce* in *It weighs an ounce.* Many nouns also become verbs, as *to paint the house, to brush the suit, to thread the needle,* but there is very little interchange between nouns and the connectives, prepositions and conjunctions. A few prepositions were formed from prepositional phrases (preposition plus noun) in the past, such as *aboard* (*on board*) and *beside* (*by the side of*), and an occasional conjunction, as *because* (*by* + *cause*), but by and large functional shift between nouns and connectives today is dormant. It is much more active among the other parts of speech. Nevertheless, as an extreme instance of how a connective can come to have a noun usage there is the story of a man who kept objecting to everything his friend wanted to do, by interrupting him with "but . . ." at each proposal. Exasperated, the friend finally retorted, "But me no more buts!" making a verb as well as a noun out of the conjunction.

[1] See Donald W. Lee, *Functional Change in Early English* (Menasha, Wis., G. Banta Company, 1948).
[2] See Fries, *The Structure of English,* Chapter V, "Parts of Speech."

For the Student

A. FURTHER READINGS

Jespersen, *The Philosophy of Grammar*, pp. 17–29; 31–57; 72; 78–79; 106–107.

Aiken, *A New Plan of English Grammar*, pp. 3–11; 158–176.

Bryant, *A Functional English Grammar*, Chapters 16–17.

Kennedy, *Current English*, pp. 316–328; 484–485; 515–516.

Curme, *Syntax*, pp. 128–130; 142–147.

Jespersen, *A Modern English Grammar*, 3rd edit., Part II, pp. 310–314.

Krapp, *Modern English, Its Growth and Present Use*, pp. 308–311.

Bryant and Aiken, *Psychology of English*, 2nd edit., pp. 81–82; 100; 123.

Roberts, *Understanding Grammar*, pp. 19–20, 491.

Lloyd and Warfel, *American English in Its Cultural Setting*, pp. 173–177.

Zandvoort, *A Handbook of English Grammar*, 5th edit., pp. 302–315.

B. FOR CLASS DISCUSSION

1. Look up the definition of *grammar* in the *Oxford Dictionary* and in Webster's *New International Dictionary*. Read Jespersen's *The Philosophy of Grammar*, pp. 31–57; also pp. 1 and 4–8 in Sweet's *A New English Grammar*, Part I, and pp. 4–7 in Aiken's *A New Plan of English Grammar*. Is the term, as they define it, a broader or narrower term than you had originally considered it? If so, what is the difference?

2. Does the grammarian differ from the lexicographer in his approach to and his treatment of language? If so, in what way?

3. Define and illustrate the terms *syntax* and *morphology*. Do they differ at all in meaning? Are there other terms for morphology? With which are you familiar? See Aiken's *A New Plan of English Grammar*, pp. 158–176.

4. Define the terms *form* and *function*. See Aiken's *A New Plan of English Grammar*, pp. 3–11.

5. Make a diagram similar to Diagram H, using other words as examples. See Jespersen's *The Philosophy of Grammar*, p. 46.

6. How many functions can you think of for the word *round*? Illustrate. Can you think of another word as versatile?

7. Is it proper to label a word out of context as a "noun," "adjective," etc.? Why not?

8. Choose a column in your daily newspaper and note down the instances of words used in more than one function.
9. Define the term *functional shift* and illustrate your definition.
10. Give four other so-called "formulas" similar to the one mentioned in par. 4. See Jespersen's *The Philosophy of Grammar*, pp. 17–29, and Aiken's *A New Plan of English Grammar*, pp. 192–196. Can these expressions be analyzed in the same way that an ordinary sentence can? Why, or why not?
11. What is the basic three-part formula for the English sentence? Does *Long Live the King!* fit into the formula? If not, how can you explain it?
12. From your reading select ten examples in which the nouns have taken over the adjective function; ten in which the adjectives have taken over the noun function.
13. Read an article in a current magazine or paper and see what proportion of the noun functions are performed by adjectives and vice versa. How many adverbial nouns can you find in the article? What other instances of functional shift can you find?
14. Make five sentences in which you use adverbial nouns. Tell what adverbial notion each expresses.
15. What pronouns can you use as adjectives? Give illustrations.
16. Why are newspaper headlines sometimes ambiguous? Bring in illustrations. What signal words have been omitted?

C. SUGGESTIONS FOR RESEARCH PAPERS

1. Adjectives as Nouns in Milton (or any other author).
2. Adverbial Nouns in Wordsworth (or any other author).
3. Nouns as Verbs in Keats (or any other author).
4. Grammatical Patterns in a Current Article (or a work of a particular author).

39

The English Inflections
and Form Words [1]

39.1 Five Inflections   As this work has already made abundantly clear, Modern English is a language of few inflections. Disregarding meaning, and looking solely at forms, we find only five living inflections (that word "living" is important in this connection, because it means that such survivals as the plural -*en* from Old English are not relevant to the present discussion). Two of the five inflections belong with verbs, one with verbs and nouns, and two with adjectives and adverbs.

What a contrast English offers in this respect to such an inflected language as Latin, for instance. In a single group of Latin nouns—those of the first declension with ā-stems—there are six different inflectional forms: -*ǽ* for the genitive and dative singular, -*am* for the accusative singular, -*ā* for the ablative singular, and -*æ* again for the nominative plural, -*ārum* for the genitive plural, -*īs* for the

[1] For Chapters 39 and 40 I have drawn freely upon my article, "The English Inflections and Form Words," *Word Study* (Vol. XXI, No. 1, October, 1945), pp. 3–5. By permission. From WORD STUDY, copyright, 1945, by G. & C. Merriam Co.

dative and ablative plural, and *-ās* for the accusative plural. And, as every student of Latin knows, there are five declensions of nouns, each with its inflectional endings, to say nothing of the inflections for other parts of speech.

Getting back to Modern English, we find its living inflections limited to *-ed, -ing, -s, -er,* and *-est.* But even these few inflections are not universally applied. For example, *-ed* is not always used in the past tense of weak verbs. We say *He hurt me yesterday,* not *He hurted me,* and even the participial *-ing* must be omitted from verbs such as *ought* (*oughting* is inconceivable). But such grammatical situations are exceptional.

39.2 Living Inflections   These five inflections are like the living patterns set forth in the preceding chapter (see par. 38.3) in that they are indefinitely capable of application to new words, so that if a new word with noun, verb, and adjective uses should come into being, such as the nonsense word *flin,* it would be easy to make up its inflected forms *flinned, flinning, flins, flinner,* and *flinnest.* These five inflections correspond to what are called by Jespersen *free expressions.*

39.3 Added Form Words [2]   If to the inflectional suffixes of Modern English are added all the separate words which have a grammatical coloring or significance besides their meaning content, the result will be a long list. The auxiliary verbs come under this head, and so do all articles, prepositions, and pure conjunctions, as well as the verb *to be* in many instances and nouns, pronouns, adjectives, and adverbs under particular circumstances. Occasionally it is difficult to distinguish inflections from form words. Certainly the *to* of the infinitive is as much an inflection as the *-ing* of the participle, although they are different in that the *to* may stand for the entire infinitive, as in *I don't want to,* and may be split from the infinitive, as in *Remember to always erase the blackboard.*

39.4 Inflectional Fossils   Although English has only five remaining free inflections, it includes a great number of surviving formula inflections which have not the power to extend their use, such as the *-ne* of *mine* and the *-t* of *left.* Just where to draw the line between such fossil inflections and formative elements like the *be-* of *be-*

---

[2] Sometimes called "function words"; sometimes "empty words"; and sometimes "structure-words."

smirch and *bedew* is hard to say, but the distinction must lie between meaning and grammar. If an affix affects a word's meaning (like *-able* in *desirable*), it is not an inflection; if it affects its grammatical coloring or implication, it is an inflection.

39.5 Implied Inflections   One of the most interesting problems in all grammar concerns the existence or nonexistence of implied inflections that are now lost. For example, there used to be a dative case in Old English, as in the sentence *Hē him þā bōc geaf, He gave him the book.* Now that the dative has disappeared from Modern English and the objective has absorbed the dative and the dative functions, should one still call *him* dative in the Modern English sentence just given?[3] Or if that is too easy to answer, how about *sheep* in *Three sheep were grazing?* Should one call the word a plural even though it is indistinguishable from the singular?

39.6 Implied Form Words   Indeed, it might reasonably be said that almost any word in English may have a morphological significance. Take, for example, the illustrative sentence just given, *Three sheep were grazing.* The plural idea is found not in the word *sheep* but in the two words *three* and *were.* Are these form words? And if one drops these so as to leave only the words *sheep grazing,* one finds that it is not the presence of a word, but the absence of some number word, which gives *sheep* its inconclusive character. Is one therefore to call the absence of a word a form word? Logically one should do so if the test is the conveying of a plural idea.

39.7 Grammatical Ideas Covered   It would be possible to pursue the notion of implied form words to the borders of absurdity by claiming as grammatical every implication of a word, as for instance the derogatory air of *timid,* while *cautious* means much the same but carries no such sense of condemnation. The way to avoid such an extreme is to define the grammatical ideas, colorings, or aspects which may be conveyed by inflectional elements.

39.8 New Term Needed   The somewhat rarely used term *aspect,* which has varied meanings for various grammarians, will be used here to denote the categories of morphology. Its application may be illustrated by the sentence *His letters came.* The first word falls into

---

[3] In Old English the accusative form for the third person singular masculine pronoun was *hine* and the dative was *him.* The accusative form has been supplanted by *him,* which now serves in both functions. See par. 3.16.

the possessive category or aspect, the second has an inflectional ending which partakes of the aspect of number, while the third is a fossil inflected form falling under the aspect of time.

39.9 Number of Aspects Indefinite   The most obvious aspects, or grammatical colorings, which may be expressed by inflections are those of number and time, the one centering mainly in the noun, as in *boy* (singular), *boys* (plural), and the other in the verb, as in *walk* (present tense), *walked* (past tense). Then come, in nouns, the aspects of gender and case, both of which are more important historically than currently. That is, in Old English nouns were masculine, feminine, or neuter, but in Modern English no noun is regarded as being of a particular gender in itself, but only as it refers to something which is, according to sex, masculine, feminine, or neuter, as *husband* is masculine, *wife* is feminine, and *house* is neuter. With regard to case, in the Old English noun there were four principal cases, nominative, genitive, dative, accusative, but in Modern English we have, from the standpoint of form, only two cases left, the nominative and genitive, *boy, boy's*. The objective (accusative) and dative have the same form as the nominative. We might even classify the genitive as an adjective and say that the English noun has entirely lost the aspect known as case. For example, in *the boy's hat, boy's* really tells which hat is designated and limits the meaning, just as much as *red* in *the red ball*.

The adjective aspect, on the other hand, is called comparison and the forms of comparison are known as degrees, the positive degree setting the norm or standard, as in *fast*. Then the comparative is formed by adding the inflection *-er, faster,* and the superlative by adding the inflection *-est, fastest*. The comparative and superlative may, however, be formed by adding the form words *more* and *most* or *less* and *least,* respectively, to the norm, as *more happy, most happy* or *less happy, least happy*. Inflections are generally employed with words of one syllable or with well-established longer words, as *slower, slowest, happier, happiest,* but *more scholarly, most scholarly*.

The verb has, besides tense, the very subtle and difficult aspects of person, mood, and voice to handle. Of the many inflections for persons in verbs in Old English the only remnant left is the *-s* which is added in the singular present indicative, to show not only number but the third person, as in *he walks; it runs.* Several verbs, however, forming their present tense from what at one time was a past, do not use the third-person -*s;* among them are *ought, must, can.* As for mood, inflections have been lost, but form words play a part. In the subjunctive mood in particular the cautious, doubting, contrary-to-fact idea is generally expressed by such auxiliaries as *would, should, might, may,* as in *If he had returned, I might have considered the offer.* Form words are employed also in turning the active voice into the passive. Passives consist of two or more words, the past participle of the verb and the auxiliary *to be* in one of its forms. For example, *should be called, have been called,* and *am called* are all passives. In these examples the auxiliaries *should be, have been,* and *am* are form words. In the aspects of mood and voice one runs into more difficulties. What are the aspects represented by the -*ing* forms of verbs? Some of the verb aspects of English are almost impossible even to define, covering as they do such notions as habit, intention, doubt, condition, and denial. For example, one of the most frequent uses of the present tense is to express habit or occupation. The question "What *is* he *writing?*" is different from "What *does* he *write?*" If the answer to the latter question is "He *writes* novels," the verb *writes* is present tense in form but also covers present and past time. It is probably his occupation. At any rate, he may not be writing a novel at the present moment but undoubtedly he has written novels in the past and is in the habit of producing them. Habit may also be expressed in the past or future tenses, as in "As a boy I *would* never *play* ball" and in "Next spring he *will be flying* planes." To express habitual action joining the past and present *has been* and *have been* are employed, as in "For a long time he *has been* (I *have been*) painting." Thus we see that in the verb there are many other aspects of thought besides time, the one usually considered.

39.10 Summary To summarize the rather difficult material of this chapter, a *form word* may be defined as a word expressing a grammatical aspect. Inflection covers the five living and many fossil forms, including affixes and internal changes, which indicate grammatical aspects. It is probably best not to recognize implied aspects such as a dative in Modern English, or the presence of a number word as a substitute for the plural inflection; but one may certainly speak of words like *three* in *three sheep* or *graze* in *sheep graze* as having a morphological significance, since they decide the question of the plural character of *sheep*.

For the Student

A. FURTHER READINGS

Sweet, *A New English Grammar*, Part I, pp. 12–35.
Aiken, *A New Plan of English Grammar*, pp. 178–191.
Robertson and Cassidy, *The Development of Modern English*, 2nd edit., pp. 109–114; 281–285.
Aiken, *English Present and Past*, pp. 215–219.
Bryant, *English in the Law Courts*, pp. 4–25.
Fries, *The Structure of English*, Chapter VI.
Francis, *The Structure of American English,* pp. 230–235.
Lloyd and Warfel, *American English in Its Cultural Setting*, pp. 93–99; 276–283.
Sledd, *A Short Introduction to English Grammar*, pp. 96–113; 213.
Whitehall, *Structural Essentials of English*, pp. 53–89.

B. FOR CLASS DISCUSSION

1. Define the term *inflection*. Name three types of inflections and illustrate. See Sweet, pp. 28–30; Aiken, *A New Plan of English Grammar,* pp. 178–179; Aiken, *English Present and Past*, pp. 215–217; Robertson and Cassidy, pp. 109–114; Sledd, pp. 220–221; Francis, pp. 196–200; Lloyd and Warfel, pp. 96–99.
2. List the living inflections in Modern English and give an example of each. What is the meaning of the term *dead inflection?* Illustrate.
3. Can you give other examples of implied inflections similar to those mentioned in par. 5?
4. Define the term *form word*. Give examples of several different types. Use them in sentences to show emphasis; negation; possession; comparison. See Sweet, pp. 22–24; Aiken, *A New Plan of English Grammar,* pp. 186–191; Bryant, "Form Words," pp. 4–25; Fries, "Function Words," pp. 87–109; Francis, pp. 231; 234–235; 424; 427–428; Lloyd and Warfel, pp. 93–96; 276–283; Sledd, pp. 96–113; Whitehall, pp. 53–89.

5. Of the two methods, the use of inflections or the use of form words, which is more characteristic of Modern English? Support your decision with examples. See Francis, pp. 230–234.
6. What has caused the change in the modern use of inflection?
7. Select a paragraph in this book and omit all the inflections. Does it make sense?
8. Take the same paragraph used in Question 7 and point out all the form words.
9. Illustrate the notions of habit, intention, doubt, condition, and denial in the verb (see par. 9).
10. Find the proportion of inflections and form words to the total number of words in passages from current writings.

C. SUGGESTIONS FOR RESEARCH PAPERS

1. Conjunctions as Form Words.
2. Adverbs and Adjectives as Form Words.
3. Nouns and Pronouns as Form Words.
4. The History of the Living Inflections of Modern English.
5. A Study of Internal Inflection.

40

Other English Form Words

40.1 Surviving Fossil Inflections The surviving fossil inflections, such as O.E. *ge-* in the archaic *yclept* and the Old English dative plural suffix *-um* in *whilom*, have been mentioned (see pars. 3.10 and 3.18, respectively), but it would scarcely be profitable to try to make a complete catalog of these. There is a survival of the Old English instrumental case in Mod.E. *why*, from O.E. *hwī*, the instrumental form of *hwā, who;* and an obscured instrumental also lingers in *the* of *the more the merrier,* which is by derivation not the definite article *the* of Modern English but the instrumental form *þȳ* or *þē* of O.E. *sē, sēo, þæt.*[1] Other scattering survivals are to be found in Modern English adverbs, verbs, pronouns, and even proper names such as *Atterbury (æt þǣre byrig).*

40.2 Near Inflections It would be easy to include under inflections the *to* of the infinitive, the *-ess* of the feminine, and even the suffix *-ly*, which turns an adjective into an adverb. But *to* is written as a separate word, *-ess* is not extending its use today, and *-ly* as an

[1] *Sē, sēo, þæt* were the three nominative singular forms of the definite article in Old English—the masculine, feminine, and neuter. See par. 3.15.

adverb-forming suffix could not be included under inflections without also bringing in other similar suffixes as inflections, among them -*ness* in *eagerness,* which turns an adjective into a noun, and -*al* of *national,* which works in the contrary direction. It seems best to exclude all past inflections and near inflections, and confine ourselves to those five which have been mentioned and described in Chapter 39.

40.3 More Form Words to Count   It is the form word list which this chapter must serve to amplify. While a few form words have been mentioned, notably the auxiliary verbs and prepositions (pars. 38.2 and 39.3), many others need to be added. Indeed, the entire concept of the form word may profitably be clarified, so that the student may understand just what separates form words from full words—a separation as difficult to define as the distinction between plants and animals in the field of natural science.

40.4 Form and Full Words   The examples given in Chapters 38 and 39 indicate that the form word is never something in itself but always acts with reference to something else which may or may not be within the particular sentence. It adds grammatical significance to some other word. This is very plain in the case of the phrase verb such as *should have done.* The first form word contributes an idea of duty and the second one of the near past, while the combination expresses condition contrary to fact, a duty unfulfilled, stated as a fact and hence of the indicative type.

40.5 Meaning Added   If the student thinks this statement will make it easy to identify form words, he is wrong. The difficulty is that the form word may add individual meaning to its grammatical function and thus place itself very much on the borderline between form word and full word. For example, the word *to* in *He threw the ball to John* is clearly a form word, disappearing if the order is changed to *He threw John the ball.* Yet in the case of *after* in *After dinner he slept* the preposition *after* has such a specific individual meaning that one might be pardoned for calling it a full word.

40.6 Another Example   In the sentence *That brother of Ann's will have been waiting for her,* we find two inflections, -'s and -*ing,* and several form words. Perhaps it is easier to select the full words; we are sure of *brother, Ann,* and *wait.* The only problem is presented by the pronoun *her.* Is this a form word or a full word? There is meaning present, to be sure, but equally certainly the word derives its meaning from outside itself. It is a word of reference, different in character from the auxiliaries *will, have,* and *been,* but like them in that its meaning is complete only through context or the joining of other words to it. Assuming that it refers to *Ann,* the student may call it another example of the form word.

40.7 Two Tests But let us assume that the word *her* in the sentence under discussion does not refer to *Ann,* and that it is stressed as one of the important words in the sentence. In this event meaning perhaps outweighs form and *her* ceases to be a form word. Thus lack of stress is one of the tests for form words, and the other test is the possibility of omission. In the original sentence the phrase *for her* (meaning *for Ann*) might easily have been understood even if it had not actually been included. It is in part at least this omissibility which makes *her* a form word. If *her* does not mean *Ann* it is essential to the sense and cannot be omitted.

40.8 Connectives as Form Words By the two tests just explained, as well as by the definition of *form word, nevertheless* and its equivalents are included in the list. *Nevertheless* may stand at the beginning, the middle, or the end of a sentence. One may say, *Nevertheless, he did it,* or *He, nevertheless, did it,* or *He did it, nevertheless.* Whether *nevertheless* is a form word or not depends upon the stress given it. If it receives strong stress, it is not a form word, but if it is merely a connective, receiving slight stress, it is a form word. Both coordinate and subordinate conjunctions, as well as prepositions, regularly are unstressed, and they can frequently be omitted. Thus *that* may be used or discarded in *I know that it is raining,* and even *nevertheless,* which sounds very meaningful and is stressed, may be left out without hurting the sense in *I know he did wrong; nevertheless, I am sure he is sorry.* Here *nevertheless,* being stressed, is not definitely a form word. It is one of the borderline instances which occur in connection with every scientific distinction.

40.9 Expletives Are Form Words The words *it* and *there* are called by most grammarians expletives [2] in their function of causing the subject to follow the verb. By a change in order *It is best to go*

_____

[2] Sometimes called "fillers" or "pattern-fillers."

becomes *To go is best,* and *There were four present* becomes *Four were present.* Thus these introductory words may always be omitted; and they are seldom stressed. They must be added to the list of form words.

For example, we can easily distinguish the adverbial of place *there* from the expletive *there* by means of intonation and stress, even if they appear in the same sentence, as "There were three books there." Here the first word and the last are spelled alike but are pronounced differently. The difference between the two words is one of stress, as shown in the phonetic transcription. The first *there*, the unstressed expletive, would be [ðər] or [ðə], whereas the adverb *there* would be [ðæər], [ðæə], [ðɛər], [ðɛə], according to the dialect used.

40.10 Substitution Words   While English grammar usually limits to pronouns its discussions of the words which are used in place of other words, the language actually includes a great variety of such substitution words. Two of the commonest are *so* and *did,* and these may be used together as in the sentence *He thought it was unfortunate and so did I.* In this sentence *did* substitutes for *thought* and *so* for *it was unfortunate.* Another ending might be *and I did too,* where *did* stands for the entire predicate of the first part. Although stress may be present on either *so* or *did* in their substitution uses, they are to be classed as form words.

For the Student

A. FURTHER READINGS

Fries, *American English Grammar,* pp. 108–127; 240–246.
Bryant, *English in the Law Courts,* pp. 4–25.
Aiken, *A New Plan of English Grammar,* pp. 10–11; 186–191.
Sweet, *A New English Grammar,* Part I, pp. 22–24.
Jespersen, *Essentials of English Grammar,* pp. 83–85.
Sledd, *A Short Introduction to English Grammar,* pp. 145–146; 148–149; 211.
Lloyd and Warfel, *American English in Its Cultural Setting,* pp. 276–283.

Fries, *The Structure of English,* pp. 97–98.
Roberts, *Understanding Grammar,* pp. 252–254; 488–489.

B. FOR CLASS DISCUSSION

1. What does Fries in his *American English Grammar,* pp. 114 ff., mean by compound function words? What three varieties does he distinguish? Do these occur most often in Standard English or in Vulgar English?
2. Give examples to illustrate the expansion type of compound function words discussed by Fries. Do you agree with his analysis of the reasons for the increasing use of such words?
3. Look up the following words in the *Oxford Dictionary: at, by, for, from, in, of, on, to, with.* How many meanings are given for each one? Read Fries' discussion in *American English Grammar,* p. 113. Do you agree with him that the meaning of these words depends on the meaning of the words which they connect?
4. Can you think of other examples of substitution words similar to those mentioned in par. 10? See Aiken's *A New Plan of English Grammar,* p. 190.
5. Point out all the simple form words used in the text of this chapter.
6. Can you find examples of compound form words in this chapter?
7. Are any substitution words employed in this chapter?
8. Bring in five sentences containing the expletive *there* and five containing the adverb *there.* Compare the adverb *there* with the expletive *there.* What is the difference? What follows *there* in the sentences containing the expletive? Note the word order. See Fries, *The Structure of English,* pp. 97–98; 160–162.
9. Bring in five sentences containing the expletive *it.* What follows *it* in the sentence? Note the word order.

C. SUGGESTIONS FOR RESEARCH PAPERS

1. Form (Function) (Structure) (Empty) Words.
2. Compound Form Words.
3. Substitution Form Words.
4. The Importance of Form Words in the English Language.
5. Frequency Study of Form Words and Inflections.
6. Expletives.

41 [1]

Order in Sentences

41.1 Importance of Sentence Order Besides inflections and form words, sentence order is of great inflectional significance. (See pars. 38.3 and 38.4.) In Chapter 37 attention was called to the sentence order of the Old English passage cited. Sentence order is at one and the same time so important and so generally slighted by earlier grammarians that I wish to treat it separately here. Sentence order is one of the chief syntactical devices of Modern English.[2] It has taken the place of ablaut, umlaut, and inflections generally. With functional shift it must stand as a key to the comprehension of the structure of the language we speak.

41.2 Natural Order? Is there such a thing as a natural order of ideas and hence a natural order of words? Kellner says that if we

---

[1] For Chapters 41 and 42 I have drawn freely upon my article, "Order in Sentences," published in *College English* (May, 1944), pp. 434–438. For permission to use this material I am grateful to W. Wilbur Hatfield, editor at that time.

[2] See Charles C. Fries, "On the Development of the Structural Use of Word-Order in Modern English," *Language* (Vol. XVI, July–September, 1940), pp. 199–208.

put into natural order such a sentence as *May I trouble you for the butter?* it would proably read *The butter—trouble you—may I?* [3] and it is quite true that in imperative constructions such as *Shut the door* the first thing usually thought of is probably the direct object, *door* in this case. But on the other hand, it is easy to imagine some irascible individual who, having perceived that the door needed shutting and having seen two students beside the door, shouted, *Hey! You fellows over there! Shut that door!* That would not be a "natural" word order in the sense of logical, as Kellner postulates, but it would be "natural" in the sense of customary for users of English.

41.3 Standardized Order If a natural order of expression were followed, the same communication might have as many different sequences as it contained individual ideas, since any one of these ideas might naturally come first in the mind of some speaker. Such a simple sentence as *Joe began the fight* might be seen in the speaker's mind with Joe, the fight, or the beginning as of greatest importance and therefore to be uttered first. To avoid this grammatical anarchy (which to a certain degree did prevail in Latin and other highly inflected languages), English adopted or rather developed a system of standardized sentence order. The advantage is that communications are more readily comprehended because the hearer knows beforehand what to expect. Standardized sentence order, in short, may be regarded as a concession made by the speaker to the hearer.

41.4 Variety in Unity But English sentence order is far from being completely standardized. It is kept flexible by numerous devices, the chief of which is functional shift. Such a sentence as Jespersen's *He moved astonishingly fast,* for example, can be transformed into a dozen synonymous structures by the use of such transformational words as *movements, astonishment, speed, his,* etc. It is quite possible, within the standardized patterns of English sentence order, to include all the divergence which the speaker may desire. There is no standardization in the choice of an initial idea in the mind of the speaker.

41.5 Many Patterns The numerous order patterns of English speech fall into two divisions, those concerned with the sentence as a whole and those concerned with individual parts within the sen-

[3] Leon Kellner, *Historical Outlines of English Syntax* (London, The Macmillan Company, 1924), p. 285.

tence. The single basic pattern of English speech and writing, one from which stem all variant patterns, is subject-verb-complement. This is the standard, or norm for the ordinary simple declarative sentence, and it will fit perhaps three-quarters of all sentences in English.

41.6 Influence of Basic Pattern on Syntax   The feeling for the standard sentence pattern in which the subject is placed first is so strong that in a sentence like *Him was given a book,* meaning *A book was given to him,* where the indirect object is placed first because of the importance of the person over the thing, the *him* has been replaced by *he,* making the indirect object into a subject and producing a normal sentence pattern in Modern English. Thus one sees, hears, or writes today *I was granted a leave, The soldier was awarded the distinguished service cross,* etc. The idea of the indirect object has been completely lost in such constructions. Another illustration may be seen in the expression *It is me* or *It is I.* The Old English equivalent was *Ic hit eom,* which changed in Middle English to *Hit am I.* In this order *hit* was felt to be the subject, not *I,* and the verb therefore shifted from the first person to the third, from *am* to *is,* giving *It is I.* Even as early as the sixteenth century, *I* had a competitor in *me,* no doubt because the objective case usually follows the verb. Today *It is me* (more often *It's me*) is good colloquial English. The position of the word in the sentence was more important than the traditional syntax in determining the inflectional form. Even Shelley lets poetry triumph over grammar in his use of *me* in

> Be thou, spirit fierce,
> My spirit! Be thou me, impetuous one! [4]

The objective case seems to be more normal and more emphatic. Much emphasis is gained by *Be thou me* instead of *Be thou I.* Shakespeare, who lived before the grammarians of the eighteenth and nineteenth centuries set down rules to be followed, was emphatic where he wished to be emphatic, as in

> Lay on, Macduff,
> And damned be him that first cries, "Hold, enough!" [5]

---

[4] *Ode to the West Wind,* ll. 61–62.
[5] *Macbeth,* V, viii, ll. 33–34.

in the First Folio reading in *Macbeth,* often replaced in school texts by *he.* The great dramatist wrote in the days when people were less afflicted with purists and his works show the effect.

41.7 Usual Sentence Order Long Established   The subject-verb-complement sentence order is of long standing in English. In the *Anglo-Saxon Chronicle,* written from about A.D. 891 to 1154, this order is frequently used, the chief exceptions being sentences opening with *hēr* (*here*) or *þā* (*then*), which adverbs induce a shifted order of verb-subject (*þā ondswarede hē, Then answered he*). Additional inversions due to the negative, the compound construction, and other causes were frequent in Old English, but there is not space to present them in detail here.

41.8 Modern Inversion   Today there are four types of sentences which most often contain inversion in the main clause. These are (1) expletive constructions with *it* and *there;* (2) sentences beginning with a prepositional phrase or an adverb, such as *never;* (3) sentences containing direct quotations with *said he, she answered,* or the like; (4) miscellaneous inversions mainly for poetic effect. Examples are:

(1) There was once a man with three sons.
(2) Never have I understood that.
(3) "Go at once," she sobbed.
(4) "Dull would he be of soul who could pass by. . . ."

Occasionally the complement is put first for emphasis: *That promise he always kept.*

41.9 Imperative Order   Order in the imperative sentence is much the same as in the declarative except that, the subject *you* being understood, there are only verb and complement (if any) besides the possible vocative, which may be placed at various points in the sentence and is most frequently found at the beginning or the end. Now and then the subject *you* is expressed. Examples are: *Speak. Speak your piece. John, you speak your piece next, please. You speak next, John, please.* The subject and vocative are likely to be stressed if they appear. Any sentence may be imperative in idea while not conforming to the imperative pattern (*You will please do this. Will you please do this?*)

41.10 Exclamatory Pattern Two words, *what* and *how,* are typically used in exclamations at the beginning of the sentence. They are followed by the complement, then the subject, and then the verb. *How clever he is!* is an example, also *What good pies she bakes!* But besides exclamations with *what* or *how* there are many which use some other order and show themselves exclamatory by the intonation in oral English and the punctuation (exclamation mark) in written English.

41.11 Interrogative Order The order in questions is determined by the nature of the question.[6] If an interrogative word (*what, who,* etc.) is used as a subject or as an adjective modifying the subject (or *how* in connection with a subject), the normal subject-verb-complement order is used (*What happened? Which boy climbed the fence? How many books are in the library?*). If the interrogative word occurs as a complement or a complement modifier, part of the verb is front-shifted. This means that the first auxiliary is placed before the subject, as in *What has he read? How many books has he read?* If there is no auxiliary, a form of *do* is supplied (*What did he want?*).

41.12 *Be* and *Have* in Questions The verbs *to be* and, to some extent, *to have* form an exception to the rule of front-shifting of the verb in questions. One says *What is his name?* and *Who is his father?* rather than *Who does his father be?* One may also say *What has he?* and *How much money had Ida?* although there is also a current tendency toward *What does he have?* and *How much money did Ida have?*

41.13 Other Questions When questions are asked without the use of an interrogative word, or with the adverbs *where, when, why,* etc., the verb is front-shifted as just explained: *Is the news on yet? Does Vera have the answer? Where shall we find it?* Notice that in a verb in which there is an auxiliary the verb is not shifted but only the auxiliary. This is a modern order device. In Old English Archbishop Ælfric wrote *Hū begǽst þū cræft þinne?*[7] (*How carriest on*

---

[6] For an analysis of the question, see Dwight L. Bolinger, *Interrogative Structures of American English,* Publication of the American Dialect Society, No. 28 (University, Ala., University of Alabama Press, 1957).

[7] Marjorie Anderson and Blanche C. Williams, *Old English Handbook* (Boston, Houghton Mifflin Company, 1935), p. 147.

thou thy craft?); *Hū gēfēhst þū fixas?* [8] (*How seizest thou the fishes?*). The same order prevails six centuries later in Shakespeare when Troilus in *Troilus and Cressida* says, "Say I she is not fair?" [9] and "Weigh you the worth and honour of a king . . . ?" [10] Also in the King James version of the Bible of the same period one finds "Fear ye not me?" [11] and "Seest thou not what they do in the cities of Judah and in the streets of Jerusalem?" [12] Thus it is evident that the front-shifting applied to the whole verb as recently as three centuries ago.

41.14 Inversion In Old English the inverted subject-verb order, even the inversion of the complement, was much more common than it is today. In addition to inverted order being caused by the placing of some modifier of the predicate before the predicate, as mentioned in par. 7, inversion was employed in interrogative sentences (*Lufast þū mē? Lovest thou me?*), in imperative sentences (*Cume ðīn rīce, Thy kingdom come*), and in negative sentences (*Ne mētte hē ær nān gebūn land, syððan hē fram his āgnum hāme fōr,*[13] *Nor did he before find any cultivated land after he went from his own home*). Notice here that the verb *mētte* is placed before the subject *hē*. As mentioned before in par. 8, in Modern English the adverb *never* may cause inversion: *Never have I seen such a thing.* It is not practicable to list all the sources of inversion in Old and Modern English; they apply, however, to a very small proportion of sentences and do not affect appreciably the regular pattern of declarative sentence order.

[8] *Ibid.,* p. 149.
[9] Act I, Sc. i, l. 81.
[10] Act II, Sc. ii, l. 27.
[11] *Jeremiah* 5:22.
[12] *Jeremiah* 7:17.
[13] Quoted from "Voyages of Ohthere and Wulfstan," in Anderson and Williams, *op. cit.,* pp. 192–193.

For the Student

A. FURTHER READINGS

Jespersen, *The Philosophy of Grammar,* pp. 26; 44; 147–150; 174; 251–252; 297–298; 304–305; 326–331; 340–341.

Jespersen, *Essentials of English Grammar,* pp. 99–105; 126–128; 297–300; 306–307; 311–312; 314; 341; 376.

Jespersen, *A Modern English Grammar,* Part V, pp. 30–37; 273–274; 443–444; 480–488; 500–504; 512–514.

Jespersen, *Language: Its Nature, Development, and Origin,* pp. 344–346; 355–364.

Aiken, *A New Plan of English Grammar,* pp. 140–149.

Sweet, *A New English Grammar,* Part II, pp. 1–7.

Curme, *Syntax,* pp. 347–353.

Kennedy, *Current English,* pp. 119; 500–502.

Kellner, *Historical Outlines of English Syntax,* pp. 285–290.

Robertson and Cassidy, *The Development of Modern English,* 2nd edit., pp. 42–44; 145; 193; 281; 285–297.

Sledd, *A Short Introduction to English Grammar,* pp. 114–182; 256; 270–271; 296–299; 304–305; 313–314.

Francis, *The Structure of American English,* pp. 230; 234; 423.

Fries, *American English Grammar,* pp. 37–39; 72; 90–91; 93–94; 147–148; 169; 200–203.

Lloyd and Warfel, *American English in Its Cultural Setting,* pp. 137–145; 207–226.

Palmer and Blandford, *A Grammar of Spoken English,* 2nd edit., pp. 220–258.

Roberts, *Understanding Grammar,* pp. 300–304.

Whitehall, *Structural Essentials of English,* pp. 8–20.

Zandvoort, *A Handbook of English Grammar,* 5th edit., pp. 270–290.

Maetzner, *An English Grammar,* Vol. III, pp. 535–571.

Einenkel, *Geschichte der englischen Sprache,* pp. 1138–1151.

B. FOR CLASS DISCUSSION

1. What is the importance of word order morphologically and syntactically? Illustrate.
2. Give the normal order of words for each of the four types of sentences with illustrations of each.

3. What is the order of words in a question if the verb has one auxiliary? More than one auxiliary? No auxiliary? Illustrate each sentence.
4. What happens to the order of words in a question if the main verb is *be*, present or past, or *have*, present? Illustrate.
5. What is the effect on the regular word order of the use of an introductory interrogative word (adjective, adverb, noun)? Illustrate.
6. Can a question be asked without an auxiliary or introductory word? Illustrate.
7. What is the typical exclamatory word order?
8. How may interrogative and exclamatory ideas be expressed other than by changing the declarative word order?
9. What is the normal word order of an imperative sentence? Illustrate. Give as many types of imperative sentence as you can.
10. Check a column of newspaper prose to see how many of the sentences have the normal word order. Classify the sentences according to type. What proportion of them is declarative? Select those out of the normal word order and explain why the order has been changed.
11. Under what circumstances is the normal order of the declarative sentence changed? Illustrate.
12. Study the word order in the Old English selection in Chapter 37. How does it differ from that of Modern English?
13. Study the word order of the first hundred lines of the prologue to Chaucer's *Canterbury Tales*. Compare it to that of the Old English selection and to that of a Modern English poetical selection. What differences do you find?
14. Compare the word order of a page of Milton's prose with that of a page of Charles A. Beard or Carl Sandburg. Do you notice any differences?

C. SUGGESTIONS FOR RESEARCH PAPERS

1. Word Order in Questions (Exclamations).
2. Word Order in Indirect Discourse.
3. Inversion in Modern (Old, Middle) English.
4. Imperative Word Order.
5. Word Order in Carl Sandburg (or any other author).

42

Order of Sentence Parts

42.1 General Tendency Books of rhetoric sometimes advise placing last in a sentence or paragraph the emphatic elements, those which the speaker desires to have linger in the mind of the hearer. But in the natural mental arrangement of sentence parts which precedes speech, the emphatic element is more likely to be placed at the first of the sentence; thus *On the piano lay the score* emphasizes *piano* rather than *score,* although any altered placing of a sentence element does tend to call attention to that element. Generally, emphasis within the sentence favors the initial position.

42.2 Second Tendency Another general rule, this one having to do with modifiers, is that light sentence elements tend to come earlier than heavy ones, *light* being defined as both shorter and less stressed. The words *the small numbers on the ticket, which indicate the price* show the light modifiers *the* and *small* first, then the phrase *on the ticket,* and finally the *which*-clause. This tendency has led to the rhetoricians' advice to place the longer members last in a series; for example, *She went to the store to buy bread, a bone for the dog, and milk for the child's supper.*

42.3 Noun-Modifier Order   For the parts of a sentence there are not one but several well-defined standard orders, which apply to modifiers and some other small units. In all of these rules, one may find exceptions, but they are observed in the great majority of cases. The first applies to the noun with its modifiers and is illustrated in the first example in the preceding paragraph *the small numbers on the ticket, which indicate the price;* it calls for the order word modifier, then noun, then phrase modifier, and last clause modifier, with a comma between the last two if both are used.

42.4 Exceptions to Rule   Exceptions to the modifier-noun order just given are of two sorts: first, certain adjectives either regularly or occasionally follow instead of precede their governing word, and there are stock and poetic phrases where the same things occur; examples are *good men and true, the church militant, something red, soldiers three, anything new.* Second, it sometimes happens that a phrase adjective, especially the passive infinitive, is placed before instead of after the noun: *a never-to-be-forgotten event; the to-me-extraordinary name of Mealy Potatoes* (Dickens, *David Copperfield*); *the anything-but-ornamental garments* (*ibid.*). Carlyle has been accused of making a habit of this shifting of the phrase modifier in his writings.

42.5 Adverb Order   The adjective is somewhat more stable in position than the adverb, partly because it modifies only one part of speech, pronouns almost never taking attributive modifiers. With a verb, most adverbs follow (*ran fast; will leave Friday*); some very common ones, including the negatives, come between the parts of a verb phrase (*will not leave, was never tempted*). But if there is a complement, most adverbs follow that; *put it there, leave town tomorrow.* And many adverbs have several possible placings in a sentence, including the opening position: (*Tomorrow*) *he will leave for Buffalo; He will leave tomorrow for Buffalo; He will leave for Buffalo tomorrow.*

42.6 Order Among Adverbs   Among adverbs themselves there is an interesting tendency which may be expressed as *Where-When-How-Why.* It is exemplified in the sentence *He came to New York yesterday by bus to see his sister.* This is the regular order, followed unconsciously by the speaker, in a group of adverbs, and it prevails generally whether or not all the questions are answered: *They left* *for Vermont last week* (or, *last week for Vermont*). *They will return tomorrow by train* (or, *by train tomorrow*). *He plans to get there so as to be in time for the opening session.* As the examples show, *Where* and *When* are sometimes transposed.

42.7 Preposition Order   In a prepositional phrase the almost invariable order is preposition plus object. This object, as a noun, comes under the modifier-order rule given in par. 3, so that one would say *to the old tumbled-down farmhouse on the hill, where he had spent his boyhood.* As a unit the prepositional phrase conforms to the order rules for adjective or adverb, depending on its function.

42.8 Indirect Object   This is one of the best standardized orders in all English grammar. The prepositionless indirect object goes between verb and direct object: *He tossed the child a ball.* The indirect object with *to* or *for* follows the direct object: *He tossed a ball to the child.* Unless an adverb intervenes (*He tossed a ball carelessly to the child*)—and this makes a slightly clumsy effect—the indirect-object order has scarcely an exception in English grammar.

42.9 Conjunction Order   The order of the coordinating conjunction is simplicity itself; it fits between the two elements equal in rank to be connected. Difficulty will arise only if there is a correlative as in *He wants not only to visit Paris but also to live there. Not only* is placed before the infinitive *to visit* and *but also* before *to live.* It is easy to say that the subordinating conjunction comes as close as possible to the opening of the clause it introduces and that ordinarily it is the first word in its clause; but this requires one reservation. When a relative pronoun or other subordinating conjunction is the object of a preposition (*the dish in which I had put the fruit*), the preposition precedes it in formal English, although in informal English the preposition may occur at the end of the clause (*the dish which I had put the fruit in*).

42.10 Clause Order   Next to be considered is word order within clauses, which in general is the normal one of subject-verb-complement. The only exception occurs when the complement word, or its modifier, is also the connective introducing the clause. Then the connective function overcomes that of complement or modifier, and the unit, complement and all, is shifted to the opening of the clause. The first two sentences of this paragraph contain examples of the normal clause order; the shifted order occurs in *the book which they lent me* and in *the book whose name I don't know* (or, *the name of which I don't know*). This last *of which* construction is exceedingly clumsy, although it is preferred to the construction with *whose* by those grammarians who hold that *whose* cannot properly serve with inanimate objects.

42.11 End-Shifted Verb Order The Old English sentence *Ne mētte hē ǣr nān gebūn land, syððan hē fram his āgnum hāme fōr* (literally translated: *Nor did he find before any cultivated land after he from his home departed*) illustrates the end-shifted verb order which was common in Old English dependent clauses; that is, the placing of the verb at the end of the clause, as in Modern German. Notice that the literal translation of the dependent clause is *after he from his own home went;* that is, the verb *fōr* (*went*) is placed at the end of the clause. This order, which seems unnatural, has been abandoned by speakers of Modern English.

42.12 Sketch Inadequate No one is more aware of the inadequacy of the foregoing sketch of English word order than the author. The subject needs to be studied both historically and in current speech and writing. Many small exceptions and shades of meaning should be accounted for; the single word *not* deserves a study in itself, as does the shifted order often substituted for the subordinating conjunction, as in *had I but known. . . .* The student is urged to pursue much further than is possible here the rewarding study of English word order.

For the Student

A. FURTHER READINGS

Curme, *Syntax*, pp. 63–66; 70–75; 77; 96–98; 115–117; 125; 130–134; 136–137; 250–251.

Aiken, *A New Plan of English Grammar*, pp. 149–156.

Sweet, *A New English Grammar*, Part II, pp. 7–28.

Kellner, *Historical Outlines of English Syntax*, pp. 290–302.

Kennedy, *Current English*, pp. 106–107; 300–301; 326; 502–508; 519–520; 541.

Jespersen, *A Modern English Grammar,* Part V, pp. 53–55; 293–294.

Kruisinga, *A Handbook of Present-Day English,* 5th edit., Part II, Vol. 3, §§ 1973 ff.; 2065 ff.; 2163 ff.; 2349 ff.; 2381 ff.

Poutsma, *A Grammar of Late Modern English,* 2nd edit., Part I, First Half, pp. 385–540.

Fries, *American English Grammar,* pp. 189–190; 247–282.

Lloyd and Warfel, *American English in Its Cultural Setting,* pp. 110–120; 145–151; 167–173; 193–203.

Pooley, *Teaching English Grammar,* pp. 87–102.

Roberts, *Understanding English,* pp. 185–223.

Sledd, *A Short Introduction to English Grammar,* pp. 285–296.

Long, "Contemporary Clause Patterns," *American Speech* (Vol. XXXII, February, 1957), pp. 12–30.

B. FOR CLASS DISCUSSION

1. Read a column of newspaper prose and see whether the emphatic elements are placed at the beginning of the sentence or at the end.
2. Read a page of literary prose and see whether you find any exceptions to the placing of the shorter elements of the sentence before the longer as described in par. 2. If so, try to explain the exceptions.
3. What is the normal order for the modifiers of nouns? Illustrate.
4. Can you think of other illustrations of exceptions to the normal order for the modifiers of nouns besides those mentioned in par. 4?
5. Read several pages of Carlyle and pick out any exceptions to the rule for the modifier of the noun. Why do you think he used a variant order so often?
6. What is the usual position for elements modifying verbs? Illustrate.
7. What are the regular positions for the adverb *not*? Illustrate.
8. What is the usual position for adverbs of manner? Illustrate. Are other types of adverbs placed in the same order?
9. Do words of frequency, such as *never, rarely, often,* behave in the same way as other types of adverbs? Illustrate.
10. What is the regular order among adverbs themselves? Illustrate.
11. What is the regular position for the preposition? When is the position altered? Illustrate each question.
12. What is the position of the prepositionless object in the sentence? Illustrate.
13. How does the presence of a preposition affect the position of the indirect object? Illustrate.
14. Where is the coordinate conjunction regularly placed in the sentence? Illustrate. What is the exception? Illustrate.

15. Where is the subordinate conjunction regularly placed in the sentence? Illustrate. What is the exception? Illustrate.
16. What is the normal word order within a clause? Illustrate. What is the exception? Illustrate.
17. Bring in examples of *whose* used instead of the phrase *of which.* Look up Leonard's *Current English Usage*, p. 103, to see the status of *whose*.
18. Analyze the order of words in a page of some modern author or of some current magazines and give your conclusions.
19. Choose a page of prose from an earlier period and do the same thing. Compare the results. Are there any differences?
20. Analyze Arnold's *Self-Dependence* below and compare the results with those of Questions 18 and 19.

> Weary of myself, and sick of asking
> What I am, and what I ought to be,
> At this vessel's prow I stand, which bears me
> Forwards, forwards, o'er the starlit sea.
>
> And a look of passionate desire
> O'er the sea and to the stars I send:
> "Ye who, from my childhood up, have calmed me,
> Calm me, ah, compose me to the end!
>
> "Ah, once more," I cried, "ye stars, ye waters,
> On my heart your mighty charm renew;
> Still, still let me, as I gaze upon you,
> Feel my soul becoming vast like you!"
>
> From the intense, clear, star-sown vault of heaven,
> Over the lit sea's unquiet way,
> In the rustling night-air came the answer:
> "Wouldst thou *be* as these are? *Live* as they.
>
> "Unaffrighted by the silence round them,
> Undistracted by the sights they see,
> These demand not that the things without them
> Yield them love, amusement, sympathy.
>
> "And with joy the stars perform their shining,
> And the sea its long moon-silvered roll;
> For self-poised they live, nor pine with noting
> All the fever of some differing soul.

"Bounded by themselves, and unregardful
In what state God's other works may be,
In their own tasks all their powers pouring,
These attain the mighty life you see."

O air-born voice! long since, severely clear,
A cry like thine in mine own heart I hear:
"Resolve to be thyself; and know, that he
Who finds himself, loses his misery!"

C. SUGGESTIONS FOR RESEARCH PAPERS

1. The Order of *Not* (or other negative adverbs) in Sentences.
2. The Order of Adverbs (Adjectives, Infinitives, Participles, Prepositions, Conjunctions) in Modern (Middle, Old) English Sentences.
3. The Placing of Prepositional Phrases as Modifiers in Modern (Middle, Old) English Sentences.
4. The Order of Clauses in the Sentence.
5. The Order of the Direct and Indirect Object.
6. The Order of Articles and Numerals.
7. The End-Shifted Verb in English and German.

43

Structure of Sentences
and Connectives

43.1 The Paratactic Construction In Old English the coordinative placing of propositions one after another was exceedingly common, as in *Ða wæs ān man rihtwīs ætforan God, sē wæs Nōe gehaten* (*There was one man righteous before God, he was called Noah*). This type of paratactic construction is still used in Modern English. One might say *I see that. You are a hunter.* These two statements are disconnected although it may be easy to see the connection in the meaning. In the next stage of development the two sentences run into one, *I see that you are a hunter,* which was in Old English *Ic sēo þæt þū eart hunta.* Although these clauses were connected in Old English, they were felt to be of equal rank, whereas in Modern English one is made the principal clause and the other subordinated.

43.2 Complex Sentences the Latest Of the three basic types of sentences, the simple, complex, and compound, the latest one to develop was the complex. In Old English there are simple and compound sentences, the compound being made up of simple sentences. For example, in *Luke* 15:23 one finds *And bringað ān fætt styric and* *ofslēað, and utun etan and gewistfullian,* a typical sentence of several ideas joined together by *and.* A translation of this verse in the King James version, *And bring hither the fatted calf, and kill it; and let us eat and be merry,* shows that Biblical Hebrew, like Old English, did not have a well-developed complex construction, but used the paratactic construction as well. The complex sentence scarcely goes back to Old English. It is a modern construction coming in with the influence of the Latin and Greek, where it was well developed. There was, however, a gradual change from the cumbrous parataxis to the smoother hypotaxis with its increase in connectives, particularly the subordinating conjunctions so common in modern speech.

43.3 Complex Equivalents Accompanying the formal complex sentence, numerous constructions which might be expanded into clauses have grown up. Among the examples of the possible constructions are the following: *When studying, use a good light (When you are studying . . .); He wishes to fly a plane (. . . that he may fly a plane); The laundress washed the clothes clean (. . . so that they became clean); I question his happiness (. . . that he is happy).* These sentences may be called semi-complex. From them one can see the many complex elements of the sentence in Modern English.

43.4 Not All Complex Although the complex construction is quite common in Modern English, a judicious mixture of simple and compound sentences along with the complex seems to be the ideal of those who consider writing as an art. There are some modern writers who minimize the use of the dependent clause. Among them are Ernest Hemingway and his followers. In the hands of an expert stylist simplicity and power may be gained, but in the hands of one who is not a master, choppiness and monotony may be the result.

43.5 Development of Prepositions With the development of the complex constructions has gone the development of connectives. According to Leon Kellner,[1] the Old English prepositions indicated place almost exclusively, but have gradually come to designate cause, time, and other relationships, some of which are even figurative. For example, the preposition *from* originally referred to space, to distance, a meaning still retained in *three thousand miles from*

---

[1] *Op cit.,* p. 269.

home. Next it came to denote extent of time, as in *from sunup to* (O.E. *til*) *sunset;* then origin, as in *He comes from the Cherokee tribe of Indians;* and finally cause—*He fell from fright.*

43.6 Cases Replaced by Prepositions As English has become more and more analytical [2] the cases have been replaced by prepositional phrases. In grammars one often finds the statement that the preposition in Modern English is virtually an inflection, for it has been substituted for what would have been an inflectional case ending in Old English. Thus *of the man* is one of the modern equivalents of what in Old English was *mannes.* Also the preposition *to* in *Pass it to the men* has precisely the same implication as the Old English dative plural *mannum* (*to the men*). It is said that the modern prepositions *of, to, for, by,* and *with* all serve to express relationships which in Old English could have been expressed by nouns without prepositions but with the case endings of the genitive, dative, and instrumental. The statement applies to these prepositions but not to the numerous prepositions that have developed since the Old English period. In these new prepositions there is much meaning content, as *across, beside,* etc. It seems improbable that case endings alone without prepositions would have taken care of the complicated relationships.

43.7 Various Objects of Prepositions Today one finds as objects of prepositions many kinds of words, phrases, and clauses, belonging to almost any part of speech. The most common object is the substantive, as *on the table, above the bridge.* Verbs and adverbs may also be objects, as in *She did everything but write* and *call up from below.* The marriage service illustrates the use of an adjective as object of a preposition: "for better, for worse, for richer, for poorer." In *The light seemed to come from around the bend, around the bend* is a phrase object of the preposition *from,* and in *This package goes to whoever gets here first,* we find a clause *whoever gets here first* as object of the preposition *to.* Verbid clauses [3] may also be objects as in *From originating a theory to putting it into practice*

[2] See par. 3.11.

[3] The present author prefers Jespersen's term *verbid* to the usual *verbal.* It may be well to explain the term *verbid clause* here. It is really a dependent clause, a clause containing a verbid with subject, complement, or subject and complement, as in "*To write a letter* is easy," "*Writing a book* is hard work," "I saw *him writing the book*," "I saw *him write.*"

is a big step where *originating a theory* is object of *from* and *putting it into practice* is object of *to*.

43.8 Phrasal Prepositions In Modern English a great many phrasal prepositions have developed, such as *because of* and *owing to*. One which is well on its way to becoming a preposition is *due to*. *Due* is designated by almost every grammarian and lexicographer as an adjective. It has this function in such a sentence as *His refusal was due to the coldness of the weather*, but in the sentence *Due to the coldness of the weather, he refused*, it seems that usage justifies calling *due to* a phrasal preposition. This use of *due to* is exceedingly common.

43.9 The Coordinating Conjunction Another type of connective is the coordinating conjunction, which joins elements equal in rank and generally of the same kind. It may connect two words, two phrases, or two clauses. Examples of coordinating conjunctions are *and* and *but*. Coordinating conjunctions sometimes go in pairs, such as *both . . . and, either . . . or, not only . . . but also,* called correlative conjunctions. This type of conjunction was common in Old English.

43.10 The Subordinating Conjunction Along with the modern development of the complex sentence came the subordinating conjunctions. None of our present subordinating conjunctions has come down from the Old English period without change, and most of them have grown up in the Modern English period. The interrogative adverbs *where, when, how,* and *why* of Old English have become typical subordinating conjunctions in Modern English as in *The platform where he spoke is now painted, He does not know when I am coming, I do not see how it can be done, He does not understand why I am here*. These words serve as adverbs within their own clauses, but are also subordinating conjunctions in the sentence.

43.11 The Conjunction *That* One of the common subordinating conjunctions is *that*, used in introducing clauses of purpose, equivalent to *in order that* or *so that*, as in *She sold that we might get out of debt*. This use of *that* traces its heritage back to Old English.

43.12 Varied Origins The origins of the subordinating conjunctions, mentioned from time to time in previous chapters, are various. *Why* is the instrumental case of the Old English interrogative pronoun *hwā, hwæt* (*who, what*); *while* is a noun from O.E. *hwīl* (*while*); *after* is an adverb in the comparative degree, the old comparative suffix *-ter* added to *of; provided* is the past participle of the verb *provide;* and *because* is a prepositional phrase (*by* + *cause*). From the imperative employed paratactically comes *suppose* as in *Suppose he writes her, will she answer?* To this group have also come numerous adverbs and prepositions as well as phrases such as *as if, as far as, as soon as,* and *provided that.*

43.13 Pairs of Subordinating Conjunctions Among the subordinating conjunctions are pairs that go together, one regularly placed at the beginning of the subordinate clause and the other at the beginning of the principal clause. These may be called correlative subordinating conjunctions. Among them are *when* (*if*) . . . *then* and (*al*)*though* . . . *yet* (*still*) as in *When it was quiet, then one should look for trouble; If one goes to the country, then one can expect to be alone; Though the telephone kept ringing, yet he was sure he would get there on time.* It should be said, however, that the second in each pair is at times omitted.

43.14 Relatives as Connectives In discussing connectives one cannot omit relative pronouns, which are connectives even though they also have other functions in the sentence. The connective function is generally shared with that of complement, subject, or adjective, as in *I saw who wrote it, I understood whom she wanted, I saw which one it was.* The connective function has developed in these words since the Old English period.

For the Student

A. FURTHER READINGS

Kruisinga, *A Handbook of Present-Day English,* 5th edit., Part II, Vol. 2, §§ 1417 ff.; 1475 ff.; Vol. 3, §§ 2071 ff.; 2246 ff.; 2253 ff.

Jespersen, *The Philosophy of Grammar,* pp. 32–33; 87–90; 95; 97–98; 102–107; 163; 297–298; 315; 340; 342.

Jespersen, *Essentials of English Grammar,* pp. 67–69; 349–373, *passim.*

Jespersen, *A Modern English Grammar,* 3rd edit., Part II, pp. 10–11; 15;

310–314; 342–346; Part IV, pp. 374–389; Part V, pp. 38–44; 92–93; 212–217; 341–399, *passim.*

Curme, *Syntax,* pp. 112–114; 161–173; 181–346; 559–571.

Curme, *Parts of Speech and Accidence,* pp. 87–104.

Bryant, *A Functional English Grammar,* pp. 105–113; 143–148; 271–291.

Palmer and Blandford, *A Grammar of Spoken English,* 2nd edit., pp. 198–215.

Roberts, *Understanding Grammar,* pp. 68–78; 222–242; 305–308.

Aiken, *A New Plan of English Grammar,* pp. 106–131; 194.

Kellner, *Historical Outlines of English Syntax,* pp. 268–278.

Ohlander, *Studies on Coordinate Expressions in Middle English.*

Kennedy, *Current English,* pp. 289–290; 507–608; 535–542; 579.

Fernald, *English Synonyms and Antonyms, passim.*

Fernald, *Connectives of English Speech,* pp. 1–313.

Aiken, *Commonsense Grammar,* pp. 143–154; 182–196.

Fries, *The Structure of English,* Chapter VIII.

Lloyd and Warfel, *American English in Its Cultural Setting,* pp. 278–281.

Sledd, *A Short Introduction to English Grammar,* pp. 98–103; 166–182; 273–306; 311–320.

Whitehall, *Structural Essentials of English,* pp. 29–77.

Zandvoort, *A Handbook of English Grammar,* 5th edit., pp. 226–269.

B. FOR CLASS DISCUSSION

1. What is the function of connectives in the structure of sentences?
2. Look up the discussion of the structure of the sentence in several grammars or handbooks. What is the method of treatment?
3. What is the meaning of the terms *parataxis* and *hypotaxis?* Illustrate.
4. Which was the more common in Old English? Which do you think is the more common in Modern English? Check your answer by reading an article in a reputable current periodical to see what proportion of the sentences are hypotactic or complex.
5. Is there any connection between the paratactic sentence and the run-on sentence?
6. What is the attitude toward the "run-on sentence," sometimes called the "comma blunder," "comma splice," or "comma fault" in grammars and handbooks? Look into several of each. Can you account for the run-on sentence? See Perrin and Dykema, *Writer's Guide and Index to English,* 3rd edit., pp. 56–60; 480–481 (*Contact clauses*). Can you think of a reason why they are common in English?
7. Would you consider the run-on sentence an error? You have already examined a number of grammars and handbooks. Now consult Leon-

ard's *Current English Usage,* pp. xvii; 17–25; 148–149. What conclusions do you draw concerning the run-on sentence? Give reasons for your answer.

8. In your daily newspaper, see how many run-on sentences you can find. See how many run-on sentences you can find in a short story in one of the reputable current periodicals. In what kind of writing do more run-on sentences occur? Why?

9. What parts of speech are connectives? Illustrate each.

10. Are there more prepositions in Old or Modern English? Can you account for your answer?

11. How do new prepositions develop? Read Kenyon's "The Dangling Participle *Due,*" *American Speech,* Vol. VI, No. 1, October, 1930, pp. 61–70. Look up *due to* in the *Oxford Dictionary.* What part of speech is it? Collect examples of its use in oral and written English and analyze them.

12. Look up the history of *from* in the *Oxford Dictionary* and see how many meanings it has. Bring in a sentence to illustrate each meaning. Do the same thing for two other prepositions. What conclusions do you draw?

13. Give three examples of preposition objects which are words not ordinarily used as nouns.

14. Look up the double genitive in a number of handbooks, including Perrin and Dykema, *Writer's Guide and Index to English,* 3rd edit., p. 540. What conclusions do you draw from your investigation?

15. Do you approve of the term double dative? Why?

16. May a sentence end with a preposition? Read an article in your daily paper or in a current magazine and see whether there are any prepositions placed at the end of sentences. Make up a good rule to cover this matter.

17. Would you classify *in addition to* in *In addition to football he played basketball* and *on the part of* (equivalent to *by*) in *A suggestion on the part of Jane was disregarded* as one preposition? How would you determine a single preposition? List other phrasal prepositions in addition to those in par. 8.

18. Look up *ask, appear, keep,* and *journey* in Fernald's *English Synonyms and Antonyms* (with the correct use of prepositions) and bring in sentences illustrating the idiomatic use of prepositions with these words.

19. Why do foreigners learning English have more trouble with the preposition than with any other part of speech? Illustrate some of their difficulties.

20. Look up *and* in the *Oxford Dictionary.* Give its history.

21. List three coordinating conjunctions and use each in sentences.
22. What are correlative conjunctions? Illustrate.
23. What is the subordinating conjunction? Examine the definitions given in several grammars and then write your own.
24. What overlapping functions may a subordinating conjunction have in a sentence? Illustrate. See Aiken, *A New Plan of English Grammar,* pp. 116–125.
25. Look up the origin of six other subordinating conjunctions in addition to the ones mentioned in par. 13.
26. Give two examples of subordinating conjunctions used in pairs. Illustrate in sentences.
27. Distinguish between correlative coordinating conjunctions and correlative subordinating conjunctions.
28. Make three sentences using the relative pronoun as a connective.
29. Would you class the relative pronoun as a subordinating conjunction? Give reasons for your answer.
30. How does the use of connectives affect the structure of the sentence? Illustrate.

C. SUGGESTIONS FOR RESEARCH PAPERS

1. A Study of Parataxis.
2. The Run-On Sentence.
3. A Study of the Types of Sentences in Milton's Prose (or any other author of your choice).
4. Parataxis (or Hypotaxis) in Milton (or any other author).
5. Thought Patterns in Swift (or any other author).
6. Style in the King James Version of the Bible (or any other classic).
7. Genesis of Our Common Prepositions.
8. A Study of *As* and *For* as Prepositions.
9. The Substitution of Prepositions for Cases.
10. The Increase of Prepositions.
11. A Study of Phrasal Prepositions.
12. The History of Prepositions (select a few and study them).
13. The Figurative Meanings of Prepositions.
14. Coordination in Middle English (Old English, Current English).
15. A Study of the Adverbial Coordinating Conjunction (choose a certain period or author).
16. A Study of the Pure Coordinating Conjunction.
17. Coordinating Conjunctions in Ernest Hemingway (or any other author).

18. Interrogative Adverbs as Subordinating Conjunctions.
19. Subordinating Conjunctions in Substantive Clauses.
20. *That* as a Subordinating Conjunction.
21. The History of Subordinating Conjunctions (select a certain group or groups).
22. Correlative Subordinating Conjunctions.
23. A Study of *Whereas* and *For*.
24. A Study of *Than* and *As*.
25. Punctuation with Subordinate Clauses (base study on a particular author or periodical).
26. Frequency of the Use of Clauses in Modern English (select periodical or author).

44

Substantives: Nouns
and Pronouns

44.1 The Substantive In English grammar the noun and the
pronoun are both substantives. One generally finds in grammars the
statement that nouns name and that pronouns are substitutes for
nouns, a statement which recent grammarians have attacked, pointing out that many pronouns, such as *none, nobody,* and the impersonal *it,* are not substitutes for anything, while many nouns are
substitutes, such as *dog* in *He called to Rover and asked the dog to
speak for his food.* Perhaps the best solution is to give the characteristics of a noun. Among the markers of nouns are the articles and
pronominal adjectives (*the, a, an, my, your, his, their, this, each,
some, any,* etc.), which modify nouns, when they modify, and precede the noun.

Nouns are likewise a part of an inflectional pattern, generally
forming the plural by adding [s], [z], or [ɪz] (*cats* [kæts], *dogs*
[dɔgz], *roses* [rozɪz]), written *-s* or *-es,* and forming the genitive
(possessive) by adding the same sounds, written *-'s, -s',* or *-es',* as *girl,
girl's* (singular), *girls, girls'* (plural), *Joneses, Joneses'* (plural).

Many nouns are also marked by derivational suffixes, such as *-er* (*baker*), -*ist* (*chemist*), -*ness* (*kindness*), -*ity* (*facility*), -*ee* (*employee*), -*ance* (*performance*), -*ence* (*precedence*), -*age* (*shortage*), -*ism* (*Quakerism*), -*ion* (*comprehension*), -*al* (*revival*), -*ment* (*assortment*), -*cy* (*illiteracy*), -*ship* (*friendship*), -*ian* (*politician*), -*ster* (*youngster*).

Nouns likewise appear in certain positions. Word order, based on fixed speech patterns resulting from the loss of inflections, often helps in determining a noun. For example, in *Boys like dogs* the first word, the subject, is a noun, placed before the verb, and so is the last word, the object, placed after the verb. (See Chapter 41.)

Occasionally, in spoken English, certain superfixes, such as the placement of stress, are significant in distinguishing a two-syllable noun from another part of speech. For example, *súbject* with the stress on the first syllable is a noun.

As it is difficult to define a noun, so it is to give a definition of the pronoun. It seems best, however, to define it as one of a special list of words more or less arbitrarily chosen, which grammarians have decided to call by this name. The term *substantive* covers both, taking in nouns and their equivalents. For example, in *Boys play ball,* the subject is *boys* and in *They are merchants* it is *they.* The function of the substantive is not restricted to the subject, but may be a complement (direct object, cognate object, reflexive object, objective complement, predicate noun, retained object), a modifier, or a connective, as in the case of the relative pronoun.

44.2 Kinds of Noun Substantives Noun substantives may be words, phrases, or clauses, sometimes called nominals.[1] For instance, in *Over the hill is a phrase,* the subject is the phrase *Over the hill;* in *Whoever knows who did it please notify the police,* the subject is the first five words, but within the subject is another clause *who did it,* used as the direct object of *knows.*

44.3 Case in Substantives Case may be defined as the change of form by which is indicated the grammatical relationship in which a noun or a pronoun stands to other parts of a communication. In Modern English, under this definition, so far as the noun is con-

---

[1] See Sledd, *op. cit.,* pp. 83–91; 101–106; 114–120; 126–143; 300–302; Sumner Ives, *A New Handbook for Writers* (New York, A. A. Knopf, 1960), pp. 35–36; 68–85; 144–146; 186–187; and Arthur M. Z. Norman, "An Outline of the Subclasses of the English Nominal," *American Speech,* Vol. XXXIII (May, 1958), pp. 83–89.

cerned, there are only two cases: the nominative and the genitive (possessive), *boy, boy's.* It is possible to classify the genitive with the adjective and say that the English noun has lost the grammatical idea of case, but when one looks at the pronoun there are six words which prevent this solution: *me, us, him, her, them,* and *whom.* These words keep alive the distinction between nominative and accusative in English. Thus we have in Modern English three cases, nominative, genitive, and accusative, the accusative appearing in word form only in the six little words mentioned.

44.4 The Noun The written English noun has one living inflection, the letter *-s,* which is used for both the plural and the possessive, having the spellings *s, es, 's, s',* and *es',* or even the apostrophe[2] alone as in *Mary Jones' dog,* and the sounds [s], [z], [ɪz], or no sound at all as in the example cited. English has no alternative way of forming a possessive other than the *of* phrase,[3] which is being replaced more and more by structures like *beef soup, chair cover, woman lawyer. Beef, chair,* and *woman,* nouns modifying following nouns, are termed by some noun adjuncts.[4]

44.5 Other Plurals in the Noun Although the methods of forming the plural without *s* are not increasing their use and the total number of nouns employing these methods is fewer than fifty English words, they apply to some of the most common words in our language. There is a weak or *-en* plural, common throughout the Old English and Middle English periods, but it has so completely disappeared that Modern English has only one true *-en* plural, *oxen.* There are, however, three double plurals remaining which include *en: children* coming from OE. *cild,* pl. *cildru,* *w*ith the added suffix *en; brethren,* from O.E. *brōðor,* pl. *brōðor* or *brōðru,* with added

---

[2] A mechanical device introduced in the late seventeenth century to distinguish the possessive from the plural.

[3] For a discussion of the inflected genitive, see C. C. Fries, "Some Notes on the Inflected Genitive in Present-Day English," *Language* (Vol. XIV, April–June, 1938), pp. 121–133, and Russell Thomas, "Notes on the Inflected Genitive in Modern American Prose," *College English* (Vol. XV, January, 1953), pp. 236–239.

[4] See Francis, *op. cit.,* pp. 299–301; Fries, *The Structure of English,* pp. 187; 196; 201; 224–226. Lloyd and Warfel, *op. cit.,* 113–114; 170–173; 241–242; 251; Sledd, *op. cit.,* pp. 92, 115–116; 163; 231. See also Anna Granville Hatcher, "Modern Appositional Compounds of Inanimate Reference," *American Speech* (Vol. XXVII, February, 1952), pp. 3–15.

en; [5] archaic *kine,* sometimes used in poetry, from O.E. *cū,* pl. *cȳ,* again with *en* added. More of these old weak plurals in *-n* were surviving in the sixteenth century, before they gave way to the usual *s*-forms. Shakespeare, for instance, at times used *eyen* for "eyes" and *shoon* for "shoes." Another method of forming the plural still found in some seven nouns, *man, woman, goose, foot, tooth, mouse, louse,* is known as the mutation plural, the fronting of the vowel in the plural in agreement with the vowel of an ending now lost. Then there are the invariable plurals, fish and game words, especially when numerals are added, such as *trout, deer, bear.* Some of these go back to the Old English neuter nouns, which had the same form in the nominative singular and plural. A few other words besides fish and game words have invariable plurals, among them *sheep, dozen, gross,* and *heathen.* Number words, however, such as *hundred, dozen,* or *gross,* use the *-s* plural when they are nouns rather than adjectives: *We bought dozens of their melons.*

44.6 The Apostrophe and the Genitive The use of the apostrophe to denote the genitive case is a modern graphic convenience. It was not employed in the Old and Middle English periods. In the Middle English period, however, the unaccented *-es* of the genitive sounded like *-is* or *-ys* and was frequently so written. Thus this ending came to be confused with the unstressed pronoun *his* which commonly lost its *h.* In pronunciation there was no difference between *wulfis* and *wulf is (his).* Wyld points out [6] that as early as the thirteenth century the ending in the genitive was at times written separately. The idea of the genitive being a contraction of a noun and the pronoun *his* is evidenced in Shakespeare's *In characters as red as Mars his heart* and it continued well into the eighteenth century, even resulting in expressions like *my friend her book* as well as *my friend his book.*

44.7 Gender in the Modern English Noun With the loss of grammatical gender (see par. 3.12) natural gender developed. To indicate gender various methods have been employed. At times a pronoun or a word designating the sex is added, as in *he-goat, she-goat; salesman, saleslady* or *saleswoman; policeman, policewoman.*

---

[5] See par. 4.22.

[6] Henry C. Wyld, *History of Modern Colloquial English,* 3rd edit. (Oxford, B. Blackwell, 1936), p. 315.

At other times separate words are used, as *buck, doe; boar, sow; lord, lady.* The present tendency, however, is to throw aside all masculine-feminine distinctions, especially in professions. For instance, *doctor, lawyer, professor, poet* are applied to either a man or woman. If sex must be distinguished, *woman* or *girl* is prefixed as *woman lawyer.* One of the most widely used gender suffixes in the past was one of French origin, *-ess,* as in *patron, patroness; hunter, huntress; heir, heiress; count, countess.* Other minor feminine suffixes were *-trix, -ina, -ine, -etta, -a,* as *executor, executrix; czar, czarina; hero, heroine; Henry, Henrietta; sultan, sultana.* Then there were the different words borrowed from other languages, such as *alumnus, alumna; beau, belle.* In *bridegroom* and *widower* we find the language playing a trick by forming the masculine from the feminine. Of the three Old English feminine suffixes *-e, -estre,* and *-en, -e* has been lost completely, *-en* survives only in *vixen,* originally the feminine of *fox*[7] but now a "shrewish, ill-tempered woman," and *-estre* remains as *-ster* in *spinster, tapster,* and proper names like *Webster.* The feminine force of this ending disappeared as is evidenced in *seamstress* and *songstress* when the second feminine suffix was added, resulting, however, in double feminines. The ending *-ster* has completely lost its feminine significance and has taken on a new meaning as can be seen from *gangster, youngster,* and *teamster.*

44.8 The First Personal Pronoun   If we disregard the dual forms of Old English which have been entirely lost, the first personal pronoun is similar in Modern English and Old English, for *I, mine, me, we, our, us* of Modern English have developed directly from Old English *ic, mīn, mē, wē, ūre, ūs* (see par. 3.16). The accusative *mē, mec* has merged with the dative *mē* and Old English *mīn* has developed a stressed form *mine* and an unstressed *my.* Stress is supposed also to have been instrumental in developing *I* from Old English *ic.* The usual explanation is that along with *ic* [ɪk], later [ɪtʃ], was an unstressed form *i* [ɪ] which came to be used in stressed positions as well as unstressed and became tense, giving first [i:] and finally [ɑɪ]. One can observe the same process at work in present-day speech, where unstressed *I* is pronounced [ə], as in *I think I'll*

7 See par. 4.36.

write [ə ðɪŋk əl rɑɪt]. In the plural of the first person pronoun, Old English *ūre* has produced two forms *our* and *ours*,[8] the latter adding the possessive *-s*, making a double possessive. Other double possessives that have developed accordingly are *yours, hers,* and *theirs* in the second and third personal pronouns.

44.9 The Second Personal Pronouns In the first personal pronoun there are eight Modern English forms as compared to eleven in Old English. In the second personal pronoun there has been much greater simplification, for only three forms remain in Modern English as compared with eleven in Old English. As in the first person, the dual forms have disappeared entirely and the Biblical forms *thou, thine,* and *thee,* from O.E. *ðū, ðīn, ðē,* have fallen into disuse, employed now only in poetry, in prayer, and among the Quakers, having been superseded by *you, your,* and *yours,* which grew out of the plural forms in Old English. The Old English nominative plural *gē* developed into the Biblical English *ye,* as in *Judge not that ye be not judged (Matthew* 7:1), for which was early substituted the dative and accusative plural form *you,* derived from O.E. *ēow.* In earliest English the difference between *thou* and *ye* was one of number, but gradually a new distinction grew up, prevalent in the thirteenth century, brought about primarily through the influence of French and the custom of court circles, in which the singular pronoun came to be used in familiar address, in conversing with one's intimate friends or members of one's family as well as persons of inferior rank, and the plural form as a mark of respect, the polite form, to address a superior. In the early Modern English period, that is, in the time of Shakespeare, and even as late as the early eighteenth century, *thou* and *you* both were employed, *thou* for use among friends and between husband and wife and *you* for more formal conversation. *You* was originally the accusative form, but early in the fourteenth century it began to replace the nominative *ye.* In the next century *ye* came to be used in the accusative case, resulting in an interchange of the two forms *ye* and *you,* until finally

[8] A third form which has developed and is heard in popular speech is *ourn* with an *-n* ending, no doubt influenced by *mine* and *thine* and perhaps by the possessive adjective *own.* Other personal pronoun forms which have developed on the same pattern are *yourn, hisn, hern,* and *theirn.* One can find examples of this form in Wycliffe's Bible, as *the eritage schal be ourun* (*Mark* 12:7) and *the kyngdom of hevenes is herne* (*Matthew* 5:3).

ye disappeared, leaving the one form *you*. Occasionally, however, we find *ye* used poetically, as in Wordsworth's "And O, ye Fountains, Meadows, Hills" from his *Ode on Intimations of Immortality*. The Quakers, even though they have retained the old singular forms, have done precisely what the standard language has done in giving up the nominative *thou* for the accusative *thee*, as in "Thee will have to get thee a book." In prayer and poetry, the other two places where these old forms are found, language tends to be conservative and traditional and thus preserve the old historical forms. *You* and *your* were formerly not used in addressing God, perhaps in the beginning because it did not seem proper to use a courtly custom for this purpose, and now that *you* has replaced the other forms, to some it may seem too familiar.

44.10 The Third Personal Pronouns Modern English in the third person, instead of having fewer forms than in Old English, has developed two more forms, making twelve instead of ten. In the masculine and feminine singular the dative and accusative have merged under one form, the dative, *him* in the masculine and *her* in the feminine. The genitive in the feminine has the same form *her*, but has developed in addition another form, a double possessive, by adding the possessive *-s*, *hers*. As was previously explained, the nominative has developed the form *she*, probably through the influence of the demonstrative *sēo* on the original form *hēo*, and Modern English in the plural for all genders has the Scandinavian forms *they*, *their*, and *them* as well as a double possessive in the form *theirs*. One of the most interesting developments, however, is in the neuter singular. In Middle English the dative *him* was replaced by the accusative *hit*, which was the same as the nominative. *Hit* in unstressed positions weakened to *it*, but the genitive *his*, identical with the genitive case of *he*, continued to be used to the middle of the seventeenth century when an analogical form *it's*, based on the possessive of nouns (*cat's*, *boy's*), came to be generally used. This form originated in the sixteenth century. The apostrophe was kept in the spelling until about 1800. The use of *his* in the neuter seemed illogical and various substitutes were tried, even *it* without the *-s*, as in *Hamlet* when Horatio describes the ghost by saying "It lifted up it head." The new form was recorded for the first time by John Florio in his Italian-English dictionary *A Worlde of Wordes*, published in

1598, so it must have been in colloquial speech for some time previous to that date, even though in the Bible of 1611 there is not a single instance of it and in the First Folio of Shakespeare's plays, published in 1623, there are only ten, seven of which were in his later plays.[9] Milton uses the form only three times in his poetry and seldom in his prose. It gained acceptance nevertheless so that *his* used as a neuter seemed archaic to Dryden (1631–1700).

44.11 Interrogative Pronouns Of the six Old English forms of the interrogative pronouns, five have been preserved, *who* developing from the Old English masculine nominative form *hwā; whose* from the genitive *hwæs; whom* from the dative *hwām,* the accusative *hwone* being replaced by the dative; *why* from the surviving instrumental *hwī;* and *what* from the nominative and accusative neuter *hwæt.* The neuter in Old English had the same form as the masculine in the genitive, dative, and instrumental. These pronouns have been retained more fully than any others, as can be seen from the following Old English paradigms with their Modern English equivalents:

	MASCULINE		NEUTER	
	Old Eng.	*Mod. Eng.*	*Old Eng.*	*Mod. Eng.*
Nom.	hwā	who	hwæt	what
Gen.	hwæs	whose	hwæs	whose
Dat.	hwām	whom	hwām	whom
Acc.	hwone		hwæt	what
Ins.	hwī	why	hwī	why

It should be said, however, that *who* is well on its way in replacing *whom* in present-day English, as in *Who did you hear?* or *I didn't know who to listen to.* Some years ago the popular newspaper columnist, author, and radio performer on Information Please (a "quiz" program) F. P. Adams took delight in ferreting out literary misuses of *whom* and citing them with the sardonic question, *"Whom are you?" said Cyril.*

Actually, the survival of the accusative form *whom* bedevils even skillful writers when the word appears in a complex sentence. So much emphasis has been placed by teachers and purists on the im-

[9] E. A. Abbott, *A Shakespearean Grammar* (London, Macmillan and Co., Ltd., 1915), pp. 151–152.

portance of *whom* in accusative or prepositional constructions, that writers now have the tendency to use it when *who* is actually required. The usually well edited *Life Magazine,* in its article on "Bilbo Hearing" in the December 16, 1946, issue (p. 32), had this statement: "His favorite target is the Negro, *whom* he claims is constantly being incited, . . ." It is easy to see how the writer, editor, and proofreaders all went astray; subconsciously they tended to regard *whom* as the object of the verb *claims,* without realizing that it actually was the subject of the succeeding verb.

44.12 Relative Pronouns The English language, in developing a more hypotactic construction of logical subordination to take the place of the loose paratactic arrangement of coordinate clauses so common in Old English, began to use *who* as a relative in the sixteenth century. In Old English there was no separate relative pronoun, the relative function being carried out by means of the demonstrative *sē, sēo, ðæt,* or the indeclinable particle *þe* and sometimes *þe* joined with the demonstrative or with a personal pronoun, *þe* becoming the most commonly employed by the end of the Old English period. In the Middle English period, however, *þæt* came to be used for all genders with the alternate *which* developing in the fifteenth century, referring principally to neuters, but occasionally to persons, a use surviving in the opening of the Lord's Prayer: "Our Father, which art in Heaven." Even though *who,* an interrogative pronoun in Old English, developed a relative function in the sixteenth century, the use of *which* for animals and things and of *who* for persons was not established until the eighteenth century. In the *Spectator* (No. 78) "Humble Petition of *Who* and *Which*" the use of the relative *that,* which to the present day is preferred by the ordinary person, was objected to as an upstart doing injury to *who* and *which.* Steele undoubtedly did not know that *that* had developed its relative function before *who* and *which. Who* grew out of the use of *whom* and *whose* as relatives. Examples of these can be found in Chaucer. *Who* was the last to join the small number of relative pronouns which play an important role in Modern English syntax.

44.13 Reflexive Pronouns There are eight reflexive pronouns, *myself, yourself, himself, herself, itself, ourselves* (*ourself*), *yourselves, themselves.* They are used as intensives (*I myself will do it*), in prepositional phrases (*He did it for himself*), as reflexive indirect objects (*He gave himself a bath*), and as reflexive objects (*He hurt himself*). The reflexive object is the direct object which coincides with the subject.

44.14 Demonstratives   The demonstrative pronouns in Modern English are four in number: *this, that, these, those.* Examples are *This is it, That is mine, These are yours, Those are his.* These same words may be used as demonstrative adjectives, as *this (that) boy, these (those) books.* The word *that* in Old English was the neuter form of an inflected demonstrative pronoun in three genders, used also as the definite article. *This* also had three genders, two numbers, and all the cases. These two demonstrative pronouns today still preserve the singular and plural distinction, one of the few remnants of number outside the plural *-s* in Modern English.

44.15 Other Pronouns   There are two other main types of pronouns: the impersonal and the indefinite. The pronoun *it* is used often in an impersonal sense as in *It snows, It is said that* . . . . *You, they,* and *one* have somewhat similar uses in *You can't always tell what is going to happen, They say that* . . . , *One must live.* The indefinite pronouns are rather numerous, consisting of a long list of words like *both, any, none, one, many, anything* (but not *any thing*), *nothing* (but not *no thing*), and *several.* These words are indefinite pronouns when employed as subjects or complements, as in *Both may come* or *I want both.* Otherwise they may become another part of speech as in *Both boys may come* (adjective), or *Both John and Henry may come* (coordinate conjunction).

For the Student

A. FURTHER READINGS

Jespersen, *The Philosophy of Grammar*, pp. 82–86; 98–99; 103–104; 173–187, *passim;* 188–243.

Jespersen, *A Modern English Grammar*, 3rd edit., Part II, pp. 8–12; 16–231; 310–314; 398–462; Part III, pp. 12–23; Part V, pp. 5–85; 137–142; 169–203.

Jespersen, *Essentials of English Grammar*, pp. 66–68; 108–114; 120–131, *passim;* 132–214; 349–354, *passim.*

Kruisinga, *A Handbook of Present-Day English*, 5th edit., Part II, Vol. 2, §§ 751 ff.; 957 ff.

Curme, *Parts of Speech and Accidence*, pp. 87–91; 97–100; 112–140; 148–161.

Curme, *Syntax*, pp. 3–19; 32–35; 38–39; 60–61; 70–92; 96–127; 146–147; 181–258; 539–558.

Kennedy, *Current English*, pp. 288–291; 447–449; 491; 498–499.

Aiken, *A New Plan of English Grammar*, pp. 57–82.

Bryant, *A Functional English Grammar*, pp. 13–45; 114–134; 152–157; 168–175.

Palmer and Blandford, *A Grammar of Spoken English*, 2nd edit., pp. 27–74; 215–216.

Aiken, *Commonsense Grammar*, pp. 50–60; 85–99, *passim;* 168–181.

Roberts, *Understanding Grammar*, pp. 25–89.

Sweet, *A New English Grammar*, Part II, pp. 71–81.

Bryant and Aiken, *Psychology of English*, 2nd edit., pp. 54–55.

Fries, *American English Grammar*, pp. 72–96; 101–103.

Kellner, *Historical Outlines of English Syntax*, pp. 126–131.

Francis, *The Structure of American English*, pp. 174–181; 237–253; 298–302.

Lloyd and Warfel, *American English in Its Cultural Setting*, pp. 93–94; 110–120; 170–173; 187–193; 233–252; 276–278.

Sledd, *A Short Introduction to English Grammar*, pp. 60–62; 64–65; 68–73; 76–79; 81–91; 101–106; 114–120; 126–143; 153–164; 228–229; 231; 243; 300–302.

Zandvoort, *A Handbook of English Grammar*, 5th edit., pp. 107–217.

B. FOR CLASS DISCUSSION

1. Examine the definition of *substantive* in several grammars and dictionaries. Bring in your own definition.
2. What is the difference between a noun and a pronoun? Are they ever confused? Why? See Jespersen's *The Philosophy of Grammar*, pp. 82–84. See also Sledd, pp. 231; 243, for the definition of noun and pronoun, and Roberts, pp. 25–29; 53–55, for the discussion of the two terms.
3. Is there any justification for grouping adjectives and nouns together as substantives? Illustrate.
4. In Modern English what words form their plurals by adding -*en* instead of the regular plural inflection? Look these words up in the *Oxford Dictionary*. Are they old or new in the language? Are they frequently or rarely used?

5. What is meant by the mutation plurals? Are they new or old in the language? Are they frequently or rarely used? Do you know of any other language that has these plurals?

6. What is the plural of each of the following words: *couple, gross, dozen, hundred, pounds, pair?* Look these words up in Webster's *New International Dictionary* and in Jespersen's *A Modern English Grammar,* 3rd edit., Part II, pp. 57–63. What do you find about the plural forms?

7. Compare other languages that you know with English in respect to their treatment of gender. Do these languages have natural or grammatical gender? Does gender in the noun affect modifying words, and if so, in what way?

8. What English words with the feminine suffix *-ess* are now in good standing? Can you list others which, although once considered equally good, are no longer approved? How do you account for the change in their status?

9. Look up the history of the suffix *-ster* in common and proper nouns, such as *spinster, tapster, Webster.*

10. Look up the definition of the term *case* in a number of grammars and compare them. After examining these definitions, form your own definition.

11. Compare English with Latin or some other highly inflected language in respect to treatment of case. Do you think it more efficient to use inflectional endings or form words to show case relationships?

12. Do you make any distinction between the *-'s* inflection of the possessive singular and the regular inflection of the plural? Between the possessive plural and the other forms of the plural? Of what value is the written form *-s'*, as in *dogs'* (plural)? Draw conclusions as to the need for this inflection.

13. Consult Leonard's *Current English Usage,* pp. 50–54. What were his findings in connection with the use of the apostrophe in the possessive case?

14. What is a double genitive? Illustrate. Is there any advantage in the use of the double genitive? See Roberts, §§ 38; 57.

15. According to Fries' *American English Grammar,* pp. 74–75, is the use of the genitive case increasing or decreasing? What is substituted for it? On what material did Professor Fries base his conclusions? What material would you use?

16. Consult Hall's *English Usage,* pp. 202–207, for a discussion of the genitive. What are his conclusions?

17. When did the pronoun *its* come into use in English? What was previ-

ously used for the neuter possessive? Why do you think the form *its* developed?

18. Why did the second person singular pronoun *thou* cease to be used? See Bryant and Aiken's *Psychology of English*, 2nd edit., pp. 54–55.

19. Make two sentences in which you use a clause as a subject; two in which you use a phrase.

20. Turn back to par. 3.16 to the tables for the personal pronouns similar to the one in par. 11. Note the differences and list them.

21. Which of the personal pronouns had a dual number? See par. 3.16. Do we have a dual number in Modern English? (See Jespersen's *The Philosophy of Grammar*, pp. 205–207.) Can you account for the disappearance of the Old English forms? See Roberts, pp. 58–59.

22. What were the forms for *it* in Old English? In the neuter third personal pronoun, what changes have taken place? Can you account for these changes?

23. Is Aiken's title in *Commonsense Grammar* "The Villain Pronoun" a good one? Why?

24. From what are the reflexive pronouns formed? Illustrate their uses.

25. Make two sentences illustrating the impersonal pronoun. See Roberts, p. 251.

26. List the interrogative pronouns. Use each in a sentence.

27. What are the demonstrative pronouns? Make sentences using each of them.

28. How was the relative function in Old English performed? What was the first relative to develop? What was the second? The third?

C. SUGGESTIONS FOR RESEARCH PAPERS

1. Words That May Be Used in the Singular and the Plural.

2. A Historical Sketch of the Nouns That Form Their Plurals by an Internal Vowel Change or by Adding *-en* or *-ren*.

3. Foreign Plurals in English.

4. Number Usage in —— (select some newspaper or periodical).

5. The Gender Suffixes.

6. Personification—Gender in Wordsworth (or other poet).

7. Gender Suffixes in Proper Names.

8. The Distinction between *Who* and *Which*.

9. Should English Abolish Case?

10. History of Case Endings in English.

11. History of the Apostrophe in English.

12. Double and Group Genitives.

13. Shakespeare's Use of the Genitive.

14. Frequency of Genitives with Inflection and *Of* Compared.
15. Use of Genitive in Hemingway (or any other modern author).
16. The Polite *You* in Various Languages.
17. The Clause-Subject or Phrase-Subject (limit to a current periodical, particular author, or particular period).
18. The Reflexive Object in Shakespeare (or any other author).
19. The Personal Pronouns in Chaucer (or any other author).
20. Reflexive Pronouns in Shakespeare (or any other author).
21. Impersonal Pronouns in Milton (or any other author).
22. A Study of the Interrogative (Demonstrative, Relative, or Indefinite) Pronoun.
23. *Who* and *Whom* in Shakespeare.
24. Shall English Eliminate *Whom?* (Consider frequencies, errors, rules, etc.)

45

Modifiers: Adjectives and Adverbs

45.1 Modifiers Adjectives and adverbs are generally grouped together in grammars as modifiers and differentiated by the statement that they modify or qualify different types of words, adjectives being used chiefly with substantives and adverbs with everything else, particularly verbs. Since the substantive is discussed in Chapter 44, it will be well to consider its modifier, the adjective, first.

45.2 The Adjective The Old English adjective inflected for all the forms for which the noun inflected (number, case, gender, and class) and in addition for strong and weak position (see par. 3.14). The Modern English adjective, however, has lost all its endings and has so simplified as to become invariable, with but one form for any case, number, or gender. The only inflections left are those of comparison: *pretty, prettier, prettiest*. There are two methods of forming the comparative and superlative, one by adding the suffixes *-er* and *-est* and the other by using the adverbs *more* and *most*, both methods going back to Old English. In Old English, however, most adjectives formed the comparative by adding *-ra* and the superlative by adding *-ost*, from which developed the Modern English *-er* and

-*est* respectively. There were in Old English also a few adjectives with mutated comparative and superlative forms, as well as a small number in which the mutated [1] comparatives and superlatives were of a different root from the positive form. The first is exemplified in *strengra, strengest,* from *strang,* "strong"; *lengra, lengest,* from *lang,* "long"; *ieldra, ieldest,* from *eald,* "old." By analogy, in Modern English, *strong* and *long* have developed the usual forms, *stronger, strongest, longer, longest,* but we have a remnant of the mutated vowel in the nouns *strength* and *length.* The one adjective comparison which shows a trace of vowel mutation is *old, elder, eldest* (besides *older, oldest*). The second type with different roots has developed into the few surviving adjectives irregular in comparison, such as *good, better, best.* Usage has changed throughout the centuries in the method of comparison employed with different words. In the works of the sixteenth century one finds words like *lenger* and *strenger,* which have been replaced by *longer* and *stronger; beautifuller, gracefullest,* now compared with *more* and *most,* the analytical forms; and the use of both methods in a phrase like *the most unkindest,* now either *most unkind* or *unkindest.* At the present time, in general, monosyllabic adjectives take -*er* and -*est,* and those of two or more syllables use *more* and *most.*

45.3 Double and Triple Inflections in Adjectives Some adjectives, such as *nearer* and *lesser,* have double inflections. *Near* is developed from the comparative *nēarra* from the Old English *nēah,* "nigh." This comparative, still used in Middle English, became confused with the positive and inflections were again added, giving *near, nearer, nearest. Nearest* is actually a comparative-superlative adjective. Another double comparative of later date is *lesser,* in addition to *less.* Along with double comparatives are found double superlatives, such as *outmost, topmost,* and *foremost,* formed from an original superlative in -*m* strengthened by a second superlative suffix -*est.* The double ending -*mest* came to be confused with the

[1] Mutation or umlaut was an important sound change that took place in Old English. It was a change produced in an accented radical vowel or diphthong by the sound of an *i* or *j* in the following syllable. For instance, the plural of *man* in Prehistoric Old English was *°manni.* Because of the *i* the *a* in the first syllable was changed to *e.* Thus *°manni* became *menn.* This mutation accounts for the plural of *man* being *men* in Modern English. The same is true with *tooth, teeth; foot, feet; goose, geese; mouse, mice.*

adverb *most,* used in the analytical superlative forms. Triple inflections may be seen in words like *uppermost, innermost,* and *furthermost.*

45.4 Adjective as Word, Phrase, or Clause Adjectives may be words (*pretty* in *a pretty dress*), phrases (*of the book* in *the pages of the book*), or clauses (*which stands* in *the house which stands*). The adjective phrase or clause is almost always placed after the noun while the word-adjective generally precedes the noun it modifies, except for a few more or less stereotyped expressions like *life eternal* and *something unforeseen* and adjectives like *alone, aloud, awake, afire, aboard, afraid.*

This inverted order of noun and modifier is not, however, necessarily obsolete or obsolescent. In designating parts of a book, for example, we still prefer *page two, Chapter Two, Part One,* etc. This order received a new lease on life in a curious practice that developed among the Allied High Command in World War II. Several "top secret" military proposals for invasions of enemy-held bases and other military objectives were studied by various groups of military strategists, and for each proposal a fanciful name, preceded by the word *Operation* was used. Thus *Operation Torch* referred to the North African invasion plans.

After the war the habit lingered on in military circles. The Bikini test of the atomic bomb became *Operation Crossroads* and the miliary maneuvers in Northern Canada to try out equipment under Arctic and sub-Arctic conditions was, humorously, dubbed *Operation Frostbite.* In the winter of 1946–47 an Army group was sent to Alaska for further tests of military equipment under Arctic conditions. It was a "task force"—a term made current in World War II— with the modifier before the word *force.* But, as a particular task force among many, it also acquired an adjective modifier placed after the noun *force,* and the full phrase became *Task Force Frigid,* not the "normal" English *Frigid Task Force.* The Space Age has continued the practice of inverting the order of the noun and its modifier with the naming of the numerous rocket programs of the National Aeronautics and Space Administration, among them *Project Vanguard; Project Mercury,* putting a man in orbit; and *Project Apollo,* putting a man on the moon. However, the original atomic bomb development was referred to as the "Manhattan District," not the "District Manhattan," all of which goes to show the wide flexibility in the uses of modifiers in Modern English.

45.5 Adjectives as Nouns Adjectives are very susceptible to functional shift. One may observe a constant interchange between adjectives and nouns. Just as one may use a noun in the place of an adjective, as in *table top, glass bottle, plastic button,*[2] so adjectives may be used in place of nouns, as in *the reds, the whites, and the blues.* Practically any adjective naming a personal quality may be used in place of a noun naming those who possess it, as in *The wise always know what to do* or *The foolish come empty-handed.* These adjective-nouns may have adjectives modifying them, as *the undeserving poor.*

45.6 The Adverb The sources of Modern English adverbs are numerous. Some were originally nouns used adverbially, either the dative or genitive case. As was pointed out, *whilom* had its origin in the dative plural, but a number developed from the genitive singular, among them *else, always, homewards, once* (O.E. *ān-es*), *twice, thrice, backwards, sometimes, sideways, upwards, nowadays, needs* in *He needs must go,* which also takes the form *He of necessity must go.* Of the adverb-forming suffixes of Old English, *-e, -linga, -longa,* and *-līce,* the only living adverbial inflection at present is *-ly* which developed from *-līce.* With the loss of the *-e,* many adverbs such as *hard* and *fast* have identical forms with the adjectives. The suffixes *-linga* and *-longa* have given rise to *darkling, groveling, headlong,* and *sidelong.* It is interesting to note that *groveling* has been taken for a present participle and has given rise to a new verb, *to grovel.* Another bit of confusion between the adjective-forming suffix *-līc* as in *frēondlīc,* "friendly," and the adverbial *-līce* resulted in both adjectives and adverbs ending in *-ly* in Modern English. We find *She is a kindly person* and *She spoke kindly to the child.*

45.7 Sentence and Clause Modifiers Although adverbs usually modify a verb or another modifier, they may also modify a sentence as a whole. For example, *fortunately* in *Fortunately, the letter did not come* modifies, not the verb *did come,* but the whole sentence. Such words as *indeed* and *surely* are sentence modifiers. Likewise a

---

[2] Called *noun adjuncts* by some. See par. 44.4.

clause as a whole may be modified by an adverb, as in *Precisely what he said is not known,* where *precisely* modifies the noun clause *what he said* which is subject of the verb *is known.* Other instances of nouns modified by adverbs are *here* in *this little tree here* and *writing carefully* in *Writing carefully is a good exercise,* where *writing* functions as a noun and *carefully* modifies it. When adverbs modify nouns, they always occur immediately after the noun. Compare the latter with *Careful Writing.* . . .[3]

45.8 Adverb Order   Adverbs do not shift their functions so easily as adjectives, but they move around more freely in the sentence. In the sentence *Carefully he wrote the letter, carefully* may be placed in several positions without affecting the sense expressed. Of particular interest is the placing of the adverb *only* in a sentence. Theoretically, it should immediately precede the word it modifies, but usually it is to be found before the verb, even if it actually modifies some later word in the sentence. Thus, *She only came for the dance* should mean that she came for nothing else except the dance, but as the sentence reads it implies that she did nothing else but come. Sometimes this misplacing of *only* can cause confusion; on the other hand, it appears to be achieving status as an idiom of the language that no amount of condemnation will be able to eradicate. As pointed out in *Psychology of English,*[4] *only* is felt to be the emphatic word in the sentence, so there is the natural tendency to put it near the start, regardless of its logical position.

45.9 Adverb or Adjective?   There are constructions in English in which it is difficult to determine the function of a particular unit. For instance, in the sentence *Thinking she was ahead of time, Mary began reading,* the first six words may be thought of as an adverb of cause or time or as an adjective modifying *Mary.* There are many such ambiguous constructions in which the function of the unit depends upon the interpretation.

---

[3] See Fries, *The Structure of English, op. cit.,* pp. 216–217; 226; Francis, *op. cit.,* pp. 304–305; Roberts, *op. cit.,* p. 212.

[4] Margaret M. Bryant and Janet Rankin Aiken, *Psychology of English* (New York, Columbia University Press, 1940; 2nd edit., Frederick Ungar Publishing Co., 1961), pp. 108–9.

For the Student

A. FURTHER READINGS

Adjectives

Jespersen, *A Modern English Grammar*, 3rd edit., Part II, pp. 4–6; 17–18; 40–44; 212; 231–245; 270; 272–282; 299; 335–343; 366–398.

Jespersen, *Essentials of English Grammar*, pp. 67–68; 76–77; 80–81; 88–89; 164–165; 170–171; 178.

Jespersen, *The Philosophy of Grammar*, pp. 72–81; 99.

Curme, *Syntax*, pp. 63–94; 159; 204–238; 329–330; 497–498; 508–538; 560–561.

Curme, *Parts of Speech and Accidence*, pp. 41–62; 103–104; 193–196.

Sweet, *A New English Grammar*, Part II, pp. 65–70.

Palmer and Blandford, *A Grammar of Spoken English*, 2nd edit., pp. 73–91; 216.

Aiken, *Commonsense Grammar*, pp. 111–126.

Kennedy, *Current English*, pp. 266–267; 291–294; 318–319; 324; 340–341; 348; 351; 476–477; 484; 502–504; 510; 519–520; 557.

Kruisinga, *A Handbook of Present-Day English*, 5th edit., Part II, Vol. 2, §§ 946 ff.; Vol. 3, §§ 2264 ff.

Bryant, *A Functional English Grammar*, pp. 182–190; 196–204.

Roberts, *Understanding Grammar*, pp. 90–109; 224–225; 309–316.

Francis, *The Structure of American English*, pp. 268–281; 298–299; 318; 320–322; 424.

Lloyd and Warfel, *American English in Its Cultural Setting*, pp. 85–86; 112–119; 140–141; 153–157; 162–164; 168–170; 172; 175–177; 180; 184; 187; 193–205; 243; 267–274.

Sledd, *A Short Introduction to English Grammar*, pp. 79–81; 92–94; 98; 103–105; 109; 115–119; 123–126; 134–135; 140–141; 170; 177; 286–287.

Hill, *Introduction to Linguistic Structures*, pp. 167–171; 175–190; 203–204; 230–239; 246–252; 264; 299–312; 318–319; 329.

Hockett, *A Course in Modern Linguistics*, pp. 204; 225 ff.

Zandvoort, *A Handbook of English Grammar*, 5th edit., pp. 218–225.

Chatman, S., "Pre-adjectivals in the English Nominal Phrase," *American Speech*, Vol. XXXV (May, 1960), pp. 83–100.

Adverbs

Curme, *Parts of Speech and Accidence,* pp. 71–86.
Curme, *Syntax,* pp. 128–142.
Jespersen, *A Modern English Grammar,* 3rd edit., Part II, pp. 4–6; 10–12; 15–16; 290–292; 318–320; 353–360; 367; 371–372; 390–391.
Jespersen, *Essentials of English Grammar,* pp. 68–69; 73; 76–77; 357–373.
Jespersen, *The Philosophy of Grammar,* pp. 100–102; 104–107; 211.
Palmer and Blandford, *A Grammar of Spoken English,* 2nd edit., pp. 171–198; 216–217.
Kruisinga, *A Handbook of Present-Day English,* 5th edit., Part II, Vol. 2, §§ 953 ff.; Vol. 3, §§ 2299 ff.
Aiken, *Commonsense Grammar,* pp. 126–142.
Kennedy, *Current English,* pp. 266; 305–307; 321; 325–326; 475; 504–505.
Bryant, *A Functional English Grammar,* pp. 190–204.
Roberts, *Understanding Grammar,* pp. 207–221; 225–226; 317–332.
Francis, *The Structure of American English,* pp. 281–288; 304–305; 314–317; 320–321; 323–324; 348; 403; 408.
Lloyd and Warfel, *American English in Its Cultural Setting,* pp. 85; 139; 141; 144–150; 153–159; 164–168; 174–177; 181; 184; 187; 204–205; 267–270; 274; 281.
Sledd, *A Short Introduction to English Grammar,* pp. 60–62; 70; 79–81; 84; 94–101; 103; 109–111; 116–117; 122–126; 136; 140; 143–148; 163; 170; 177; 287–288; 290–291; 303–306; 313.
Hill, *Introduction to Linguistic Structures,* 149–150; 170–171; 182–184; 199; 222–231; 236–244; 246; 250; 252; 255; 264–265; 276; 283–291; 309; 312–318; 329–334; 389; 391–405.
Hockett, *A Course in Modern Linguistics,* pp. 193; 204; 210 ff., 226; 258.
Zandvoort, *A Handbook of English Grammar,* 5th edit., pp. 218–225.

B. FOR CLASS DISCUSSION

1. Look up the inflection of the adjective in any Old English grammar, or turn to par. 3.14, and compare it with the present-day adjective. What differences do you note? Compare with the Middle English adjective of par. 4.23 and note the differences.
2. Does the adjective in Modern English have any inflections left? If so, what?
3. Can you account for the forms *old, elder, eldest* and *old, older, oldest?*
4. What accounts for the forms *good, better, best?*

5. What accounts for words like *lenger* and *strenger* in sixteenth-century works?
6. Shakespeare uses adjectives like *honester* and *violentest*. Are the same forms found in Modern English? Can you account for present-day usage?
7. What rule would you make for forming the comparative and superlative in Modern English?
8. What is meant by double and triple inflections in adjectives? Illustrate.
9. Make as many sentences as you can with a different type of adjective in each. How many types do you have? Where is the adjective placed in the sentence in each instance? What general conclusions would you draw from your illustrations?
10. Read an article in a current magazine and mark each adjective, whether a word, or a phrase, or a clause. What do you observe concerning the order of the adjectives in the sentence?
11. What is the difference between an adjective and an adverb? Read discussions of Francis, Hill, Hockett and Sledd.
12. Look up the definition of each in several grammars and then write your own definition.
13. How many sources for adverbs can you give? Illustrate each.
14. List three words each of which can be used both as an adjective and as an adverb. Can adjectives be interchanged with other parts of speech? Give illustrations.
15. Read an article in a current periodical and mark all the adverbs. In each instance note what the adverb modifies. How many different types of modifiers do you find for the adverb?
16. Did you find any sentence or clause modified by an adverb? What is the proportion of sentence or clause modifiers?
17. In the same article, note the order of the adverbs in the sentence. What conclusion would you draw concerning adverb order?
18. Are there any instances in the article in which it is difficult to determine whether the modifier is an adverb or an adjective? Can you give such an illustration of such a construction?
19. Is the ending *-ly* a good test for the adverb? Give reason for your answer.
20. What is the function of *just* in *Just why you are going I do not know?*

C. SUGGESTIONS FOR RESEARCH PAPERS

1. A Study of Adjectives (or Adverbs) in Milton (or some other author).
2. The Adjective Phrase (or Clause) in Shakespeare (or any other author).
3. Adjectives as Adverbs (or Nouns) in Shakespeare (or any other author).

4. Adverbs as Sentence Modifiers in Shakespeare (or any other author).
5. Adverbs as Modifiers of Words Other than Verbs.
6. The History of Adverbs.
7. The Order of Adverbs (or Adjectives).
8. Classifying Adverbs.
9. The Adjectival (or Adverbial) Phrase (or Clause) in Shakespeare (or any other author).
10. Order in Phrases (or Clauses).
11. The History of the Phrase.
12. The Frequency of Adjective (or Adverbial) Phrases (or Clauses).

46

Verbs

46.1 The Verb The Modern English verb continues the two separate divisions of the verb characteristic of the Germanic languages: the weak and the strong. The weak is characterized by adding the suffix *-ed, -d,* or *-t,* the strong by the ablaut series or internal change of the vowel.[1] In English the weak verbs have always been the larger group and they continue to be since any recently created or recently borrowed verb is conjugated as a weak verb and since verbs once strong at times become weak, as in the case of *helped* superseding *holp* or *sowed* superseding *sew.* In early Modern English one also finds forms like *blowed* and *growed,* still heard in popular English, which failed to replace the strong form in literary English. On the other hand, in a few instances, by analogy with some strong verb, a few weak forms have been replaced by strong ones, as in *stuck* for *sticked* and *dug* for digged. On the whole, however, the simpler pattern of the weak verbs has been the dominant ones. These changes take place more readily among the illit-

[1] See pars. 2.5 and 3.17.

erate and among children who are not bound by conventions but make use of analogy in their speech. ⎡Analogy combined with the leveling off of inflections and the loss of them in the Middle English dialects reduced the several forms of the present tense so that in Modern English there is only one, as *I, you, we, you, they love*, except for the third singular, *he loves*, having the inflectional -*s*, taken over from the Northern dialect.[2] The conservative language of archaic poetry or prayer, however, preserves in the singular the different forms *I love, thou lovest, he loveth*, but has in the plural the same form as the standard, *we, you, they love*. The third person singular ending -*eth*, the ending of the Southern dialect in the Middle English period and the ending universally found in Chaucer, was still common in the early Modern English period as can be observed in the Bible. The use of the -*s* ending began to increase in the sixteenth century, especially in colloquial speech, and by the end of the century it prevailed, although in a few words like *hath* and *doth* the older form may have been more common. In present-day English the -*eth* ending is felt to be definitely archaic whenever employed. ⎦

46.2 Auxiliaries   Besides the strong and weak verbs there are a number of helping verbs which must be considered separately. They are known as auxiliary (Latin *auxilium*, "help") verbs and are used in verb phrases to qualify in some way the meaning expressed by the final word of the phrase. For example, in *I can play the piano*, *can* adds the idea of possibility to *play*. The playing is possible, but is not taking place. The words used as auxiliaries only are *can, could, may, might, must, shall, should, will*, and *would*. There are also a few special verbs which are used as main verbs as well as auxiliary. These are *be, do*, and *have*. In addition, there are several semi-auxiliaries which are developing and have developed. Among them are *go* (*He is going to write*) and *ought* followed by *to* (*He ought to write*). Others are *come* (*He came to be admired*), *get* (*He will get hit*), *let* (*Let him be considered*), and even *be able to* (*He is able to walk*).

46.3 The Past-Present Verbs   In the English language there seems to be a tendency toward bringing past time up to the present.

---

[2] This statement does not apply to the intensive *do love* and the progressive *am loving*.

That is, verbs originally past in tense take on a present meaning. This tendency can be observed particularly with auxiliary verbs. In Old English five of these verbs had developed presents from former pasts: *ought, must, may, shall,* and *can.* One will notice that these verbs omit the inflection in the third person singular present tense (he *must,* not he *musts*) like forms of the past tense rather than of the present. *Could, might,* and *should* have become past-presents since the Old English period. So has *would,* which was not one of the Old English group. *Ought* today is doubly past-present in that it was the Old English past-present verb *āgan* (*to owe*) and has now developed a present tense.[3] So has *must.* The original strong preterits, *āh* and *mōt,* became present in meaning and developed new weak preterits, *āhte* and *mōste* (Mod.E. *ought* and *must*). *Ought* and *must* have in turn become present in use.

46.4 Voice   In Modern English facts may be looked at from two points of view, from that of the doer and from that of the thing done. When facts are looked at from the vantage point of the doer, the verb is in the active voice; if they are considered from what is done, the verb is in the passive. The sense of the sentence is the same but there is a different word order, a different form of the verb, and the addition of the preposition *by.* For instance, in the sentence *Joan painted a picture, painted* is in the active voice, for the subject *Joan* is the doer; but in the sentence *A picture was painted by Joan,* the same idea is expressed with the order of the words changed, *by* added, and *was painted* substituted for *painted.* Here the subject of the verb receives the action. In the latter example the verb is in the passive voice, a late linguistic development in English, commonly used in writing, perhaps because of its impersonality. It is also employed in popular speech, as "Boy, was he thrown for a loop!" and "O.K., O.K., maybe I was licked, but I ain't goin' to stay licked." According to Kellner[4] it developed out of the reflexive construction. Although grammarians do not agree on how it developed,[5] one may observe that all passives are phrase verbs, consisting of two or

---

[3] For fuller treatment, see the author's "The Preterite-Present Verbs of Present-Day English," *College English* (February, 1944), pp. 259–264.

[4] *Op. cit.,* p. 224.

[5] See C. Alphonso Smith, *Studies in English Syntax* (Boston, Ginn & Company, 1906), pp. 66–71, and George O. Curme, "The Proper Subject of a Passive Verb," *Modern Language Notes* (April, 1913), pp. 97–101.

more verbs; that the final word in the phrase is the past participle
of the verb, a form usually ending in -*ed;* and that generally the
auxiliary *to be* in one of its forms is placed before the final or stem
verb. Compare the following forms of the verb *order* in the two
voices:

Tense	Active	Passive
1. Present	I order	I am ordered
2. Present perfect	I have ordered	I have been ordered
3. Past	I ordered	I was ordered
4. Past perfect	I had ordered	I had been ordered
5. Future	I shall (*or* will) order	I shall (*or* will) be ordered
6. Future perfect	I shall (*or* will) have ordered	I shall (*or* will) have been ordered

The passive in colloquial English sometimes employs other verbs
besides the verb *to be,* such as *get* and *become,* as in *If he should
get promoted, we could go abroad,* or *The man is becoming fatigued.*

46.5 Mood   In English there are three moods: the imperative,
the mood of command or request; the indicative, the mood of fact or
reality; and the subjunctive, the mood employed in special constructions of wish, condition, command, and the like. The subjunctive
identified as such by a difference in form is disappearing. In Old
English the subjunctive was commonly employed, but with the passing of the centuries the forms have gradually dropped out. We have
left one form *were* used in sentences such as *If I were you, I would
not do that* and *I wish I were in Europe.* Even here the tendency
today is to use the indicative *was,* the *were* being principally a
literary idiom. The one other form left, *be,* after such verbs as *recommend, ask, order, direct, agree, require, urge, insist, demand, pro-
pose* is being replaced by *should be.* Instead of *He insisted that
Mary be given the scholarship* one may hear *He insisted that Mary
should be given the scholarship.* Other examples are archaic. Perhaps the grammars of tomorrow will omit the subjunctive entirely.

46.6 Tenses   In Old English, as in Primitive Germanic, there
were two basic tenses, present and past. At that time, however, the
future tense was developing. It has since been established as one of
the basic time distinctions, but makes use in literary English of the
auxiliaries *shall* and *will* in its formation, whereas the present and

past have definite forms for each. It should be said, however, that the auxiliary *shall* in popular speech is being replaced by *will*. The future may be expressed by the present, as in *I go tomorrow*. Other means of expressing the future are *I am going, I am to go,* and *I am going to go*.

The next step in building the tense structure was to add the perfect tenses, one to each of three principal tenses, present,[6] past, and future. Thus we have present perfect, *I have gone;* past perfect, *I had gone;* and future perfect, *I shall have gone*. These tenses indicate previous time in each instance. For instance, *had gone* in *I had gone when you arrived* shows "past in the past." That is, *arrived* indicates past time, but *had gone* shows past in that past time. These six tenses indicate completed action, but English needed a way of expressing continuing action and developed the so-called progressive tenses, one for each of the six tenses:

Present progressive	I am ordering today.
Present perfect progressive	I have been ordering . . .
Past progressive	I was ordering yesterday.
Past perfect progressive	I had been ordering a month . . .
Future progressive	I shall be ordering another month too.
Future perfect progressive	I shall have been ordering a month . . .

The progressive forms are made by adding *to be* to the present participle.

46.7 Progressive Tenses One of the most significant developments in the modern period is the wide use of the progressive tenses.[7] In Middle English one rarely found a progressive form. These forms have grown up chiefly since the sixteenth century. Leah Dennis in her study of the progressive tense counted the progressives in 411 different extracts (56,500 lines) from 1466 to 1932, using the writings of the time. In her investigation of the prose

---

[6] See Edward Calver, "The Uses of the Present Tense Forms in English," *Language* (Vol. XXII, October–December, 1946), pp. 317–325; Dwight L. Bolinger, "More on the Present Tense in English," *Language* (Vol. XXIII, October–December, 1947), pp. 434–436.

[7] See discussion of Anna Granville Hatcher, "The use of the Progressive Form in English: A New Approach," *Language* (Vol. XXVII, 1951), pp. 254–280.

fiction, prose drama, poetry, verse drama, and formal prose of the various periods she found 3 instances in the period from 1466–1499; 3 from 1500–1532; 5 from 1533–1565; 14 from 1566–1599; 6 from 1600–1632; 16 from 1633–1665; 15 from 1666–1699; 14 from 1700–1732; 24 from 1733–1765. She also found a preponderance of progressive forms in colloquial usage as evidenced by the 198 instances in colloquial prose as opposed to 72 for poetry (including verse drama) and 56 for formal prose. All of these extracts were British, but beginning with 1766 American English was used as well and in each period approaching the present in both British and American English the use of the progressive is more and more common. One may compare the 24 instances in British English of the period 1733–1765 to the 60 instances in 1900–1932. The American English for the same period 1900–1932 had 95 instances.[8] The progressive tense grew out of the use of the participle as a noun with the preposition *on*, which weakened to *a-* and then disappeared. For instance, *He was on-fighting* became *He was a-fighting* and finally *He was fighting*. The extension of the progressive forms to the passive, joining the past participle to *being* as in *is being fought*, came as an even later development, starting at the end of the eighteenth century. The earliest instance which has been recorded is from the year 1769.[9]

Let us look for a moment at such a normal and (to us) natural phrase as "The house is being built." We are hardly conscious of it as progressive passive form; it is, to our mind, the proper way of expressing the idea. But only eighty-eight years ago (when this revision of *Modern English and Its Heritage* was made) a distinguished linguist wrote, indignantly: [10]

"The phrase 'the house *is being built*' for 'the house *is building*' is an awkward neologism, which neither convenience, intelligibility, nor syntactical congruity demands, and the use of which ought therefore to be discountenanced, as an attempt at the artificial improvement of the language in a point which needed no amend-

[8] Leah Dennis, "The Progressive Tense: Frequency of Its Use in English," *PMLA* (Vol. LV, September, 1940), pp. 855–865.

[9] *OED, s. v. be.*

[10] George P. Marsh, *Lectures on the English Language,* 4th edit. (New York, Scribner, Armstrong & Co., 1874), p. 649.

ment." Whether needed or not this progressive passive construction has prevailed, until today it seems artificial to say "the house is building" instead of "the house is being built."

In common speech the present progressive has all but replaced the formal present tense. To say, "John, what do you?" and to expect the answer "I work" is not current English. The present tense now generally indicates ability, as in *I paint, I teach, I play*, or customary action, seen in *I work on Saturdays*. But action currently going on is almost always expressed in the present progressive (*He is writing; I am reading*), except for *I think, I doubt*, etc.

The history of the progressive tenses, now well established in Modern English, gives evidence of the fact that grammar is ever changing along with the other changes that take place in the language.

For the Student

A. FURTHER READINGS

Jespersen, *The Philosophy of Grammar*, pp. 164–168; 254–264; 265–289; 313–321.

Jespersen, *Essentials of English Grammar*, pp. 230–270; 293–295.

Jespersen, *A Modern English Grammar*, Part IV, pp. 352–363; Part V, pp. 504–512.

Curme, *Parts of Speech and Accidence*, pp. 203–237; 252–333.

Curme, *Syntax*, pp. 22–26; 354–447.

Fries, *American English Grammar*, pp. 61; 63–64; 103–107; 130–149; 172–198.

Sweet, *A New English Grammar*, Part I, pp. 105–114; Part II, pp. 84–117.

Kruisinga, *A Handbook of Present-Day English*, 5th edit., Part II, Vol. 1.

Palmer and Blandford, *A Grammar of Spoken English*, 2nd edit., pp. 91–171.

Bryant and Aiken, *Psychology of English*, 2nd edit., pp. 51–54; 103–105; 151–154; 206–214.

Aiken, *A New Plan of English Grammar*, pp. 48–53; 162–176.

Pooley, *Grammar and Usage in Textbooks on English*, pp. 61–64.

Bryant, *A Functional English Grammar*, pp. 53–86; 205–253.

Kellner, *Historical Outlines of English Syntax*, pp. 247–265.

Roberts, *Understanding Grammar*, pp. 110–180.

Francis, *The Structure of American English*, pp. 252–268; 424.

Lloyd and Warfel, *American English in Its Cultural Setting*, pp. 94; 120–145; 157–158; 255–267; 278.

Sledd, *A Short Introduction to English Grammar*, pp. 73–76; 89–92; 106–111; 128–129; 153–164.

Hill, *Introduction to Linguistic Structures*, pp. 152–164; 191–229; 273–291.

Zandvoort, *A Handbook of English Grammar*, 5th edit., pp. 7–106; 364–375; 380–383.

Ives, "Concerning Verbs," *American Speech*, Vol. XXXII (December, 1957), pp. 264–270.

Twaddell, *The English Verb Auxiliaries*.

B. FOR CLASS DISCUSSION

1. Are the terms "regular" and "irregular" as applied to verbs appropriate terms? Give reasons for your answer.

2. Look up J. and E. M. Wright's *Old English Grammar*, 2nd edit., pp. 98–103, and explain what is meant by ablaut.

3. Which group of verbs is the larger? How can you distinguish between the two types?

4. What type is *teach, taught, taught?* Why?

5. What type of verb is *help* in Modern English? Look up the history of this verb and explain what has happened since the Old English period.

6. Why do children say *teached* for *taught?*

7. When new verbs come into the language today, what type are they? Illustrate.

8. What accounts for the use of *swang* in the past tense? Can you think of other similar uses?

9. Read a chapter in the Bible and note the endings of the third person singular. What endings do you find? Are they all alike? If not, what is the proportion of one to the other? Do we employ the same endings today? Explain what has happened here.

10. Is the *-eth* ending in the verb ever found in Modern English? If so, where? What attitude do present-day speakers have toward this form?

11. What is meant by auxiliary verbs? Name the true auxiliaries and use each in a sentence, showing how it performs its function as an auxiliary verb. See Twaddell, *The English Verb Auxiliaries*.

12. What verbs may be used as main verbs as well as auxiliary? Illustrate in sentences.

13. How many semi-auxiliaries can you list? Illustrate.

14. What is meant by a past-present verb? Illustrate. Look up preterite-present verbs in an Old English grammar and read Bryant's "The Preterite-Present Verbs in Present-Day English," *College English,* February, 1944, pp. 259–264.

15. Why is *ought* doubly past-present? Look up the history of *ought.* Can you explain the use of *had ought?* Is it a past in idea and in form?

16. Look up the definition of *voice* as applied to the verb in the dictionary. Examine several grammars and see what is said about voice. Read Jespersen, *The Philosophy of Grammar,* pp. 164–165, on this subject. What term does he prefer? What conclusions do you draw?

17. What is the difference between the active and passive voice? How is the difference shown between the two?

18. Look up the verb in an Old English grammar. What voices, moods, and tenses do you find?

19. Read an article in a reputable current periodical and pick out all passive verbs. Try to account for the use of each one (Jespersen's *The Philosophy of Grammar,* pp. 167–168, may be of help). What proportion of the verbs are active? What proportion passive?

20. Handbooks of writing often advise against the use of the passive. Do modern writers avoid the passive? Present evidence.

21. Read a scientific or technical article and a story, picking out the passive verbs in each. From this investigation, in what form of writing do you conclude that the passive is most useful?

22. Which forms of the passive were used most in the article you read? See also Fries' *American English Grammar,* pp. 188 ff. What conclusions do you draw concerning the relative frequency of the forms of the passive?

23. Look up mood in various grammars and dictionaries. What do you think of the definitions you find?

24. Read an article in a reputable current periodical and pick out the subjunctives according to form (see any grammar for the conjugation of the verb and the form of the subjunctive). Pick out the imperatives and the indicatives. What is the proportion of each? What are your conclusions in regard to the subjunctive? What did Fries find in his investigation of the subjunctive (*American English Grammar,* pp. 103–107; see also Leonard, *Current English Usage,* p. 120, and Thyra Jane Bevier, "American Use of the Subjunctive," *American Speech,* Vol. VI, February, 1931, pp. 207–215)?

25. Read a piece of prose by Milton or some other standard prose writer of the seventeenth century. Do you find a more frequent use of the

subjunctive than in present-day prose? Are there instances of the subjunctive which would be expressed by the indicative in present-day English? Compare the results of this investigation with that in Question 24.

26. Look up tense in several grammars. In what sense is it used? Look up the history and derivation of the word *tense* as applied to verbs.

27. Name and illustrate the three simple tenses in English and the three perfect tenses. How are the perfect tenses formed?

28. What is meant by the progressive tenses? How are they formed? When did they develop? Illustrate the different forms.

29. Does a single tense represent only one time of action? What conclusions would you draw from the following sentences?
    (1) I hear a train.
    (2) The earth revolves around the sun.
    (3) He goes to San Francisco tomorrow morning.
    (4) She broadcasts on the radio.
    (5) He walks into the store; the thieves stick a gun into his face; he holds up his hands and they rob him.

30. Make sentences similar to those in Question 29. How many times of action can you represent by a single tense?

31. Do verb forms have other uses besides showing time? See Aiken, *A New Plan of English Grammar*, pp. 162–176; Bryant and Aiken, *Psychology of English*, 2nd edit., 1962, pp. 206–214; and Bryant, *A Functional English Grammar*, pp. 221–228.

C. SUGGESTIONS FOR RESEARCH PAPERS

1. The Future of the Strong Verbs in English.
2. The Past-Present Verbs.
3. The Origin of *Could, Would,* and *Should* (or *May, Can,* and *Must*).
4. The History of the Verb *Be.*
5. A Study of *Ought* (or *Might*).
6. *Go* in Modern English.
7. The Semi-Auxiliaries in Current English.
8. *Do* as an Auxiliary.
9. English as an Indicative Language.
10. Does English Need a Subjunctive Mood?
11. Uses of the Subjunctive in Old English.
12. A Comparison of the Attitudes of Various Grammarians Toward the Subjunctive.
13. Comparative Frequency of Indicative and Subjunctive in Current Periodical Literature.

14. The Frequency of the Imperative in Modern Narrative or Dramatic Literature.
15. The History of Passive Forms in English.
16. The Use of the Passive in Newspaper Editorials.
17. The Use of the Passive in Shakespeare (or any other author).
18. The Future in English.
19. Substitutes for the Future Perfect.
20. Teaching Foreigners the Present-Perfect Tense.
21. The Progressive Tenses in English.
22. The Infinitive (or Participle) in Modern English (Middle English or Old English) or in Shakespeare (or some other well-known author).

47

Usage

47.1 Language Always Changing To many educated persons, grammar appears to be one of the few remaining eternal verities. They know that the meanings of words change, that slang is ephemeral (yesteryear's "23, skidoo" has given way to "Scram," "Take a powder," "Hit the road," or "Get lost"), and that to a certain extent styles alter with regard to spelling and even punctuation, but they have the comforting belief that syntax in the language, like the multiplication table in arithmetic, is fixed and immutable. But just as the meanings, spelling, and sounds of words change with the years, so does syntax. What is good English today will not with any certainty be good English tomorrow. This fact may be observed from reading the literature of past centuries. Old English seems practically a foreign language, and a modern reader needs a great many notes even for understanding a play by Shakespeare. Shakespeare, for example, omitted articles where we include them, as in *creeping like snail* and *in table of my heart,* and included them where we omit them, as in *at the least* and *at the last.* Likewise the negative

occupied a different position in the sentence, as in *I not think* and
it not appears to me. The double and sometimes triple use of the
negative for emphasis, common in Old English, still survived in
Shakespeare as in *say nothing neither* and *Nor this is not my nose
neither.* This intensive use of the negative can still be heard among
the illiterate. These examples are sufficient to show that language is
in a constant state of flux.

47.2 Usage, the Sole Arbiter   As changes gradually come about
in language, the only arbiter to be considered in linguistic matters
is usage. The purist may like to hold on to the expression he learned
in his early days, but he will find that his wishes are disregarded.
Language change is a democratic process, and the few invariably
make way for the many. Horace, the great Latin poet, recognized
that "use is the sole arbiter and norm of speech," a tenet upheld by
John Hughes in his essay *Of Style* (1698) when he wrote "general
acceptation . . . is the only standard of speech." Dr. Johnson in the
Plan for his dictionary stated that he would "endeavour to discover
and promulgate the decrees of custom." He was too intelligent a
student of language not to know the power of usage. So did Lord
Chesterfield, who said "Every language has its peculiarities; they are
established by usage, and whether right or wrong, they must be
complied with." In the eighteenth century, however, the chief ex-
ponent of this doctrine was the philosopher, theologian, and chemist,
Joseph Priestley, who stressed the significance of usage in his *Rudiments of English Grammar* (1761) and in his *Theory of Language*
(1762), a point of view promoted by George Campbell in his *Philosophy of Rhetoric* (1776). Thus one can see that throughout the centuries students of language have recognized the fact that usage is
the most important criterion of language.

47.3 *It Is Me*   The history of the phrase *It is me* well illustrates
the change in syntax and the force of usage. In Old English we find
Ic hit eom (*I it am*), which changed in Middle English to (*H*)*it am I.*
Since *it* was felt to be the subject *am* was changed to *is,* resulting in
It is I. It is I has now shifted to *It is me,* the *me* being used, no
doubt, because of its position after the verb, for the accusative case
generally follows the verb. *Me* was competing with *I* for supremacy
as early as the·sixteenth century, and one can find instances of it in

the work of such writers as Sir Richard Steele, Jane Austen, Joseph Conrad, as well as in more modern books.[1] William Ellery Leonard termed *It is I* "suburban English,"[2] suggesting that the phrase is overcorrect. *It is me* or *It's me* is now the phrase employed in informal, colloquial speech and writing and *It is I* is reserved for formal, literary style.

47.4 *Me*, *Him*, *Her*, *Us*, and *Them*   If *me* has come to be the form after the verb in *It is me*, one wonders about the other pronouns, *him*, *her*, *us*, and *them*. *It is me* is far more common than *It is him*, *It is her*, and *It is them*. On the other hand, one may take note of an opinion expressed by H. G. Wells in one of his novels: "'That's him,' said Ann Veronica, in sound idiomatic English."[3] One may cite other examples from authors[4] such as James Stephens, A. A. Milne, J. Middleton Murray, but the dictum of C. T. Onions is interesting. He says the one [*It is me*] is "used even by educated speakers" but the others are "generally regarded as vulgar or dialectal."[5] Weekley also says, "Personally I say 'That's me,'" hesitate at 'That's him (*or* her)' . . ."[6] Sterling A. Leonard shows in *Current English Usage* that *It is me* is established in usage but that *If it had been us, we would admit it* is a borderline expression, approved by 29 judges and condemned by 19, and that *I'll swear that was him*, *I suppose that's him*, *I am older than him*, and *It seems to be them* are all disputable.[7] One can find the objective forms of the pronouns in good present-day speech and writing where the purist would use the nominative, as, for example, ". . . which is not simply *us*" (*Yale Review*, Summer, 1958, p. 529) and ". . . people who . . . are us . . ."

[1] See George H. McKnight, *Modern English in the Making* (New York, D. Appleton and Company, 1930), pp. 532–533.

[2] W. E. Leonard, "Concerning the Leonard Study," *American Speech* (Vol. VIII, No. 3, October, 1933), p. 58. See also Wallace Rice, "Who's There?—Me," *ibid.*, pp. 58–63.

[3] H. G. Wells, *Ann Veronica* (London, T. F. Unwin, 1909), Chapter VI.

[4] See list in McKnight, *op. cit.*, pp. 532–533.

[5] C. T. Onions, *An Advanced English Syntax*, 4th edit. (New York, The Macmillan Company, 1927), p. 34.

[6] Ernest Weekley, *Cruelty to Words* (New York, E. P. Dutton & Co., 1931), p. 79.

[7] Sterling A. Leonard, *Current English Usage*, published for the National Council of Teachers of English (Chicago, Inland Press, 1935), pp. 108–111. The meanings of "established" and "disputable" are explained on p. 99 of this monograph.

(*Saturday Review*, August 30, 1958, p. 28). The *Linguistic Atlas* records also afford available evidence from cultivated informants.[8] Jespersen explains as follows what is actually happening to pronouns: "On the whole, the natural tendency in English has been towards a state in which the nominative of pronouns is used only where it is clearly the subject, and where this is shown by close proximity to (generally position immediately before) a verb, while the objective is used everywhere else." [9] He proceeds to cite examples from Jane Austen, Strachey, Bennett, and Stevenson of the use of the objective in an independent position, such as *Me!, Dear me!, No, not me, And him sixty!* From these instances one can see that *him, her, us,* and *them* are gaining strength and that there is nothing sacred about case in pronouns. Instead, word-order is the determining factor.

47.5 *Who* and *Whom* After discussing the personal pronouns, one immediately thinks of the interrogative pronouns *who* and *whom.* Just as the objective case is used after the verb so there is a strong tendency to use the nominative before the verb. *Who*, therefore, is often found instead of *whom* in sentences like *Who did you call? Who is the letter from?* In both instances word order dictates the case. There is, however, more involved here than word order; that is, the tendency to substitute the nominative *who* for *whom* in every position. A note under *whom* in the *OED* reads "no longer current in natural colloquial speech." Jespersen likewise says that "the form *who* is generalized, so that it is now practically the only form used in colloquial speech." [10] He continues by showing that this has been true for at least three centuries, citing examples from Shakespeare, Marlowe, Addison, Sheridan, and George Eliot. He also points out that many people have become so conscious of the *who* and *whom* controversy that they feel proud at remembering to use *whom*,[11] a symptom of the decadence of the form. Kemp

---

[8] See Jean Malmstrom, *A Study of the Validity of Textbook Statements About Certain Controversial Grammatical Items in the Light of Evidence from the Linguistic Atlas* (a dissertation at the University of Minnesota, 1958), Microfilm 58–7012.

[9] Otto Jespersen, *Essentials of English Grammar* (New York, Henry Holt and Company, 1933), p. 136.

[10] *Ibid.*

[11] *Ibid.*, p. 137.

Malone, however, considers the use of *who* and *whom* a matter of style. That is, in unstudied style one will use *who* in sentences like "*Who* will you choose?" and "*Who* will you speak to?" but in a studied style *whom* will be substituted for *who*.[12]

47.6 The Relative *Who* and *Whom*   There is at present a state of confusion also in regard to the form of the relative pronoun to be employed in sentences like *We hire persons whom we think are good.* Here the form *whom* is used as the subject of *are*. This use, no doubt, occurs as a result of an attempt to be "correct," and is one of the best evidences of the disappearance of the form, for it is a use against the tendency of the language—the caseless use of *who*. Collections of this use have been made by various students of the English language, among them Weekley, Jespersen, Fowler, and Robertson,[13] to show what is happening to one of the few remaining case forms in Modern English.

47.7 Other Confusion of *Who* and *Whom*   Another place where *whom* is often used as the subject of a verb is in a clause introduced by a preposition such as *There was considerable doubt as to whom should be elected.* Here *whom* is used as the subject of *should be elected.* The whole clause, and not *whom*, is object of the preposition *to*. There must be a consciousness of the different forms *who* and *whom* in the mind of the speaker or writer who employs *whom* in this construction. The use is not so natural that there is no confusion, one of the first indications of the departure of a form. The same confusion exists in the use of *whomever*, as in *Write this to whomever asks for a book.*

47.8 *Only*   In discussing the cases of the pronouns we have seen the importance of word order, one of the chief syntactical devices of Modern English, often determining the appearance of a particular construction.[14] To avoid grammatical anarchy English has developed

---

[12] "Whom," *College English* (Vol. X, October, 1948), pp. 37–38. See also discussion by James B. McMillan, " 'Who' and 'Whom'," *College English* (Vol. VII, November, 1945), pp. 104–105.

[13] See Weekley, *Cruelty to Words, op. cit.*, pp. 23–27; Jespersen, *Essentials of English Grammar, op. cit.*, p. 137; H. W. Fowler, *A Dictionary of Modern English Usage* (Oxford, Clarendon Press, 1926), pp. 724–725; Stuart Robertson, *The Development of Modern English* (New York, Prentice-Hall, Inc., 1934), pp. 502–503.

[14] See Chapter 41.

a system of standardized sentence order, and in Modern English the modifying words generally come immediately before the words they modify. One of the most familiar sentence patterns is made up of the subject, adverbial modifier, verb, and object, as *He carefully did the work*. This pattern tends to be followed even when the adverb does not logically refer to the verb as in *We only had one left*, an order objected to by purists but found by Leonard to be established in Modern English.[15] Palmer and Blandford in their *Grammar of Spoken English* state: "In spoken English it [*only*] generally occupies the pre-verbal position. . . ."[16] The great majority of speakers place *only* before the verb and even in literature one can find instances of it. Matthew Arnold's *Dover Beach* will serve as an example:

> But now I only hear
> Its melancholy, long, withdrawing roar.[17]

Marckwardt and Walcott call this usage literary English.[18]

47.9 Split Infinitive The pattern of putting the adverb before the verb has produced a strong tendency to place the adverbial modifier of an infinitive immediately before the infinitive and after the *to,* the sign of the infinitive, which was originally a preposition meaning "toward" and governing the dative case, and not properly a part of the infinitive. The prepositional force of *to* ceased to be felt as early as the fourteenth century, and then by analogy the adverb began to take its place after the *to* and before the infinitive and has been employed by good writers for several centuries. In Modern English, however, the split infinitive has been the subject of a great deal of controversy because of the authoritarian grammarians of the eighteenth and nineteenth centuries, who selected it as something to be avoided under all circumstances. The persons who have come under the sway of those authoritarians are not aware of the changes that have gone on in the English language since the death of Dryden and are willing to run the risk of ambiguity and awkwardness rather

[15] S. A. Leonard, *Current English Usage, op. cit.,* pp. 136–137.
[16] P. 186.
[17] Ll. 24–25.
[18] A. H. Marckwardt and F. Walcott, *Facts About Current English Usage,* NCTE Monograph, No. 7 (New York, D. Appleton-Century Company, 1938), p. 35.

than split an infinitive. Those same persons do not object to verb phrases being divided by an adverb as in *He does not write to me,* or *She is always working for others;* or to subjects and predicates being separated as in *He always writes, He generally reads at night;* or to the separation of the preposition from its object in a verbid phrase such as *of successfully writing* in *He told of successfully writing the book.* Then *to always write* is not very different from *he always writes.* Despite the authoritarian hold, good writers and speakers have continued to split the infinitive where avoiding it would have caused ambiguity or patent artificiality, and at last students of English usage have shown that the split infinitive is established.[19] The more recent handbooks and grammars are willing to acknowledge it. One even goes so far as to say that it is "no longer considered one of the seven deadly sins of college composition." [20] The literary precedent for it has been pointed out by many students of language.[21] With all the evidence that has been piled up in the last half century, it would seem that even the "die-hard purist" would be willing to accept a few split infinitives in preference to awkwardness and ambiguity. In the long run the great forces of analogy, clarity, and word order win against the authoritarian.

47.10 Group Genitive Along with the split infinitive may be considered another locution, which could be called a *split genitive* but is termed *the group genitive.* In the *Duke of York's hat,* the genitive undoubtedly belongs with Duke although the inflection is two words removed, preceding *hat.* The genitive belongs with *Duke, of York* being an adjective phrase modifying *Duke.* Phrases of this type are common today, having, like the split infinitive, the sanction of educated speakers and writers. Thus in the *Mayor of New York's car* it is clear that the car belongs to the Mayor and not to New

[19] S. A. Leonard, *Current English Usage, op. cit.,* pp. 122–124.

[20] John M. Kierzek and Walker Gibson, *The Macmillan Handbook of English,* 4th edit. (New York, The Macmillan Company, 1960), p. 390.

[21] T. R. Lounsbury, *The Standard of Usage in English* (New York, Harper & Bros., 1908), pp. 240–268; Fowler, *op. cit.,* pp. 558–561; G. O. Curme, *Syntax* (Boston, D. C. Heath & Company, 1931), pp. 458–467 and "Origin and Force of the Split-Infinitive," *Modern Language Notes,* Vol. XXIX, No. 2, pp. 41–45 (February 1914); Otto Jespersen, *A Modern English Grammar,* Part V, *Syntax,* Vol. IV (Copenhagen, Ejnar Munksgaard, 1940), p. 330; H. Poutsma, *A Grammar of Late Modern English,* Part I, *The Sentence,* 2nd edit. (Groningen, P. Nordhoff, 1928), p. 462.

York. Bradley points out that in colloquial English this construction assumes grotesque extremes as in his example *That was the man I met at Birmingham's idea,* where *the man I met at Birmingham* is considered for the time as a unit, a word, and to it is added the *'s*.[22] Other group genitives that are now well established are *someone else's, nobody else's, everybody else's,* etc. despite the fact that Leonard found in the preparation of *Current English Usage* that the teachers he consulted placed the artificial *everybody's else* among "established" usages. They must have been influenced by handbooks which were still under the influence of the authoritarian, for the expressions with the *'s* added to *else* are now idiomatic. The linguists, on the other hand, considered *everybody's else* as "illiterate or semi-literate."[23]

47.11 One   Another pronoun about which there has been a great deal of discussion is the indefinite *one,* used impersonally. It is not quite parallel to the French *on* or the German *man* in the phrases *on dit* and *man sagt,* but handbooks once insisted that the form should be consistently employed throughout a sentence, as in *One rarely enjoys one's luncheon when one is tired.* This is called the established form in *Current English Usage.* The comments on this sentence, however, implied that even though it was correct, it was somewhat stilted. One linguist wrote: "*One* followed by one or more *one's* never wholly excluded *one* followed by one or more *he's.* A series of *one's* strikes many (including me) as a kind of pedantry. As a matter of fact, probably most people who stick rigidly to *one* have acquired it by effort."[24] More recent handbooks with the up-to-date viewpoint accept *he* after *one.* Marckwardt and Cassidy say: "Writers today do not hesitate to insert forms of the pronoun *he.*"[25] Perrin and Dykema make a distinction between formal English where *one* may be used and informal English where it is not. They then add: "American usage stands firmly by older English usage in referring back to *one* by *he, his, him* (or *she, her*),"[26] giving as an

[22] Henry Bradley, *The Making of English* (New York, The Macmillan Company, 1904), p. 61.
[23] S. A. Leonard, *Current English Usage, op. cit.,* p. 112.
[24] *Ibid.,* p. 106.
[25] A. H. Marckwardt and F. G. Cassidy, *Scribner Handbook of English,* 3rd edit. (New York, Charles Scribner's Sons, 1960), p. 348.
[26] *Op. cit.,* p. 612.

example: *One is warned to be cautious if he would avoid offending his friends and bringing their displeasure down upon his head.* This statement may be further substantiated by a sentence from Professor Fries' *American English Grammar,* in which he writes: "If one could conjure up Shakspere or Spenser or Milton, he would find their English strange to his ears not only in pronunciation but in vocabulary and grammar as well." [27] In early Modern English *one* was followed by *his, him,* and *himself* and today everyone prefers to carry on the tradition. Sentences are usually recast to avoid the excessive use of *one,* but the problem arises because the English language does not possess a generalized pronoun that does duty for *he, she,* and *it.*

47.12 None   There has also been a great deal of discussion as to whether *none* is singular or plural. Those who insist that *none* is properly a singular use the argument that it is equivalent to *no one. No one* and *not one* are now used when we wish to emphasize the singular, but *none* may be singular or plural, and its use in the plural is more common. *None* with the plural verb can be traced back to the Middle English period. It was not, however, until the end of the period and the beginning of the early Modern English period that *none* came to be followed or preceded immediately by a plural verb form. The idea uppermost in the speaker's mind determines the use of a plural or a singular verb. Professor Fries found in his investigation of this usage that with but one exception *none* was used with the plural verb as were *any* and the disjunctive pronouns *neither* and *either.*[28] S. A. Leonard in *Current English Usage* shows that *None of them are here* is established usage.[29] He quotes an author saying, "It is pure priggishness to pretend that *none* is always singular." Recent dictionaries point out that it is generally used with a plural verb. An example of the plural usage is: "*None* of these people would be doing what *they were* doing if *they* knew what was in store. . . ." [30]

47.13 Concord   The discussion of *none* with a singular or plural verb brings one to the question of concord or agreement. Those who

[27] *Op. cit.,* p. 6.
[28] *Ibid.,* pp. 50, 56.
[29] *Op. cit.,* pp. 103–104.
[30] *Saturday Review* (April 9, 1955), p. 20/3.

try to superimpose Latin syntax upon the English language insist upon complete agreement in number, gender, person, and case, wherever it is possible to show the agreement by distinctive forms. That is, they insist that a plural subject shall be followed by a plural verb, a singular subject by a singular verb, and so on. Good prose of today, however, does not always observe the theoretical rule of concord established in the eighteenth century. One may often find sentences in which a singular verb is used with a plural subject, such as: "But the assault and robbery *is* at least equally likely to have been a reason for his voluntary resignation." [31]

47.14 Agreement in Number Between Subject and Verb If a group of words, even though plural in form, creates one conception in the mind of the person using them as a subject, a singular verb follows. In Modern English where there is a conflict between form and meaning, meaning tends to triumph.[32] In the verb, however, except for the single instance of *was* and *were*, number is distinguished in the present tense only, and even there, only in the third person, the ending generally being -*s*. As Jespersen phrases it, ". . . singular and plural in verbs has nothing at all to do with the verbal idea: when we say 'birds sing' with the plural form of *sing* . . . this does not denote several acts of singing, but is only a meaningless grammatical contrivance showing the dependence of the verb on its subject."[33] He feels that it is "superfluous to have separate

---

[31] F. N. Robinson (ed.), *The Works of Geoffrey Chaucer*, 2nd edit., "Introduction" (Boston, Houghton Mifflin Company, 1957), pp. xxiii–xxiv. For discussions of concord see Russell Thomas, "Concord Based on *Meaning* versus Concord Based on *Form:* The Indefinites," *College English* (Vol. I, October, 1939), pp. 38–45, and "Concord of the Verb in Relative Clauses After *One of*," *College English* (Vol. XIII, October, 1951), pp. 43–44; F. Christensen, "Number Concord with *What*-Clauses," *American Speech* (Vol. XXX, February, 1955), pp. 30–37; J. S. Kenyon, "One of Those Who Is . . . ," *American Speech* (Vol. XXVI, October, 1951), pp. 161–165; Roberts, *op. cit.*, pp. 274–291.

[32] For a fuller discussion of this topic, see Bertha M. Watts, "Discordant Views on Concord," *College English* (Vol. VIII, April, 1946), pp. 420–422. For *there is* (*are*), *was* (*were*) followed by a compound subject, see E. Bagby Atwood, *op. cit.*, pp. 29–30; R. J. Geist, "There Is One and . . . ," *College English* (Vol. XIV, November, 1952), pp. 115–116; " 'There Is' Again," *College English* (Vol. XVI, December, 1954), 188–189; J. Malmstrom, *op. cit.*, pp. 203–204; V. G. McDavid, *op. cit.*, pp. 54–55.

[33] Jespersen, *Essentials of English Grammar, op. cit.*, p. 216.

forms in the verb for the two numbers" and "that English has lost
nothing in clearness, but has gained in ease, through the dropping
of nearly all the forms that in former stages of the language distinguished the two numbers in verbs." The question of concord or
agreement in number between the subject and the verb is, therefore,
a limited one.

47.15 Collective Nouns   Meaning also predominates over form
where collective nouns, such as *audience, committee, family, class,
crowd, troop, army,* are used. *Class* may be followed by a plural verb
as in *The class were all present* if the meaning stresses the individuals making up the group. If, however, the class is thought of as a
unit, as in *The class goes out at eleven o'clock,* the singular verb is
employed. This tendency was apparent in Old English except that
the plural form practically never immediately followed or preceded
the collective noun, as may be seen in *Hēr cuōm micel sciphere on
West Walas, ond hīe tō ānum gecierdon, ond wiþ Ecgbryht, West
Seaxna cyning, winnende wǣron* (Anglo-Saxon Chronicle, 835) and
*Hēr rād sē here ofer Mierce innan East Engle ond wintersetl nāmon
æt Ðeodforda* (Anglo-Saxon Chronicle, 870). You will note that several words come between the collective *sciphere* and the plural
pronoun *hīe* and plural verbs *gecierdon* and *wǣron* in the first example. Likewise in the second example seven words intervene between the collective *here* and the plural verb *nāmon*. By the Middle
English period the collective noun singular in form was placed next
to a verb plural in form and ever since the concord of number has
depended upon the meaning rather than on the form of the noun.
Even words like *number, part, rest, remainder* may be followed by
a plural verb, as in *A number of letters were written but not mailed.*
On this subject, Jespersen writes: "According as the idea of plurality
is more or less prominent in the mind of the speaker, there is in all
languages and at all times a tendency to forget the fact that collectives are grammatically singular, and we often find plural constructions, partial or total. . . . In Modern English the tendency is perhaps stronger than in most languages, because so few verb forms
and hardly any adjectives show any distinction at all between the
two numbers. . . . And then also distance plays some part, the plural construction occurring more easily at some distance from the

singular substantive (*they* in the next sentence, etc.) than in immediate contact with it." [34]

47.16 This, These, That, Those *This, these, that, those* as demonstrative adjectives generally agree in number with the number of the noun following, as *this* (*that*) *book* and *these* (*those*) *books*. This agreement occurs even with collective nouns, as in *This crowd of soldiers is here to see the fleet*. On the other hand, with two words *kind* and *sort*, the plural forms *these* and *those* occur, especially in cases followed by an *of* phrase, in which the noun is plural, such as *these kind of books, those sort of pictures*. *Kind* and *sort* are so closely connected with the noun they are placed before that they seem like adjectives and thus the demonstrative adjective used with them is chosen in conformity with the plural idea expressed in the principal noun in the *of* phrase rather than with the singular word *kind* or *sort*. Professor Fries found that this usage commonly appeared in the Standard English that he investigated but not once in the Vulgar English.[35] In Vulgar English he found *them kind of books*, the demonstrative of plural number being *them* instead of *these* and *those*. Jespersen suggests that we look upon *kind* and *sort* as unchanged plurals and therefore accept the construction as correct,[36] but at present the expression has only colloquial standing.

47.17 Possible Origin of These Kind *These* and *those kind* or *sort* may have had their origin in the characteristic Old English order of the genitive regularly preceding its governing word, so that instead of *wise men of all kind*, we have *of-all-kind wise men: alles cynnes witan*. Historically *these* and *those* are not plurals but genitives in expressions like *these kind of books*. This phrase may be the modern descendant of *þisses cynnes béc: of-this-kind books*. There was no *of* expressed in Old English, but it entered this genitive construction early, about the thirteenth century, and was standard usage by Shakespeare's time.[37]

47.18 Kind of a, Sort of a The use of *kind of* and *sort of* sug-

---

[34] Otto Jespersen, *A Modern English Grammar*, Part II, "Syntax," Vol. I (Heidelberg, Carl Winter's Universitätsbuchhandlung, 1914), p. 94, § 4.813.

[35] Fries, *American English Grammar, op. cit.*, pp. 51, 58.

[36] Jespersen, *Essentials of English Grammar, op. cit.*, p. 202.

[37] Bryant and Aiken, *Psychology of English, op. cit.*, pp. 69, 95 ff.

gests the colloquial *kind of a* and *sort of a*, as in *a kind of a hammer* and *a sort of a barn*, which are very common in informal, colloquial English. Perrin and Dykema point out that these expressions are also fairly common among respected writers.[38] They cite examples from John Jay Chapman's *Letters*, Gilbert Murray's *The Rise of the Greek Epic*, and Sally Benson's *People Are Fascinating*. In formal writing, however, one usually finds *a kind of hammer* and *a sort of barn*.

47.19 Quite   A similar expression to *kind of a* is *quite a* which grows out of the informal and colloquial use of *quite* meaning "to some extent, somewhat, very, rather" as in *I am quite happy*. From this meaning develop the colloquial phrases *quite a few*, *quite a little*, *quite a lot*, as well as *quite some time*. In formal English the meaning of *quite* is "completely, wholly."

47.20 Adjective or Adverb   There are other expressions in English with divided usage, such as *I feel bad* or *I feel badly*. The question concerns the use of the adjective or the adverb. The theory behind the use of the adjective is that *feel* is a copula or a linking verb, joining the subject *I* with the predicate adjective *bad*. The person who employs *badly* has a feeling that an adverb is more "correct." The adverb is identified to him by an *-ly* suffix and so by analogy he uses *badly* instead of *bad*. S. A. Leonard found that *badly* is established in good colloquial English in sentences like *I felt badly about his death*, and some of the judges approved the expression as appropriate to formal literary English.[39] There are numbers of similar expressions in current English, such as "to rest easy," "easy come, easy go," "to sit quiet," "to shine bright," "to stand firm," in which the adjective is preferable. Curme numbers about sixty linking verbs in present-day English which have the adjective after them and says, "Their wide and varied use is the most prominent feature of our language."[40] Among them are *appear, become, taste, sound, look, grow,* and *act*.

47.21 Slow or Slowly   Another question of usage arises with *slow* and *slowly*. The choice is not between adjective and adverb as with *bad* and *badly*, but between adverb and adverb. *Slow* is an

[38] *Op. cit.*, 573.
[39] *Current English Usage, op. cit.*, pp. xv, 136.
[40] G. O. Curme, *Parts of Speech and Accidence* (Boston, D. C. Heath and Company, 1935), p. 67.

old adverb, going back to the Old English adverbs that ended in *-e* instead of to those that ended in *-lice*. The latter has given us the modern ending *-ly,* but the former has disappeared, leaving a number of adverbs with the same forms as adjectives, among them *hard, fast, first, much, loud, low,* and *slow.* The purist may object to *Go slow,* but history and universal usage sanction it. *Go slow* is a more vigorous expression than *Go slowly;* however, in making the choice rhythm and euphony generally determine the decision. Note both forms in one poetic line from Arthur Hugh Clough: "In front the sun climbs slow, how slowly" ("Say Not the Struggle Naught Availeth").

47.22 Shall and Will   There may be a question concerning *slow* and *slowly,* or *bad* and *badly,* or *these kind* and *those kind,* but when one looks up *shall* and *will,* he is completely bewildered. The literary uses of *shall* and *will* provide one of the most vexatious—and ludicrous—situations in the study of English. The rules are so intricate, and so artificial, that H. W. and F. G. Fowler took more than twenty pages of their book *The King's English* [41] to expound the exact procedures prescribed by grammarians for various circumstances. For more than a hundred years there have been many vigorous discussions and much written on this subject. Professor Fries, who has devoted a great deal of time to this question, writes: [42] "In all this mass of material there is hardly a general statement . . . for which a direct contradiction cannot be found coming from a source that merits careful consideration. Thus, after a century . . . there are no accepted views of what the actual usage of these two words is, of the meaning and trend of the development of that usage, and of the causes that gave rise to it." Editors and writers in formal English generally use *shall* in the first person and *will* in the second and third for the simple future, following the rules laid down in most handbooks, and reverse the process for the emphatic future. However, in speech and informal writing in America one generally finds *will* in all persons. In the emphatic future there is a tendency to use *shall* in all persons. In speech, however, determination is shown by stress rather than by the word. Either *shall* or *will* may be heard. The use of the contractions *I'll, you'll, he'll,* etc. has undoubtedly helped in

[41] H. W. and F. G. Fowler, *The King's English* (Oxford, Clarendon Press, 1924), pp. 133–154.
[42] Fries, *American English Grammar, op. cit.,* p. 151.

establishing *will.* The speaker may think he is avoiding the issue when he employs the contraction, but he is really establishing the usage of *will,* for *I'll* is a contraction, phonetically, of *I will,* not of *I shall.* No one follows the rules laid down in most grammars and handbooks. The users of the language have for the most part ignored the many fine-spun distinctions, even in writing. For instance, who uses *shall* with *you* in questions, such as *Shall you be in your office this morning?* This construction has no place in present-day grammars. *Shall,* however, is often employed in the first person in questions, as *Shall I open the door? Shall we get the food?* [43]

47.23 The Passive and Its Subject Another question in connection with the verb concerns itself with the passive and its subject. Here we may see again word order determining the case. The original *Him wæs gegiefen ān bōc, Him was given a book, him* being the indirect object and placed first because the person is more significant than the thing, became *He was given a book,* now accepted by all grammarians. The normal sentence pattern consists of the subject placed before the verb. Therefore by analogy *him* was changed to *he* in early Middle English. Also, when a proper name such as *Mary* was used instead of *him,* there was no formal change in the word and *Mary* was felt to be the subject instead of the indirect object. Finally, the pull of analogy was so great that the change was accepted. Along with this acceptance came another complication for the grammarian, for the meaning of *I was given a chair* and *A chair was given me* was the same and he could not explain the construction logically. After generations of condemnation by the textbook writers, a name *retained object* was applied to the complement after the passive verb, and today there is little objection to the passive constructions. The passive voice and the nominative case before a passive verb have both been established in Modern English.[44]

47.24 *Like* as a Conjunction The purist opposes converting *like*

[43] For the discussion of *shall* and *will,* see Charles C. Fries, "The Periphrastic Future with *Shall* and *Will* in Modern English," *PMLA* (Vol. 40, 1925), pp. 963–1024; "The Expression of the Future," *Language* (Vol. 3, 1927), pp. 87–95; *American English Grammar, op. cit.,* pp. 150–168. For a fairly good picture of present-day usage, see Perrin and Dykema, *op. cit.,* pp. 693–695, and Roberts, *Understanding Grammar, op. cit.,* pp. 147–153.

[44] See Roberts, *op. cit.,* pp. 125–131, and Sledd, *op. cit.,* pp. 106–107; 131–132; 255; 302–303; 306.

into a conjunction; that is, using it in place of *as* and *as if* in introducing clauses, as in *It looks like it will rain. Like,* however, is accepted in Standard English when the verb is omitted from the clause, as *It looks like rain, It fits him like a shoe.* The grammarian explains *like* here as a preposition, overlooking the fact that *like* as a preposition was converted from *like* as an adjective. The *OED* comments concerning the substitution of *like* for *as:* "Now generally condemned as vulgar or slovenly, though examples may be found in many recent writers of standing." In spoken English *like* is increasing in usage. One hears it daily, even on the lips of cultivated speakers, as evidenced by a study of the Linguistic Atlas records of the Upper Midwest and North Central States.[45] It must be said, however, that it occurs more frequently in the West and South than in the East. Were it not for the editors and publishers who follow stylebooks, *like* would probably become established in standard literary English. Professors Perrin and Dykema say, "Historically both forms are good, since both are parts of the older *like as* ('Like as a father pitieth his children . . .'). Some speakers have taken *as,* others *like. Like* is preferable from the standpoint of meaning, because *as* has several different meanings and several functions in the language and so is relatively weak. *Like* is more exact and more emphatic in a comparison than *as* can be." [46]

47.25 Observation Necessary The examples of divided usage cited in this chapter serve to show that in the study of the English language more observation is necessary and less prohibition. We need grammars based on what is true of the language we use rather than on some person's idea of what it should be. Some progress has been made in this direction by recent studies, but we need more. In fact we should have a comprehensive survey of syntactical usage in present-day English. Each person must also learn to observe the language he uses and hears in order to know what is good current English.

Each person must also decide for himself what grammatical and word forms he will accept for his own writing and speaking. The choice is not so easy as it may seem, because in some circumstances it cannot be made on the basis of one's own knowledge or taste,

[45] See Malmstrom, *op. cit.,* pp. 40–42; 266–268.
[46] *Op. cit.,* pp. 582–583.

however superior or informed. If, for instance, one is writing for a
periodical that adheres to the eighteenth- and nineteenth-century
grammatical taboos, the splitting of infinitives is almost certainly going to provoke the wrath of the powers that be. Even if one is an
independent author, the splitting of infinitives and the use of "like"
as a conjunction will cause large segments of the public to regard
the writer as careless or ignorant of the niceties of the language. In
conversation, too, the choice is sometimes difficult. One may feel
perfectly justified in saying "like I did," but the listener may draw
the inference that the speaker "doesn't know any better." The purist
is always around, and it is not easy to make him admit that usage is
the "sole arbiter and norm of speech."

For the Student

A. FURTHER READINGS

Jespersen, *A Modern English Grammar*, Parts II, III, IV, "Syntax," *passim.*
Jespersen, *Essentials of English Grammar, passim.*
Curme, *Syntax, passim.*
Curme, "Are Our Teachers of English Properly Prepared?" *PMLA* (Vol.
      XLVI, Supplement for 1931), pp. 1415–1426.
Leonard, *Current English Usage, passim.*
Marckwardt and Walcott, *Facts About Current English Usage, passim.*
Bryant, *Current American Usage, passim.*
Fries, *The Teaching of the English Language, passim.*
Fries, *American English Grammar, passim.*
Fries, "Usage Levels and Dialect Distribution," *American College Dic-
      tionary*, pp. xxvii–xxviii.
Robertson and Cassidy, *The Development of Modern English*, 2nd edit.,
      pp. 279–326.
Dean and Wilson, *Essays on Language and Usage.*
Kennedy, *Current English, passim.*
American Speech, passim.
Hall, *English Usage, passim.*
Baugh, *History of the English Language*, 2nd edit., Chapters 9 and 10.
Poutsma, *A Grammar of Late Modern English, passim.*

Kruisinga, *A Handbook of Present-Day English,* 5th edit., Part II, "English
   Accidence and Syntax," *passim.*
Pound, "Extensions of Usage of a Pronoun" in Language Monographs
   (*Curme Volume of Linguistic Studies*), No. VII, December, 1930,
   pp. 118–119.
Pooley, *Grammar and Usage in Textbooks on English, passim.*
Pooley, *Teaching English Usage, passim.*
Hall, *Leave Your Language Alone! (Linguistics and Your Language).*
Kenyon, "Cultural Levels and Functional Varieties of English," *College
   English* (Vol. X, October, 1948), pp. 31–36; "Linguistics and Usage,"
   Part IV (17 articles and an introduction), in *Readings in Applied
   English Linguistics,* ed. by H. B. Allen, pp. 193–291.
Horwill, *A Dictionary of Modern American Usage, passim.*
Oxford (New) English Dictionary, Vol. I, pp. xxvii–xxxiv.
Wyld, *Universal Dictionary of the English Language.*
Webster's *New International Dictionary,* 3rd edit.
B. and C. Evans, *A Dictionary of Contemporary American Usage, passim.*
Kurath (ed.), *et al., Linguistic Atlas of New England.*
McDavid, R. I., Jr., "American Dialects" in Nelson Francis, *Structure of
   American English,* pp. 480–543.
Kurath, *Word Geography of the Eastern United States.*

B. FOR CLASS DISCUSSION

1. What is meant by good usage? See Fries, *American English Grammar,*
   pp. 1–15; *The Teaching of English* (Ann Arbor, Mich., George Wahr,
   1949), Chapter 5; Hall, *Leave Your Language Alone!* pp. 1–28; Otto
   Jespersen, *Mankind, Nation and Individual from a Linguistic Point of
   View* (Oslo, Aschehoug, 1925), Chapters V and VI; Perrin and Dykema, *op. cit.,* pp. 26–35; Pooley, *Teaching English Usage,* pp. 3–31.
2. Does usage change? Illustrate.
3. What are the chief varieties of English usage? Give the characteristic
   uses of each (see Baugh, *op. cit.,* pp. 378–382; Bloomfield, *Language,*
   pp. 52; 149 ff.; Fries, *American English Grammar;* Kenyon, "Cultural
   Levels and Functional Varieties of English"; Marckwardt and Walcott, *Facts About Current English Usage;* L. M. Myers, *American
   English,* Englewood Cliffs, New Jersey, Prentice-Hall, Inc., 1952, pp.
   28–41; Perrin and Dykema, *op. cit.,* pp. 15–26; Pooley, *Teaching
   English Usage).*
4. What is archaic English? Illustrate.
5. Is there a difference between American and British usage? Illustrate.
   See Simeon Potter, *Our Language,* London, Penguin, 1954.

6. Is there a difference between Canadian English and that of the United States? See Morton W. Bloomfield, "Canadian English and Its Relation to Eighteenth Century American Speech," *Journal of English and Germanic Philology* (Vol. XLVII, 1948), pp. 59–67.

7. Are there differences within the United States? Illustrate. What are the main dialects? See McDavid, R. I., Jr., "American Dialects," in Nelson Francis, *Structure of American English.*

8. What section or sections of the United States does your speech represent?

9. What influences are there on your speaking or writing?

10. List the types of books and periodicals that you read. What newspaper or newspapers do you read? What parts of the newspaper do you read? In what way does reading influence you?

11. Analyze the speech you hear at college, at home, or in your vicinity and note down the characteristics of it.

12. What is the difference between formal and informal English? Where is each used? Bring in illustrations of each (see Perrin and Dykema, *op. cit.,* pp. 18–24).

13. What is Vulgar English? Bring in illustrations of it.

14. Read an article or story in a magazine and comment on the use of words. Are there archaic words in it? Localisms? Dialect? Foreign words? What level of usage does it represent?

15. Look up *ain't* in Webster's *New International Dictionary,* 3rd edition. What is its standing today? What level of usage does it represent?

16. Bring in a paragraph showing formal usage and one showing informal usage. What is the difference?

17. See Louise Pound's "Extension of Usage of a Pronoun" for the extension of the usage of the third person singular pronoun *it.* Can you think of other extensions of usage?

18. What do you think is the possibility of *It's him* becoming good usage? See Leonard's *Current English Usage,* pp. 108–109. Can you find other evidence?

19. If in doubt would you use *who* or *whom?* See Leonard's *Current English Usage,* pp. xv and 111–112, for the status of such a sentence as *Who are you staring at?* See also Myers, *op. cit.,* p. 126.

20. Of what importance is word order in bringing about changes in constructions? Illustrate.

21. What is meant by the group genitive? Illustrate.

22. What is meant by concord? Illustrate.

23. Does a verb always agree with the subject in number? Illustrate. What determines the number of the verb?

24. Would you accept as good usage *these kind* and *those sort?* Give reasons for your answer.
25. Do you say *I feel bad* or *I feel badly?* Which do you hear?
26. Analyze your own speech for *shall* and *will.* Which do you use and under what circumstances?
27. Do you use *like* as a conjunction? Do you think it should be established in Standard English? Why?
28. List other questions of usage that might have been included in this chapter. Analyze each and determine to what level of usage each belongs.

C. SUGGESTIONS FOR RESEARCH PAPERS

1. Select any one of the questions of usage mentioned in this chapter, or some other question of divided usage, and make a study of it in a reputable current periodical or in a modern author.
2. Compare a particular usage of today with an earlier century and see what changes have occurred.

Appendix

Important Dates

FIRST PERIOD

449   Coming of the English to England. Date given in the *Anglo-Saxon Chronicle* for the landing of Hengist and Horsa on British soil.

597   Coming of the missionaries who introduced the Roman tradition of Christianity into England. This date marks the early Latin influence which has given us several ecclesiastical and general terms.

787   Coming of the Danes. This influence, which culminated over a century later, gave English not only a large part of its vocabulary of common words, but a good deal of its grammmar. For example, the third person plural pronouns come from Danish.

901   Death of King Alfred. This king largely advanced the study and practice of the English language in England.

1066   Date of the Norman Conquest. Again this conquest had its full influence perhaps a century later than this year. It stands for the introduction of the enormous number of French words in present-day English.

1154   End of the first period of the development of the English language. This is the date of the ending of the *Anglo-Saxon Chronicle*.

SECOND PERIOD

1327–77   Flemish influence in English, through the importation of Flemish weavers.

1362   The return to the use of English in the law courts, where French had previously been used. This marks the re-establishment of English as the national language.

1400   End of the Second Period; death of Chaucer, the Father of English Poetry and a very real contributor to the language itself.

THIRD PERIOD

1477   Introduction of printing in England. This date indicates the beginning of the standardization of English spelling, grammar, and expression.

1558   Accession of Queen Elizabeth. This date stands for the Renaissance, with its rediscovery of the classics and its exploration of all fields of thought.

1600 (*or* 1616)   This date stands for the life and work of Shakespeare, the greatest English writer. The first date may stand for the culmination of his powers, the second date is that of his death. In countless ways Shakespeare has enriched the English language.

1607–1620   Colonization of Virginia and New England. These dates mark the world-wide extension of English, particularly to North America. Since the seventeenth century there has grown up a distinct standard dialect of English in America, supplementary to the standard English spoken in England.

1611   Date of the translation of the Scriptures into English, the King James version of the Bible. It has been said that during this century and the one following, England was a nation of one book, and that book was the Bible. The Bible has had a very definite and far-reaching influence upon the English language.

1727   Death of Sir Isaac Newton. This date may stand for modern science, with its tremendous accession of new words in the English vocabulary.

1757   Conquest of India by the British. This date stands for British colonial expansion over the globe.

1783   Invention of the steam engine by James Watt. It marks the opening of the Industrial Revolution, with modern invention adding countless new words to the English vocabulary.

1803   The Louisiana Purchase. This date stands for American expansion, with the consequent extension of American English.

1914–1918   World War I. This date typifies increased American and British influence in world affairs, with the consequent extension of the use of English all over the world.

1920 *on*   There is no specific date for the invention of the radio and the talking motion pictures, but the years of their development are important ones in the history of the English language, since they have shown themselves an extending and standardizing influence in English.

1939–1945   World War II. This date has brought even greater American and British influence in world affairs, with the resulting extension of the use of English all over the world.

1945 *on*   Invention of the atomic bomb. It marked the opening of the Atomic Age, with modern invention adding innumerable new words to the English vocabulary.

1957 *on*   First successful launching of a space manmade vehicle in orbit— the advent of the Space Age with its satellites, rockets, missiles, and other numerous inventions. This date indicates a new frontier to influence the English language in countless ways.

Selected Bibliography

Aiken, Janet Rankin, *A New Plan of English Grammar*, New York, Henry Holt and Company, 1933.

Aiken, Janet Rankin, *Commonsense Grammar*, New York, Thomas Y. Crowell Company, 1936.

Aiken, Janet Rankin, *English Present and Past*, New York, The Ronald Press Company, 1930.

Aiken, Janet Rankin, *Why English Sounds Change*, New York, The Ronald Press Company, 1929.

Allen, H. B. (ed.), *Readings in Applied English Linguistics*, New York, Appleton-Century-Crofts, 1958.

Anderson, Marjorie, and Blanche Colton Williams, *Old English Handbook*, Boston, Houghton Mifflin Company, 1935.

Arnold, Thurman W., *The Folklore of Capitalism*, New Haven, Yale University Press, 1937.

Arnold, Thurman W., *The Symbols of Government*, New Haven, Yale University Press, 1935.

Atkinson, B. F. C., "Alphabet," *Encyclopaedia Britannica* (Chicago and London, 1959), Vol. I, pp. 677–685.

Atwood, E. Bagby, *A Survey of Verb Forms in the Eastern United States*, Ann Arbor, University of Michigan Press, 1953.

Avery, Elizabeth, Jane Dorsey, and Vera Sickels, *First Principles of Speech Training*, New York, D. Appleton Company, 1930.

Baugh, Albert C., *A History of the English Language*, 2nd edit., Appleton-Century-Crofts, 1957.

Bender, Harold H., *The Home of the Indo-Europeans*, Princeton, Princeton University Press, 1932.

Bense, J. F., *A Dictionary of the Low-Dutch Element in the English Vocabulary*, Parts I–V, London, H. Milford, 1926–1939.

Berrey, Lester V., and Melvin Van den Bark, *The American Thesaurus of Slang*, New York, Thomas Y. Crowell Company, 1942.

Bloch, Bernard, and G. L. Trager, *Outline of Linguistic Analysis*, Baltimore, Linguistic Society of America, 1942.

Bloomfield, Leonard, *An Introduction to the Study of Language*, New York, Henry Holt and Company, 1914.

Bloomfield, Leonard, *Language*, New York, Henry Holt and Company, 1933.

Bloomfield, Leonard, "Language or Ideas?" *Language*, Vol. XII, pp. 89–95 (April, 1936).

Bradley, Henry, *The Making of English*, New York, The Macmillan Company, 1904.

Bradley, Henry, *On the Relations Between Spoken and Written Language With Special Reference to English*, London, Published for the British Academy by H. Milford, 1913.

Bréal, Michel J. A., *Semantics*, translated by Mrs. Henry Cust, London, W. Heinemann, 1900.

Bright, James W., *An Anglo-Saxon Reader*, New York, Henry Holt and Company, 1929. Revised and enlarged by James R. Hulbert, 1935.

Brugmann, Karl, and B. Delbrück, *Grundress der vergleichenden Grammatik der indogermanischen Sprachen*, 3 vols., 2nd edit., Strassburg, Trübner, 1897–1916.

Brunner, Karl, *Altenglische Grammatik* (based on E. Sievers), Halle, M. Niemeyer, 1942.

Brunner, Karl, *Abriss der mittelenglischen Grammatik*, 4th edit., Tübingen, M. Niemeyer, 1959.

Bryan, W. F., "The Midland Present Plural Indicative Ending -e(n)," *Modern Philology*, Vol. XVIII, pp. 457–473 (January, 1921).

Bryant, Margaret M., *A Functional English Grammar*, Boston, D. C. Heath and Company, 1959.

Bryant, Margaret M., *Current American Usage*, New York, Funk & Wagnalls Company, 1962.

Bryant, Margaret M., *English in the Law Courts*, New York, Columbia

University Press, 1930; 2nd edit., New York, Frederick Ungar Publishing Co., 1962.

Bryant, Margaret M., and Janet Rankin Aiken, *Psychology of English,* New York, Columbia University Press, 1940; 2nd edit., New York, Frederick Ungar Publishing Co., 1962.

Bryant, Margaret M., "Semantics Today," *Word Study,* pp. 6–7 (December, 1944). Reprinted in *Hispania,* Vol. XXVIII, No. 4, pp. 564–566 (November, 1945).

Bryant, Margaret M., "The Preterite-Present Verbs in Present-Day English," *College English,* pp. 259–264 (February, 1944).

Bryant, Margaret M., "What One Word Can Do," *College English,* pp. 284–290 (December, 1941).

Campbell, Alistair, *Old English,* New York, Oxford University Press, 1959.

Carnap, Rudolf, *Formalization of Logic,* Cambridge, Mass., Harvard University Press, 1943.

Carnap, Rudolf, *Introduction to Semantics,* Cambridge, Mass., Harvard University Press, 1942.

Carnap, Rudolf, *Meaning and Necessity: A Study in Semantics and Modal Logic,* Chicago, Chicago University Press, 1947.

Carnap, Rudolf, *The Logical Syntax of Language,* New York, Harcourt, Brace and Company, 1937.

Carr, Charles T., *The German Influence on the English Vocabulary,* Society for Pure English, Tract No. XLII, Oxford, Clarendon Press, 1934.

Carroll, John B., *The Study of Language,* Cambridge, Mass., Harvard University Press, 1953.

Chase, Stuart, *The Tyranny of Words,* New York, Harcourt, Brace and Company, 1938.

Clark, G. N., *The Dutch Influence on the English Vocabulary,* Society for Pure English, Tract No. XLII, Oxford, Clarendon Press, 1935.

Clodd, Edward, *The Story of the Alphabet,* New York, D. Appleton-Century Company, 1938.

Collingwood, R. G., and J. N. L. Myres, *Roman Britain and the English Settlements,* 2nd edit., *Oxford History of England,* Vol. I, Oxford, Clarendon Press, 1937.

Cook, Albert S., *Literary Middle English Reader,* Boston, Ginn and Company, 1915.

Coulton, G. G., *Medieval Panorama,* New York, The Macmillan Company, 1938.

Craigie, Sir William A., "An American Language," *Saturday Review of Literature,* Vol. VII, No. 31, pp. 614–615 (February 21, 1931).

Curme, George Oliver, "Are Our Teachers of English Properly Prepared?"

Publications of the Modern Language Association, Vol. XLVI, Supplement for 1931, pp. 1415–1426.

Curme, George Oliver, *Parts of Speech and Accidence,* Boston, D. C. Heath and Company, 1935 [Vol. II of Curme and Kurath, *A Grammar of the English Language*].

Curme, George Oliver, *Syntax,* Boston, D. C. Heath and Company, 1931 [Vol. III of Curme and Kurath, *A Grammar of the English Language*].

Curry, Robert O. L., *The Mechanism of the Human Voice,* New York, Longmans, Green & Co., 1940.

Daryush, A. A., *Persian Words in English,* Society for Pure English, Tract No. XLI, Oxford, Clarendon Press, 1934.

Davis, H. W. C. (ed.), *Medieval England,* Oxford, Clarendon Press, 1924.

Dean, Leonard F., and Kenneth G. Wilson, *Essays on Language and Usage,* New York, Oxford University Press, 1959.

Dickins, Bruce, and R. M. Wilson, *Early Middle English Texts,* London, Bowes & Bowes, 1956.

Edwards, Violet, *Group Leader's Guide to Propaganda Analysis,* New York City, Institute for Propaganda Analysis, Inc., 1938.

Einenkel, E., "Syntax," *Geschichte der englischen Sprache,* in Hermann Paul, *Grundriss der germanischen Philologie,* Vol. I, Strassburg, Karl J. Trübner, 1901, pp. 1138–1151.

Emerson, Oliver Farrar, *A Brief History of the English Language,* New York, The Macmillan Company, 1902.

Emerson, Oliver Farrar, *A Middle English Reader,* new and revised edit., London, Macmillan and Company, Ltd., 1932.

Emerson, Oliver Farrar, *The History of the English Language,* New York, The Macmillan Company, 1897.

Etc.: A Review of General Semantics, Vol. I, No. 1 (August, 1943, to date).

Evans, Bergen, and Cornelia Evans, *A Dictionary of Contemporary American Usage,* New York, Random House, 1957.

Fernald, James C., *Connectives of English Speech,* 37th edit., New York, Funk & Wagnalls Company, 1904.

Fernald, James C., *English Synonyms and Antonyms with Notes on the Correct Use of Prepositions,* 37th edit., New York, Funk & Wagnalls Company, 1914.

Firth, J. R., "The Technique of Semantics," *Transactions of the Philological Society,* London, 1935, pp. 36–72; also in *Papers in Linguistics 1934–1951,* London, Oxford University Press, 1958.

Fowler, H. W., *A Dictionary of Modern English Usage,* Oxford, Clarendon Press, 1924.

Francis, W. Nelson, *The Structure of American English,* with a chapter on "American English Dialects" by Raven I. McDavid, Jr., New York, The Ronald Press Company, 1958.

Frank, Jerome, *Law and the Modern Mind,* New York, Brentano's, 1930.

Fries, Charles C., *American English Grammar* (NCTE Monograph, No. 10), New York, D. Appleton-Century Company, 1940.

Fries, Charles C., "The Expression of the Future," *Language,* Vol. 3, 1927, pp. 87–95.

Fries, Charles C., *The Structure of English,* New York, Harcourt, Brace and Company, 1952.

Fries, Charles C., *The Teaching of the English Language,* New York, Thomas Nelson and Sons, 1927.

Funke, Otto, *A Middle English Reader* (texts from the 12th to the 14th c.), Bern, A. Francke Ag., 1944.

Giles, Peter, "Alphabet," *Encyclopaedia Britannica,* 11th edit., Vol. I, pp. 723–732.

Gleason, H. A., Jr., *An Introduction to Descriptive Linguistics,* rev. edit., New York, Holt, Rinehart and Winston, 1961.

Glicksberg, Charles I., "General Semantics and the Science of Man," *Scientific Monthly,* Vol. LXII, pp. 440–446 (May, 1946).

Graff, Willem L., *Language and Languages,* New York, D. Appleton and Company, 1932.

Gray, G. W., and C. M. Wise, *The Bases of Speech,* 3rd edit., New York, Harper & Brothers, 1959.

Gray, Louis H., *Foundations of Language,* New York, The Macmillan Company, 1939.

Greenough, James Bradstreet, and George Lyman Kittredge, *Words and Their Ways in English Speech,* New York, The Macmillan Company, 1901.

Gummere, F. B., *Founders of England,* with Supplementary Notes by F. P. Magoun, Jr., New York, G. E. Stechert & Co., 1930.

Hall, J. Lesslie, *English Usage,* Chicago, Scott, Foresman and Company, 1917.

Hall, John R. Clark, *A Concise Anglo-Saxon Dictionary,* 2nd edit., Cambridge, University Press, 1916.

Hall, Joseph Sargent, "The Phonetics of Great Smoky Mountain Speech," Monograph No. 4, *American Speech,* New York, King's Crown Press, 1942.

Hall, Robert A., Jr., *Linguistics and Your Language,* New York, Doubleday, Anchor Books, 1960 (Reissue of *Leave Your Language Alone!* Ithaca, New York, Linguistica, 1950).

Hatcher, Anna Granville, *Modern English Word-Formation and Neo-Latin,* Baltimore, The Johns Hopkins Press, 1951.

Hayakawa, S. I., *Language in Action,* New York, Harcourt, Brace and Company, 1941.

Hayakawa, S. I., *Language in Thought and Action,* New York, Harcourt, Brace and Company, 1949.

Hayakawa, S. I. (ed.), *Language, Meaning and Maturity* (Review of General Semantics, 1943–1953), New York, Harper & Brothers, 1954.

Hayakawa, S. I., *Our Language and Our World* (Review of General Semantics, 1953–1958), New York, Harper & Brothers, 1959.

Heffner, R-M. S., *General Phonetics,* Madison, University of Wisconsin Press, 1952.

Hill, A. A., *Introduction to Linguistic Structures,* New York, Harcourt, Brace and Company, 1957.

Hirt, Herman, *Indogermanische Grammatik,* 7 vols., Heidelberg, Carl Winter, 1921–1937.

Hockett, Charles F., *A Course in Modern Linguistics,* New York, The Macmillan Company, 1958.

Hodgkin, R. H., *A History of the Anglo-Saxons,* 2 vols., 3rd edit., New York, Oxford University Press, 1953.

Horwill, H. W., *A Dictionary of Modern American Usage,* Oxford, Clarendon Press, 1935.

Hubbell, Allan F., *The Pronunciation of English in New York City,* New York, King's Crown Press, 1950.

Hulbert, James R., *Dictionaries British and American,* New York, Philosophical Library, 1955.

Huse, H. R., "Reading and Understanding," *Studies in Language and Literature,* ed. by George R. Coffman, Chapel Hill, University of North Carolina Press, 1945.

Huse, H. R., *The Illiteracy of the Literate,* New York, D. Appleton Company, 1933.

Jackson, Kenneth, *Language and History in Early Britain,* Cambridge, Mass., Harvard University Press, 1954.

Jespersen, Otto, *A Modern English Grammar,* 7 vols., Copenhagen, Ejnar Munksgaard, 1909–1949.

Jespersen, Otto, *An International Language,* London, G. Allen & Unwin, Ltd., 1928.

Jespersen, Otto, *Essentials of English Grammar,* New York, Henry Holt and Company, 1933.

Jespersen, Otto, *Growth and Structure of the English Language,* 4th edit., revised, Oxford, B. Blackwell, 1923; 8th edit., Leipzig, B. G. Teubner, 1935; New York, Doubleday, Anchor Books, 1955; 9th edit., Oxford, B. Blackwell, 1956.

Jespersen, Otto, *Language: Its Nature, Development, and Origin,* New York, Henry Holt and Company, 1933.

Jespersen, Otto, *Negation in English and Other Languages,* København, A. F. Høst & Søn, 1917.

Jespersen, Otto, *The Philosophy of Grammar,* London, G. Allen & Unwin, Ltd., 1935.

Johnson, Charles F., *English Words,* New York, Harper & Brothers, 1892.

Johnson, Wendell, *People in Quandaries: A Semantic Approach to Personality Adjustment,* New York, Harper & Brothers, 1946.

Jones, Daniel, *Everyman's English Pronouncing Dictionary,* 11th edit., New York, E. P. Dutton & Co., 1956.

Jones, Daniel, *An Outline of English Phonetics,* 8th edit., Cambridge, England, W. Heffer & Sons, Ltd., 1957.

Jones, Daniel, *The Pronunciation of English,* 4th edit., Cambridge, England, Cambridge University Press, 1956.

Jordan, Richard, *Handbuch der mittelenglischen Grammatik,* Part I, 2nd edit., Heidelberg, Carl Winter, 1934.

Judson, L. S., and A. T. Weaver, *Voice Science,* New York, D. Appleton-Century Company, 1941.

Kantner, Claude, and Robert West, *Phonetics,* rev. edit., New York, Harper & Brothers, 1960.

Kellner, Leon, *Historical Outlines of English Syntax,* London, The Macmillan Company, 1924.

Kendig, M. (ed.), *Papers from the Second American Congress on General Semantics,* Chicago, Institute of General Semantics, 1943.

Kennedy, Arthur G., *Current English,* Boston, Ginn and Company, 1935.

Kenyon, John Samuel, *American Pronunciation,* 10th edit., Ann Arbor, Michigan, George Wahr, 1951.

Kenyon, John Samuel, and Thomas A. Knott, *A Pronouncing Dictionary of American English,* Springfield, Mass., G. & C. Merriam Company, 1953.

Kökeritz, Helge, *Shakespeare's Pronunciation,* New Haven, Yale University Press, 1953.

Korzybski, Alfred, *Science and Sanity: An Introduction to Non-Aristotelian Systems and General Semantics,* Lancaster, Pennsylvania, The Science Press Printing Company, 1933; 2nd edit., 1941.

Krapp, George Philip, *A Comprehensive Guide to Good English,* Chicago, Rand McNally & Company, 1927.

Krapp, George Philip, *Modern English: Its Growth and Present Use,* New York, Charles Scribner's Sons, 1909.

Krapp, George Philip, *The English Language in America,* 2 vols., New York, The Century Co. for the Modern Language Association of

America, 1925; 2nd edit., New York, Frederick Ungar Publishing Co., 1960.

Krapp, George Philip, *The Pronunciation of Standard English in America,* New York, Oxford University Press, 1919.

Krapp, George Philip, *The Rise of English Prose Style,* New York, Oxford University Press, 1915.

Kruisinga, E., *A Handbook of Present-Day English,* 5th edit., Part II, 1, 2, 3, "English Accidence and Syntax," Groningen, P. Noordhoff, 1931, 1932.

Kurath, Hans, *A Word Geography of the Eastern United States,* Ann Arbor, University of Michigan Press, 1949.

Kurath, Hans, *et al., Handbook of the Linguistic Geography of New England,* Providence, R. I., Brown University, 1939.

Kurath, Hans (Director and Editor), *et al., Linguistic Atlas of New England,* 3 vols. in 6, sponsored by the American Council of Learned Societies and assisted by Universities and Colleges in New England, Providence, R. I., Brown University, 1939–1943.

Kurath, Hans, and Raven I. McDavid, Jr., *The Pronunciation of English in the Atlantic States,* Ann Arbor, University of Michigan Press, 1961.

Kurath, Hans, and Sherman M. Kuhn (eds.), *Middle English Dictionary,* Ann Arbor, University of Michigan Press, 1952 (in progress).

Laird, Charlton G., *The Miracle of Language,* Cleveland, The World Publishing Company, 1953.

Lee, Donald W., *Functional Change in Early English,* Menasha, Wis., G. Banta Publishing Co., 1948.

Lee, Irving J., *Language Habits in Human Affairs: An Introduction to General Semantics,* New York, Harper & Brothers, 1941.

Lee, Irving J. (ed.), *The Language of Wisdom and Folly,* New York, Harper & Brothers, 1949.

Leonard, Sterling A., *Current English Usage* (NCTE Monograph, No. 1), Chicago, Inland Press, 1932.

Leonard, Sterling A., *The Doctrine of Correctness in English Usage, 1700–1800,* Madison, University of Wisconsin Studies in Language and Literature, No. 25, 1929.

"Linguistics and Usage" (17 articles and an introduction) in *Readings in Applied English Linguistics,* ed. by H. B. Allen, New York, Appleton-Century-Crofts, 1958.

Lloyd, Donald J., and Harry R. Warfel, *American English in Its Cultural Setting,* New York, Alfred A. Knopf, 1956.

Long, Ralph B., "The Clause Patterns of Contemporary English," *American Speech,* Vol. XXXII, pp. 12–30 (February, 1957).

Macaulay, T. C., *Interlanguage,* Society for Pure English, Tract No. XXXIV, Oxford, Clarendon Press, 1930.

Maetzner, E., *An English Grammar,* 3 vols., translated by C. J. Grece, London, John Murray, 1874.

Malone, Kemp, "When Did Middle English Begin?" *Curme Volume of Linguistic Studies, Language Monograph No. 7,* Baltimore, Waverly Press, Inc., 1930.

Marckwardt, Albert H., *American English,* New York, Oxford University Press, 1958.

Marckwardt, Albert H., *Introduction to the English Language,* New York, Oxford University Press, 1942.

Marckwardt, Albert H., and Fred G. Walcott, *Facts About Current English Usage* (NCTE Monograph, No. 7), New York, D. Appleton-Century Company, 1938.

Marsh, George P., *Lectures on the English Language,* 4th edit., New York, Scribner, Armstrong & Co., 1874.

Mathews, M. M., *A Survey of English Dictionaries,* London, Oxford University Press (Humphrey Milford), 1933.

McKnight, George H., *English Words and Their Background,* New York, D. Appleton-Century Company, 1923.

McKnight, George H., *Modern English in the Making,* New York, D. Appleton and Company, 1930.

Meillet, A., *Introduction à l'étude comparative des langues indo-européennes,* 7th edit., Paris, Hachette, 1934; new edit., corrected and augmented by Émile Benveniste, 1953.

Meillet, A., and Marcel Cohen (eds.), *Les langues du monde,* 2nd edit., Paris, Société de Linguistique de Paris, 1952.

Mencken, H. L., *The American Language,* 4th edit., Alfred A. Knopf, 1937; *Supplement I,* 1945; *Supplement II,* 1948.

Meyer, Ernst, *Die Indogermanenfrage,* Marburg, Elwert-Gräfe und Unzer, 1948.

Moore, Samuel, *Historical Outlines of English Sounds and Inflections,* rev. by Albert H. Marckwardt, Ann Arbor, Michigan, George Wahr, 1957.

Moore, Samuel, and Thomas A. Knott, *The Elements of Old English,* 10th edit., Ann Arbor, Michigan, George Wahr, 1960.

Moorhouse, A. C., *Writing and the Alphabet,* London, Cobbett Press, 1946.

Morris, Charles W., *Signs, Language and Behavior,* Englewood Cliffs, New Jersey, Prentice-Hall, Inc., 1946.

Mossé, Fernand, *A Handbook of Middle English,* translated by James A. Walker, Baltimore, The Johns Hopkins Press, 1952.

Myers, L. M., *American English: A Twentieth Century Grammar*, Engle-wood Cliffs, New Jersey, Prentice-Hall, Inc., 1952.

Ogden, Charles Kay, and I. A. Richards, *The Meaning of Meaning*, New York, Harcourt, Brace and Company, 1923.

Ohlander, Urban, *Studies on Coordinate Expressions in Middle English*, Lund, C. W. K. Gleerup, 1936.

Paget, Sir Richard, *Human Speech*, New York, Harcourt, Brace and Com-pany, 1930.

Palmer, Harold E., and F. G. Blandford, *A Grammar of Spoken English*, 2nd edit., Cambridge, England, W. Heffer & Sons, Ltd., 1955.

Pedersen, Holger, *Linguistic Science in the Nineteenth Century*, trans-lated by J. W. Spargo, Cambridge, Mass., Harvard University Press, 1931.

Philbrick, F. A., *Understanding English: An Introduction to Semantics*, New York, The Macmillan Company, 1942.

Pike, Kenneth L., *The Intonation of American English*, Ann Arbor, Uni-versity of Michigan Press, 1946.

Pike, Kenneth L., *Phonemics: A Technique for Reducing Languages to Writing*, Ann Arbor, University of Michigan Press, 1947.

Pollock, Thomas Clark, *The Nature of Literature: Its Relation to Science, Language and Human Experience*, Princeton, New Jersey, Princeton University Press, 1942.

Poole, Austin L., *From Domesday Book to Magna Carta 1087–1216*, in *Oxford History of England*, Vol. 3, Oxford, Clarendon Press, 1951.

Pooley, Robert C., *Grammar and Usage in Textbooks on English*, Bulletin 14, Bureau of Educational Research, University of Wisconsin, 1933.

Pooley, Robert C., *Teaching English Grammar*, New York, Appleton-Century-Crofts, 1957.

Pooley, Robert C., *Teaching English Usage* (NCTE Monograph, No. 16), New York, D. Appleton-Century Company, 1946.

Potter, Simeon, *Our Language*, London, Penguin, 1954.

Pound, Louise, "Extensions of Usage of a Pronoun," in *Language Mono-graphs (Curme Volume of Linguistic Studies)*, No. VII, pp. 118–119 (December, 1930).

Pound, Louise, "Word Coinage and Modern Trade Names," *Dialect Notes*, Vol. IV, The American Dialect Society, 1913, pp. 29–41.

Poutsma, H., *A Grammar of Late Modern English*, Part I, First Half, 2nd edit.; Part I, Second Half, 2nd edit.; Part II, Section I, A; Part II, Sec-tion I, B; Part II, Section II, Groningen, P. Noordhoff, 1928, 1929, 1914, 1916, 1926.

Pyles, Thomas, *Words and Ways of American English*, New York, Ran-dom House, 1952.

Quirk, Randolph, and C. L. Wrenn, *An Old English Grammar*, New York, Henry Holt & Co., Inc., 1957.

Rapaport, Anatol, *Fights, Games and Debates*, Ann Arbor, University of Michigan Press, 1960.

Rapaport, Anatol, *Operational Philosophy*, New York, Harper & Brothers, 1953.

Rapaport, Anatol, *Science and the Goals of Man*, New York, Harper & Brothers, 1950.

Reiser, Oliver L., *The Promise of Scientific Humanism Toward a Unification of Scientific, Religious, Social and Economic Thought*, New York, Oskar Piest, 1940.

Richards, I. A., *Interpretation in Teaching*, New York, Harcourt, Brace and Company, 1938.

Roberts, Paul, *Understanding English*, New York, Harper & Brothers, 1958.

Roberts, Paul, *Understanding Grammar*, New York, Harper & Brothers, 1954.

Robertson, Stuart, *The Development of Modern English* (1934); 2nd edit., rev. by Frederic G. Cassidy, Englewood Cliffs, New Jersey, Prentice-Hall, Inc., 1954.

Robinson, F. N. (ed.), *The Works of Geoffrey Chaucer*, 2nd edit., Boston, Houghton Mifflin Company, 1957.

Russell, G. Oscar, *The Vowel, Some X-Ray and Photo Laryngoperiskopik Evidence*, Columbus, The Ohio State University Press, 1928.

Sapir, Edward, *Language*, New York, Harcourt, Brace and Company, 1921 (Harvest Books, 1960).

Schlauch, *The Gift of Language*, New York, Dover Publications, 1955 (Reissue of *The Gift of Tongues*, New York, Modern Age Books, 1942).

Schreuder, Hindrik, *Pejorative Sense Development in English*, Groningen, Noordhoff, 1929.

Schrijnen, J. K. F. H., *Einführung in das Studium der indogermanischen Sprachwissenschaft*, translated by W. Fischer, Heidelberg, Carl Winter, 1921.

Sheard, J. A., *The Words We Use*, New York, Frederick A. Praeger, 1954.

Shenton, Herbert N., Edward Sapir, and Otto Jespersen, *International Communications: A Symposium on the Language Problem*, London, Kegan Paul, Trench, Trubner & Co., Ltd., 1931.

Skeat, Walter W., *Etymological Dictionary of the English Language*, 4th edit., Oxford, Clarendon Press, 1910.

Skeat, Walter W., *Principles of English Etymology*, 2 vols., Oxford, Clarendon Press, 1887–1891.

Sledd, James H., *A Short Introduction to English Grammar,* Chicago, Scott, Foresman and Company, 1959.

Sledd, James H., and Gwin J. Kolb, *Dr. Johnson's Dictionary: Essays in the Biography of a Book,* Chicago, University Press, 1955.

Smith, Logan Pearsall, *The English Language,* New York, Henry Holt and Company, 1912.

Stanley, Oma, *The Speech of East Texas, American Speech,* Monograph, No. 2, New York, Columbia University Press, 1937.

Starnes, D. T., and Gertrude E. Noyes, *The English Dictionary from Cawdrey to Johnson,* 1604–1755, Chapel Hill, University of North Carolina Press, 1946.

Stenton, F. M., *Anglo-Saxon England,* 2nd edit., *Oxford History of England,* Vol. 2, Oxford, Oxford University Press, 1947.

Stewart, George R., *Names on the Land,* rev. edit., Boston, Houghton Mifflin Company, 1958.

Sturtevant, Edgar H., *An Introduction to Linguistic Science,* New Haven, Yale University Press, 1947.

Sturtevant, Edgar H., *Linguistic Change: An Introduction to the Historical Study of Language* (1917), Chicago, The University of Chicago Press, 1961 (Phoenix Books).

Sweet, Henry, *A Handbook of Phonetics,* Oxford, Clarendon Press, 1877.

Sweet, Henry, *A New English Grammar,* Oxford, Clarendon Press, 1925.

Taylor, Isaac, *The Alphabet,* 2 vols., London, Kegan Paul, Trench & Co., 1893.

Taylor, Walt, *Arabic Words in English,* Society for Pure English, Tract No. XXXVIII, Oxford, Clarendon Press, 1933.

The Oxford English Dictionary (OED) (1884–1928; reissued, with Supplement, 1933) (originally known as *A New English Dictionary on Historical Principles: NED*).

Thomas, Charles K., *An Introduction to the Phonetics of American English,* 2nd edit., New York, The Ronald Press Company, 1958.

Trager, G. L., and H. L. Smith, *An Outline of English Structure,* Norman, Oklahoma, Battenburg Press, 1951; 4th printing, New York, Columbia University Press, 1961.

Tucker, Gilbert Milligan, *American English,* New York, Alfred A. Knopf, 1921.

Turner, Lorenzo D., *Africanisms in the Gullah Dialect,* Chicago, University of Chicago Press, 1949.

Twaddell, W. Freeman, *The English Verb Auxiliaries,* Providence, Rhode Island, Brown University Press, 1960.

Ullman, Stephen, *The Principles of Semantics,* Glasgow University Publications, No. LXXXIV, 2nd edit., New York, Philosophical Library; London, Blackwell, 1957.

Van Dongen, G. A., *Amelioratives in English,* Rotterdam, De Vries, 1933.

Walpole, Hugh R., *Semantics: The Nature of Words and Their Meanings,* New York, W. W. Norton Publishing Company, 1941.

Warfel, Harry R., *Noah Webster, Schoolmaster to America,* New York, The Macmillan Company, 1936.

Webster's *New International Dictionary,* 2nd edit., Springfield, Mass., G. & C. Merriam Co., 1934; 3rd edit., 1961.

Weekley, Ernest, *An Etymological Dictionary of Modern English,* London, J. Murray, 1921.

Weekley, Ernest, *Cruelty to Words,* New York, E. P. Dutton & Company, 1931.

Weekley, Ernest, *The Romance of Words,* 4th edit., London, J. Murray, 1928.

Welby, V., "Significs," *Encyclopaedia Britannica,* 11th edit., Vol. 25, pp. 78–81, 1911.

Welby, V., *Significs and Language,* London, Macmillan & Co., Ltd., 1911.

Wentworth, Harold, *Blend-Words in English* (abstract of Cornell thesis), Ithaca, New York, 1933.

Wentworth, Harold, and Stuart Berg Flexner, *Dictionary of American Slang,* New York, Thomas Y. Crowell Company, 1960.

Wetmore, Thomas, *Low Back and Low Central Vowels in the English of the Eastern United States,* Publications of the American Dialect Society, XXXII, 1960.

Whitehall, Harold, *Structural Essentials of English,* New York, Harcourt, Brace and Company, 1956.

Whitney, William Dwight, *Language and the Study of Language,* New York, Charles Scribner and Company, 1867.

Wright, Joseph, and Elizabeth M. Wright, *An Elementary Middle English Grammar,* 2nd edit., Oxford, Oxford University Press, 1928.

Wright, Joseph, and Elizabeth M. Wright, *An Elementary Old English Grammar,* Oxford, Clarendon Press, 1923.

Wright, Joseph, and Elizabeth M. Wright, *Old English Grammar,* 3rd edit., Oxford, Oxford University Press, 1925.

Wyld, Henry Cecil, *A Short History of English,* 3rd edit., New York, E. P. Dutton and Company, 1927.

Wyld, Henry Cecil, *History of Modern Colloquial English,* 3rd edit., New York, E. P. Dutton and Company, 1937.

Wyld, Henry Cecil, *The Universal Dictionary of the English Language,* London, G. Routledge & Sons, Ltd., 1932.

Zachrisson, R. E., *Pronunciation of English Vowels, 1400–1700*, Göteborg, Sweden, Zachrisson, 1913.
Zandvoort, R. W., *A Handbook of English Grammar*, 5th edit., London, Longmans, Green and Co., 1957.

For other readings see:

Bibliographie linguistique des années 1939–1947, 2 vols., Utrecht-Brussels, 1949–1950, and its annual supplements, published with the support of UNESCO.
Kennedy, Arthur G., *Bibliography of Writings on the English Language*, Cambridge, Mass., Harvard University Press, 1927.
Modern Humanities Research Association, *Annual Bibliography of American Language and Literature*, Cambridge, England (1920, to date).
Annual Bibliography in *Publications of the Modern Language Association of America*, New York, New York University.

Index